VINE'S
TOPICAL
COMMENTARY

CHRIST

VINE'S
TOPICAL
COMMENTARY

CHRIST

W. E. VINE
WITH C. F. HOGG

THOMAS NELSON
Since 1798

Vine's Topical Commentary: Christ

© 2010 W. E. Vine Copyright Ltd. of Bath, England

Published in Nashville, Tennessee, by Thomas Nelson. Thomas Nelson is a registered trademark of HarperCollins Christian Publishing, Inc.

Thomas Nelson titles may be purchased in bulk for educational, business, fundraising, or sales promotional use. For information, please e-mail SpecialMarkets@ThomasNelson.com.

Library of Congress Cataloging-in-Publication Data

Names: Vine, W. E. (William Edwy), 1873-1949, author. | Hogg, C. F.
Title: Vine's topical commentary : Christ / W. E. Vine with C. F. Hogg.
Other titles: Christ.
Description: Nashville : Thomas Nelson, 2022.
Identifiers: LCCN 2022008989 (print) | LCCN 2022008990 (ebook) | ISBN 9780310144922 (paperback) | ISBN 9781418560546 (ebook)
Subjects: LCSH: Jesus Christ—Person and offices—Biblical teaching. | Bible. Gospels—Commentaries.
Classification: LCC BT203 .V56 2022 (print) | LCC BT203 (ebook) | DDC 232—dc23/eng/20220502
LC record available at https://lccn.loc.gov/2022008989
LC ebook record available at https://lccn.loc.gov/2022008990

22 23 24 25 26—5 4 3 2 1

CONTENTS

Section 2: The Life of Christ

Section 3: The Teachings of Christ

INTRODUCTION

*We may well hesitate to write anything upon the infinitely great and sacred
subject of the person and work of the Son of God. The place whereon we
tread is holy ground; we may not approach it save with unshod feet, lest we
make ourselves of the number of those who have desecrated it by erroneous speculations and by perversions of the truth. The apprehension of the
numerous onslaughts being made upon the doctrines of the faith concerning
our adorable Lord, and the command given us "to contend earnestly for
the faith once for all delivered to the saints" (Jude 3), provide additional in-
ducement to handle this holy theme, and so to continue the witness already
faithfully given by those who have held and taught the truth.*

—C. F. Hogg

Undoubtedly William Edwy Vine was qualified in many fields. As well as
being a theologian and a man of outstanding academic intellect, he had a heart
for all humanity that made him a master of communication.

Born in 1873, at the time when C. H. Spurgeon, D. L. Moody and F. B. Meyer
were enjoying popularity on both sides of the Atlantic, Vine was brought up in a
boarding school owned by and governed by his father as its headmaster. This was
a major contribution to his interest in teaching. At the age of seventeen he was a
teacher at his father's school while attending the University College of Wales in
preparation for his eventual London University degree, an M.A. in classics.

At the age of twenty-six he spent an Easter vacation at the home of a godly
couple, Mr. and Mrs. Baxendale, where he met their daughter Phoebe; a few
years later, they married. It was a marriage made in heaven. They had five children: Helen, Christine, Edward (O.B.E.), Winifred, and Jeanette. During the time
of their engagement, Vine's reputation as a clear Bible expositor was growing. It
was not long before he accepted the joint headmastership of his father's school.
In 1904, after his father died, his brother Theodore became joint headmaster
with him.

It was during this time, in conjunction with Mr. C. F. Hogg, that he produced
three classic commentaries on 1 and 2 Thessalonians, followed by Galatians.
These master works display the full scope of Vine's scholarship.

While Vine was teaching in the school, preparing for his M.A., and writing
in-depth commentaries, he also developed a lifetime habit of teaching classes in
New Testament Greek grammar. This laid the foundation for his all-time classic
works, *An Expository Dictionary of New Testament Words*, and later, *An Expository
Dictionary of Old Testament Words*. His dictionaries are classics—copies are in
excess of 3 million worldwide—proof that his scholarship and clarity of expression is as relevant today as when first published.

EXPOSITORY COMMENTARIES

Vine applies a "microscopic" approach to expository teaching—a word approach that takes into consideration every reference to that word in the Bible as well as its use in contemporary and classic Greek. Vine's verse-by-verse exposition reveals a depth of understanding that commentaries many times the size of his fail to give. He explains the meaning of the key words in each verse and links them with the complete passage.

This volume is compiled from the writings on Christ found in the five-volume series *The Collected Writings of W. E. Vine*. In some cases these articles have been condensed from their original form. Introductory paragraphs in italic type have been added to assist the reader.

THE
PERSON AND
WORK
OF CHRIST

THE SON OF GOD

In the Gospel of John, the writer emphasizes his declaration that Jesus is both eternal and equal with God the Father. The Father and the Son are one, yet distinct. The Father, the Son, and the Holy Spirit aren't three separate beings; each possessed the attributes of Deity. That there is only one God remains an essential doctrine of the Christian faith. This emphasis is seen in greater focus in John's prologue. Not only are there amazing theological statements about Jesus Christ and His relationship to the Father, but there are also very practical assertions about His qualities and characteristics, many of which can be seen in the original Greek, which you will read about below.

THE ETERNAL WORD

"In the beginning was the Word, and the Word was with God, and the Word was God" (John 1:1). The first of these three statements declares His preexistence. In whatever way the phrase "In the beginning" may be understood (it probably refers to the creation of the universe), the paramount fact is that He, the Word, was preexistent to it. Whensoever creation had a beginning He was already there. There was no beginning to His being.

The second statement declares the distinctiveness of His person. He was "with God." The preposition is not *sun*, which signifies "accompaniment," nor *meta*, which suggests accompaniment with mutual interest, but *pros*, which is expressive of a personal attitude toward and occupation with the One whose presence is being experienced.

The third statement predicates His Deity, His oneness in Godhood with Him whom the second statement spoke of as God. The three declarations stress the personal nature of Him who is the Word. That this bears the implication of the existence of two Gods is refuted by this very Gospel, which declares that the Father and the Son are one, and by other Scriptures which predicate that there is one God.[1]

THE SIGNIFICANCE OF REPETITIONS

These initial statements are followed by a repetition of the first and second, with emphasis on the demonstrative pronoun: "The same (or rather, "This One") was in the beginning with God." But why this repetition? There are no mere

---

[1] The same applies to the Holy Spirit. The doctrine of the Unity of the Godhead is prominent in the Old Testament, and is maintained in the New. The New, however, consistently with the progress of docrine in the Sacred Volume, plainly unfolds the truth of the Trinity of Persons in the Unity of the Godhead. A Unitarian recently made the following remark in a conversation with one who holds the truth of the Trinity in Unity: "If what *we* believe is true, you are idolaters; if what *you* believe is true, we are not Christians." Now the doctrine of the Trinity, woven as it is into the very texture of the New Testament, precludes Tritheism and invalidates any imputation of the worship of three Gods. Yet to deny the Deity of Christ is to be devoid of title to be a Christian.

repetitions in the Scriptures. Sometimes a reiterated statement is confirmatory of what has been stated; sometimes it is also introductory to what immediately follows. This is the case here; for, immediately after the repeated statement that the Word was in the beginning with God, the existence of the universe is attributed to Him. "All things were made by Him."

This again is reiterated and expanded: "And without Him was not anything made that hath been made." This also is not simply a repetition. It is preparatory to a declaration that He is the Author of life: life, which exists in Him essentially, is bestowed through Him upon His creatures. "In Him was life, and the life was the light of men." Upon the fact that in Him life is unoriginated and essential rests the dependence of His creatures upon Him for it. The order of life and light is significant. In nature, life in its full activity depends upon light; light is the life of the animate physical creation. In spiritual matters the position is reversed. The Life is the light. We do not receive spiritual life simply because Christ is the light. He brings light into our darkness because He brings life, the life that becomes ours when we are born of God, that is to say, when we receive Christ by faith (v. 12).

These subjects, the Word, the Life, and the Light, as set forth in verses 4–13, lead to a resumption of the title "The Word" in verse 14, and to the statement, "The Word became flesh and dwelt among us." The Revisers have rightly rendered by "became" instead of "was made."[1] The statement that He "became flesh" declares the voluntariness, on the part of Him who is the Word, of the act of His Incarnation. Further on in the Gospel, as also in the first Epistle of John, we learn that this voluntary act was likewise the sending by the Father. The counsels of grace were mutually designed and carried out; this is true in respect also of the Holy Spirit, whose part in the Incarnation is declared in Matthew 1:18–20 and Luke 1:35.

THE OMISSION OF THE DEFINITE ARTICLE

The apostle bears witness for himself and his fellow-apostles that they "beheld His glory, glory as of the only begotten from the Father." There are certain facts to be noted in this phraseology. The definite article is absent in the original before both "only begotten" and "Father." According to a well-known principle in regard to the Greek definite article, its omission before certain descriptions of persons or objects serves to stress the particular feature or character mentioned in the description; whereas, on the other hand, the insertion of the definite article simply points the reader to the person or object as one well-known, or one to be recognized. Thus, had the definite articles been used here, the apostle would simply have been pointing out (as is frequently the case) that the two persons whom he was mentioning were those well-known to his readers as "the only begotten Son" and "the Father." But that is not the case, for he is giving a description of the particular kind of glory which he and his fellow-apostles had seen. The nature

---

1 *Ginomai* should never be rendered "to make," except in the passive voice where English requires it.

of the description, then, shows that the definite articles were purposely omitted in order to lay stress upon the particular characteristics, of the One as an Only Begotten, and of the Other as a Father.

THE MEANING OF "GLORY"

We may here notice the significance in Scripture of the word "glory," as used of God and of Christ. From what is said in the passages where this word is found, we learn that glory, in this respect, is the manifestation of characteristics or character, and of power. For instance, when in the second chapter we read: "This beginning of His signs [a sign is a miracle with a meaning or message] did Jesus in Cana of Galilee, and manifested His glory," the glory which He revealed in His kindly act at the wedding feast was the expression both of His power and His character.

So, then, the glory which the apostles witnessed in Christ was the visible expression of what is indicated in the relationship of "an only begotten from a Father."

Further, the Revisers have rightly rendered the preposition by "from" and not "of." The word in the original is *para*, which signifies, in this construction, "from the presence of," "from with [a person]." The same preposition is used in the Lord's own words in 7:29, "I am from Him, and He sent Me."

This preposition "from," together with what has already been set forth concerning the glory as that of a Father's Only Begotten, indicates that He Who became flesh, was Himself, in virtue of the previously existing relationship, the unique and perfect representative and manifestation of the being and character of the Father from whose presence He came. In other words, the glory to which John refers was the outshining of a unique, eternal only begotten sonship.[1]

THE TERM "ONLY BEGOTTEN"

The term "only begotten," used in verse in connection with the definite article, is one which, with reference to Christ, is found only in the writings of the apostle John, and, as we have seen in the former instance in verse 14, the term does not refer to generation in respect of His humanity. There are other statements relative to His Sonship which do not contain the title "only begotten," and which do

---

1 That John the Baptist is said to have been "sent from [*para*] God," does not adversely affect the intimation in 1:14 that Christ stood prior to His Incarnation in unoriginated relationship as Son to the Father, and that the glory which the apostles beheld was the glory of One who held this relationship. What requires consideration is both the contextual phraseology, concerning Christ's glory in its manifestation in this respect, and the teaching of Scripture elsewhere concerning the eternal relation between the Father and the Son. There is all the difference between the circumstances of the Baptist and what Scripture teaches about the person of Christ. The latter precludes our pressing the analogy on the ground of the similar use of the preposition. Angels and prophets are said to stand in the presence of God, and in this sense John the Baptist was sent from God, but the truth relating to Christ as "only begotten from the Father" is different. *Para* with the genitive with reference to Him has to do with that which is antecedent to His birth.

refer to His Incarnation; but that is not the case with *monogenēs*, "only begotten." This speaks of that relationship as Son in which He stands alone, coequal and eternal with the Father, yet distinct in personality as the Son.

Again, the term as used of the Son's relationship to the Father in the ideal and intimate affections involved therein must be distinguished from generation as applied to human beings. The phrase "eternal generation" finds nothing to correspond to it in Scripture. It does not serve to explain the doctrine of the eternal relationships in the Godhead. Human limitations prevent a full comprehension of the eternal. Yet God has in grace conveyed the facts relating to Himself in language the phraseology of which we can understand, though the facts themselves lie beyond the range of human conception.

The term here, as frequently in Scripture, signifies both uniqueness and endearment. Thus of Isaac in Hebrews 11:17, the writer, quoting from the Septuagint of Genesis 22:2, instead of from the Hebrew which, translated, reads, "Thy son, thine only son, whom thou lovest, even Isaac," says that Abraham offered up (lit., "was offering") "his only begotten son."

Plainly therefore only begotten is in that passage the equivalent of "only." Now, by actual relationship Isaac was not Abraham's only son. Ishmael had been born before, but Isaac stood in unique relation to Abraham, and in a place of special endearment.

The significance of the word "only begotten," in a sense altogether apart from birth, is strikingly exemplified in two passages in the Psalms. In that part of Psalm 22 which is anticipatory of the Lord's utterances on the cross, the appeal is made, "Deliver My soul from the sword, My darling from the power of the dog." According both to the Hebrew and the Greek, the word for "darling" is "only begotten." The same is the case in Psalm 35:17, where the English translation gives "rescue My soul from their destructions, My darling from the lions." Plainly there can be no connection here with natural relationship of father and son; what is intimated is that that part of the being which is referred to holds the position of preciousness and uniqueness. So with the use of the term in regard to the infinite and unoriginated relationship between Father and Son.

In addition to the thought of uniqueness and endearment, the term when coupled with the word "Son" conveys the idea of complete representation, the Son manifesting in full expression the characteristics of the Father. This is borne out by what is further said in John 1:18.

IN THE BOSOM OF THE FATHER

The plain implication of the preexistent sonship of Christ given in verse is confirmed in verse by the description of the Son as the One who is "in the bosom of the Father." The phraseology employed is that of the definite article with the present participle of the verb "to be," lit., "the [one] being in the bosom . . ." This form of phrase provides what is virtually a titular description, and is to be distinguished from the use of the relative pronoun with the present tense of the verb to be ("who is"). Had it been the intention of the writer to state that the Son is at the present time in the bosom of the Father, in contrast to a time in the past when He was not in that position and relationship, the relative clause, that is to say, the relative pronoun with the present tense, would have been used (i.e., *hos esti*, "who is"). The participial construction (the definite article with the present participle "being") is not thus limited in point of time. Here the construction conveys a timeless description, expressing a condition and relationship characteristic, essential and unoriginated.

The phrase "in the bosom of the Father" conveys the thought of affection, and is indicative of the ineffable intimacy and love essentially existent between the Father and the Son, the Son sharing all the Father's counsels, and ever being the object of His love.

The preposition *eis* ("in") expresses something more than the similar preposition *en*.[1]

What is suggested is not only "in" as indicating the essential union of the Son with the Father, but the further thought of His absolute competency to respond to the Father's love. Of none other could the phrase be used. Nothing is to be gained by rendering the preposition by "into," as if in a more literal sense.

The use of the definite article in this construction points, then, to the uniqueness and the essential nature both of the position and the relationship of Christ.

As in verses 1–14, the doctrines relating to Him as the Word culminate in the statement of His Incarnation, "the Word became flesh," so now verse 18, recalling the description "only begotten" from verse 14, and distinguishing the Son by that designation, leads on, while terminating the prologue, to the witness of John the Baptist. This is introduced by the particle "and" connecting verse 19 with verse 18, and this witness brings before us the culminating truth of Christ as the Lamb of God (v. 29).

FURTHER ILLUSTRATIONS OF THE OMITTED ARTICLE

The principle of the stressing of the character or description of a person by means of the omission of the article, as exemplified in the clause "an only begotten from a Father," is well illustrated in certain passages in the epistle to the Hebrews in connection with the sonship of Christ.

HEBREWS 1:1, 2

In the opening words of the Epistle, "God, having of old time spoken unto the fathers in the prophets by divers portions and in divers manners, hath at the end of these days spoken unto us in *His* Son, Whom He appointed Heir of all things, through Whom also He made the worlds," the insertion of the word "His" in italics is sufficient indication that there is no definite article in the original. Literally,

---

1 Etymologically *eis* (really *ens*) was thus a more comprehensive word than the simple *en*.

therefore, the statement reads "hath at the end of these days spoken unto us in a Son." The stress is put upon the relationship. He in whom God has spoken to us is marked out as One standing in relation to Him as Son to Father. In verse 8, in contrast to this, the article is used: "Of the Son He saith, Thy throne, O God, is forever and ever." The use of the definite article here marks the Son as the person who has already been spoken of in this respect.

The design in the stress on the word "Son" in verse 2 is not to convey the idea that God has spoken to us in one who became His Son, but that he has done so in one whose relationship to Him as Son stands in antecedent existence both to creation and to His Incarnation. The appointment of Christ as heir was a matter of the divine counsels in Eternity.

The passage is itself a testimony to the preexistent Sonship of Christ; for not only has God spoken to us in Him who is His Son, but by Him, "the Heir of all things," he "made the worlds" (the ages). The plain implication is that He by whom God made the worlds stood in relationship to Him in this respect as His Son. If there was no such relationship before the Incarnation, the conclusion seems unavoidable that one God made use of another God to make the worlds. There are not two Gods, nor are there three acting together. Deity is monotheistic. He by whom all things were created (Col. 1:16), was the Son of the Father's love (v. 13), and one with Him in Godhood as Creator as in all other attributes of Deity.

The Father, the Son, and the Holy Spirit were never three separate beings each possessed of the attributes of Deity, each self-existent, and possessed of similar character and power. That there is only one God remains an essential doctrine of the Christian faith. That there are three distinct persons in the Godhead is consistent with the foundation truth of the unity of the Godhead. The very titles given in Scripture are evidences of this. Yet each is God, that is to say, possessed of Godhood, and all subsist together as the One God. Denial of the eternal Sonship of Christ lays one open to the Tritheistic idea that, as to presence, place, and glory, divine persons were together, coequal and coeternal, and yet that the Father and the Son were not related as Father and Son. It leads also to the erroneous view that the relationships of the Father and the Son belong simply to the sphere of revelation.

It will be helpful here to quote Liddon's remarks on the use of the word *persons* in reference to the Father, the Son, and the Holy Spirit. Speaking of the truth relating to the Godhead, he says: "It postulates the existence in God of certain real distinctions having their necessary basis in the essence of the Godhead. That such distinctions exist is a matter of Revelation. . . . These distinct forms of being are named persons. Yet that term cannot be employed to denote them, without considerable intellectual caution. As applied to men, 'persons' [this word is not in quotes in the original but the style in Vine's is to put quotes on words used as words] implies the antecedent conception of a species, which is determined for the moment, and by the force of the expression, into a single, incommunicable modification of being. But the conception of species is utterly inapplicable to

That One Supreme Essence which we name God; the same essence belongs to each of the divine persons. Not, however, that we are therefore to suppose nothing more to be intended by the revealed doctrine than three varying relations of God in His dealings with the world. On the contrary, His self-revelation has for its basis certain eternal distinctions in His nature, which are themselves altogether anterior to and independent of any relation to created life. Apart from these distinctions, the Christian Revelation of an Eternal Fatherhood, of a true incarnation of God, and of a real communication of His Spirit, is but the baseless fabric of a dream. These three distinct 'Subsistences,' which we name Father, Son, and Spirit, while they enable us the better to understand the mystery of the self-sufficing and blessed life of God before He surrounded Himself with created beings, are also strictly compatible with the truth of the divine unity. And when we say that Jesus Christ is God, we mean that in the Man Christ Jesus the second of these persons or subsistences, one in essence with the first and with the third, vouchsafed to become Incarnate."

THE OMITTED DEFINITE ARTICLE IN HEBREWS 1:5

Again, in Hebrews 1:5, in the quotation, "I will be to Him a Father, and He shall be to Me a Son," the omission of the definite article places the emphasis upon the relationship expressed in the terms "Father" and "Son." This statement is not a prediction about a time when the relationship would begin. The beginning of the relationship is not in view. What is set forth is, firstly, its distinct character in contrast to its nonexistence in the case of the angels; and secondly, the adequate realization of it in His life of entire obedience to the Father's will; and not only then, but its continuance ever afterwards. The relationship which had eternally existed found a new expression in the Son Incarnate.

There is a love which had no beginning involved in the relationship. Never would the love of the Father to the Son and that of the Son to the Father have become known and adoringly apprehended by the redeemed, had it not been for the Incarnation of the Son. The manifestation of the relationship gives us to appreciate in measure what the Father is to the Son and what the Son is to the Father. In the statement, then, "I will be to Him a Father, and he shall be to Me a Son," we have the assurance that the relationship was to be realized in a perpetual fulfillment in the divine actings on behalf of man, and in an ineffable appreciation therein of the fatherhood of the Father by the Son, and of the sonship of the Son by the Father.

The word *huios*, "son," is not simply, nor indeed always, indicative of offspring; it signifies expression of character. We read, for instance, of "sons of this world," and "sons of light" (Luke 16:8, R.V.). Used of the Lord Jesus, the single title "Son" generally signifies, as in the passages we have just considered regarding Him, that He shares in unoriginated subsistence the Father's nature, and is the revealer of His character. Thus He says to Philip, "He that hath seen Me hath seen the Father" (John 14:9). Plainly what is in view in such a statement is not the inception of the relationship.

HIS SONSHIP AS THE SENT ONE

Jesus was sent by the Father, and He is called the Son of God. The following focuses on the relationship between Father and Son—coexistent and coequal members of the divine Trinity—as it is described in the New Testament. The Sonship of Jesus is also a critical element in our understanding of the faithfulness of Jesus.

There are many passages which speak of the sonship of Christ in respect of His having been the One sent by the Father; these call for our contemplation, especially in connection with what is involved as to the glory and grace of our blessed Lord. The first of these in the Gospel of John is in chapter 3, verses 16 and 17: "For God so loved the world, that He gave His only begotten Son, that whosoever believeth on Him should not perish, but have eternal life. For God sent not the Son into the world to judge the world, but that the world should be saved through Him." Neither does this Scripture nor any other state that it was as the Son of God in manhood that He was given and sent. The statement does not mean that the sending into the world took place after His birth and His having grown up into manhood. Both the gift and the sending were from heaven. The greatness of the love of God in giving and sending is measured in terms of the preexistent relationship expressed in the title "only begotten."

That the Lord was in the presence of Nicodemus when He spoke of himself in this way provides no support for the view that the sending into the world was subsequent to His birth. Nor again does the fact that John the Baptist began his public career as a man sent from God afford an analogy for the sending of Christ in the same way. John had no antecedent existence; Christ was eternally preexistent.

Nor does the fact that Christ came in a mediatorial character provide an argument against His preexistent Sonship. His relation as Son to the Father is not contingent upon His mediatorship. On the contrary, as we shall see from Colossians 1:15, 18, His mediatorial acts, in regard both to creation and redemption, were consequent upon His already existing Sonship.

"SANCTIFIED AND SENT"

In His controversy with the Jews the Lord speaks of Himself as the one "Whom the Father sanctified and sent into the world" (John 10:6). The order is significant, and is sufficient to show, when taken with other Scriptures, that the sending was from heaven to earth. The order is "sanctified and sent," not "sent and sanctified." The sanctification, that is, the setting apart for the purpose, was not a matter of time. It was in the counsels of God before the foundation of the world, that the Son was set apart for His mission of redeeming grace.

The testimony in 1 John 4:9, concerning God's love to us can only rightly be understood in the same way: "Herein was the love of God manifested in us, that God hath sent His only begotten Son into the world, that we might live through Him. Herein is love, not that we loved God, but that He loved us, and sent His Son to be the propitiation for our sins." The love of the Father for the Son, implied in the term "only begotten," was a love of which the Son Himself, in addressing the Father as the Father, says, "Thou lovedst Me before the foundation of the world" (John 17:24). If that preexistent love was not between the Father and the Son, what can have been the relationship in which it was exercised? It does not suffice that the divine persons were coequal and coeternal. God did not send one who was simply God.

PREEXISTENT GLORY WITH THE FATHER

The love involved in the relationship prior to the Incarnation marks the sending as taking place, not out into public life after Christ had grown up, but from the glory of which He says, "And now, O Father, glorify Thou Me with Thine own self with the glory which I had with Thee before the world was" (17:5). Such words are surely a testimony against an interpretation that the glory which was His was with one who eventually became His Father when He was born. True, we cannot define that glory, but we can accept the truth of the eternal existence of the relationship and the eternal love involved in it. That He received honor and glory from the Father in the days of His flesh affords no testimony to the contrary. So again the apostle's statement, "We have beheld and bear witness that the Father hath sent the Son to be Savior of the world" (1 John 4:14), does not mean that having become the Father, He sent the one who had become His Son to be the Savior of the world.

HIS SONSHIP ESSENTIAL IN HIS GODHOOD

It is evident from the Lord's Prayer recorded in John 17 that His relationship as the Son to the Father subsists essentially in His divine personality. His Sonship, therefore, must have subsisted in the eternal Godhead, and unchangeably so, for a change in His Godhood is impossible.

The preexistent relationship is expressed in the Lord's words in John 16:28: "I came out from the Father, and am come into the world: again, I leave the world and go unto the Father." The twofold course, both in the coming and the return, is clear. His return to the Father was in the reverse order of procedure to that of His coming. He came from heaven to the world; He returned from the world to heaven. He speaks of the one from whom He came as "the Father," not in the sense that He came out from one who subsequently became the Father at His birth, but from one who was the Father when He came out. Nor can His statements mean that His coming into the world was an entrance into public life, as in His manhood, after God has become His Father. His leaving the world, by way of His exaltation to the Father's right hand, was in direct antithesis to the stoop which He took when, coming forth from the glory which He had with the Father, He humbled Himself to become Incarnate.

AN ANALOGY CONCERNING THE HOLY SPIRIT (GAL. 4:4-6)

The word "sent forth" is used both of the Son and of the Holy Spirit in Galatians 4:4-6: "When the fullness of the time came, God sent forth His Son, born of a woman, born under the Law, that He might redeem them which were under the Law, that we might receive the adoption of sons. And because ye are sons, God sent forth the Spirit of His Son into our hearts, crying, Abba, Father."

The use of the word "send" with reference to the Holy Spirit throws light upon the significance of the word as used of the sending of the Son by the Father. The Lord said that the Father would send the Holy Spirit, and that He Himself would likewise do so. He was not the Holy Spirit because He was sent; He did not become the Holy Spirit upon the occasion of His mission. So neither did Christ become the Son in being sent from the Father.

The analogy, then, confirms the preexistent Sonship of Christ. But not only so, the very title, "the Spirit of His Son," expresses that essential relation and characteristic of the Holy Spirit with regard to the Son by reason of which He produces the spirit of sonship within us.

Even grammatically, the statement may not be read as if it meant that "God sent forth His Son, having been born of a woman." The construction in the original is against such a rendering. The construction is precisely the same, for instance, as in Philippians 2:8, where "becoming" translates the same word as that here rendered "born" (*ginomai*), the form of the verb being the same. The statement, "He humbled Himself, becoming obedient even unto death," could not mean that He humbled Himself after having become obedient unto death. On the contrary, His self-humbling was expressed in His becoming obedient. The particular form of the verb rendered "becoming" signifies the mode of the humbling.

So the preceding verse, where the same word is rendered "being made," sets forth the mode of His self-emptying. "He emptied Himself, taking the form of a servant, becoming in [see margin] the likeness of men." He did not empty Himself after taking the form of a servant and becoming in the likeness of men. These acts specify how His self-emptying[1] took effect.

This construction, then, throws light upon the statement in Galatians 4:4. The clause, "born of a woman," particularizes the act, not the antecedent, of the

---

1 The construction is the aorist participle following a main predicate in the past tense. The aorist (or indefinite) participle in such a construction does not mark an event which took place prior to that expressed by the preceding verb; it serves to specify the mode of the action signified by that predicate.

sending. He was not sent forth after His birth. The sending forth took effect in His birth. The one who was sent forth was already the Son of the Father. He was and is the Son, not because He began to derive this relationship from the Father at His Incarnation, but because He ever was, in that relationship, the expression of what the Father is, as confirmed in His own statement, "He that hath seen Me hath seen the Father" (John 14:9).

RELATIONSHIP NOT DETERMINED BY REVELATION

The fact that no names such as "the Son," "the Son of God," were actually given till the New Testament in no way serves to disprove the preexistent relationship. Did not Jehovah, for instance, exist as Jehovah before the title was revealed to man? Was God, "the Almighty God," simply from the time when He first made Himself known by this title? Does His existence as the Father begin simply from the time when that title was revealed to man? Far from it. The existence of the attributes and character of God, and the relation of the Son to the Father, did not depend upon their revelation to man. Certainly it is because God has made Himself known as the Father, and has provided the means by which we become His children, that we can regard Him in that relationship and through grace can address Him so. But that fact does not afford us any ground for the supposition that He was not the Father till He was made known in that relationship. Neither are we to suppose that Christ was the Son only when He was revealed as Son, any more than God was God only when He was made known as such. Facts of deity are not contingent upon human knowledge. To regard the relationship of Fatherhood and Sonship as being contingent upon the revelation of the persons in the Godhead to creatures, is to conceive of the subject in the reverse order of that revealed in Scripture. The eternal relationship of the Father to the Son was entirely compatible with the equality of the persons in the Godhead. It was compatible, too, with the fact that God as God is invisible, and with the truth of the inscrutability of the Godhead as such.

SUBORDINATION NOT INFERIORITY

The question arises whether the position of subjection which Christ took in His life of perfect obedience to the Father involved His inferiority in the divine relationship. Now, even in earthly relationships sonship does not necessarily involve inferiority. When a son is grown up to manhood, and undertakes responsibilities which formerly belonged to his father, he is frequently in a position of equality with his father. Solomon was king of Israel while yet his father David was alive. If this may be so in human relationships, how must more in regard to relationships in the Godhead? Christ became subordinate in His Incarnation for the purpose of the fulfillment of the Father's will, and in divine grace toward man, but His subordination did not involve His inferiority, as the Son of God. In becoming man He did not abrogate His attributes of Deity. In His birth, and without intermission, His Godhood remained. Accordingly He said, "I and the Father are one"

(John 10:30), and enjoined that all were to honor the Son "even as they honor the Father," declaring likewise that "he that honoreth not the Son honoreth not the Father which sent Him" (5:23).

If in human affairs the sending of a person may mean authority on the part of the sender and inferiority on the part of him who is sent, we are not justified in pressing the analogy to hold good in the case of divine persons. For the fact remains that in absolute deity the Son, as such, was sent by the Father, as such, into the world, without any change in equality of the persons as in the Godhead. The fact of the eternal equality does not render the relationship, and what was involved in the sending, incompatible with the continued equality, in respect of Deity.

The same is true of the Holy Spirit. In deity He always was and ever remained on equality with the Father and with the Son, and yet the Holy Spirit was sent at pentecost both by the Father and by the Son (John 14:26; 15:26; 16:7). The sending did not involve inferiority in His case. In regard, therefore, to the persons in the Godhead, the term "sent" does not imply such a relative position as is inconsistent with equality in deity.

The new condition into which Christ entered in becoming man was, indeed, one of subordination (Heb. 2:9; 5:8; 1 Cor. 15:27). Accordingly He said, "My Father is greater than I" (John 14:28). With this statement we may compare His word concerning His sheep: "My Father, which hath given them unto Me, is greater than all" (John 10:29). The context in each passage shows that there is a difference. The statement in 10:29 is not relative to the Son as Incarnate, but is absolute. For He says that the sheep are as secure in His hand as they are in the Father's (v. 28), and proceeds to say, "I and the Father are one" (v. 30). In 14:28, however, the context points to the statement, "My Father is greater than I," as being relative to the Son as Incarnate. Here the Lord has in view His return to the Father. He would then enter into a glory which He had not in the days of His flesh. He is regarding His return in the light of the completion of what He came to do in His servant character, and in fulfillment of the Father's will. His subordination in the days of His flesh did not therefore involve His inferiority.

THOU ART MY SON, THIS DAY HAVE I BEGOTTEN THEE

Psalm 2:7 is quoted three times in the New Testament. This Old Testament reference is illustrative of Jesus' incarnation, but also of His Priesthood. Beginning in the Psalms, we are able to trace the Sonship of Christ as it pertains to His role as a Priest of the order of Melchizedek.

PSALM 2:7 AND ITS QUOTATIONS
The First Quotation: Acts 13:33

The declaration, "Thou art My Son, this day have I begotten Thee," quoted in Acts 13:33; Hebrews 1:5, and 5:5, from Psalm 2:7, indicates a distinct act accomplished at a given time. As to the occasion referred to, the context both in Acts 13 and Hebrews 1 gives intimations. In Acts 13 Paul is addressing the men of Israel in the synagogue at Antioch in Pisidia; in briefly narrating the history of the people, he speaks of David as having been "raised up" to be their king (v. 22). Obviously not resurrection from the dead is there in view, but the raising up of a person through birth and childhood into manhood, to occupy a particular position in the nation. In the same sense Moses had spoken of Christ as follows: "The Lord thy God will raise up unto thee a Prophet from the midst of thee, of thy brethren, like unto me." This is quoted by the apostle Peter in addressing the people in Solomon's Porch (Acts 3:22), and by Stephen in addressing the Council (7:37). This prophecy received its fulfillment in that Christ was raised up as a prophet in the nation as the result of His Incarnation. That ministry He fulfilled in the days of His flesh.

In Acts 13:33, the apostle Paul speaks in the same way in the synagogue at Antioch concerning Christ. He says: "We bring you glad tidings of the promise made unto the fathers, how that God hath fulfilled the same unto our children, in that He raised up Jesus" (v. 33). That is to say, God raised Him up in the midst of the nation in the same sense as in the other passages just noted. The word "again" in the A.V. has nothing corresponding to it in the original. The translators of the A.V. added the word "again" by way of interpretation. The reference in this verse (unlike that in the next), is not to resurrection, but to what has already been stated. In verse 34 the additional statement of His resurrection is made with stress upon it: "And as concerning that He raised Him up from the dead, now no more to return to corruption, He hath spoken on this wise, I will give you the holy and sure blessings of David." His having been raised from the dead stands thus in emphatic contrast to, and as the counterpart of, what was stated in verse 33 as to His being raised up in the nation. Emphasis is imparted by the addition of the words "from the dead."

Now in verse 33 the statement as to the raising up of Jesus in the midst of the nation is confirmed by the quotation from the second psalm: "Thou art My Son, this day have I begotten Thee." Accordingly, the reference in this quotation would be to His Incarnation. The order is significant: His Incarnation in verse 33, His resurrection from the dead in verse 34. In these two respects the apostle says that God both has fulfilled His promise made unto the fathers, and has given the sure blessings of David.

The Second Quotation: Hebrews 1:5

That the reference in the declaration, "Thou art My Son, this day have I begotten Thee," is to the Incarnation, is confirmed by the quotation in Hebrews 1:5, and its relation to the 6th verse. The clause, "And when He again bringeth in the Firstborn into the world" (R.V.) looks on to the Second Advent (see Heb. 5, in connection with the subject of Christ as the Firstborn). That event, yet future, is set in contrast to the birth of Christ, His First Advent. It was then that God brought His Firstborn into the world the first time. To this, accordingly, the quotation refers in the preceding verse, "Thou art My Son, this day have I begotten Thee."

What is stated in regard to the Incarnation in this declaration can only rightly be viewed in the light of the existent and eternal relationship of the Father to the Son. This preexistent relationship found expression in that act of grace by which the Son became man through the operation of the Holy Spirit according to the counsels of the triune God.

That the Lord Jesus was the Son of God in that special phase of His existence by which He "partook of flesh and blood" (Heb. 2:14), being born of the Virgin Mary, does not involve His not having preexisted in relationship as Son to the Father. That act, accomplished with the purposes of redemption in view, was effected by those who stood the one to the other in unoriginated relationship and divine nature as Father and Son, as well as by the Holy Spirit. The declaration, "Thou art My Son, this day have I begotten Thee," was made in view of the fact that now, in the scheme of redemption, He who was the Son had become Incarnate, combining in Himself humanity and Deity.

His Incarnation constituted a new and distinct phase in the existence of Him who, in unoriginated personality in the Godhead, was antecedently "the only begotten Son in the bosom of the Father." That preexistent relationship but enhances the glory of the grace of His Incarnation. His had been the eternal glory which He had with the Father, and His was now the additional glory of that condescending grace by which He stooped to become Man. The very infinitude of His person in relationship to the Father forbids the deduction that, because the Father, in view of what took place at Bethlehem, said, "Thou art My Son, this day have I begotten Thee," His Sonship therefore began at that time.

The Third Quotation: Hebrews 5:5

The third quotation is set in connection with the High Priesthood of Christ, which forms the central theme of the epistle. It was introduced at the beginning of the third chapter, and is continued from the 14th verse of the fourth chapter into the fifth, and from the seventh to the tenth. In chapters 5 and 7 two points stand out prominently in the presentation of the perfect fitness of the Lord Jesus for His High Priestly ministry. The one relates to His Incarnation, His experiences in the days of His flesh, His death and resurrection and exaltation. The other relates to the eternal character of His Sonship.

In regard to the first, and with a view to expanding the character of the Priesthood of Christ, the writer shows how He fulfilled all that was foreshadowed concerning Him in the Levitical priesthood (ch. 5:1–4). Two qualifications marked the high priest of old. He was taken from among men, and was appointed by God for man (v. 1). This was fulfilled in the person of the Lord Jesus Christ. He became man, and has been appointed by God the Father: "and no man taketh the honor unto himself, but when he is called of God, even as was Aaron. So Christ also glorified not Himself to be made a High Priest, but He that spake unto Him, Thou art My Son, this day have I begotten Thee" (vv. 4, 5). The passage stresses the fact of His humanity, the days of His flesh, His strong crying and tears, His perfect obedience as Son, and His sufferings. His sacrificial death was the foundation upon which He perfectly fulfills His office as High Priest.

THE MELCHIZEDEK CHARACTER OF HIS PRIESTHOOD

But this further is added, that His priesthood is not after the Aaronic order, but after the order of Melchizedek (vv. 6–10). This subject is extended at the close of the sixth chapter and the beginning of the seventh.

Now it is in connection with the Melchizedek character of the Lord's High Priesthood that His eternal Sonship is intimated. For Melchizedek is "made like unto the Son of God" in this, that he stands before us in the Genesis record, "without father, without mother, without genealogy, having neither beginning of days nor end of life" (Heb. 7:3). If the Sonship of the Lord began at His Incarnation, then the analogy fails in the respect that He had beginning of days at His birth. It is significant that in this comparison He is called "the Son of God," for only just before, in 6:20, He is spoken of simply as "Jesus," and at the beginning of the chapter as "Christ." The title "Son of God" is purposely chosen in order that, this relationship being presented, He may, in not having beginning of days or end of life, fulfill the analogy with Melchizedek. The very glory of Christ's High Priesthood lies in this, that He stands in His relationship as the Son of God, and that in this respect He has neither beginning of days nor end of life. It was an obligation with the Aaronic priests to declare their genealogy, but Melchizedek stands before us in the narrative in Genesis not only with an absence of these details, but likewise without mention of human parentage, and in this his likeness to the Son of God also exists.

It is in His divine relationship, then, to the Father, that Christ has neither beginning of days nor end of life. This stands in striking contrast to the period spoken of as "the days of His flesh" (5:7), which began with His birth and ended with His death. But that is not the case with His Sonship, and in this respect it is a significant feature of the Gospel of John, the object of which is to present Him as the Son of God, that it gives no record of His birth.

Thus the perfections of our High Priest lie in this, among other respects, that He is possessed both of Godhood and manhood. His deity is set forth in the Hebrews epistle, as well as in other Scriptures, in that He was the Son of God, not simply in time but in the eternal past; His humanity is set forth in this that, being already the Son of the Father, He became man by an act of grace, being "born of a woman" by divine operation. This stupendous condescension received the divine declaration, "Thou art My Son, this day have I begotten Thee."

It is true that the word "eternal" is not used in Scripture in connection with the Sonship of Christ, but that affords no proof that the relationship did not exist in the eternal past. Phraseology that is endorsed by the general teaching of Scripture is sound, and the Scriptures give abundant evidence that the relationship was eternal.

THE SIGNIFICANCE OF THE TITLE "THE FIRSTBORN"

Jesus is not only called the only begotten Son of God; He is also referred to as the Firstborn of all creation. Here we explore the biblical significance of being "firstborn," and look in detail at five different passages where the term appears. In being examining this title, we gain a greater understanding of Jesus' relationship with the Father, His priority, His creative prowess, and His position over all creation.

1. THE FIRSTBORN WITH REFERENCE TO CREATION

There is a significant passage which, like the first chapter of the Gospel of John, speaks both of His Creatorship and of His relationship with the Father, and teaches plainly that He gave creation its being in virtue of His preexistent Sonship. This is Colossians 1:16, 17, where Christ is described as "the image of the invisible God, the Firstborn of all Creation."[1]

It is necessary first to consider the objective character of the phrase "of all creation." We say "objective" in contrast to "subjective," as if He were Himself the subject of creative power, and so were to be classed with creation; whereas, on the contrary, the construction is plainly objective, signifying that the universe owes its existence to Him as its Creator. This is confirmed by the succeeding context, which declares that "all things were created by Him, things visible and invisible, whether thrones or dominions or principalities or powers." Accordingly, to class Him with creation is to imply that He created Himself, which is an absurdity. The phrase means, then, that as the Firstborn He was the producer of creation.[2]

---

1 For a paper on the subject see "Echoes of Service," October, 1910; also a booklet, "Christ the Firstborn."

2 This objective genitive construction is quite frequent in the N.T. Thus in John 2:17, "the zeal of Thine House" means "the zeal for Thine House." In John 10:7, "the door of the sheep" signifies "the door for the sheep to enter by." Acts 4:9 literally reads, "the good deed of an impotent man," which plainly is "the good deed done to an impotent man." In John 17:2, where, literally, the phrase is "authority of all flesh," the only possible rendering is "authority over all flesh." There is a further striking example of the objective genitive in the description of Christ as "the Beginning of the creation of God" (Rev. 3:14). This does not class Him with the creation referred to there, but speaks of Him as the originator, the prime cause and head of it.

We may note, in passing, the three prepositions in verse 16. The R.V. gives these correctly: "All these things have been created in Him . . . through Him, and unto Him." The first preposition "in" signifies that He personally was the center of the divine counsels concerning creation before it actually had being, just as an architectural design exists in the mind of the architect before the actual building is constructed. The second preposition "through" marks Him as Himself the instrument in bringing creation into existence. The third, "unto," signifies that He is the object for whose glory the universe has been brought into being.

The Term "Firstborn"

The term "firstborn," while sometimes used in Scripture in its literal sense, is, on the contrary, frequently used without reference to primogeniture, and in order to indicate preeminence. This is clear, for instance, from the Mosaic Law in Deuteronomy 21:16, which decreed that a man who had two wives, the one beloved and the other hated, who had both borne him children, must not, when dividing his inheritance among his sons, "make the son of the beloved the firstborn before the son of the hated, which is the firstborn." Clearly the term is used to signify a position of preeminence or headship above others. Sometimes indeed the word is used without reference to natural birth at all. Thus God says to Pharaoh, "Israel is My son, My firstborn" (Exod. 4:22). Again, in Jeremiah 31:9, He speaks in the same way of Ephraim: "I am a Father to Israel, and Ephraim is My firstborn."

Now, while the term does involve the relationships of fatherhood and sonship, yet the passages in Exodus and Jeremiah are sufficient to illustrate the fact that with reference to the Lord Jesus Christ the title does not refer to any inception of His relationship to the Father. On the contrary, it is used to signify His priority and His preeminence over created beings. It marks Him as the ideal pattern to which they were designed to conform.

The Firstborn of All Creation

The form of expression illustrated by the phrase "Firstborn of all Creation" was frequently used to distinguish a person from others in declaring his priority to them in time, and his superiority over them in position. The literal rendering, for instance, of the words of John the Baptist in John 1:15, 30, is: "He was the first of Me." Now John expressly combats the idea that he himself was the Christ, and certainly the phrase he used does not class Christ with the order of beings to which he himself belonged. So the Greek historian Xenophon speaks of a war as "the most notable of wars previously waged." The "of" clearly implies distinction, not association. For a war is not itself of a number of those waged before it. In English literature, too, this distinctive use of the word "of" may be illustrated by Milton's line, "Adam, the goodliest man of men since born." Adam was not one of the men born after him, so the "of" is again used in the sense of distinction, not identification.

Just so Christ, as the Firstborn, is distinct from and prior to all created beings, and the phrase marks His superiority over them as their Creator. In the phrase, "the Firstborn of all Creation," however, the special import is not only His priority to and preeminence over creation, but His relationship to the Father while acting as Creator.

Merely temporal priority is to be excluded from the phrase in this verse. Headship is the dominant idea, but this again not without that of the essential, and therefore unoriginated relationship to the Father. The phrase, and indeed the passage itself, show that in the creation of the universe Christ acted not only in virtue of His Godhead, but as the Son accomplishing His work for the glory of the Father. The term "Firstborn" beautifully combines, as no other term would do, the two subjects, both that of His relationship to the Father and that of His headship over creation. His resurrection is not here in view, for it was not in resurrection that He became the Firstborn. Nor did the natural creation owe its existence to Him in virtue of His prospective resurrection from the dead.

The Five Passages Viewed Chronologically

With the term "Firstborn" as thus used in Colossians 1:15, we may connect the four other places where it is used of Christ. We will take them according to the chronological order of the events connected with the title. The first has to do, as we have noticed, with His work as Creator. The second and third have reference to His death and resurrection. The fourth is associated with His position among His saints in their future glorified state; the fifth with the manifestation of His Person and glory at His Second Advent.

2. THE TERM "FIRSTBORN" IN CONNECTION WITH HIS RESURRECTION (FIRST ASPECT) COLOSSIANS 1:18

In verse 18 of this first chapter of Colossians, Christ is called "The Firstborn from the dead." While verse 15 speaks of His power and headship in regard to the natural creation, this verse speaks of the same in regard to the spiritual: "He is the Head of the Body, the Church: Who is the Beginning, the Firstborn from the dead; that in all things He might have the preeminence." This does not imply that Christ entered upon this relationship to the Father either at His birth or in His resurrection. Just as in regard to the creation, so His was priority in resurrection. Unlike others previously raised, He has been raised to die no more.

That He is the Firstborn from the dead does not imply that He was the Firstborn because He has been raised from the dead. What is conveyed in the phrase is the fact that, had He not been raised from the dead, no others could have had resurrection, and the Church could never have been brought into being. Again, as we have seen with regard to the natural creation, the term combines the twofold idea of His unoriginated relationship to the Father and His headship over the spiritual creation.

"The Beginning"

Further, in connection with His saints, as the Firstborn from the dead He is here called "The Beginning." In His resurrection lie the source and potentiality of their spiritual life; His resurrection is the pledge and earnest of theirs. That He is the Firstborn with regard to them is not a matter of primogeniture, but of superiority to and headship over them, the object being that "in all things He might have the preeminence." In relation to the Church, He is the source and Creator of the spiritual life of the saints who form His body. As the Head He rules, guides, unites, sustains them; He is the mainspring of their energy and the power of their activity.

With reference to the new creation, the Lord speaks of Himself as "the Beginning of the Creation of God," in addressing the Laodicean church (Rev. 3:14). As already observed in connection with the objective sense of the phrase, He is not Himself included in that which is created. But being divinely appointed in the counsels of the triune God, as the Head over all things to the new Creation, He Himself makes known the character of its glory as being from God. "If any man is in Christ, He is a new creature (or, as in the margin of the R.V., "there is a new creation") . . . But all things are of God" (2 Cor. 5:17, 18). Whatever place the Church occupies is due to Christ, and He both is the source of it and gives it its true character.

3. The Second Aspect of His Resurrection: Revelation 1:5

This passage again speaks of Him as the Firstborn in connection with His death and resurrection. Here He is called "the Firstborn of the dead." There is no preposition in the original, according to the best MSS., in contrast to Colossians 1:18, where the preposition *ek*, "out of," is used. Here, as there, the term does not bear the sense of primogeniture, but of priority, superiority, and Headship, in virtue of His relationship with the Father. The distinction between the two passages is this, that the phrase in Revelation 1:5 lays special stress upon the fact that Christ *was* dead (cp. v. 18), while Colossians 1:18 lays stress upon the fact that He rose from the *midst of* the dead. Just as in Colossians 1:15, where the term "Firstborn" is used objectively to denote that creation owes its existence to Him and is maintained under His dominating power, so here, the fact that the saints are to be raised from the dead is due to His resurrection. By reason of His resurrection His saints are called "the Church of the firstborn [ones] who are enrolled in Heaven" (Heb. 12:23). For theirs is a position both of relationship to the Father and to the Son, and of preeminence in regard to others.

The firstborn in Israel were the representatives of the whole people as a nation set apart by God for Himself. Israel is similarly described as "My son, My firstborn" (Exod. 4:22; Jer. 31:9). In each case the thought is that of preeminence in relationship to God. In regard to Israel, other nations are to be brought into divine favor hereafter because of the relationship which God established between Himself and His chosen people. In this sense they are His firstborn.

We may compare the term "firstfruits," which signifies a special position as the outcome of the favor of God and His dealings of grace. Two Hebrew words are thus translated, one meaning the chief or principal part (Num. 18:12; Prov. 3:9, etc.); the other the earliest ripe part of the crop or of the tree (Exod. 23:16; Neh. 10:35, etc.); they are found together in Exodus 23:19, etc.: "the first of the firstfruits."

As the whole land of Canaan was consecrated to God by the consecration of the firstfruits, so the whole nation of Israel was acknowledged as belonging to God by the setting apart of the firstborn (Exod. 13:12–16). Subsequently, the tribe of Levi was substituted for the firstborn of the families, to minister to the Lord (Num. 3:12, 45–50).

So the Church is the peculiar possession of God. It is not His only possession, but, as it is "the Church of the firstborn ones," they are, in their special relationship, a token that all else belongs to Him. Their union with Christ in His resurrection life obtains for them this distinction over other members of the human race. The title identifies them immediately with Christ Himself. All others who are brought into divine favor are viewed in this term. Just as Christ as "the Firstfruits" is the earnest and pledge of the future resurrection of saints, so believers, "a kind of firstfruits," are the earnest and pledge of the eventual restoration of Creation.

4. HIS POSITION AMONG THE GLORIFIED SAINTS: ROMANS 8:29

"Whom He foreknew, He also foreordained to be conformed to the image of His Son, that He might be the Firstborn among many brethren." This points to the consummation of the divine counsels in Christ, when, with bodies conformed to His body of glory, the saints will be in His complete likeness: "Whom He foreordained, them He also called: and whom He called, them He also justified: and whom He justified, them he also glorified" (v. 30). This past tense is prospective, the future event being presented as accomplished, in line with the preceding statements. That Christ is spoken of as "the Firstborn among many brethren" indicates that He is the pattern, or type, to which they are to be conformed in a relationship in which, since He is the only begotten Son, He stands in priority and superiority to them, and, being the Firstborn, He stands in His glorified position as preeminent over them. Their divine relationship is a matter of pure grace. He will not stand alone, in His absolute, unoriginated glory as the only begotten Son; on the contrary, divine grace having related us to Him, He will be seen in His preeminence as the Firstborn among those whom "He is not ashamed to call His brethren," the many sons who will have been brought to glory through His death. In that consummation of grace He will say, "Behold, I and the children which God hath given Me" (Heb. 2:10–13).

5. HIS MANIFESTED GLORY: HEBREWS 1:6

In point of time the last passage in which Christ is called "the Firstborn" is Hebrews 1:6: "And when He again bringeth in the Firstborn into the world (the habitable earth), He saith, And let all the angels of God worship Him."

The R.V. rendering is important for a proper understanding of the meaning. The word *palin*, "again," is not used in verse 6 in the same way as in verse 5, to introduce an additional quotation. In verse 6 it comes, in the original, inside the adverbial clause which begins with the word "when." Another instance of this use of the word is in 2 Corinthians 12:21, "when I come again."

Accordingly, in verse 6, instead of simply introducing a fresh quotation, it points to the future event, when God will again bring His Firstborn into the world, that is to say, at the Second Advent. The time referred to is marked by the divine decree: "And let all the angels of God worship Him." At His birth there was "a multitude of the Heavenly host praising God" (Luke 2:13), but upon His return to the earth in His manifested glory, all the angels will worship Him. They will accompany Him when He comes in the glory of His Father (Matt. 16:27; 25:31; 2 Thess. 1:7; Rev. 19:14). Now the quotation, "Let all the angels of God worship Him," is from the Septuagint Version of Deuteronomy 32:35–43. That passage speaks of the time of the Second Advent. It tells of the judgment of the foes of Israel, the final deliverance of that nation and the blessing granted to the Gentiles. The Septuagint is frequently quoted in the New Testament.

The following is a rendering of the salient parts of the passage: "In the day of vengeance I will recompense. For the Lord shall be comforted over His servants. For I will sharpen My sword like lightning . . . and I will render judgment to Mine enemies, and will recompense them that hate Me. . . . My sword shall devour flesh . . . from the blood of the wounded . . . from the head of their enemies that rule over them. . . . Rejoice ye heavens with Him, and let all the angels of God worship Him; rejoice ye Gentiles with His people . . . the Lord shall purge His people's land." The head of the enemies of Israel, as in the R.V. of verse 42, "the head of the leaders of the enemy," is the man of sin, the first beast of Revelation 13. With this prophecy may be compared Psalms 96 to 100; Isaiah 11:4; Daniel 7:11; Zechariah 14; 2 Thessalonians 2:8; Revelation 19:20, and other passages relating to the circumstances of Christ's Second Advent.

The Five Passages Reviewed

To summarize the five passages, He who was the Father's Firstborn before the creation of the Universe, to which He Himself gave being, He who is the "Firstborn among many brethren," will, when He comes to overthrow the foes of God and of His people the Jews, and to set up His kingdom of peace upon the earth, occupy, as the Firstborn, His preeminent position in the very place of His former humiliation and rejection.

Distinguishing, then, between the two titles, "Only begotten" and "Firstborn," the former speaks of His unoriginated relationship to God the Father, as expressive of His delight in His Son, and looks beyond the limits of human thought to the eternity of the past. Referring as it does to His divine, unique, and absolute relationship, it is not used with reference to created beings. The title "Firstborn" is used, however, with reference to created beings, but distinguishes Him (1) from all creatures absolutely, and (2) relatively from those who form the Church and will be brought into the glory of complete conformity to His likeness. The fourfold teaching of the title may be set forth thus: it indicates (1) His divine relationship, a relationship essential and unoriginated in itself; (2) His priority to created beings in the matter of time; (3) His creative power as the source of their existence; (4) His preeminence and Headship over them, He being the ideal type whose glory they are designed to set forth, in being conformed thereto.

"The Image of the Invisible God"

The mention of Christ as the Firstborn with regard to creation in Colossians 1:15 has a special significance in connection with the preceding statement, "Who is the image of the invisible God." That predicates His Deity. For *eikōn*, "image," is not mere likeness or resemblance, it involves visible and adequate representation. Thus, when used of Christ, it expresses in the one word what is said of Him in John 1:18, with regard to the Father, that "He hath declared Him"; that is to say, has visibly and completely represented Him. Its use in Hebrews 10:1, in contrast to *skia*, "a shadow," suggests the idea of substance. The Law had "a shadow of the good things to come, not the very image of the things," i.e., not the substance of the things themselves.

With this in view, then, He is called "the Firstborn of every creature" (the absence of the article before "Firstborn" throwing stress upon this relationship to the Father). Now the epistle to the Colossians was written to counteract the heretical teachings promulgated in Western Asia and elsewhere, that matter was the origin and abode of evil, that therefore God and matter were antagonistic to each other, and had no communication with each other, and that the creation and government of the world were due to the agency of a series of intermediate beings, angels, or emanations, acting as mediators.

To combat these speculative errors, the apostle sets forth the truth that Christ, the Firstborn, the one eternal Son, was, as such, the sole mediatorial agent both in creation and in the maintenance of the universe, and is, likewise, as the Firstborn (with the significance of the term as mentioned), the one mediator in regard to the spiritual creation, the Church. Just as later on, in instructing Timothy, who was working in that very district, as to what he was especially to inculcate, he says, "For there is one God, one Mediator also between God and Men, Himself man, Christ Jesus" (1 Tim. 2:5). Just as, again, the apostle John, combating the same error, shows that the eternal Word, the only begotten Son, became Incarnate, for the purposes of redemption. The eternal Son was the one answer to all cosmical speculations, the solution to all mystical problems.

While creation was a mediatorial act, and Christ is also the one mediator in regard to redemption and the spiritual creation, the subject of His mediatorship is not actually mentioned in the Gospel of John. This omission is appropriate to that special feature of this Gospel, which sets forth believers as children of God. Christ is the mediator of the covenants (Gal. 3:19, 20; Heb. 8:6; 9:15; 12:24); He is the mediator between God and men; He will be the mediator of the Kingdom of God in its future phase (1 Cor. 15:24–28). But He is not said to be the mediator between God the Father and His children.

IN HIM WAS LIFE

John's Prologue says "in Him was Life." We also know that Jesus is called "the Way, the Truth, and the Life," and He brings the hope for eternal life to all people. Christ is eternal, and the evidence for his eternality is carefully laid out from the great "I AM" of Genesis to the "First and Last" of Revelation. The source of eternal life to the believer is directly related to Jesus's eternal nature Himself; indeed the Eternal One is the only one able to provide eternal life.

Like the Father, the Son has life in Himself, as being one with Him in the Godhead. "In Him was life" (John 1:4). He is "the Life" (11:25; 14:6; 1 John 5:20). Yet the life essentially in Him was not possessed independently of the Father. He says, "As the Father hath life in Himself, even so gave He to the Son to have life in Himself" (5:26). The very comparison, "As the Father hath life in Himself," precludes the idea that the Lord was referring simply to the human life upon which He entered at His birth. It is not a case of cause and effect, or of consequence upon a condition. In other words, the statement does not convey the idea that since the Father hath life in Himself, on that account He gave to the Son to have life in Himself. The statement is one of comparison; the measure of the life of the Son is the measure of the life of the Father. The Father did not give life to the Son as He gives it to creatures. The unity of the two persons in the Godhead forbids the thought. Life essentially resides in the Son, and has ever done so, as One possessing an eternal communication of it from the Father, in virtue of the unoriginated relationship in the Godhead.

The special tense of the verb in the original rendered "gave" (the aorist, which is, literally, the undefined tense) is not here equivalent to the perfect tense, "He hath given."[1]

---

1 The aorist tense in Greek is the normal method of expressing "indefinite or undefined action." It is often culminative, not expressing action from the point of view of an act carried out at a precise or definite occasion, but describing an event as a whole without reference to the time taken in its accomplishment. "The Green aorist takes no note of any interval between itself (i.e., what is expressed in the tense) and the moment of speaking. . . . The Green aorist and the English past do

That the Son has life from the Father cannot be dissociated from the eternal relationship. It has been well said, "The Father from all eternity giveth it, the Son from all eternity receiveth it." That the Lord Jesus is the giver of life to man does not rest simply and solely upon the fact that He became man with a view to giving Himself in propitiatory sacrifice. Eternal life is bestowed indeed on that ground, but that not without the primary and essential fact that the Son was coeternal and coexistent with the Father in life and relationship. So with reference to the same use of the word "gave" in the next verse, where the Lord says, "And He gave Him authority to execute judgment because He is the Son of man." The giving of authority to Him to execute judgment is indeed in view of His being the Son of man as well as the Son of God, but no specific point of time is indicated as to the giving. It does not say that the Father gave this authority to the Son after He had become Son of man. We gather, then, that His statement is to be viewed in the eternal light of the counsels of God, with whom the future is as real and assured as the present.[1]

The opening of the first epistle of John gives further testimony to the Lord's preexistent Sonship. The apostle says, "We . . . declare unto you the life, the eternal life, which was with the Father and was manifested unto us. "That the eternal life is, the person of our Lord Jesus Christ is clear not only from the context, which shows that He was one whom the apostles had seen and handled, but from the identification of "the eternal life" with Christ, in what is said at the end of the epistle, namely, "We are in Him that is true, even in His Son Jesus Christ. This is the true God and eternal life." As "the eternal life," He was with "the Father." The apostle does not here say that He was with God, but with "the Father." Not that He was in the eternal past with One who subsequently became the Father at the Incarnation, but that, as "the Life," He was with One who stood to Him in the relationship of Father. The manifestation was temporal, the presence with the Father was eternal. He did not begin to be the life at His birth, neither did He then begin to be the Son.

His Eternal Preexistence

In the contemplation of this subject our thoughts are carried by the Scriptures into the measureless eternity of the past, and from thence to what constitutes the period of greatest crisis in the history of the human race, and again onward to the

---

not exactly correspond. . . . The aorist is so rich in meaning that the English labors to express it." (A. T. Robertson's *Grammar of the Greek New Testament*, pp. 831, 832, 848.)

If this is so in natural circumstances and conditions, how much more in matters concerning the inscrutable relationships in the Godhead and conditions relative to the life of the persons in the Godhead. We have no hesitation therefore in regarding the use of the aorist tenses in John 5:26 and 27 as pointing, not to specific events in time, but of the Son and His redemptive work and judicial functioning.

1 That He is the Son of God conveys the fact of His essential Deity; that He is the Son of man expresses not simply His humanity, but the fact that He is ideally the representative man, fulfilling in His person the divine purposes regarding man.

timeless, endless future. Two of these, and sometimes all three, are in some passages put into conjunction. For instance, the prophetic utterance which predicted the locality of the Lord's Incarnation declared at the same time His unoriginated existence in the past eternity: "But thou, Bethlehem Ephratah, which art little to be among the thousands of Judah, out of thee shall One come forth unto Me that is to be ruler in Israel; whose goings forth are from of old, from everlasting" (Mic. 5:2). There can be no mistaking who is meant. The person indicated is He who was "born in Bethlehem of Judaea, in the days of Herod the king" (Matt. 2:1). The chief priests and scribes knew full well that Micah's prophecy spoke directly of the Messiah, for they quoted it in answer to Herod's inquiry where the Christ should be born (vv. 4-6). The phrase, "from everlasting to everlasting," is the same in the original as in the words of the Psalm of Moses, "From everlasting to everlasting Thou art God" (Ps. 90:2).

HIS OWN TESTIMONY

Christ Himself declared His eternal preexistence when He said to the Jews: "Verily, verily, I say unto you, Before Abraham was, I am" (John 8:58). Strictly rendered it is: "Before Abraham came to be, I am." He sets Himself in contrast to Abraham in this, that Abraham's existence had an inception. His own existence was marked by no beginning; Abraham's was limited by the condition of time, His had been eternal. Conscious of His limitless, timeless existence in the past, He speaks of Himself by the eternal title of Jehovah, the great "I AM." The Jews had no misunderstanding about that. The discussion closes with dramatic suddenness. This self-acclaimed deity on Christ's part demanded, in their view, His immediate death by stoning, according to the Law. Had His claim been unintentional He could easily have protested and explained. Instead, He simply "went forth out of their hand."

Again, He declares that when He, the Son of man, ascends to heaven, He will be "where He was before" (John 6:62). Often did He say that He came forth from the Father, and that the Father had sent Him into the world; and in His closing prayer He places His preexistence prior to creation, stating of His past glory that it was His with the Father "before the world was" (John 17:5).

THE PERSONAL WORD

It is in the light of these statements of the Lord Himself that we find an explanation of the opening words of the Gospel of John. Only in the sense of His eternal and personal preexistence can we rightly understand the declaration, "In the beginning was the Word." However the phrase "In the beginning" may be taken, whatsoever time our finite mind may conceive of, He who is the Word then "was." The statement does not predicate that He had beginning, that at any time He began to be, it says that in the beginning He was already existent, implying that He was unoriginated.

This passage, like others that have been mentioned, associates the past eternity of His Being with His Incarnation. "The Word was with God, and the Word was God . . . and the Word became flesh, and dwelt among us" (John 1:1, 2, 14). There is not the slightest suggestion here that "The Word" was an abstract, impersonal quality. The whole passage cries out against the idea. This Gospel itself is a witness against it. He who is here called "The Word," who was "with God" and "was God," in union and yet distinction in the Godhead, is at the same time spoken of as the Creator. "All things were made by Him" (v. 3). In a similar manner the passage speaks of Him as "the Light," not an impersonal emanation, but a Being, who, as the Light, came into the world (v. 9, R.V.), and again in this respect, He is spoken of as the Creator: "the world was made by Him" (v. 10). He called Himself "the Light of the World." Personal as the Light, He was likewise personal as the Word. And then, further to emphasize His personality, the apostle shows that He who is "the Word" is none other than the only begotten Son of God (v. 18). This title, "only begotten," we must consider later. The identification of the Word with the Son is of itself sufficient to refute any idea that the Word, or Logos, ever was anything but a personal being. His preexistence, then, must have been coeternal with that of the Father.

The Testimony of the Epistles

The epistles are likewise explicit as to this. The apostle John, in his first epistle, speaks of Christ as "the Word of Life . . . the eternal life, which was with the Father, and was manifested unto us" (1 John 1:1, 2). In the epistle to the Colossians, Paul says, "He is before all things, and in Him all things consist" (Col. 1:17). There is therefore nothing that does not owe its existence to Him, nor anything that exists independently of Him. Again, in the introduction of the epistle to the Hebrews, Christ is presented in His preexistence as the Creator and as the Sustainer of all things, as the Sin-Purger at Calvary (Heb. 1:3), and as the unchanging, everlasting One in the future (v. 12). This passage associates the three, the eternal past, the central point of time, and the eternal future. The past eternity and the future eternity of His being find their focus at the Cross.

And of Christ in the Apocalypse

In the closing book He speaks from the glory, declaring three times that He is "The First, and the Last, and the Living One," the One who was dead and is "alive forevermore" (Rev. 1:17, 18; 2:8; 22:13). His title, "the First," does not imply that He had a beginning, any more than "the Last" implies that He will have an end. These terms could not possibly signify that He belongs to the order of created beings. On the contrary, they are the terms which three times in Isaiah Jehovah uses of Himself (Isa. 41:4; 44:6; 48:12). They therefore declare, in respect of the Son, what is true of the Father, His unoriginated and unending self-existence, His divine power as the originating cause of all creation, and His absolute supremacy over all.

The testimony of the Scriptures we have been considering as to Christ's pre-existence constitutes at the same time a witness to His essential deity. That His goings forth were "from everlasting" could not be said of a created being. The prologue to John's Gospel not only shows that he was personally the Word, but definitely states that He was God (ch. 1:1), and since He Himself declares that He came forth from the Father, and that He and the Father are One, He must have been eternally one with the Father in the Godhead. Again, both this Gospel and the epistles state that He was the Creator of all things, a power which belongs alone to deity.

As we contemplate the essential and eternal glory of Christ in the past eternity, we thereby learn to value more intelligently and adoringly His redemptive work on the cross. May we thus be helped to take the low place at His feet, and, responding to God's grace in Him, worship and serve in fear and filial love all our days!

> Lord Jesus Christ, Eternal Word,
>   The Father's well-beloved Son,
> Thyself Creation's Source and Lord,
>   Thou living, life-imparting One,
> For life and pardon through Thy Blood
> We praise Thy Name, O Son of God.
>
> Thou Who from glory didst descend,
>   The Father's glory, yet Thine own,
> To shameful death Thy way to wend,
>   That we might share Thy glorious Throne,
> For "grace abounding" through Thy Blood
> We praise Thy Name, O Son of God.
>
> Thou uncreated Life and Light,
>   By Whom the heavens and earth were made,
> On Calvary's tree, in death's dark night,
>   By Thee our ransom price was paid.
> For our redemption through Thy Blood
> We praise Thy Name, O Son of God.
>
> Exalted high at God's right hand,
>   For Thy redeemed Thou soon wilt come,
> Fulfilling all that grace has planned,
>   Thy Father's House our destined home.
> And all we owe to Thy shed Blood!
> Blest be Thy Name, Thou Son of God.

THE ETERNAL SONSHIP OF CHRIST

Was Jesus "the Son" before He was born as a man? Many today struggle over what it means for Jesus to be both eternal, begotten, and firstborn. Here we look in great detail at the answer to these questions, considering the relationship between the Father and the Son, Jesus's role as the "only begotten," the reality of Christ's humanity, and His sinless life.

The question now before us is whether in Christ's preexistence He was the Son of God, or whether He became so at His Incarnation. Many Scriptures which testify to His divine sonship might, apart from passages to the contrary, be regarded as suggesting (and have been so understood) that He became the Son of God at His birth, and that this title applies to Him only from that time onward. Should we find, however, that there are Scriptures which demonstrate His eternal Sonship in the past, we must understand the other passages in this light.

In the Epistle to the Galatians the apostle states that "When the fullness of time came,

GOD SENT FORTH HIS SON,

born of a woman, born under the Law" (Gal. 4:4). The reference plainly is to His being sent forth from heaven to earth by Incarnation, and not to any subsequent mission in the days of His flesh. This passage clearly indicates that God sent forth one who was already His Son. We may not read it as if it meant that "God sent forth One who in His birth became His Son," any more than the parallel statement in verse 6, "God sent forth the Spirit of His Son" (R.V.), could be taken to mean that God sent forth one who became His Spirit at the sending. The Spirit of God, sent forth at Pentecost, had ever been His Spirit. Similarly, verse 4 implies that He whom God sent forth was already His Son.

THE LORD'S TESTIMONY

With this agree the Lord's own statements recorded in the Gospel of John. He says to the disciples: "Ye . . . have believed that I came forth from the Father. I came out from the Father, and am come into the world; again, I leave the world, and go unto the Father" (John 16:27, 28). In this He gives a plain intimation of His preexistent relationship as the Son prior to the Incarnation. Some have considered His statement, "I came out from the Father," as pointing to an eternal procession from the Father in the past, or what has been termed the "eternal generation" of the Son. This, however, does not seem to be the Lord's meaning here. His statement, "Again, I leave the world and go unto the Father," expresses the reversal of His procedure mentioned in the first part of the verse. His going unto the Father is the antithesis of His coming out from the Father. What the Lord is teaching in this passage is not the interrelations of Deity in the abstract, but His mission from the Father as having been sent by Him into the world.[1]

His words to the disciples are to be compared with His previous utterance to the Jews, "I came forth and am come from God; for neither have I come of Myself, but he sent Me." Here again the reference is plainly to His mission, and not to His person.

THE TESTIMONY OF JOHN'S FIRST EPISTLE

The apostle John, in the introduction to his first epistle, says, "The Life was manifested and we have seen, and bear witness, and declare unto you the Life, the Eternal Life, which was with the Father, and was manifested unto us" (1 John 1:2). He does not here say that He who was the Life was "with God," but that He was "with the Father." The term "Father" implies the existence of a Son. The terms "father" and "son" are correlative. In no other sense than that of preexistent Fatherhood and Sonship can the apostle have made such a statement.

There is no hint in the Scriptures of any time at which God began to be a Father; yet the above Scriptures make clear that His Fatherhood in relation to Christ was preexistent to the Incarnation. The Fatherhood of the one being eternal, the Sonship of the other must likewise have been eternal. In the light of this introductory statement in the Epistle, we are to understand the subsequent statement in chapter 4:14, "The Father hath sent the Son to be the Savior of the world." It was a Father who sent and a Son who came.

HIS ONLY BEGOTTEN SON

These Scriptures provide us with the interpretation of other passages. When we read, for instance, that "God so loved the world, that He gave His only begotten Son" (John 3:16), the statement may not be taken to mean that Christ became His only begotten Son by incarnation. That would rob the verse of its meaning and force. The value and greatness of the gift lay in the Sonship of Him who was given. His Sonship was not the effect of His being given.

The expression, "only begotten," which, as used of Christ, is found only in John's Gospel and his first epistle, does not refer to His Incarnation. In the Gospel he says, "We beheld His glory, glory as of the [lit., an] only begotten from the [lit., a] Father" (1:14)—not as in the Authorized Version, "*of* the Father." "From" rightly translates the word *para*; the same preposition is used in His words in chapter 7:29, "I am from Him, and He sent Me." The glory was that of a Father's Only Begotten, the sole representative and manifestation of the being and character of the one who sent Him in virtue of the relationship. In other words, the

---

1 It is true that the preposition *para* is used at the end of verse 27, while a different preposition, *ek*, is used in verse 28. We may not, however, press the meaning of *ek* as being "out of," and as denoting eternal generation. It states still more strongly than in the preceding clause His coming forth from heaven to earth. Indeed, the Lord may here be emphasizing the fullness of His self-sacrificing love in leaving the glory to come into the world.

glory to which John refers was the outshining of a unique, eternal, only begotten Sonship. In this relationship He came from heaven to earth on His Father's mission.

In that same eternal sense we are to understand the statements that "the only begotten Son . . . is in the bosom of the Father" (1:18), and that of chapter 3:16 already quoted (cp. 3:18). This is made clear from what the apostle says in his first epistle, that "God hath sent His only begotten Son into the world, that we might live through Him" (1 John 4:9). The sending was by way of His Incarnation, and not subsequent to it. That He is "the only begotten Son, which is in the bosom of the Father," expresses both His eternal union with the Father in the Godhead, and the ineffable intimacy and love between them, the Son sharing all the Father's counsels and enjoying all His affections. The form of expression used in the original, and rendered "which is," indicates that "the bosom of the Father" ever has been and ever will be the Son's dwelling place.

Only then in the sense of unoriginated relationship are we to understand the term "only begotten" when used of the Son. The word "Son," in the case of the Son of God, speaks of Him as the perfect archetype of all that the word connotes, whether in human relation or divine; the expression, "only begotten," tells of the uniqueness of that relation in His case.

The Term, "Begotten"

That the word "begotten" should be used of the Son's relationship to the Father does not imply any beginning to His sonship. It suggests relationship indeed, but must be distinguished from generation as applied to man. To endeavor to shape our ideas of divine relationship according to our knowledge of human relationships is simply to betray our ignorance. The finite mind cannot conceive of that which is infinite. Our limitations of time and sense forbid our full apprehension of the eternal. Yet God has conveyed the facts relating to Himself in language the phraseology of which we can understand, though the facts themselves lie outside the range of human conception.

The Father's utterance, predictively recorded in Psalm 2:7: "Thou art My Son; this day have I begotten Thee," and quoted in Acts 15:33; Hebrews 1:5; and 5:5, is to be distinguished from those passages which we have been considering, which speak of Christ as the only begotten. This latter signifies, as we have seen, an eternally preexisting relationship; the utterance in Psalm 2 and its quotations point to a distinctive occasion, whether the Incarnation or the Resurrection.

The Term "Firstborn"

Again, the title "firstborn" (Col. 1:15, 18; Rom. 8:29; Heb. 1:6; Rev. 1:5), as used of Christ, does not imply a beginning of His being, nor does it class Him with His creatures; it indicates the dignity of His preeminence over them. When, for instance, the apostle Paul speaks of Him as "the Firstborn of all creation" (Col. 1:15), the mode of expression in the original and the context of the passage, sufficiently guard against the idea that Christ is to be classed with the Creation itself. The idiomatic form of expression distinguishes Him from all created beings, and declares His priority and superiority to them. The next verse is explanatory of this title, and shows that instead of being created, He was Himself the creator. The term, "only begotten," is absolute; as such, Christ stands alone in timeless relationship with the Father. The term "firstborn" is relative; it does distinguish Him from all creatures, but it brings them in view so as to show His infinite superiority to them.

HUMAN RECOGNITION OF HIS SONSHIP

In the days of His earthly ministry the recognition of His divine relationship as the Son of God, in whatever connection the title was used, was not based upon a recollection of His superhuman birth, but upon the exhibition of His divine attributes; for even in His manhood while on earth these were always His, even though they might not always be in exercise. For instance, Nathanael's confession, "Rabbi, Thou art the Son of God" (John 1:49), drawn from him by the display of the Lord's omniscience, was contingent, not upon Nathanael's possible acquaintance with the fact of the divine character of Christ's birth, but upon a recognition of His divine personality. Still more suggestive is Martha's confession, the result of the evidences of His divine attributes, "I have believed that Thou art the Christ, the Son of God, even He that cometh into the world" (John 11:27), a recognition at once of His preexistence as well as His divine sonship. The same is true of the effects of His omnipotence in stilling the storm, when the disciples worshiped Him, saying, "Of a truth Thou art the Son of God" (Matt. 14:33). Such is the case also with the testimony of those who were possessed of demons, who, at the putting forth of His power to deliver the victims of this thralldom, cried out, "Thou art the Son of God" (Luke 4:41). What Christ had been in the past eternity was now known among men.

THE SON PRIOR TO CREATION

The writer of the Hebrews epistle states that the words of Psalm 102:25, "Of old hast Thou laid the foundations of the earth, and the heavens are the works of Thy hands; they shall perish, but Thou shalt endure," were addressed by the Father to the Son. That is to say, the utterance was spoken to the Son as such, long prior to His Incarnation. He was, then, already the Son when He created the heavens and the earth (Heb. 1:8, 10). This makes clear the meaning of verse 2. It is "in a Son" that God has spoken to us. The omission of the definite article or pronoun serves to emphasize the relationship. It is true that he has spoken to us through a Son incarnate, but it is also through Him that "He made the worlds," proving that His Sonship did not begin in His Incarnation.

Again, the epistle to the Hebrews states that the brief biography of Melchizedek in Genesis was so shaped that, by the omission of his parentage and his death, he was made (i.e., in the inspired narrative) "like unto the Son of God," and the similarity lay in this, that he had "neither beginning of days nor end of life." Accordingly it was as the Son of God that Christ was without beginning of days. His Sonship was therefore unoriginated and eternal.

"HE THAT CONFESSETH THE SON"

Disbelief in the eternal preexistent Sonship of Christ, while acknowledging God as everlasting Father, is transgression of His express Word, that all should "honor the Son even as they honor the father" (John 5:23). To deny the eternity of the Son while admitting it in the case of the Father, cannot be ascribing equal honor to Them. "Whoso denieth the Son, the same hath not the Father: he that confesseth the Son hath the Father also." Let us see to it that we abide in the truth, that we may "abide in the Son and in the Father" (1 John 2:23, 24). Only as we rightly consider the excellences of His eternal glory as the Son of God can our hearts be bowed in due adoration of Him who stooped to the death of the Cross in order to bring us nigh to God.

THE INCARNATION OF OUR LORD

What is said of the meal offering in the second and sixth chapters of Leviticus reminds us that the Incarnation can only rightly be considered in the Holy Place, and that it is a subject of meditation for those alone who are in the relationship of priests to God. As we ponder it let us worship and adore.

"When the fullness of the time came, God sent forth His Son, born of a woman, born under the Law" (Gal. 4:4). "Born of a woman!" A special significance attaches to this. The apostle hereby distinguishes the birth of Christ from that of all others. Were it not so he would just be stating a fact of common experience and wasting his words on a mere superfluity of detail. That is not Paul's way. His argument has no room for a simple truism. No one, in writing a biographical sketch of an ordinary man, would think of saying he was born of a woman. No! For the apostle thus to speak of Christ is both to distinguish Him in accordance with His divine and preexistent Sonship as just set forth by him, and at the same time to testify both to His real humanity and His supernatural birth.

"THE WORD BECAME FLESH"

This statement of the Incarnation of Christ is in the closest agreement with other passages of Scripture relating to the subject. The word rendered "born" is not *gennaō*, the ordinary word to describe "birth," but *ginomai*, "to become," and this is the word used in the declaration in John 1:14, "the Word became flesh," and again in Philippians 2:7, "becoming in the likeness of men" (R.V., margin). In the former passage, as we have previously observed, "the Word" is not an impersonal *Logos*, but "the only begotten Son of God." So the opening of the Gospel identifies Him. He whom God sent forth was His Son. God did not send Him forth into the body of a man. He "was manifested in the flesh" (1 Tim. 3:16). He became flesh, possessing full and perfect manhood, body, soul and spirit. These three constitute the totality of all that is essential to manhood, and this is here the meaning of the word "flesh." Christ Himself speaks of His body and of His soul, and of His spirit. Of the emblematic significance of the loaf in the Lord's Supper He said, "This is My *body*." In the dark hour of Gethsemane He said, "My *soul* is exceeding sorrowful." And on the cross, "Father, into Thy hands I commit My *spirit*." He did not come into flesh, He became flesh, and what he became He is now and ever will be, for He is coming in flesh (2 John 7), which plainly refers to the Second Advent.

The Reality of His Manhood

is expressed also in the Philippians passage referred to above. Christ Jesus, "being in the form of God, counted it not a thing to be grasped (or a means of self-aggrandizement) to be on an equality with God, but emptied Himself, taking the form of a servant, becoming in the likeness of men" (see margin). There is fuller reference to this passage later, when we consider the Servant-character of Christ. His becoming in the likeness of men explains how He took the form of a servant. The expression "likeness of men" in no way negatives the reality of His manhood. The apostle does not say "the likeness of a man," but "the likeness of men," i.e., as they actually are—a mode of existence new to Him. Only of One who was more than man could this be predicated. True manhood was His, and not a mere resemblance thereto. In becoming—what He was not before—man, He did not cease to be what He ever had been—God.

The Incarnation of Christ was

Not the Union of Two Persons,

one divine and the other human. The seat of His personality was His ever-existing deity. He said, "Before Abraham was I am," and "He that hath seen Me hath seen the Father." His manhood was not at any time independently personal. In our case the seat of personality is found in the human spirit, but the man Christ Jesus was identical in person with the Eternal Word. In Him there was no personal subsistence but one, and that from everlasting. By taking manhood He still continues and remains one and the same person, changing only the manner of His subsisting. He who before was in the nature of the Son of God alone, became also, and now is, in the nature of man. Hence we prefer to say that He became "man" and not "a man." If He were not the same person, the Son of God, who, being in the form of God, took the form of a bondservant and became obedient even to the death of the Cross, then the whole point of the passage in Philippians, namely His grace in thus acting, would be lost.

It is of Christ himself that everything is predicated, and not of His divine nature on the one hand and of His human nature on the other. He acted personally, not by this or that nature, but as one in the unity of whose person the two natures are inseparably combined, "without confusion or conversion," as against the Eutychians, who supposed that the humanity of Christ was absorbed into His deity, and "without division, without separation," as against the Nestorians, who divided and separated the natures. It is the same being who acts all through. Nor, again, did either the Father or the Spirit become incarnate, as the Patripassians taught. Manhood is predicated only of the Son. "In Him dwelleth all the fullness of the Godhead bodily" (Col. 2:9).

The two questions now arise:

HOW WAS THE INCARNATION POSSIBLE?

and, how was it accomplished? The first receives an answer at the beginning of the Old Testament, the second at the beginning of the New. "God created man in His own image" (Gen. 1:27). Man marred the divine handiwork by his self-will. That was the effect of the Fall. The narrative which describes it records the divine plan for the recovery of the guilty and the restoration of the broken harmony of man's being. The Lord God himself uttered the initial prophecy of the Incarnation. It was the seed of the woman who would bruise the serpent's head (Gen. 3:15). The apprehension of this led Adam to call his wife's name Eve, "the living one." The giving of that name was faith's response to the divine promise. "Living," not because her own life was spared, but because of her motherhood (v. 20). Life by means of the seed of the woman, that is the message latent in the name of the mother of mankind.

HOW WAS THE INCARNATION ACCOMPLISHED?

As to the second question—how the Incarnation became an accomplished fact, the sanctity of the theme demands the reverence of unshod feet. Speculation is banned. The Gospel narratives with their unencumbered statement of fact provide all that is necessary for faith. Matthew's Gospel records the divine message to Joseph, given him in a dream: "Joseph, thou son of David, fear not to take unto thee Mary thy wife: for that which is conceived in her is of the Holy Ghost. And she shall bring forth a Son; and thou shalt call His name Jesus; for it is He that shall save His people from their sins. Now all this is come to pass, that it might be fulfilled which was spoken by the Lord through the prophet, saying, Behold, the virgin shall be with child, and shall bring forth a Son, and they shall call His name Immanuel" (Matt. 1:20–23, r.v.).

Luke's Gospel records the message given to the Virgin Mary personally by the angel Gabriel. Replying to her inquiry how the promise of a Son could be fulfilled in her unmarried state, he said, "The Holy Ghost shall come upon thee, and the power of the Most High shall overshadow thee: wherefore the holy thing which is to be born shall be called the Son of God," (marginal rendering).

The faith of betrothed Joseph and Mary was remarkable. The naturally troubled state of Joseph's mind at finding that Mary was with child before they came together is intimated by Matthew (1:20). That, notwithstanding, he took Mary to wife, was the obedience of faith. Still more striking was the faith of Mary herself, when in her response to the divine communication she said, "Behold, the hand-maid [rather, "the bondmaid," *doulē*] of the Lord; be it unto me according to Thy word." Mere human considerations might have led her at least to refrain from such a ready acceptance of a situation which would naturally be misunderstood by people and be made a matter of idle talk.

By the overshadowing power of the Most High, and through the Holy Spirit, the Son of God became Incarnate, partaking with us in blood and flesh, the Creator Himself becoming part of the very creation He had called into existence (Heb. 2:14). The Christ was truly "born" of the woman. The language of Scripture precludes the ancient Monophysite (one nature) theory, that He did not partake of her substance, a denial, in other words, that he became incarnate through His mother.

The truth of the Virgin Birth of Christ is

ESSENTIAL TO THE CHRISTIAN FAITH,

it stands in inseparable connection with His acknowledged sinlessness and with the other evidences of the supernatural character of His person. The Gospel narratives of His acts and His teaching banish all incongruity from the initial and preliminary statements of His supernatural birth. His own claims as the Son of God would be invalidated if He were not of the Virgin born. Accept as facts the records of His life, and the unbiased reader is compelled to accept the statements of His virgin birth. Deny the latter, and doubts must be entertained as to the character and attributes of the person who stands before us in the Gospel narratives. Disbelief in the virgin birth and professed acceptance of the remainder of the records concerning Him are entirely inconsistent.

The accounts of the birth of Christ in the Gospels of Matthew and Luke are undeniably genuine parts of these Gospels respectively. The chapters giving the record of the nativity are found in all the manuscripts. In each Gospel the first chapters come to us on precisely the same authority as the remaining chapters. The genuineness of these writings has been fully vindicated. The internal evidences are sufficient to show that the story of the virgin birth of Christ could never have been invented.

It is argued that the virgin birth of Christ does not help to explain His sinlessness and that the taint of sin might have been conveyed by Mary, since hers was a sinful nature. The argument is groundless, however. The overshadowing of the Most High, the power of the Holy Spirit, and the act of the Son of God Himself in the Incarnation, were sufficient to secure absolute freedom from taint of sin. As we have remarked above, the birth of Christ was not the generation of a new being. It was the entrance, on the part of one who was already God, upon a new mode of existence, and hence "the Holy One" remained holy.

"THE GRACE OF OUR LORD JESUS CHRIST"

"Ye know the grace," says the apostle, "of our Lord Jesus Christ, that though He was rich, yet for your sakes He became poor, that ye through His poverty might become rich." This is the meaning and message of the Incarnation. It is not a matter of cold theology. Never can we rightly contemplate the theme without the stirring of our deepest gratitude and affection. Nay, more, be it ours, constrained by such wondrous grace, to render to Him in loving devotion "all we have and are."

> "He has come! the Christ of God
> Left for us His glad abode,
> Stooping from His throne of bliss
> To this darksome wilderness.
>
> "He the Mighty King has come!
> Making this poor earth His home;
> Come to bear our sins' sad load,
> Son of David, Son of God.
>
> "Unto us a Son is given!
> He has come from God's own heaven,
> Bringing with Him from above
> Holy peace and holy love."
> —H. Bonar

THE PERFECT SERVANT

The main reason Jesus came into the world was to do His Father's will. He came to serve, and His obedience to His Father was perfect. His role was foretold: "Behold My Servant." His sacrifices were explained: "Obedient even unto death." And His example is there for us to follow: "As the Father hath sent Me, even so send I you."

The purposes for which Christ Jesus came into the world are variously stated in Scripture. He came "to seek and to save that which was lost" (Luke 19:10). He came to call sinners to repentance (5:32), and to save them (1 Tim. 1:15). His primary object, however, was to do the will of His Father. "I am come down from Heaven," He says, "not to do Mine own will, but the will of Him that sent Me" (John 6:38). This was His very sustenance, His "meat" (4:34). He alone could say absolutely, "I delight to do Thy will, O My God: yea, Thy Law is within My heart" (Ps. 40:8).

His path of undeviating obedience to the Father marked Him as the one of whom Jehovah had said through the prophet Isaiah, "Behold My Servant, Whom

I uphold; My chosen, in Whom My soul delighteth" (Isa. 42:1). "Who, being[1] in the form of God [not a resemblance to God, but that mode of being which reveals the essential nature and character of God[2]] counted it not a prize [more accurately as in the margin, "a thing to be grasped" (the true meaning probably is "a means of self-aggrandizement")] to be on an equality with God, but emptied Himself, taking the form of a servant, being made [lit., becoming] in the likeness of men" (Phil. 2:6, 7).

A BONDSERVANT

He took the form of a "bondservant." This He never was said to be in relation to men, for the word implies the complete yielding of the will to the one served. He was indeed the servant (*diakonos*) of men; so He spoke of Himself, for instance, when, correcting the ambitious rivalry of the disciples, He said, "Whosoever would become great among you shall be your minister (*diakonos*): and whosoever would be first among you, shall be servant of all. For verily the Son of man came not to be ministered unto, but to minister, and to give His life a ransom for many" (Mark 10:43–45). So again in the Upper Room, setting Himself in contrast to their questioning as to which of them was the greatest, He says, "I am in the midst of you as He that serveth" (Luke 22:27). *Diakonos* implies activity in ministry directed by one's own judgment, while *doulos* implies subjection to the will of another, and hence the latter word is said of Christ solely in relation to His service to Him who sent Him. He was the *diakonos* of men, the *doulos* of God. Precisely as the phrase, "the form of a servant," expresses the reality and the character of His position as a servant, for that He undeniably was, so "the form of God" expresses the reality of His deity. He was as truly God, both in His preexistence and subsequently after becoming Incarnate, as He was a servant when on earth.

HIS DIVINE ATTRIBUTES

Since the phrases, "taking the form of a servant, becoming in the likeness of men" (Phil. 2:7), explain the preceding statement that "He emptied Himself," it is important to observe carefully the testimony of the Gospel narratives concerning His attributes and ways as Jehovah's servant. That He remained in the fullest sense God, is, as we have seen, made clear throughout this passage. It is also directly stated in several places in the New Testament. The Gospels present Him

---

1 Or rather, "existing"; the word *huparchō* carries with it a twofold idea, firstly, that what is predicated of this person characterised Him in a special manner both before and at the time referred to, and, secondly, that He continued so to be characterized after the particular event stated of Him. To take an illustration, "Joseph, who was (*huparchōn*, being) a councilor . . . went to Pilate, and asked for the body of Jesus" (Luke 23:50, 52). He did not cease to be a councilor after his request from Pilate. So Christ did not cease to be "in the form of God" after becoming man.

2 That is the meaning of the word *morphē*, form; it denotes the manifestation of the reality inseparable from the person or thing mentioned.

as one who, while possessed of the divine attributes, exercised these in dependence on, and subjection to, the Father. The power He displayed was that which
belongs only to God. Nature was completely subject to His control. He walked
on the water, He stilled the tempest with a word, He turned water into wine, He
supernaturally provided bread. Again, He had absolute power over disease and
death; He healed "all manner of disease and all manner of sickness" (Matt. 4:23),
and He raised the dead. A single utterance from His lips caused His would-be
captors to fall backward to the ground (John 18:6).[1]

Again, "He knew all men," "He knew what was in man" (John 2:24, 25). He
knew the secret history of people's lives (4:16–19), and their destiny (5:24–29;
8:21). He perceived men's thoughts (Mark 2:8; Luke 5:22). He displayed a knowledge of the future impossible to men. His forecast of future events has so far been
fulfilled with absolute precision.[2]

Deeply significant, too, is the fact that the Lord could see what was going on,
though in bodily presence He was not there to behold it. He says to Nathanael,
"Before Philip called thee, when thou wast under the fig tree, I saw thee" (John
1:48). It was nothing but the evidence of Christ's divinely supernatural powers that
drew from Nathanael the exclamation, "Rabbi, Thou art the Son of God; Thou art
King of Israel." And the Lord admitted the evidence of His deity by His recognition of the man's faith; He says, "Because I said unto thee, I saw thee underneath
the fig tree, believest thou? Thou shalt see greater things than these."

HIS OBEDIENCE TO THE FATHER

Now the passage in Philippians 2, which shows that deity was still His in and after
His Incarnation, likewise states that He became "obedient even unto death." His
whole life was one of undeviating obedience to the Father, and His death was the
culminating act thereof. "He learned obedience [it does not say that He learned
to obey] by the things which He suffered" (Heb. 5:8). He never did anything
independently of the Father. He said, "The Son can do nothing of [lit., from]
Himself, but what He seeth the Father doing" (John 5:19). This did not signify
intrinsic limitations in His case; His limitations were only such as He voluntarily
imposed upon Himself. For, He further says, "for what things soever He doeth,

---

1 The miracles of Christ are to be distinguished from those wrought by apostles, prophets, and
others. In their case a miracle was accomplished by divinely imparted power. Compare Peter's
statement as to the healing of the lame man, "Why marvel ye at this man? Or why fasten your eyes
on us, as though by our own power or godliness we had made him to walk?" (Acts 3:12). Christ was
Himself one in the Godhead and, therefore, had all the attributes of Deity, while, being also man,
He acted in the power of the Spirit.

2 In this connection we may notice what the Lord says about His knowledge of the Father. IN one of
the discussions with the opposing Jews He says, "Ye have not known Him; but I know Him" (John
8:55). In the former statement the word is *ginōskō*, indicating knowledge derived from experience;
in the latter it is *oida*, signifying intuitive knowledge. He thus differentiates Himself entirely from
the Jews. It is true that He uses the word *ginōskō* of His knowledge of the Father, as He does also
of the Father's knowledge of Himself, as, for instance, in John 10:15, where He syas, "Even as the
Father knoweth Me, and I know the Father."

these the Son also doeth in like manner." All that He did was done in inseparable union with the Father. He said, "I and the Father are One," and again, "My Father worketh even until now, and I work." Supernatural power, therefore, inalienably belonged to Him as the Son. Yet He ever acted as one who in virtue of His manhood was dependent on, and in subjection to, the will of His Father.

HIS ANOINTING

Again, He declared that He wrought signs by the Spirit of God (Matt. 12:28). The apostle Peter also, referring to the time of Christ's baptism in the Jordan, states that "God anointed Him with the Holy Ghost and with power" (Acts 10:38). This does not imply that Christ was in Himself void of supernatural power, or not possessed of the attributes of Godhead prior to His being so anointed, nor does it imply that He was without the Holy Spirit up to that time. His works were wrought as a result of a divine unction. And herein we learn more fully the glory of His grace as the Perfect Servant; for it shows that, while His deity gives to all He did a unique character and value, He did not act merely in virtue of His Godhood, but, continuing the position of dependence on, and subjection to, the Father, He lived and taught and wrought and offered up Himself, and won His mighty victory, in the power of the Spirit. Had it not been so He would have failed to preserve perfectly the place of a bondservant, which He took so really in this world.

HE LAID DOWN HIS LIFE

In His "becoming in the likeness of men," His body itself became the instrument of His fulfillment of the Father's will. This Psalm 40 foretold, as quoted in Hebrews, "When He cometh into the world, He saith, Sacrifice and offering thou wouldest not, but a body didst Thou prepare for Me: in burnt offerings and sacrifices for sin Thou hast had no pleasure. Then said I, Lo, I am come (in the roll of the book it is written of Me), to do Thy will, O God" (Heb. 10:5–7). He could and did restrict the use of His divine attributes. He allowed His captors to bind Him after the display of His divine power in prostrating them with His Word. He subjected Himself to human violence and indignity. He permitted those who had charge of His crucifixion to carry out their deed. "He was crucified through weakness" (2 Cor. 13:4), not through helplessness, nor through weakness caused by maltreatment, but by the voluntary suspension of His essential power as the Son of God. Human force itself was absolutely unavailing against Him save as it was His will to submit thereto. In proof whereof He said of Himself, what could not possibly be true of any mere man, "I lay down My life, that I may take it again. No one taketh it away from Me, but I lay it down of Myself. I have power [or authority] to lay it down, and I have power to take it again. This commandment received I from My Father" (John 10:17, 18).

The restrictions He imposed on Himself are consistent with His true manhood. At the same time in these very restrictions He constantly displayed His supernatural power. Nowhere is this more strikingly exhibited than on the cross. Certain details regarding His death distinguish it from the crucifixion of a mere man, as, for example, His mighty shout, the dismissal of His spirit, and prior to it the bowing (or rather, reclining) of His head, in contrast to the natural order in which the last breath is followed by the drooping of the head. His death could not have been the death of a mere man. It is useless to argue that God cannot die and therefore Christ was not God. He who was God could become also man in order to die, and this He did. His death was the supernatural death of one who was both man and God.

"OF THAT DAY AND THAT HOUR"

As with His divine power, so with His divine knowledge, referring to His Second Advent He said, "But of that day or that hour knoweth no one, not even the angels in Heaven, neither the Son, but the Father" (Mark 13:22). This was not failure in knowledge. Indeed, it is quite possible that the original conveys the thought that the Son's knowledge is only in conjunction with the Father's. This would be in keeping with His statements, "My judgment is true; for I am not alone, but I and the Father that sent Me" (John 8:16); "I speak that which I have seen with My Father" (5:38). The Lord's statement in Mark 13 is proof that He possessed powers of knowledge which belong to God alone. It likewise displays His character as the perfect Servant of Jehovah. John 1:17–34 is another instance of this. It was in the path of the Father's will that after Lazarus's death, He waited two days before going, and on arriving inquired how long he had been buried and where. All this evinced His compassionate tenderness toward those who were in sorrow.

The Scriptures plainly teach, then, both that the Lord never abandoned His divine attributes, and that He sat as a scholar in the Father's school and learned from Him His daily will. It was of Christ that Isaiah wrote, "The Lord God hath given me the tongue of them that are taught . . . He wakeneth morning by morning, He wakeneth mine ear to hear as they that are taught" (Isa. 50:4, 5).

THE BARREN FIG TREE

In the case of the fig tree recorded in Mark 11:13, He decided to make use of the ordinary means of investigation common to men. "Seeing a fig tree afar off having leaves, He came if haply He might find anything thereon." Here the fig tree was fruitless. "The season was not of figs." The figs should have been there before the leaves if there was to be fruit at all. Immediately, and with a view to the moral significance of His act, He dooms the fig tree to destruction. Both in the investigation and in the destruction He fulfilled the Father's will in perfect communion with Him.

All such instances, while evidences of the true humanity of our Lord, are at the same time to be regarded in the light of His essential deity. Not that the attributes of the divine were communicated to the human nature; the Lord's acts were those of one who was in the possession of both natures. He never acted at one time as man and at another as God. The two natures were, and are, perfectly and inseparately combined in Him. The restrictions He imposed upon Himself illustrate then the apostle's statement that Christ "emptied Himself, taking the form of a servant." They reveal the essential reality of His Servant character, and only so can they be rightly considered. They are not matters of mere Christology.

HIS EXAMPLE TO US

We behold Him, therefore, as One who undeviatingly delighted to do the will of the Father, never permitting anything to mar the glory of His filial service and obedience. This was His greatest joy, the joy that breathes through His statements, "I can of Myself do nothing; as I hear I judge: and My judgment is righteous; because I seek not Mine own will, but the will of Him that sent Me" (John 5:30).

So, again, when leaving the Upper Room with His disciples, with the horrors of Gethsemane, His betrayal, His trial, and death, before Him, He says, "I love the Father, and as the Father gave Me commandment even so I do" (14:31). This was the spirit that found expression at the hour of His dark Gethsemane conflict, in His utterance of sublime resignation, "Father, if Thou be willing, remove this cup from Me: nevertheless not My will, but Thine be done."

May our contemplation of the Son of God ever lead our hearts to worship and adore Him, and, while we consider Him in the perfection of His ways, let us remember that He "left us an example that we should follow His steps." And let us find our delight in doing His will. For to us His word applies, "As the father hath sent Me, even so send I you."

THE SINLESSNESS OF CHRIST

Jesus came into this world as a man, yet He lived without sin. There is no doubt as to the flawlessness of His character; Scripture supports the fact that He "knew no sin." Here we trace the biblical claims, testimony, and evidence that support the sinlessness of Christ.

The witness of the writers of the New Testament to the sinlessness of Christ is varied yet unanimous. And the witness is the more cogent in that neither the variety nor the unanimity can possibly have been prearranged. Even the most critical reader, be he candid, is compelled to admit the impossibility that the writers can have agreed to a consensus of opinion upon this subject. Indeed the very diversity of the testimony is against the idea.

We will take first the direct statements of the writers themselves. We might have expected to find assertions as to the sinlessness of Christ made by the writers of the Gospels. Their testimony, striking in itself, is however, of a different sort. It is true that certain of the characters in their writings make definite pronouncements, but for assertions on the part of those who wrote the New Testament we must turn to the epistles. And here the testimony is strikingly appropriate to the character or circumstances respectively of those writers who predicate His sinlessness.

THE TESTIMONY OF THE APOSTLES

The apostle Peter's testimony is that He did no sin (1 Pet. 2:22). This comes appropriately from one who was characteristically a man quick to act. He adds, "neither was guile found in His mouth," perhaps with a recollection of his own waywardness of utterance on the night of His betrayal. John says, "*In Him* is no sin" (1 John 3:5). The Gospels make clear that to this apostle was granted a special nearness to, and intimacy with, the Lord in the days of His flesh, as, for instance, when at the Supper he leaned on Jesus' breast (John 13:23–26). He, then, testifies, not to the outward acts, but to the inner being of the Lord.

A third form of testimony comes from Paul's pen, namely, that Christ "*knew no sin*" (2 Cor. 5:21). This is peculiarly fitting on the part of one to whom it was committed to communicate so much of the Lord's mind, and who says, "we have the mind of Christ" (1 Cor. 2:16), and later exhorts the saints to have the mind which was in Him (Phil. 2:5).

The fullest statements are made by the writer of the epistle to the Hebrews, and this is consistent with the fact that practically the whole epistle is occupied with the glories of Christ. Here we read that He was "in all points tempted like as we are, yet *without sin*"; that He was "holy, guileless, undefiled, separated from sinners" (Heb. 4:15; 7:26).

THE WITNESS OF THE GOSPELS

We turn now from direct statements of this sort to the testimony of the Gospels. The Gospels provide a threefold witness; (1) that of the character and ways of Christ; (2) the utterances of Christ Himself; (3) the testimony of His adversaries.

HIS CHARACTER AND WAYS

(1) The writers of the Gospels, as we have said, do not themselves state therein that Christ was sinless. How readily could they have done so! How easily they might have sounded His praises, discoursed on His perfections, or spoken with admiration of His flawless character! The absence of all such remarks makes their presentation the more striking. With unvarnished naturalness and simplicity they state facts seen by them or communicated to them, and the person whom they each present, independently of one another indeed, and yet with perfect consistency, is seen to be the very archetype of holiness, whose stainless beauty and unsullied glory stamp with imperfection everything apart from Himself.

Christ did not become sinless, He was so from the beginning. He never gave a trace of strife against inward moral contradictions. The closest scrutiny can never detect the slightest degree of repentance or remorse on His part. He never prayed for forgiveness, for He had no sin to confess. No sentence He ever uttered could be construed to indicate a consciousness of guilt, or an admission of unworthiness. In urging repentance upon men, it was for their own sins; He never identified Himself with them in this need. When overtaken by calamity men spontaneously admit their sinfulness. Never did Christ, in the hours of His greatest distress, betray in the least degree, in the outpourings of His soul, a consciousness of error.

CONTACT WITHOUT CONTAMINATION

Nor again could it ever be said that His holiness was preserved by avoiding contact with defilement. He lived not the life of a recluse. He neither turned aside from conflict with the tempter, nor did He avoid the company of the sinful. It was a taunt of His archcritics that He was "the friend of publicans and sinners." The Gospels present Him as truly man, a member of the human race, belonging as such to all races and all generations of mankind, identifying Himself with humanity in everything but sin. He is found continually in the closest contact with the degraded and defiled, surrounded constantly by a multitude of malignant influences, yet He remained absolutely untainted by their defilement. In this He was essentially distinct from even the holiest of ordinary men. Those who were nearest to Him in character were those who felt themselves at the greatest moral distance from Him.

Yet His was by no means a mechanical faultlessness; He was "tempted in all points like as we are." The question is often raised, how could temptation be real to Christ, considering His absolute sinlessness? The Scripture says that "He suffered being tempted," and that on this account it is that He is "able to succor them that are tempted" (Heb. 2:18). He suffered being tempted! His very power to suffer and His moral perfection made the force of temptation the more real and terrible to Him. The trustworthy chain that stands the strain is as much tested as the untrustworthy chain that breaks. The greater the reliability the greater the test. It is the chain that cannot break that has the greatest testing. It is the one who never yields who feels the fullest force of a temptation and suffers the most.

HIS OWN CLAIMS

(2) Christ Himself claims that He was sinless. With an incontestable challenge to His keenest adversaries, and a certainty that the challenge could not be accepted, He says, "which of you convicteth Me of sin?" (John 8:46). To His disciples He says, "The prince of this world cometh: and he hath nothing in Me" (John 16:30). There was nothing in Him which could respond to the suggestions or instigations of the Evil One.

It has been urged that when, to the ruler who inquired what he should do to inherit eternal life, the Lord said, "Why callest thou Me good? None is good save One, even God," He was disclaiming the title of good. Such a conclusion is due to a misunderstanding of the circumstances. The ruler used the word "good" with an inadequate perception of the meaning of the term; his use of it indicated a misapprehension of his own sinfulness. Christ intimated in His reply that if the term were to be applied to Him at all, it must be used in its highest sense, namely, as it is applicable to God. So far, therefore, from suggesting a consciousness of imperfection or failure on His part, the Lord was intimating the very reverse. The pedestal on which the young man placed Him was not really high enough (Matt. 19:16–22).

Here, as in other instances, He showed Himself in conflict with the customary views of what was good. As has been said, "He came into violent collision with them, and with creative originality set forth, in His teaching, life and suffering, a view of the good directly opposed to the prevailing one," and that in a way "only possible if He Himself was possessed and filled by the glory of the truly and essentially good which He knew and brought to light," the good which was divinely and intrinsically His own.

THE TESTIMONY OF HIS FOES

(3) The witness of His adversaries is varied, again, and yet concordant. Demons acknowledged Him as "the Holy One of God" (Mark 1:24), an appellation applicable to none other save Christ Jesus; it predicates His absolute freedom from taint of sin. Negatively, His bitterest foes the Pharisees, assiduously watching through the whole course of His public ministry to find even the slightest fault in Him, plotting to catch Him in His words, prying frequently even into His private life, could at length raise no charge against Him but the baseless accusation of showing disrespect to Caesar, a charge declared void by the Roman judge who sat to hear the case.

His betrayer remorsefully said, "I have betrayed innocent blood."

His judge declared, "I find no fault in this man."

His executioner exclaimed, "Certainly this was a righteous man."

DID HE ADAPT HIS TEACHINGS TO HUMAN IGNORANCE?

Under the weight of this threefold array of evidence the imputation falls to the ground that Christ, upon occasion in His teachings, adjusted His ideas to the ignorance of the people, or made use of Jewish myths to give instruction and warning; as when, for instance, He narrated the circumstances of the death and destinies of the rich man and Lazarus (Luke 16:19–31). How gross a misconception to imagine that He, "in whose mouth there was no guile," concerning whom the testimony that He was "holy, guileless, undefiled" has been vindicated from every point of view, descended to adopt methods of deception! That He, whose heart was itself the very shrine of divine holiness, who declared with unchallengeable authority that the judgment of all men had been committed to Him, ever trifled with men's ignorance, and that, too, in matters relating to human destiny in the other world! The imputation is an outrage upon His sacred name.

In the life of every other man there is disharmony: the disintegrating effects of sin are universal to the human race. With Christ alone it is different. His nature is disclosed to us as that of the sublimest and purest harmony. Reason and will were never divorced in His case. Never with Him did any mental or moral faculty unduly preponderate. For example, He exhibited vitality of emotion and feeling, but never so that they passed into passionate excitement. All His ways were characterized by a sublime dignity. The unbroken harmony of His nature was in keeping with His unbroken harmony with the Father. In this, as to His Godhood, His words apply, "I and the Father are One."

INEVITABLE CONCLUSIONS

From the sinlessness of Christ certain considerations follow. His uniqueness in this respect involves the uniqueness of His birth. Birth by natural generation has produced no exception among men to invalidate the pronouncement that "All have sinned, and fall short of the glory of God." Not so with Christ Jesus. His sinlessness vindicates the doctrine of His virgin birth, and explains the fact. Again, His sinless life gave Him a claim, by the divine law, to exemption from death. Yet He died. His death must, therefore, have been vicarious. "Christ died for our sins." "He was wounded for our transgressions, He was bruised for our iniquities." Further, His sinlessness determined His resurrection as His rightful prerogative. God's Holy One could never see corruption. In His case "Death could not hold its prey." Hence to His perverted and arbitrary judges He declared, with the knowledge of the death which lay before Him, that He would be raised to "the right hand of the power of God" and would appear in divine glory and majesty.

The character of His life on earth showed that He was perfectly fitted to undertake the work of redeeming grace in the atoning sacrifice on the cross. We are redeemed "with precious Blood, as of a lamb without blemish and without spot, even the Blood of Christ" (1 Pet. 1:19). "Him who knew no sin, He made to be sin on our behalf; that we might become the righteousness of God in Him" (2 Cor. 5:21).

> "In His spotless soul's distress,
> I perceive my guiltiness;
> O how vile my low estate,
> Since my ransom was so great."

THE MORAL GLORIES OF CHRIST

Christ's perfection was, not merely the absence of sin, but the presence of harmony. Jesus' character was free from the taint of sin, so everything existed in balance—meekness and majesty, power and mercy, justice and benevolence. His gentleness was never characterized by weakness nor His love by mere sentimentality. His zeal never degenerated into impulsiveness nor His calmness into indifference. Indeed, the life of Christ was characterized by the ninefold Fruit of the Spirit.

> *"Join all the glorious names,*
> *Of wisdom, love, and power,*
> *That mortals ever knew,*
> *That angels ever bore;*
> *All are too mean to speak His worth,*
> *Too mean to set our Savior forth."*

The perfections which mark the life and testimony of the Lord Jesus answer to the prophetic description of His character given by the Spirit through the psalmist, "Thou art fairer than the children of men; grace is poured into Thy lips" (Ps. 45:2). The full apprehension of His moral glories lies beyond human ken. For the first time the eyes of the Father rested upon One on earth with infinite satisfaction and appreciation. He grew up before Him "as a tender plant, and as a root out of a dry ground." From the earliest days of His life on earth, and at every stage of His growth into manhood, He gave that unmingled delight to the Father which found expression at His baptism in the voice out of the heavens, saying, "This is My beloved Son, in Whom I am well pleased" (Matt. 3:17).

The successive stages of His childhood and youth are briefly summed up in the statement in Luke's Gospel: "The child grew, and waxed strong, filled with wisdom: and the grace of God was upon Him," and "Jesus advanced in wisdom and stature, and in favor with God and men" (Luke 2:40, 52). Truly child, youth, man, He was at every stage possessed of the full orb of moral perfections, and that complete blending of those traits of character which marked Him as "the Holy One of God."

THE HARMONY OF HIS CHARACTER

The perfectly adjusted combination and correlation of virtues exhibited in His life, distinguish Him from all others. The greatest and best of men give evidence of some amount of unevenness in disposition, some preponderance of one trait of character over another. There was no such disproportion in the Lord Jesus. His character never received modification nor readjustment. It was the same throughout, possessing always the same even balance and harmony. In Him majesty was perfectly blended with meekness, dignity with condescension, conscious greatness with unostentatious simplicity, power with mercy, justice with benevolence, holy indignation against sin with tender compassion for the sinner. His gentleness was never characterized by weakness, nor His love by mere sentimentality. His zeal never degenerated into impulsiveness, nor His calmness into indifference. The complete constellation of virtues shone in His character with undimmed luster, irradiating all His utterances and ways, and imparting an unexampled unity to His different actions. No situation, however critical, found Him at variance with Himself. "Grace and truth came by Jesus Christ." His untiring interest in the welfare of man was at the same time characterized by undeviating devotion to the Father.

THE INITIAL GOSPEL RECORDS

The glories of His character, which are so considerably veiled from us as regards His early years in the home at Nazareth, shine forth in all their beauty immediately the Gospel records begin to depict His public life and testimony. One's first thought is to speak of those deeds of grace and truth in the marriage feast at Cana of Galilee and the cleansing of the temple. But on considering these as following upon His temptation in the wilderness a striking connection becomes evident. How much is lost by failure to compare the various Gospel narratives one with another! Not merely with reference to the same incidents recorded in them, but in the arrangement of the order of different incidents! Quite recently it occurred to the writer that there might be a certain correspondence between the moral glories of the Lord in the circumstances of His threefold temptation by Satan, as recorded in the earlier Gospels, and the character of His first public acts and teachings as narrated by John. A comparison at once revealed coincidences obviously designed by the Spirit of God, and possibly present also to the mind of John. The correspondence is with the order of the temptations as given in Matthew's Gospel. That order is chronological. Where Luke's order differs from that of the other Gospels, there is no discrepancy in point of fact. Luke purposely groups his subjects, connecting them in a different way from that of the actual order of events.

THE TEMPTATIONS AND THEIR COUNTERPART

Now the Lord's first acts of benevolence and faithfulness, as narrated in the Gospel of John, are the counterpart respectively of His three victories over the Evil One in the wilderness. And in this we can discern a divine determination that the hidden glories of His triumph over the Adversary should be displayed immediately in His deeds of grace and faithfulness, and in His teaching.

The First Temptation and the First Miracle

This first victory in the wilderness lay in resisting the devil's suggestion to turn stones into bread, that is to say, in refusing to transform one substance into another of greater value so as to meet an immediate need. His first public miracle was precisely after this manner, though the substances were different. At the wedding feast in Cana He turned water into wine, and in so doing He performed the very kind of act which He had refused to do at the instigation of Satan. In the divine counsels the character of His victory over the spiritual foe found its counterpart in His act of blessing at Cana. "This beginning of His signs did Jesus . . . and manifested His glory" (John 2:11). That glory, previously unseen by man, which expressed itself in refusal to act in a certain way, was now displayed in a corresponding manner in service to the Father on behalf of men. Surely we may trace a divine recompense in this, a joy in the display of grace after the trial of conflict.

The Second Temptation and the Temple Cleansing

The second way in which the Lord overcame the Adversary in the wilderness was in His refusal to cast Himself down from a pinnacle of the temple so as to vindicate (probably before the public gaze) the fact of His divine sonship. It can scarcely be regarded as an undesigned coincidence that His second recorded public act after the marriage at Cana of Galilee was in connection with the temple in Jerusalem. Instead of casting Himself down from the outside He cleanses the inside. His faithfulness in the former case finds its counterpart in His faithfulness in maintaining the character of His Father's house. Instead of relying, at the devil's suggestion, upon God's provision of angelic care to prevent the destruction of His body, He now predicts the destruction of "the temple of His body," and declares that He will raise it up. Having refused to display His glory by the advice of the Evil One, in the preservation of His body, He will devote it to the redemptive sacrifice of the Cross, and manifest His glory in His resurrection. Satan's scheme to preserve the body of Christ was but a subtle effort to prevent the greater glory of the resurrection of His body. Here again is a divine compensation. For it was in His resurrection that the Father vindicated His sonship. "He was declared to be the Son of God . . . by the resurrection of the dead" (Rom. 1:4).

In the case of the first temptation and the first miracle the Lord, having refused to supply His own needs, displayed, in meeting the needs of others, His sympathy and tenderness; in the second instance, in cleansing the temple in His zeal for His Father's house, He manifested His holiness and faithfulness.

The Third Temptation, the Kingdom, and Worship

The third victory in the wilderness was the Lord's refusal to receive from Satan the kingdoms of this world and their glory, on condition of doing him an act of worship (Matt. 4:8–10). Here, again, we find a similar correspondence the narrative in John's Gospel. For the kingdom of God and the worship of God are the subjects of which the Lord treats respectively in the next events in that Gospel, namely, in His conversations with Nicodemus and the woman of Samaria. The devil had sought to frustrate the divinely appointed display of the glories of the kingdom by an arrangement which would anticipate its manifestation. According to the divine counsels, the powers of the spiritual kingdom must be in operation first. The kingdom of God must be in mystery before it comes in manifestation. When the spiritual kingdom, the kingdom which is entered by the new birth, is completed, then will the usurper, over whom the Lord triumphed, be cast out of the earth, and the kingdom of the world which Christ refused at his hands will become His own possession, by the decree and power of God.

How marvelous, again, that to the poor degraded woman of Samaria, the slave of sin and Satan, the Lord should give instruction concerning worship! It cannot have been very long after the time when He repulsed His adversary by His "It is written, thou shalt worship the Lord thy God," that He spoke to the woman concerning the true worshipers, who "shall worship the Father in Spirit and in truth."

"HE THAT OVERCOMETH"

There are lessons for us in all this, that is to say, in the fact that the moral glories of the Lord in overcoming temptation issued, with such precise correspondence, in the character of His earliest ministry among men. Faithfulness in resisting the spiritual foe is the sure precursor of power in service for God. And the character of the service is often determined by the nature of the victory over temptation. Joseph, who refuses to stain his character and mar his overseership of Potiphar's house by yielding to the enticement of his master's wife, becomes the prime minister over the whole country, and receives a wife by royal appointment. Daniel, who refuses to dishonor God by conforming to the arrangements of the Eastern court and defiling himself with the king's meat, becomes governor over the whole province of Babylon and president over the hundred and twenty satraps of the entire dominion. Fidelity to the will of God, under pressure of temptation, brings its recompense in this life and will receive its eternal reward hereafter. He who in the days of His humiliation resisted every effort to allure Him from the path to the Cross, is "crowned with glory and honor," and from His place of majesty and power encourages His tempted saints to overcome, "even as He overcame." They who refuse to defile their garments here shall walk with Him "in white."

He who is the subject of the Gospel records stands therein before the reader as one who belongs to no special type or class of man. Christ is the representative man. He unites in Himself every trait that is characteristic of man, apart from sin and its effects. Every strong and manly virtue shines in Him, as well as every tender and softer quality. He comprehends in Himself the ideals of both sexes. As Westcott says: "Whatever there is in man, of strength, justice, and wisdom; whatever there is in woman of sensibility, of purity, and insight, is in Christ, without the conditions which hinder among us the development of contrasted virtues in one person. Jesus is the single universal man, in the closest kinship with men of all time and climates."

The Gospels present Him as one who is free from the characteristic limitations, whether of race, or nation, or family. This is the more remarkable as there was everything, both in nationality and in the family circumstances in which He was born and brought up, conducive to the production of a distinct type. There are two influences which specially make for this. They are heredity and environment. Their effects are separative, sectionalizing, isolating.

HEREDITY

Christ was born into the Jewish nation. Of all national types the Jewish is one of the most persistent; yet there is nothing in either the character or teachings of Christ which mark Him conspicuously as a Jew. In this He is unique, exceptional. His teachings find an audience which is coextensive with humanity, and an answer in the inner experiences of all men. He is the connecting link between men of the most divergent nationalities. The circumscribing laws of heredity do not find an illustration in Him.

ENVIRONMENT

Take again the subject of environment. The circumstances and surroundings of a person's upbringing tend to exert a characterizing influence which distinguishes him according to his locality. The district of Galilee was no exception. On the contrary, the references to this place, in the Gospels and the Acts, mark it out particularly as of a specializing character. "Behold, are not all these which speak Galileans?" said the people who were listening to the testimony of the disciples on the day of pentecost. That the locality was also signalized by provincialisms, is plain from Matthew 26:73. There was everything, then, in His early environment to affect the life of Christ in such a way as to indicate the place of His upbringing. Yet how free He was from all specialization of this sort!

Consider again the handicraft at which He wrought, the family means of livelihood. After He entered upon His public life and testimony, those who had known Him asked, "Is not this the carpenter?" (Mark 6:31). Ordinarily speaking such an environment is not conducive to universality of type. Yet how worldwide are His affinities! The barriers that tend to separate men of one nationality from those of another are broken down in Him. No matter by whom or where the Gospel narratives are read there is nobody who does not find in Him the nearest kinsman, one in whom there is, sin excepted, a point of contact, such as is shared by no other.

THE NINEFOLD FRUIT

We will now contemplate the moral glories of Christ from another point of view. The Word of God declares that "The fruit of the Spirit is love, joy, peace, longsuffering, kindness, goodness, faithfulness, meekness, temperance (or self-control)," nine virtues combined in a perfect harmony of character. This passage, which speaks indeed of the effects of the Spirit's work in the believer, provides at the same time a commentary upon the character of the Lord as revealed in the

Gospels. In His case these moral excellences were the display of glories essential in His manhood. To illustrate each trait from the records of the four evangelists would occupy a large volume. We will here consider the witness of Christ Himself to His character in these respects. Nor will space permit us to refer to the whole of His teaching. One passage must suffice. It contains within its compass every trait enumerated in the verse in the Galatians epistle, and almost, though not precisely, in the same order. It is His discourse to the disciples in the Upper Room on the night of His betrayal. Here, too, He speaks significantly of fruitfulness. If the disciples are to bear fruit, it will of necessity be the outcome of His own fruitfulness.

The first in the list of virtues spoken of is

Love

Now in the fifteenth chapter of John's Gospel the Lord immediately follows His statement as to bearing fruit by speaking of His love. "Herein," He says, "is My Father glorified, that ye bear much fruit, and so shall ye be My disciples. Even as the Father hath loved Me, I also have loved you: abide ye in My love" (15:8, 9). His love was not mere sentiment, it consisted in keeping His Father's commandments. And our love is to be no different; it is to express itself in obedience to His own commandments, and so in loving one another (vv. 10–12). His was the "greater love," exhibited in the laying down of His life.

The next item in the fruit of the Spirit is

Joy

This finds correspondence in the Lord's next utterance, "These things have I spoken unto you, that My joy may be in you" (v. 11). One of His objects in speaking to the disciples was that they might have His joy fulfilled in themselves (17:13). His joy lay in abiding in the love of the Father and so in doing His will, and only so can our joy be fulfilled.

The third quality is

Peace

Of His peace the Lord speaks earlier in His discourse: "Peace I leave with you: My peace I give unto you" (15:27). This is "the peace of Christ" of which the apostle writes in Colossians 3:15 (R.V.), which is to rule, or rather, to arbitrate, in our hearts, removing our anxieties and fears, and settling our troubles. How dark and terrible were the Lord's circumstances on the night of the betrayal! The traitor was already engaged in his murderous plot. The agony of Gethsemane lay immediately before Him, to be followed by the terrible experiences of His trial and the more terrible sufferings of the Cross. All were known to the Lord beforehand. Yet it is in these circumstances that He speaks to the disciples of "My peace."

As we read on in the fifteenth chapter the other qualities mentioned under the fruit of the Spirit come before us in due order. They are not specifically mentioned, but we cannot read the Lord's words concerning Himself without readily discerning these traits in His character, and especially as He speaks of the treatment He received from men. The world, He says, had hated Him (v. 19), and this in itself serves to remind us of His

Longsuffering

This is particularly seen in His controversies with the opposing Jews as recorded in John's Gospel, chapters 5 to 11. It was only after they had sinned away all their opportunities that He finally departed from them (11:54).

Men had persecuted Him (v. 20). Their persecutions served to draw forth a display of His

Gentleness

His gentleness, which never ran into weakness, was the expression of His sympathy, His tender compassion for all in feebleness, distress, and need.

In spite of the hardness of heart and the willful resistance and antagonism of His enemies, He had "come and spoken unto them" (v. 22), and in this He veritably displayed His

Goodness

"Their ill but drew His goodness forth."

In addition to this He had "done among them the works which none other did" (v. 24). In this He exhibited His

Faithfulness

For all His works were done in "faithfulness and truth" (see Isa. 25:1, R.V.).

The malice His enemies had displayed against Him had fulfilled as He says, the word that was written in their Law, "They hated Me without a cause" (v. 25), and the trait of character which stands out in Him conspicuously under it all is His

Meekness

"He was as a Lamb that is led to the slaughter, and as a sheep that before her shearers is dumb." "The meekness and gentleness" of Christ fastened themselves indelibly upon Paul's heart. How tellingly he makes them the basis of his appeal to the Corinthian saints to rectify their relations with himself! (2 Cor. 10:1). Christ's meekness was never disunited from His majesty. The incomparable splendor of His greatness shone especially through His meekness. He gained the mastery over injustice while suffering it. Never were words more impressively grand and yet tender in their meekness and love than when, while undergoing crucifixion, He said, "Father forgive them: for they know not what they do."

The last of the nine in the Galatians epistle is

Self-control

Strikingly is this exhibited in the Lord's character in the discourse in the Upper Room! How patient were His dealings with these disciples, with their misunderstandings and slowness of heart! How much He had to tell them! His heart was yearning to unlock its secrets to them in fuller measure. "I have yet many things to say unto you," He says, "but ye cannot bear them now" (16:12). He felt indeed a tender sympathy toward them in their weakness, and hence His self-restraint. But this is only one instance of that same quality which manifests itself throughout the discourse, with a sublime majesty, an inexpressible grandeur.

All that perfection of character which is summed up in the phrase "the fruit of the Spirit" stands forth in its full beauty of combined virtues in the self-witness of the Lord's teaching here, as indeed it does in all His ways. The effect upon the disciples, itself an evidence of the ascendancy the Lord gained over them, was at the same time a proof of His moral strength. He who at first was recognized by them as a teacher, not differing much perhaps from a rabbi, was now their Lord. Is His ascendancy absolute over our own hearts? Is His character being stamped upon us, changing us from glory to glory, as into His own image? May it be so for His name's sake!

THE ATONING SACRIFICE OF CHRIST

Jesus came into this world in order to save sinners, and the only way to accomplish His goal was by sacrificing Himself. He was the fulfillment of God's plan of redemption, which included a guilty people, a perfect substitute, an atoning sacrifice, and ultimately, reconciliation with the Father.

The object for which the Son of God came into the world is conveyed in His Name "Jesus," which signifies "Jehovah (is) salvation." The inspired interpretation of it is, "For it is He that [or, literally, He Himself] shall save His people from their sins." In the words of one of His apostles, "Christ Jesus came into the world to save sinners" (1 Tim. 1:15). The means of accomplishing this end was His death. He said that He had come "to give His life a ransom for many" (Matt. 20:28), that He would "lay down His life for the sheep" (John 10:11–15). He was manifested "to put away sin by the sacrifice of Himself" (Heb. 9:26). His sacrifice was

DIVINELY PREORDAINED

Christ was "delivered up by the determinate counsel and foreknowledge of God" (Acts 2:23). His death was therefore not accidental, it was an essential part of the divine scheme of redemption. He Himself said to His disciples, "Thus it is written that Christ should suffer, and rise again from the dead the third day: and that repentance and remission of sins should be preached in His Name" (Luke 24:46, 47).

He came, then, not merely to teach men how to live, though that He did, nor so to tell them about God's love that they might forsake sin. He came that "through death" He might bring salvation to men (Heb. 2:14, 15). He "suffered for sins once, the righteous for the unrighteous, that He might bring us to God" (1 Pet. 3:18). His sacrifice was therefore

Vicarious

and this is borne out by the following facts: Christ lived a sinless life, even His adversaries and His critics being witnesses. On this ground alone freedom from death was His perfect right, and that by divine decree. The Law of God promised life to him who fulfilled it. Alone of men Christ absolutely carried out the conditions. Yet He died! Now His death was not simply the result of His encountering human antagonism. He could have avoided it. This He demonstrated when His conspirators came to bind Him (John 18:6; cp. 8:59; 10:39; Luke 4:29, 30), and thus He confirmed His own statement, "I lay down My life, that I may take it again. No one taketh it away from Me, but I lay it down of Myself. I have power to lay it down, and I have power to take it again. This commandment received I from My Father" (John 10:17, 18). To the judge who sentenced Him, He said, "Thou couldest have no power against Me, except it were given thee from above" (19:11). His death was unique, in that, in His case alone, the choice lay between dying and never dying at all. He could have refrained from drinking the bitter cup. It follows that, death being the consequence of sin (Rom. 5:12; 6:23), the death of Christ was substitutionary. "He died to atone for sins not His own." "He was wounded for our transgressions," "Jehovah laid on Him the iniquity of us all" (Isa. 53:5, 6).

THE CHARACTER OF SIN

False ideas of the atonement are largely due to light views both of sin and of the holiness of God. Sin is neither a temporary misadventure, nor is it simply a disease or a disaster, nor again is it "a necessary stage to higher things." "Sin is lawlessness" (1 John 3:4, R.V.). It is disregard of the will of God. It is due to unbelief (Rom. 14:23; John 16:9). God, as moral governor of the universe, gave to man a law which was the reflection of His righteous character, a law the fulfillment of which was for man's highest welfare. The breach of that law was culpable disregard of the Creator's beneficent will, and rendered man liable to God's righteous retribution. The very attributes of God demanded the execution of the penalty.

To refrain from exacting it would be to nullify the law and belie the divine character. Divine forgiveness could be imparted only in a manner consistent with God's claims of justice, the rectitude of His administration and His irreconcilability to evil.

THE PERSON REQUISITE

Atonement is impossible to man. Repentance would be ineffectual, for it could not restore the broken legal relation to God. An amended life could not do so, for it could not cancel previous guilt. Man in his unregenerate state cannot please God (Rom. 8:8). Nor could the sinner make atonement by death, either for himself or for his fellowmen. Expiation is demanded on a righteous basis. In order to make such expiation a person was required who had an adequate apprehension of the nature and claims of God. He must likewise be proved to be free from all taint of sin. He must be one who would bear the curse of the broken law, or his suffering would be on his own account, and consequently no judicial advantage could accrue to others therein. He must, moreover, put himself in connection with the law, that he might be tested thereby.

Now there was only one being who could and did fulfill all these conditions, and that was the Son of God. Being Himself one in Godhood with the Father, He, and He alone, had a perfect understanding of the nature and claims of God. The other conditions were likewise fulfilled by Him, for, though He was Himself the Creator and Sustainer of the Universe (Col. 1:16, 17), Whose goings forth had been "from of old, from everlasting" (Mic. 5:2), He became Incarnate, was born under the law, submitted to all its tests and fulfilled it without deviation, "becoming obedient, even unto death, yea, the death of the Cross." Such a One alone could bear our sin. And this He did, "being made sin for us, . . . that we might become the righteousness of God in Him" (2 Cor. 5:21). It was necessary that God should deal with Him, His sinless Son, as He would with sin. That is the significance of the lifting up of the brazen serpent, as the Lord Himself explained to Nicodemus. Jehovah made "His soul an offering for sin" (Isa. 53:10).

In this way alone could God "Himself be just and the Justifier" of the sinner. This is the grand plan of divine grace in the atonement. Whereas "all have sinned, and fall short of the glory of God," man can through faith be "justified freely by His grace through the redemption that is in Christ Jesus." For God "set Him forth to be a propitiation, through faith, by His blood . . . that He might Himself be just and the justifier of him that hath faith in Jesus" (Rom. 3:23–26). "He [this word has the emphasis] is the propitiation for our sins" (1 John 2:2).

AN OBJECTION

Objection is raised against the character of the atonement, in that such a substitutionary death for sin is, it is urged, impossible, since guilt is untransferable, and the innocent remains innocent. The objection is invalid. Personal blameworthiness is indeed untransferable, but to suffer for the sins of another is possible to anyone and is a common fact in human experience. It was to deliver men from a deserved penalty that Christ suffered. For this He bore the stroke of divine justice. "Jehovah laid on Him the iniquity of us all." There are depths in the sufferings of Christ on the cross which the human mind can never fathom. None will ever be able to measure or explain the mystery of that anguish which, under the weight of sin and the wrath due to it, drew forth the cry, "My God, My God, why hast Thou forsaken Me." Nor will anyone ever fully apprehend the other great truth, equally essential in the doctrine of the atonement, that "God was in Christ, reconciling the world unto Himself." This alone precludes any attempt to reduce the subject to terms of mere human jurisprudence, or to explain the work of the Cross by any illustration of the law courts.

The facts of the unity of the Son with the Father show at what an incalculable cost God gave up His Son to die for us. "He spared not His own Son." "Herein was the love of God manifested in us [i.e., in regard to us], that God hath sent His only begotten Son." "Herein is love . . . that He loved us and sent His Son to be the propitiation for our sins" (1 John 4:8–10).

Another Objection

Again, it is urged that a substitutionary sacrifice is contrary to moral rectitude, since for another person to die to secure freedom from future punishment could effect no radical change in the moral character of the guilty. That, however, is contrary to Scripture and to the facts of Christian experience. The gospel cries out against continuance in sin. The death of Christ enables the believer to say with the apostle Paul, "I have been crucified with Christ . . . who loved me and gave Himself up for me" (Gal. 2:20), to reckon himself to be "dead to sin" and "alive unto God," and so to walk "in newness of life." In suffering judgment and death to deliver us from the merited penalty, Christ suffered also to deliver us from sin, which was the cause of our condemnation. Such love begets a love that hates the sin on account of which the Savior died. Again, Christ did not die merely to show God's benevolence toward man. His life alone could have done that, and then the full expression of God's character would not have been exhibited. Nor was His death merely a manifestation of God's love. His death revealed God's justice in carrying out therein all that was due to sin, and His love and mercy in doing so in the person of His Son. "God commendeth His own love toward us, in that, while we were yet sinners, Christ died for us" (Rom. 5:8). Thus the divine love glorified the divine holiness and righteousness. "Mercy and truth met together. Righteousness and peace kissed each other."

That Christ became a sin offering for us, that we might be delivered from the merited execution of the sentence due to our guilt, involved no compromise of the righteousness of divine administration. In inflicting the sentence on the sinner's voluntary surety, Jehovah, "while He cleared the sinner, did not clear his sins," but executed His righteous sentence upon them. The ends of divine justice were fully assured.

THE NATURE OF HIS DEATH

His death then was not that of a martyr to a cause. Nor did He die merely to secure a blessing for man. His death was expiatory. He became incarnate, partaking of flesh and blood, in order to present Himself to be made sin and to become a curse for us, and so to remove the curse which was ours by the righteous judgment of God. Voluntarily He submitted to the death of the cross in order that on a righteous basis man might be restored to fellowship with God.

Again, His death fulfilled, and more than fulfilled, all that was foreshadowed by the offerings of animal sacrifices upon the altar. The death must be by the shedding of blood. "The life of the flesh is in the blood." Man had forfeited his life through sin. Death came by sin. Hence the divine appointment of animal sacrifices, which, though they were substitutionary, could not themselves clear the conscience from sin. The blood of bulls and goats could not take away sins (Heb. 10:4). No animal sacrifices could provide atonement for a sinner's future sins. The blood of Christ "cleanseth from all sin"; it has made a complete atonement.

Reconciliation

The words in the original, rendered "atonement" and "reconciliation," are not to be explained by the English "at-one-ment." The Hebrew word denotes "to cover," i.e., by interposition for the removal of guilt. The Greek word suggests propitiation, the gaining of pardon. Christ did not die to reconcile God. "God was in Christ, reconciling the world." Not that God was reconciled to man's sin. That could never be. And as to His attitude toward the sinner, while His love provided a remedy in that "while we were yet sinners Christ died for the ungodly," yet the wrath of God still abides on him who does not believe on the Son (John 3:36, margin). The sinner is therefore called to be reconciled to God not "to bend his pride to God's benevolence," but to secure His pardon.

Redemption

On this ground it is that God pardons the guilty, a pardon complete and immediate upon acceptance of Christ. Thus God delivers from the death sentence and gives the believing sinner acceptance in Christ. This is redemption. In Christ "we have our redemption through His blood (i.e., His death by the shedding of His blood), the forgiveness of our trespasses, according to the riches of His grace" (Eph. 1:7).

Redemption has two sides to it, one the ransom paid, the other the liberation of the sinner from his position of condemnation and death. The two are to one another as cause and effect. The ransom price of the blood of Christ was paid to the claims of divine holiness and justice. The ransom was paid for all men. But all men will not accept the provision made. Only those who do so are actually redeemed and find in Christ their substitute.

The Scope of the Atonement

The language of Scripture is precise here. Only twice is the word *anti*, "instead of," which denotes actual substitution, found in the New Testament, namely, in Matthew 20:28, and Mark 10:45, and there it is "a ransom for [instead of] *many*." In 1 Timothy 2:6 the word *antilutron* occurs: "Who gave Himself a ransom [*antilutron*, a substitutionary ransom] for [*huper*, on behalf of] all." That expresses the substitutionary character of the ransom, but the apostle does not say "instead of all." The provision made was *on behalf of* "all," it is *instead of* "many," that is to say, those who are no longer in death and condemnation, because, through acceptance of Christ as their substitute, they are actually delivered from that position.

"He is the propitiation [i.e., the person through whom by His expiatory death God shows mercy to sinners] . . . for the sins of the whole world." The actual remission takes place only in the case of those who avail themselves of the propitiation. Only believers can say that their sins have been atoned for by Christ. Those who refuse it must perish eternally. There is no Scripture to show that Christ bore away every man's sins on the cross. John the Baptist's statement, "Behold the Lamb of God which taketh away the sin of the world," means that sin was so dealt with there, that now all who accept God's terms may be freed from guilt, and that hereafter in the new heavens and new earth there will be no trace of sin. Christ was manifested "to put away sin by the sacrifice of Himself" (Heb. 9:26). We must in such verses distinguish between sin and sins (1 Cor. 15:3). Christ "died for our sins," "suffered for sins" (1 Pet. 3:18). The provision is universal, the application is made good only in the case of those who receive Christ by faith, on the ground of His finished work on the cross.

THE RESURRECTION OF CHRIST

Everything about Christianity hinges upon the resurrection of Christ. Without it, there is no Gospel. It confirms Jesus' teachings, validates His claims, and underscores His promises. The following traces the evidence for the Resurrection and its effects upon those who believe.

The resurrection of Christ is the keystone of the arch of historical evidences relating to His person and work. The fact of His Resurrection confirms the truth of His deity, His supernatural birth, His sinlessness, and His substitutionary sacrifice on the cross. Apart from His resurrection there would be no Christian faith to declare. There would remain a system of morals, but that is not Christianity. Christianity involves the operation of a personal power producing effects inexplicable by the laws of nature. The very basis of Christianity is supernatural. Admit the existence of God, and thereby is admitted that miracles are likely exhibitions of His power. Disprove the possibility or credibility of the supernatural, and the foundations of the Christian faith vanish. The message of the Resurrection comprehends and sums up all that the gospel declares. If the Resurrection is not a fact there is no gospel to preach. "If Christ hath not been raised, then is our preaching vain, your faith also is vain [*kenos*, void of result]," says the apostle (1 Cor. 15:14). Again, "if Christ hath not been raised, your faith is vain [*mataios*, void of reality]; ye are yet in your sins" (v. 17).

Christ's Resurrection was at once

THE VINDICATION OF HIS DIVINE SONSHIP

He was "declared to be the Son of God with power, according to the Spirit of holiness, by the resurrection of the dead" (Rom. 1:4). It was also the vindication of His sinlessness, of which, indeed, it was the inevitable complement. Life was assured to him who fulfilled the law. Christ's perfect fulfillment of it not only involved the vicarious character of His death, for there was nothing in Him for which to atone, it also rendered resurrection His presumptive right. In this He stands alone. Being God's "Holy One" it was not possible for Him "to be holden of death" (Acts 2:24). The Psalmist had prophesied of Him, "Thou wilt not leave My soul in Sheol: neither wilt Thou suffer Thine Holy one to see corruption. Thou wilt shew Me the path of life" (Ps. 16:10, 11).

Again, His resurrection was

THE RATIFICATION OF THE ATONING EFFICACY OF HIS DEATH

"He was delivered up for [on account of] our trespasses, and was raised for [on account of] our justification." Our justification having been secured in His death—for "we are justified by His blood" (Rom. 5:9)—God raised Him from the dead. The significance attaching to the death of Christ finds its adequate explanation in His resurrection. His resurrection was also the display of His authority over death. All others had been, or will be, raised solely by a power from without. Not so with the Lord. He was raised by His own power as well as by that of the Father. Of His body He said to His foes, "Destroy this temple, and in three days I will raise it up" (John 2:19). This itself constitutes an inarguable testimony to His resurrection as being that of His body and not merely that of His Spirit. Of His life he said, "I have power to lay it down, and I have power to take it again. This commandment received I from My Father" (10:18). As the ascended and exalted one He declares to the beloved apostle, "I am the first and the last, and the Living One: and I was dead, and behold, I am alive forevermore, and I have the keys of death and Hades" (Rev. 1:17, 18).

THE BASIS OF THE GOSPEL

The first preachers of the gospel made the fact of Christ's resurrection the foundation of all their testimony. Peter bases upon it the fact of the sending of the Spirit at pentecost (Acts 2:33), the power of faith (3:15, 16), repentance, forgiveness of sins, and salvation (2:30–38 with 4:12). So with Paul; the gospel he preached was that "Christ died for our sins, according to the Scriptures; and that He was buried; and that He hath been raised on the third day, according to the Scriptures" (1 Cor. 15:3, 4). The confession of Jesus as Lord, and the belief that God raised Him from the dead are, he says, essential to salvation (Rom. 10:9). His resurrection is the guarantee of that of the saints (Rom. 8:11; 1 Cor. 15:20–23), and of their complete reunion (1 Thess. 4:14), and of the overthrow of God's foes and the establishment of His kingdom (1 Cor. 15:25). It provides the divine assurance that by Him God will judge the world in righteousness (Acts 17:31). The resurrection of Christ then was both the climax of past developments of grace and the beginning of new developments of life, involving the formation, progress, and destiny of the Church, and the eventual deliverance of Creation from the bondage of corruption.

THE EVIDENCE

The limited character of the present article precludes anything like a review of the evidences of the Lord's resurrection, nor can we here dwell upon the subject of the well-established veracity and integrity of the New Testament records. Any difficulties which are considered to beset the character of the evidence are far less than those relative to other historical facts. In no other case are there so many convergent lines of evidence. With what convincing naturalness, for instance, the fact emerges in each Gospel narrative from those events which led up to it! The way in which the writers treat it is as unaffected and inartificial as everything else they record. They evince no such idea as that this event, though unique and startling in itself, requires any more detailed authentication than the undoubted facts that Christ lived and died. There is no attempt at impressiveness.

Take, for instance, the discovery of

The Cloths in the Empty Tomb

The body of the Lord had been bound[1] in linen cloths with about one hundred pounds weight of spices (John 19:39, 40). John describes Peter as entering into the tomb, and seeing the linen cloths lying, and the napkin that had been around the Lord's head, not lying with the linen cloths, but "rolled round in a place by itself." There is no suggestion that the head napkin had been folded up and put in another part of the tomb. That cloth was still lying in its folded shape where the head had been. So were the body cloths. Neither friends nor foes had touched them. Friends would not have moved the garments from the body; foes would not have left them in the position in which they were found. Nor again was there any indication of a struggle to obtain release. The Lord had simply left

---

1 John here uses the word *deō* (to bind), the same word as in the case of Lazarus (11:44), and as in the act of those who with hands of hate bound Christ as a captive (18:12–24). Matthew uses *entulisso*, "to fold round," as dos John later in 20:7; Mark uses *eneileō*, "to wind round closely." Evidently John's first word *deō*, in 19:39, is used purposively, in order to set in greater contrast in 20:7 the evidences of the Resurrection as seen by him in the position of the cloths.

the cloths as they had been bound around Him. This is the significance of John's statements as to the binding of the body and the position of the cloths, and of his testimony concerning himself, "he saw[1] and believed." The evidence was clear. What had occurred was not a removal of the body, but a resurrection. How marvelous was the sight! How unique the event! Yet how simply the narrative is told! And this is characteristic of the records not only of the Resurrection, but of the Lord's subsequent appearances to His disciples. The writers obviously are not seeking to add to literature, but are simply recording facts which they know to be true. Their sincerity cannot be doubted. The character of the evidences makes it impossible that they were victims of delusions. There was nothing in their thoughts and experiences which would inspire an ardent desire for such an event and so an anticipation of it. Whenever the Lord had spoken about it they did not understand Him (Luke 18:34). His closest disciples did not anticipate it, yet only a few days afterwards the whole company were absolutely assured of its certainty.

THE EFFECT ON THE DISCIPLES

Moreover, the occasions of His appearances were many and varied, and were of sufficient length for considerable intercourse and personal contact. The overwhelming power of these realities produced such a conviction, that their character became changed, their faith was transformed, and a few days after the final evidence had been provided they were all making it the business of their lives to proclaim the facts. Again, they were men of intelligence and probity. Their very incredulity marks them as the victims neither of superstition nor imposition. Besides, they had no worldly advantage to gain from the publication of the Resurrection. The very reverse. They knew that they must suffer for their testimony.

Take again the testimony of Paul. The truth which he himself had "received" he taught with the intenseness of a personal conviction gained through experience. "He appeared to me also," he says. And again, "Have not I seen Jesus our Lord?" He does not labor to prove the truth of the Lord's resurrection. His argument in 1 Corinthians 15 is against a denial of the resurrection of the dead, though not of Christ's resurrection. There is no evidence that the latter was denied, and so he uses the common belief of that fact as a proof of a future resurrection of the saints.

THE VERACITY OF THE WRITERS

The narratives in the four Gospels are clearly independent one of another, and yet are harmonious. Whatever differences there are, there are no discrepancies. Careful study of the details makes clear both the consistency and the

1 In reference to Peter, John uses two other words for seeing, *blepō* (v. 5), which means the act of seeing (cp. V. 1), and *theoreō* (v. 6), to view attentively (cp. vv. 12–14): in reference to himself he uses *eidō*, which indicates a perception of the meaning of what is seen.

independence of the records. If the story were invented it must have been either in collusion or independently. That the records were not fabricated by collusion is clear from the apparent discrepancies. That they were independent fabrications is impossible. The points of agreement are too many.

Again, the character of the records bears irrefutable testimony to the evidence as having been derived from eyewitnesses. There are a number of incidental details which serve to establish the veracity of the writers. For instance, that Christ was not recognized first when He appeared to the disciples (Luke 24:16; John 21:4), and again that He is not stated to have appeared to one of His enemies, or represented as confounding them by such a manifestation, are all contrary to the fabrication theory. An appearance to His foes, with its convincing effects, would have been a great point with one who was inventing the story. That Christ is recorded as having appeared solely to His followers substantiates the genuineness of the narratives. So also does the very limited number of the occasions of His appearing during the forty days. Men who were fabricating the story would have elaborated such manifestations both in number and point of detail. They would have depicted Christ as appearing in a body as glorious as on the occasion of the Transfiguration. There is nothing of this, however. With perfect naturalness the Lord shows His wound prints. The Roman spear, the *pilum*, had a shaft four inches wide, and inflicted a wound so large that a hand might be thrust into it. Even had He not died already, survival was impossible; yet He appears in perfect strength, not as a man miraculously saved from dying of wounds, but as one who had overcome death in resurrection.

The brevity of the narrative in each case is a testimony to its being a presentation of facts. Then, too, the modes of action on the part of the disciples in connection with their discovery of the empty tomb, and the subsequent details, are all in keeping with the differing characteristics of the persons as exhibited in the Gospels. The incidental touches of coloring in the picture are perfectly true to life.

NOT MERELY A SPIRITUAL RESURRECTION

The theory that the resurrection of Christ was merely spiritual represents an old error which has reappeared with widespread propagation in recent times. The teaching of Scripture entirely refutes the error. Firstly, when the apostle asks, "How are the dead raised," he says at the same time, "With what manner of body do they come?" Then, using the illustration of the death of seed sown in the ground, he says, "But God giveth it a body even as it hath pleased Him, and to each seed a body of its own . . . So also is the resurrection of the dead" (1 Cor. 15:35–42). So then the dead saints are to be raised with bodies. Now their resurrection is to be in the likeness of Christ's (Rom. 6:5). It follows that His was a bodily resurrection.[1]

---

1 See also what is said above concerning John 2:19.

Secondly, the apostle speaks of Christ as "the last Adam," "the second man." Now man as such is constituted a tripartite being, body, soul, and spirit. This then is the constitution of the second man, the Adamic head of the new race of the redeemed. His being, as possessed of true manhood, is conditioned both by His incarnation and His death, and His resurrection.

Thirdly, when speaking of His deity the apostle says, "In Him dwelleth all the fullness of the Godhead bodily" (Col. 2:9). As Moule says, "He rose, identical yet with differences. His body risen was the same as His body buried. But we need not insist on an identity of particles, which certainly is not necessary to our own continuous bodily identity. That identity appears to rest on personal spiritual identity. The sameness of a hand at two times of life lies, not in its consisting of the same matter, but in its holding the same relation to the same spirit. What the Gospels make clear, on the one hand, is the reality and permanence of Jesus Christ's resurrection body, under tests of sense, to which the all-truthful Lord Himself appeals. On the other hand it is plain that the body's mode of being and action was new. It appears that it was capable of transition, inconceivable to us, through material mass."

Fourthly, the Gospel records bear clear witness against the theory of a mere spiritual resurrection. "See My hands and My feet, that it is I Myself," He says to His disciples, "handle Me and see; for a spirit hath not flesh and bones, as ye behold Me having" (Luke 24:39). His appearances to His disciples are not to be explained by the supposition of temporary materializations. Such an idea is a gratuitous and unfounded assumption, representing the unsuccessful attempts of finite minds to explain the infinite and almighty. All that belonged to the Lord's humanity was retained in resurrection, while at the same time all was transfigured. The fact that He vanished at will does not involve the impossibility of His being permanently corporeal. His raised and transfigured body was and is under conditions not expressed by the laws which govern this creation. The Lord entered on His new mode of existence with His perfect manhood in permanent completeness.

THE EFFECTS

In the risen, exalted Christ our whole life and being are centered. Our bodies are "members of Christ" (1 Cor. 6:15), and the Church is the body of Christ (Eph. 1:23), in whom the members find a common principle of action in the discharge of their varying functions, a union in life which lies deeper than the controversies which here tend to divide them, a fullness of truth and power which consecrates their beings to their living Redeemer. "The body is . . . for the Lord; and the Lord for the body; and God both raised up the Lord, and will raise up us through His power" (1 Cor. 6:13, 14).

Such are the effects of a teaching, itself the outcome of the solid conviction of the truth of Christ's resurrection. His resurrection was the beginning of a new and permanent relation between the Lord and His people, a relation yet to be manifested in their resurrection life and glory and in the establishment of His kingdom on earth. He is the "faithful Witness, the Firstborn of the dead, and the Ruler of the kings of the earth." "To Him be the glory and the dominion forever and ever. Amen."

THE ASCENSION OF CHRIST

After the resurrection, Jesus remained, appearing to the disciples over a period of forty days. Upon reviewing the Gospel accounts, the significance, the response of the Lord's disciples, the evidence, and the effects of the Ascension, the reader will be engaged in the character and qualities that Jesus displays to all He comes into contact with in these forty days. Truly He desires a close and personal relationship with His people.

The occasion of the Lord's ascension was the tenth recorded appearance to His disciples after His resurrection, though the New Testament Scriptures do not indicate that there were no other appearances. In the enumeration given in 1 Corinthians 15 the instance mentioned in verse 7, when Christ appeared "to all the apostles" was no doubt that which issued in the Ascension, as recorded in considerable detail in the last chapter of Luke's Gospel and in the first of the Acts. It receives but a brief mention at the close of the Gospel of Mark, in a statement quite consistent with those of Luke. The brevity of the record in Mark's Gospel is no indication of ignorance of the facts on his part.

THE FIRST AND THE FOURTH GOSPELS

Again, that Matthew and John do not narrate the ascension, affords no justification for the inference which has been drawn therefrom against its historicity. With both writers the ascension was clearly a matter of course, following naturally upon the Resurrection. The close of Matthew's Gospel makes plain that in the writer's mind the ascension was imminent. Moreover he records Christ's declaration to Caiaphas, "Henceforth ye shall see the Son of man sitting at the right hand of power, and coming on the clouds of Heaven" (26:64). John tells us of the Lord's statement to the disciples that they would see Him "ascending where He was before" (6:62), and His words to Mary Magdalene, "Touch Me not [or rather, "do not cling to Me"]; for I am not yet ascended unto the Father: but go unto My brethren, and say to them, I ascend unto My Father and your Father and My God and your God" (20:17).

THE GOSPEL OF LUKE

Luke's record passes at once from the day of the Resurrection to that of the ascension, whereas in the Acts he states explicitly that Christ appeared to the disciples during forty days, at the end of which he gives full details of the ascension. There is, however, no discrepancy between the narratives. There is no hint whatever that Luke intended in his later account to correct anything in the former. The evidence is to the contrary. For he says that his former treatise embraced "all that Jesus began both to do and to teach, until the day in which He was received up." Plainly, therefore, though in the Gospel he did not specify the time, he intended the ascension to be regarded as having taken place after the interval mentioned. He certainly was not speaking of the ascension as occurring on the evening of the day when Christ arose, and as there must have been an interval, there is no difficulty in supposing one of forty days in the Gospel narrative.

THE CHARACTER OF THE RECORDS

The same simplicity, sincerity, and dignity which are conspicuous features of the records of the Lord's resurrection, characterize those of His ascension. To a reader who looks for grandeur and imagery the narrative would be disappointing. How naturally the story is told! How briefly too! The circumstances could have filled volumes had the writers been mere historians. Here again is that marvelous economy of detail, combined with sufficiency for faith, which marks the historical parts of Scripture as essentially doctrinal, and makes the Bible unique. The more the spiritually interested mind dwells upon the narratives, the more manifest are the inherent glory of the event and the spiritual instruction provided in the records. Certainly a master hand is narrating the incident. Like the Resurrection itself and the Lord's subsequent appearances, the great event was hidden from the world. Conviction of sin and of the truths of redemption were not to be borne in upon the hearts of men by means of an outward display of the Lord's person and glory. The divine wisdom had planned a more effectual means than that. Unregenerate humanity needs something more than the manifestation of divine glory to accomplish the work of grace in the heart.

THE PLACE

We may gather from Luke's narratives that the disciples had assembled in Jerusalem by the Lord's appointment (Acts 1:12 says they returned there), and that after appearing in their midst He led them forth to the Mount of Olives, until they were "over against Bethany" (Luke 1:50), a place dear to His heart by the ties of hospitality and friendship. There, where a home had been opened to Him in the days of His public life and testimony, He would now ascend to His own home, the Father's dwelling place on high. From that mountain, too, the garden slope of which had often witnessed His prayers, and finally His deep prostration and agony, He would now arise to His highest exaltation, to minister thence to His followers in their sufferings and sorrows.

THE DISCIPLES

Though there is no hint that the disciples were immediately anticipating the event, yet He had fully prepared them for what was to come, banishing their misconceptions and establishing their faith. He had opened their minds to understand the Scriptures concerning Him, had foretold the character of the work that lay before them, preventing any immature enthusiasm which might impel them to separate and undertake their appointed enterprise without the power of the promised Spirit, assuring them that the testimony of John the Baptist was about to be fulfilled and that they would be "baptized with the Holy Ghost not many days hence." With His own exquisite skill and tenderness He had disengaged their thoughts from the freshly awakened anticipation that the kingdom was immediately to be restored to Israel, and had imbued them with a due consciousness of the nature and purpose of the work appointed to them and the power requisite for it (Acts 1:4–8). He had given them the promise of a kingdom far surpassing their own expectations and had now prepared them for that path of faith and love, patient suffering and invincible hope, which would lead to that kingdom.

THE EVENT

And now with the significant words upon His lips, "in Jerusalem and all Judaea and Samaria, and unto the uttermost parts of the earth," indicating the outgoing of His thoughts to the lost world for which He had given His life, the transcendent moment came. His conversation suddenly passed into words of benediction. Lifting up His hands upon them in an act of blessing, He parted from them, ascending in sublime and noiseless majesty until "a cloud received Him out of their sight." Thence immediately He "passed through the heavens" (Heb. 4:14) and "sat down at the right hand of the Throne of God" (12:2).

THE EVIDENCES

His departure from the world was in keeping with the circumstances of His life on earth. No pomp and ceremony attended His exit. No multitude assembled to witness the startling spectacle. The evidences of the fact of His ascension were to depend, not on that which would appeal to the natural mind, but on the Spirit-empowered witness of His followers. The evidences are as reliable as those for the Resurrection. The account both in the Gospel of Luke and in the Acts, is that of one who, if he did not see the event, at least heard it from one who had done so. Every detail bears the stamp of genuineness, and imparts the character of undeniable credibility to the whole narrative. The subsequent descent of the Holy Spirit, the apostolic witness, the testimony of Stephen at his martyrdom, of Paul at his conversion, and of John in the Apocalypse, as to their having individually seen the ascended Lord, all add their confirmation to the angelic testimony immediately given in response to the worship and the upward gaze of the disciples after the cloud had received the Lord out of their sight. For them no lingering doubt, no lurking suspicion remained. It was "with great joy" that they returned to Jerusalem.

THE EFFECTS

Little as they had apprehended His statements in the Upper Room that it would be expedient for Him to go away, they were now to realize the full significance of the fact. The endowment of the personal power of the Holy Spirit, the diffusion of the spiritual presence of Christ Himself in the hearts of believers, the experience of all that the authority of His headship in the glory meant, as well as His gracious ministry as the shepherd and bishop of their souls, and in addition the assurance that this same Jesus, who had gone into heaven, would come again in like manner as they had seen Him go, all this, and much more besides, not only removed the pain of separation, but filled them with abiding peace, imperishable joy, and unconquerable endurance.

THE PERSON

As His resurrection was corporeal so was His ascension. His was a spiritual body—a body, not a spirit—free from all limitations imposed by natural conditions, yet still bearing the marks of His crucifixion and of the spear wound in His side. No dematerialized being entered heaven. The Lord was still truly man and as such was possessed of all the constitution and attributes of man—body, soul, and spirit. When the apostle says, "He that descended is the same also that ascended" (Eph. 4:10), he is simply stating the fact of the Lord's unchanged personality. He also states that the one who was "received up in glory" was "He who was manifested in the flesh" (1 Tim. 3:16). Not only was His personality unchanged, but the corporeal nature which He had assumed in Incarnation, so far from being discarded, remained in that same transformed condition into which His body was changed in Resurrection by the almighty power of God, who "raised Him from the dead and made Him to sit at His right hand in the heavenly places" (Eph. 1:20, 21).

THE DISPENSATIONAL SIGNIFICANCE

His ascension was both the crowning evidence of the completeness and value of His redeeming work on the cross, and at the same time marked an epoch in human history relative to the work of the gospel and the formation of the Church. For now, the Father having put "all things in subjection under His feet," "gave Him to be head over all things to the Church" (Eph. 1:22). "When He ascended on high He led captivity captive,[1] and gave gifts unto men." The ascension, then, marked a turning point in the divine dispensations. Hitherto God had had a visible dwelling place on earth. Now all was to be changed. He was about to adopt another mode of tabernacling among men, the indwelling of the Spirit in His saints, whether individual or collective. Now had come the time when "the

---

1 It has been supposed that this suggests that the saints of former ages who were in Sheol were now set free therefrom and brought by the Lord into the very presence of the throne of God. Possibly this is so.

Lord dwelleth not in temples made with hands" (Acts 17:24). The external, the ceremonial, the ritualistic in worship must now yield place to the spiritual. "The hour had come when the true worshipers must worship the Father in spirit and in truth." Finally, the ascension of the Lord both marks the fact that the saints are already spiritually raised and seated with Him in the heavenly places, and is the guarantee of their ascension in one united, redeemed, and glorified company when His resurrection shout is heard, and He receives them to be forever with Himself.

THE HIGH PRIESTHOOD OF CHRIST

In the book of Hebrews, Jesus is called a "Priest of the order of Melchizedek." He is a priest-king, and His priesthood is shown to be superior to that of Aaron. Christ is our mediator and intercedes on our behalf. Because He is our High Priest, the throne of glory has become the throne of grace. This should take much of the mystery out of some of the more difficult passages in Hebrews, while all the while clearly demonstrating Jesus' attributes.

The glories of the High Priesthood of Christ were prefigured in a twofold way in the distinct priesthoods of Melchizedek and Aaron. Both were required in order to set forth the perfections of the dignity and ministry of Christ. We can here enter only briefly into these aspects of the subject. To begin with, let us notice how the Epistle to the Hebrews points to the first, and perhaps the greatest, teaching of the Old Testament regarding it, so as to set forth the glories of the Melchizedek order of Christ's priesthood as superior to those of the Aaronic order. This presentation in Hebrews provides at the same time many a clue as to the typical character of the Aaronic priesthood, as set forth in connection with the tabernacle, the consideration of which would overstep the limits of this chapter.

The superiority of

THE MELCHIZEDEK ORDER

of Christ's priesthood is vividly brought out in the seventh chapter. The ancient King-priest is there seen in the mysterious majesty of his person and in the dignified grace of his ministry. We are shown how his biography, given in Genesis 14, was so framed, both by omission and by insertion of detail, that he might prefigure the person and work of Christ. His regal name, "King of righteousness," and his locality, Salem (or peace), show how the priesthood of the Lord Jesus is characterized by peace bestowed on a basis of divine righteousness. The parentage of Melchizedek, the length of his ministry, and his death are all withheld. And thus, by curtailment of the narrative, he is "made like" Him who, in point of fact, as "the Son of God," is without beginning of days or end of life.

The superiority of Christ's priesthood is next seen with reference to Melchizedek's ministry.

Firstly, under the Law the people paid tithes to the Levitical priests. But Abraham, their forefather, paid tithes to Melchizedek. So virtually, Levi paid tithes to him (vv. 4–9).

Secondly, Abraham was blessed by Melchizedek, and the lesser is blessed by the greater (v. 7).

Thirdly, those who received tithes under the Law were "men that die"; not so with the record concerning Melchizedek (v. 8).

Fourthly, Christ sprang from the royal tribe of Judah, which had no connection with the Levitical priesthood; and a change in the order of the priesthood necessitates a change in regard to the Law. Christ, though born under the Law, was not made a priest under it, as Aaron was. The change lies in this, that the Levitical priests were made "after the Law of a carnal commandment," but Christ "after the power of an endless life" (lit., an indissoluble life, neither changing nor passing away). So there is "a disannulling of the foregoing commandment, and a bringing in thereupon of a better hope, through which we draw nigh to God" (vv. 18, 19). That is to say, the change in both Law and priesthood is not only constitutional, it is also administrative, not only in character but also in effect. The Law could never make men fit for God, nor bring them nigh to Him. Through Christ both are effected (vv. 11–19).

Fifthly, no oath accompanied the appointment of the Aaronic priesthood. Its transitory character was unsuited to that. Inviolability is an essential feature of Christ's priesthood. The divine oath, uttered after the Law (see Ps. 110:4) "appointeth a Son, perfected forevermore" (vv. 20–28). God's oath confirms the inviolable character of that for which it is given. The Levitical priesthood was purely official, Christ's has a greatness that is personal. Herein lies its attractiveness.

Sixthly, for this reason Christ has become "the Surety of a better Covenant" (vv. 20–22). The measure of the superiority of the new covenant is the measure of the superiority of the priesthood of Christ. Human need was not met under the old; it is fully met under the new. God's oath and Christ Himself are the guarantee thereof.

Seventhly, the former priests were many; death prevented their continuance; Christ's priesthood does not pass from one to another (v. 24). By reason of all this "He is able to save to the uttermost them that draw near to God through Him, seeing He ever liveth to make intercession for them."

ANTICIPATIONS IN THE DAY OF HIS FLESH

It may be that in the Gospel narratives intimations are given concerning the priesthood of our Lord. There is something suggestive in the fact that it was when He was "about thirty years of age" that He was baptized[1] (Luke 3:23). This

---

1 The narrative in verse 23 is to be connected immediately with the account of the baptism rather than with His teaching, as in R.V. The word "to teach" is absent from the original, which reads, "And

was the age at which the priests, after their consecration, were manifested to the nation (Exod. 29:35; Lev. 8:33). While then His baptism was a symbolic anticipation of the significance of His death and resurrection, and likewise a fulfillment of the divine obligations under the Law, it was at the same time a ceremonial introduction to His public ministry, which in some respects was anticipative of His present priestly function. The Baptist perhaps gave some intimation of this in saying that, though he knew not Jesus personally, yet he had come baptizing with water in order that He might "be made manifest to Israel" (John 1:31).

There are other priestly acts of the Lord in the days of His flesh, such as His prayer on the night of the betrayal (John 17). His great act of the offering up of Himself on the cross was priestly in character. This is made clear in the epistle to the Hebrews as follows: "Such a High Priest became us . . . who needeth not daily, like those priests, to offer up sacrifices, first for his own sins, and then for the sins of the people: for this He did once for all, when He offered up Himself."

HIS OFFICIAL GLORY

The Lord Jesus entered officially on His High Priesthood when he "sat down on the right hand of God" (Heb. 10:12). "He glorified not Himself to be made a High Priest." He thrust not Himself into the position. The Father appointed Him (5:5, 10).

His entire suitability and His efficacy are based on the following facts:

Firstly, on the intrinsic excellence of His person and His proved sinlessness; He is "holy, guileless and undefiled" (7:26).

Secondly, upon the fact of His manhood, "It behoved Him in all things to be made like unto His brethren, that He might be a merciful and faithful High Priest" (2:17).

Thirdly, upon His sufferings as man, in the days of His flesh; "having offered up prayers and supplications with strong crying and tears unto Him that was able to save Him out of [see margin] death, and having been heard for His godly fear, though He was a Son [literally, and more expressively, "although being Son," as just mentioned in 5:5], yet learned obedience [i.e., in the experience of doing the Father's will] by the things which He suffered; and having been made perfect [not morally—that He ever was—but officially, by reason of His experiences], He became unto all them that obey Him the author of eternal salvation; named of God (i.e., officially appointed) a High Priest after the order of Melchizedek" (5:7–10). Thus He has knowledge of all human need and trial, of every person and every case.

Fourthly, upon the value of His atoning sacrifice; "through His own blood He entered in once for all into the holy place" (9:12). Not that He actually took blood into heaven; the taking of the blood of animal sacrifices by the Aaronic high priests within the veil on the day of Atonement, symbolized indeed the

---

Jesus Himself was beginning about 30 years, that is, when what has just been narrated took place.

entire acceptance by God of the perfect sacrifice of Christ, but was not intended to suggest the carrying of literal blood by Christ into heaven.

Fifthly, upon His resurrection. He was "separated from sinners, and made higher than the heavens" (7:26).

Sixthly, upon His relationship with those whom He represents. They are His redeemed, His own possession. They, the sanctified, are one with Him, the sanctifier; "for which cause He is not ashamed to call them brethren."

Seventhly, His Godhood invests His priesthood with an incalculable efficacy, for He thus has perfect knowledge of all the claims of divine righteousness, and maintains them, while at the same time securing the welfare of those on whose behalf He acts.

Eighthly, the character and efficacy of His priesthood rest upon the validity of the divine counsels. These are exhibited in the terms of the new covenant, of which He is the mediator (9:15–10:17). His priesthood is thus shown to be merciful, faithful, sympathetic, authoritative and continuous.

HIS INTERCESSION

In all the power and virtue, then, of His own person and work He ever lives to make intercession[1] for His people. He enters into all their concerns, their needs, and sorrows, and desires. He offers up their prayers and praises, freed from any imperfections which may characterize them, so that they ascend, like the holy incense in the golden censer, in all the perfume of His own acceptance with the Father. He pleads for their consolation and their welfare. As of old the smoke of the burnt offering mingled with the fragrance of the incense, so His intercession ascends in the savor of His sacrifice on the cross. Moreover, every request He makes has the force of a claim; it constitutes a veritable petition of right. He, and He alone, in His prayer can say, "Father, I will that . . ." (John 17:24). His intercessions never fail in their object. On earth He could say, "Thou hearest Me always" (John 11:42). What He did for His disciples here below He does still with unwearying constancy. His place has changed, but not His affection.

With such a High Priest acting on our behalf there is no room for unbelief. We are to draw near to the throne of grace "with a true heart in fullness of faith." The apprehension of the purpose and value of His ministry will rid us of all self-sufficiency and keep us in self-abasement, and in entire dependence upon His power and mercy. The throne of glory has become a throne of grace. There we "may receive mercy and may find grace." There the believer's cup of comfort is filled to overflowing and the divine consolations abound in his soul, for the refreshment of his spirit and the renewal of his strength.

---

1 The word *entunkanō*, to intercede, primarily signified to fall in with a person; then, to have intimate dealings with him, so as to gain his ear; and hence, to make an entreaty, or interpose on behalf of others.

CHRIST THE FIRSTBORN

Jesus Christ is the eternal, only-begotten Son of God; He is the Creator, the very "image of God," and the one true Head of the Church. Not only will the concept of "firstborn" be discussed, but the topics of Christ's eternality and His distinct role as Son will be addressed in the following pages. In addition, myths that other religions have espoused about Jesus will be dispelled.

The title "Firstborn," as used in Scripture with reference to the Son of God, has a certain association with the other title of His divine relationship to the Father, "the only begotten." It will be well, therefore, in the first place to consider the teaching of Scripture regarding the latter. That title is found only in the Gospel of John and in his first epistle. The passages are as follows:

1. "And the Word became flesh, and dwelt among us, (and we beheld His glory, the glory as of the Only Begotten from the Father), full of grace and truth" (John 1:14, R.V.).
2. "No man hath seen God at any time; the only begotten Son, which is in the bosom of the Father, He hath declared Him" (John 1:18).
3. "For God so loved the world, that He gave His only begotten Son, that whosoever believeth on Him should not perish, but have eternal life" (John 3:16).
4. "He that believeth on Him is not judged; he that believeth not hath been judged already, because he hath not believed on the Name of the only begotten Son of God" (John 3:18).
5. "Herein was the love of God manifested in us, that God hath sent His only begotten Son into the world, that we might live through Him" (1 John 4:9).

THE GLORY OF HIS RELATIONSHIP

In speaking of "the glory as of the Only Begotten from the Father" the apostle intimates that the Son of God was the sole representative of the being and character of the One who sent Him. In the original the definite article is omitted both before "only begotten" and before "Father," and its absence in each case serves to lay stress upon the characteristics referred to in the terms used. The apostle's object is to demonstrate what sort of glory it was that he and his fellow apostles had seen. Yet he is not merely making a comparison with earthly relationships. This is at once indicated by the word "from," which rightly translates the original *para*.

The glory to which John refers was that of a unique relationship. It was a Father's Only Begotten who came, the only One who could truly represent such a Father in being, in nature, and love. In this relationship He came down from heaven to earth on His Father's mission. With this agrees His statement to the disciples, "Ye . . . have believed that I came forth from the Father. I came out from the Father, and am come into the world: again, I leave the world and go unto the Father" (16:27, 28). Here He plainly declares His preexistent relationship as the

81

Son, prior to His Incarnation. Obviously He means that He came forth from the presence of One who was already His Father prior to His coming. The mode of His coming forth is suggested by His statement, "Again, I leave the world and go unto the Father." For this expresses the reversal of His procedure mentioned in the first part of the verse. His going unto the Father is the antithesis of His coming out from the Father.

ETERNAL SONSHIP

Again, the same writer, in the introduction to his epistle, says, "The Life was manifested, and we have seen and bear witness, and declare unto you the Life, the eternal Life which was with the Father, and was manifested unto us" (1 John 1:2). John does not say that He who was the Life was "with God," but that He was "with the Father." The terms "father" and "son" are correlative. That of "father" implies the existence of a son. There is no hint in the Scriptures as to any time at which God began to be a Father, yet the Scriptures make clear that His fatherhood in relation to Christ was preexistent to the Incarnation. Was the fatherhood of the One eternal? Then the sonship of the Other must likewise have been eternal.

So again in the same epistle, where the apostle says, "The Father hath sent the Son to be the Savior of the world" (4:14). It was a Father who sent, and a Son who came. Accordingly, we can only rightly understand the term "the only begotten" when used of the Son, in the sense of unoriginated relationship. "The begetting is not an event of time, however remote, but a fact irrespective of time. The Christ did not *become*, but necessarily and eternally *is* the Son. He, a Person, possesses every attribute of pure Godhood. This necessitates eternity, absolute being; in this respect He is 'not after' the Father" (Moule).

A DISTINCTION

Though the word "begotten" is used of the Son's relationship to the Father, it does not imply any beginning of His Sonship. It suggests relationship indeed, but must be distinguished from generation as applied to man. To endeavor to establish our ideas of divine relationship in accordance with our knowledge of human relationships is simply to betray our ignorance. The finite mind cannot conceive of that which is infinite. Our limitations of time and sense preclude our full apprehension of the eternal. God has conveyed the facts relating to Himself in language the phraseology of which we are able to understand, though the facts themselves lie outside the range of human conception. The word "Son," when used of the Son of God, speaks of Him as the perfect archetype of all that the word connotes, whether in human relations, or divine. It signifies all that goes to make up the true idea of the word "Son," viz., the same essence (Heb. 1:3; John 5:18; 10:33–36), dignity (Heb. 1:2), likeness (Heb. 1:3; Matt. 5:45, R.V.), love (John 1:18; Ps. 22:20, margin), and obedience (Heb. 5:8), as distinguished from the mere idea of "child." The expression "only begotten" tells of the uniqueness of that relation in His case. The expression also suggests the thought of the deepest affection, as in the case of the Old Testament word variously rendered, "only one" (Gen. 22:2, 12), "only son" (Jer. 6:26; Amos 8:10; Zech. 12:10), "only beloved" (Prov. 4:3), and "darling" (Ps. 22:20; 35:17). These are evidently the thoughts conveyed to us by the apostle's statement that "the Word was made flesh and dwelt among us (and we beheld His glory, glory as of an Only Begotten from a Father) full of grace and truth." He emphasizes the lowliness of Christ in deigning, with all the majesty of His eternal Godhood, to become flesh and dwell among us, and it is consistent with His glory and His lowliness that He tabernacled among us "full of grace and truth."

THE SON'S ETERNAL DWELLING PLACE

(2) The second statement is, "The Only Begotten Son, which is in the bosom of the Father, He hath declared Him" (John 1:18). This expresses both His eternal union with the Father in the Godhead and the ineffable intimacy and love between them, the Son sharing all the Father's counsels and enjoying all His affections. The form of expression used in the original, and rendered "which is," is the present continuous participle. Expressed literally in English it would be "the One being" (in the bosom). We are to understand, therefore, that the bosom of the Father ever was, and never ceased to be, the dwelling place of the Son.

THE MEASURE OF GOD'S LOVE

(3) Thirdly, the statement that "God so loved the world that He gave His Only Begotten Son" (John 3:16), cannot be taken to mean that Christ became the Only Begotten Son by Incarnation. That would rob the verse of its meaning and force. The value and greatness of the gift lay in the sonship of Him who was given. His sonship was not the effect of His being given. We must distinguish from this the declaration uttered predictively and recorded in Psalm 2:7: "Thou art My Son; this day have I begotten Thee," and quoted in Acts 13:33, Hebrews 1:5 and 5:5. These utterances point to a distinct occasion, whereas the title Only Begotten indicates, as we have seen, the unoriginated relationship of the Son to the Father.

A moment's consideration as to the character of the gift will show us how essentially the Son was one with the Father in the Godhead. It was not one whom God had created that He gave. Had He given a Son who was one of His creatures, His love would have been less than that of a man who lays down his own life for his fellows. For had Christ been created, God could have replaced His gift by another Son. Creation is no difficulty with God. He could have replaced such a gift without a drain on His resources.

No! The Father and the Son are One in the Godhead. Whatever distinction there is between them does not affect their unity. "God was in Christ reconciling the world unto Himself" (2 Cor. 5:19). "God commendeth His own love toward us in that, while we were yet sinners, Christ died for us" (Rom. 5:12). In the person of Christ God came to save us. But more than this, He gave "His only begotten Son" (with all that lies in that unique relationship). "He spared not His Son" (Rom. 8:32; 1 John 4:9). Such a gift was an "unspeakable gift" and the love was "His own," something peculiar to Himself, having no affinity with human love, which depends upon something in another to call it forth. His love was displayed toward those who were sinners.

THE SIN OF UNBELIEF

(4) Fourthly, the importance of that eternal relationship is emphasized by the apostle in the statement, "He that believeth on Him is not judged: he that believeth not hath been judged already, because he hath not believed on the name of the Only Begotten Son of God" (3:18). He might have said simply, "because he hath not believed on the Son of God." Instead he lays stress upon the full revelation of God's character and will, His love and grace, as conveyed in the name of One who, being in such a unique relationship to Him, was provided by Him as the object of faith. The sin of unbelief is seen to be the greater in proportion to the greatness of the One who came in order that men might be saved from the judgment they deserved.

NOT SONSHIP BY INCARNATION

(5) Fifthly, in his first epistle the apostle similarly stresses the greatness of the person as measuring the greatness of the love that sent Him: "Herein was the love of God manifested in us, that God hath sent His Only Begotten Son into the world, that we might live through Him" (1 John 4:9). In sending His Son He sent His all. He could give no greater gift. The infinite value of the person indicates the transcendent way in which such love was manifested. The words "in us" disclose the sphere in which God's love was exhibited. We are by nature dead through trespasses and sins.

This passage again shows the sending to have been by way of His Incarnation and not subsequent to it. The statement does not mean that God sent out into the world one who at His birth in Bethlehem had become His Son. By means of the Incarnation He sent into the world One who was already His Son. The apostle Paul, writing to the Galatians, says, "When the fullness of the time came, God sent forth His Son, born of woman, born under the Law" (Gal. 4:4). The reference plainly is to His being sent forth from heaven to earth by Incarnation, and not to any subsequent mission in the days of His flesh. We may not read the words as if they meant that God sent forth One who at His birth became His Son, any more than the parallel statement in verse 6, "God sent forth the Spirit of His Son," could be taken to mean that God sent forth One who became His Spirit when He sent Him. The Holy Spirit had ever been the Spirit of God prior to Pentecost. So in regard to the statement in verse 4, He whom God sent forth to be born of a woman had ever been His Son. This is made clear, too, by the statement in 1 John 1:2, "The Life was manifested, and we have seen, and bear witness, and declare unto you the Life, the eternal Life, which was with the Father, and was manifested unto us." The writer does not say that He who was the Life was "with God," but that He was "with the Father." Since He was with the Father, and was at the same time the eternal Life, His Sonship must have been eternal.

THE TITLE "FIRSTBORN"

With this truth before us, of the eternal relationship involved in the term "Only Begotten," we now turn to consider the other title, "Firstborn," which is to be distinguished from it, though it is associated with it. Here again, there are five passages in the New Testament, and in addition, one in the Old Testament, where this title is used of Christ. It will be useful to set these out as we did in the other case, in detail, but now in chronological order, the successive periods or points of time being indicated in the context. The passages are as follows:

1. "Who is the image of the invisible God, the Firstborn of all creation" (Col. 1:15).
2. "And He is the Head of the body, the Church; who is the beginning, the Firstborn from the dead; that in all things He might have the preeminence" (Col. 1:18).
3. "Jesus Christ, who is the faithful witness, the Firstborn of the dead, and the ruler of the kings of the earth" (Rev. 1:5).
4. "For whom He foreknew, He also foreordained to be conformed to the image of His Son, that He might be the Firstborn among many brethren" (Rom. 8:29).
5. "And when He again bringeth in the Firstborn into the world He saith, And let all the angels of God worship Him" (Heb. 1:6).
6. "I also will make Him My Firstborn, the highest of the kings of the earth" (Ps. 89:27).

A COMPARISON AND A CONTRAST

It will be seen from the above passages that the title "Firstborn," while used with reference to created beings, distinguishes Him, firstly, from all creatures absolutely as such, and then relatively from them as those who are subordinate to Him. Yet it is this reference to created beings which distinguishes the title from that of "Only Begotten." The two have this in common, that neither of them classes Him with created beings. While "Only Begotten" speaks of His absolute and unique relationship to the Father, the title "Firstborn" brings other beings into view, not implying a beginning of His being, not classing Him with His creatures, but denoting His preeminence over them in time and dignity.

The six passages above quoted have reference to the following subjects respectively, which are given in chronological order: (1) His work in creation; (2) His resurrection (first aspect); (3) His resurrection (second aspect); (4) His position among His glorified saints; (5) His manifested glory; (6) His millennial reign.

I. CHRIST THE FIRSTBORN WITH REFERENCE TO CREATION

In the first passage Christ is described as "The image of the invisible God, the Firstborn of all creation," and the explanation of the latter clause is that "In Him were all things created, in the heavens and upon the earth, things visible and things invisible, whether thrones or dominions or principalities or powers; all things have been created through Him, and unto Him" (Col. 1:16, 17).

"The Image of God"

The apostle first speaks of Him here in relation to His Godhood. He is "the Image of the invisible God." Similarly in 2 Corinthians 4:4 he describes Him as "the image of God." On the word *eikōn*, rendered "image," Bishop Lightfoot remarks, "Beyond the very obvious notion of likeness, the word involves two other ideas; (1) representation. In this . . . it implies an archetype of which it is a copy; (2) manifestation . . . the underlying idea being the manifestation of the hidden." It is to be distinguished therefore from our word "likeness," which merely denotes a resemblance.

What the apostle John says of the Son of God as the Word is likewise applicable to this term "image." "No man hath seen God at any time; the only-begotten Son, which is in the bosom of the Father, He hath declared Him" (John 1:18). Here in the Colossian passage Paul similarly predicates the invisibility of God, and virtually states that the Son, in being both the representation and manifestation of God, has declared Him. As Liddon says, "The expression 'image of God,' supplements the title of 'the Son.' As 'the Son,' Christ is derived eternally from the Father, and He is of one substance with the Father. As 'the Image' Christ is, in that one substance, the exact likeness of the Father, in all things except being the Father. The Son is the image of the Father, not as the Father, but as God: the Son is the Image of God . . . God's unbegun, unending reflection of Himself in Himself, but also the organ whereby God, in His essence invisible, reveals Himself to His creatures. Thus the *eikōn* is, so to speak, naturally the Creator, since creation is the first revelation which God has made of Himself. Man is the highest point in the visible universe: in man, God's attributes are most luminously exhibited; man is the image and glory of God. But Christ is the adequate Image of God, God's self-reflection in His own thought, eternally present with Himself."[1]

Christ the Creator

The Son, then, in His very person and nature, makes God known. He is the full revelation both of the being and character of God. As the apostle says in the next chapter, "In Him dwelleth all the fullness of the Godhead bodily" (Col. 2:9). This would in itself be sufficient to show that the expression "the Firstborn of all creation," does not imply that He is ranked among created beings. The

---

1 Liddon, "The Divinity of our Lord," pp. 321, 322.

apostle definitely refutes this implication in his succeeding explanation, "For in Him were all things created . . . all things have been created through Him and in Him all things consist." Since the Son of God is Himself the Creator, whatever the title "Firstborn" signifies, it is evident that it does not mean that He, the Creator, is at the same time to be classed with His creatures.

Further, the form of expression exemplified in the phrase "Firstborn of all creation," was not infrequently used to distinguish a person from others, in declaring his priority to them in time and his superiority over them in position. The literal rendering, for instance, of the statement of John the Baptist, "He was before me" (John 1:15–30) is, "He was first of me." The margin of the Revised Version has "first in regard of me." It was far from the Baptist's thought to class the Lord Jesus with the order of beings to which he himself belonged. With this idiomatic use of the preposition "of" we may compare Milton's line, "Adam, the goodliest man of men since born," and the words of the historian Thucydides, who speaks of a war as "the most notable of wars previously waged." In these cases "of" obviously implies distinction, not association.

A Fourfold Position

The apostle's statement, then, does not mean that Christ is ranked as the first among created beings. He existed before them, not only as their Creator, but in eternal relationship to the Father as His Firstborn. That He is "the Image of God" defines His relation in the Godhead; that He is "the Firstborn of every creature" defines His position with regard to creatures. They owe their origin and condition to Him. The position is fourfold. All things were created (*a*) firstly, in Him; (*b*) secondly, by Him; (*c*) thirdly, unto Him; and (*d*) fourthly, by His power all things consist (vv. 16, 17).

(a) "In Him"

With regard to the first of these, namely, that all things were created *in* Him, the preposition expresses that the Son of God was the center from whom, in the divine counsels, creative power should proceed. As Liddon says, "There was no creative process external to and independent of Him, since the archetypal forms after which the creatures are modeled, and the sources of their strength and consistency of being, eternally reside in Him." He was the Divine Designer.

(b) "By Him"

Secondly, they were created *by* Him. He was the Divine Instrument (Rev. 4:11, R.V.). "Without Him was not anything made that hath been made" (John 1:3). In this sense we are to understand the description the Lord gives of Himself in the letter to the church at Laodicea, where He calls Himself "The beginning of the creation of God." This expression, in the original, does not signify that He was Himself created, it means He is the source of all that has been created.

In the same sense He speaks of Himself as "the Alpha and Omega, the first and the last, the beginning and the end" (22:13; cp. 1:8, 17). The same expressions are used by God the Father of Himself in chapter 21:6, as also He had done through the prophet Isaiah: "Who hath wrought and done it, calling the generations from the beginning? I the Lord, the First and with the Last, I am He" (Isa. 41:4; cp. 44:6). Again, "I am the First, I also am the Last. Yea, Mine hand hath laid the foundation of the earth, and My right hand hath spread out the heavens" (48:12, 13). Thus the very expressions which declare the Deity of God are applied by Christ to Himself.

These expressions unfold the great name "Jehovah," and especially in two respects: "The First" or "the Alpha," as the One by whose power all things had their beginning, and "the Last," "the Omega," as indicating that He will see to it that all the divine counsels will at length be completely fulfilled. In the Apocalypse the Lord Jesus declares that His are all the prerogatives of Godhood. There is no hint in any part of the Scriptures that Christ was the first of created beings. The testimony is clear and explicit throughout that He was the Creator, Himself being uncreated.

(c) "Unto Him"

Thirdly, "All things were created *unto* Him." He is the Divine Object. "He is not, as Arianism propounded, merely an inferior workman, creating for the glory of a higher Master, for a God superior to Himself. He creates for Himself: He is the End of created things, as well as their immediate Source." In the epistle to the Romans the apostle predicates these things of God. He says, "Oh, the depth of the riches, both of the wisdom and the knowledge of God! How unsearchable are His judgments, and His ways past tracing out! For who hath known the mind of the Lord, or who hath been His counselor? Or who hath first given to Him, and it shall be recompensed unto him again? For *of* Him, and *through* Him, and *unto* Him, are all things. To Him be the glory forever. Amen" (Rom. 11:33–36). What is there said of the Father is here in Colossians said of the Son, a testimony therefore to His Deity and His oneness with the Father in the Godhead. The Son is not only a divine agent in creation, He is its final Object. The Father has determined "to sum up all things in Christ, the things in the heavens, and the things upon the earth" (Eph. 1:10). All things are to be subjected to Him (1 Cor. 15:27). The Son is "able even to subdue all things unto Himself" (Phil. 3:21).

(d) "In Him All Things Consist"

This fourth the apostle introduces by the statement, "He is before all things." Herein he declares not only Christ's preexistence, but likewise His absolute existence. He and He only *is*. All else is created. Further, He is "before all things," including time itself. This the Lord Himself stated when He said, "Before Abraham was, I am." He did not say, "Before Abraham was, I was," as He would have done had He merely intended to state His preexistence. He says instead, "I am," taking up the language of Jehovah to Moses, when He commanded him to say to the children of Israel, "I AM hath sent me unto you."

The second statement that, "in Him all things consist," signifies that every creature finds in Him "the explanation and law of its being." As Lightfoot says, "He is the principle of cohesion in the universe. He impresses upon creation that unity and solidity which makes it a cosmos instead of a chaos. Thus, to take one instance, the action of gravitation, which keeps in their places things fixed, and regulates the motion of things moving, is an expression of His mind." Similarly in the Hebrews epistle Christ is described as "upholding all things by the word of His power." Plainly these Scriptures teach that, apart from Christ, creation could neither have come into being, nor could its order be maintained. The Son of God, "the effulgence of the Father's glory and the very image of His substance," maintains all things by His word of power (Heb. 1:2, 3). The Scriptures make clear, then, that not only does the world of nature owe its existence to a direct act of creation on the part of the Son of God, but that He Himself, by whose decree, indeed, the natural laws which regulate the universe were established, sustains the universe by His might. That there are increasing evidences of this is admitted today in the scientific world. Here is what a recent writer has to say on the subject: "The Bible . . . comes in to show the rational *via media* between Deism and Pantheism, avoiding the absurdity of both extremes. There is a place where God abides in a sense in which He is not to be found in any other place. Yet His powers and perfections are such that, by His Spirit and by His Word, He is present everywhere throughout His universe. His Word is as effective at the remotest distances as near at hand, for the simple reason that matter has no "properties" which He has not imparted to it, and therefore it can have no innate inertia or reluctance to act which God's Word would need to overcome in order to induce it to act, even when this Word operates across the boundless fields of space. He has created free personalities, and He leaves the mind of each of His creatures free to serve Him or not to serve Him, these free intelligent beings becoming thus true second causes. More than this, provision for almost innumerable second causes seems to have been made even among other departments of nature, without, however, interfering with the direct action of the Word of the Infinite One in guiding and controlling them all."

His Preeminence in Dominion

When, therefore, the apostle says that Christ is "The Firstborn of all creation," he is using a term which is perfectly consistent with the fact of His preexistence before all created beings, His superiority to them, as being the source of their existence, and His preeminence over them as the One to whose power they owe their very condition and maintenance. All this lies in the meaning of the word *prōtotokos*, "firstborn," as applied to the Son of God. It is likewise connected with the principles of primogeniture with reference to dominion. The idea of dominion had a tendency, owing to the sense of priority, to outweigh the initial meaning of simple priority of birth. Indeed the thought of priority of birth was not infrequently last in the idea of preeminence. Thus, in his argument with Job, Bildad speaks of the "firstborn of death" (Job 18:13), signifying thereby the one who has preeminent power over death. So again, Isaiah, speaking of days of millennial peace and glory, says, "The firstborn of the poor [that is to say, the one who is preeminently poor] shall feed, and the needy shall lie down in plenty" (Isa. 14:30). Under the Mosaic economy it was possible for a man to make any one of His sons his "firstborn" other than the one who was actually so (Deut. 21:16, 17). This idea of preeminence in authority and dominion is then the predominant thought in the use of the word as applied to the Son of God. In coming into creation in manhood and thus taking part with that which He had Himself created, allying Himself the infinite with the finite, it could only be as "the Firstborn of all creation." This now comes before us in the remaining passages.

II. CHRIST THE FIRSTBORN WITH REFERENCE TO HIS RESURRECTION (FIRST ASPECT)

Following the description of Christ's creative power and glory as the Firstborn in regard to the natural creation, the apostle makes a similar statement with reference to the spiritual creation: "And He is the Head of the Body, the Church; who is the Beginning, the Firstborn from the dead; that in all things He might have the preeminence" (Col. 1:18). The fourfold teaching of the title, as intimated in the previous sections, is again before us here, namely (a) divine relationship; (b) priority to others in time; (c) source of their existence; (d) preeminence over them.

Resurrection His Presumptive Right

(a) Here He is described as the "Firstborn from the dead," lit., "out from among the dead." Stress is laid upon the fact of His resurrection. To Christ, as the Son of God, resurrection was not only a fact of foreordained fulfillment, it was a presumptive right; it was His Father's vindication of His Sonship, the vindication at the same time of Christ's claim to be the Son of God. He had announced it beforehand to His critics and opponents, the Scribes and Pharisees, as the one sign which would be given to them. His reply to their request for some token of the validity of His claims, was that no sign would be given them but the sign of Jonah the prophet; "For as Jonah was three days and three nights in the belly of the whale, so," He said, "shall the Son of man be three days and three nights in the heart of the earth" (Matt. 12:38–40). His resurrection was the crowning evidence of His Deity as the Son of God, and of the divine character of His mission. In His resurrection was fulfilled the Messianic prophecy uttered by Isaiah, "He is near that justified Me" (Isa. 50:8). That the statement was directly predictive of the Lord Jesus Christ, is clear from the context: "The Lord God hath opened Mine ear, and I was not rebellious, neither turned away backward. I gave My back to the smiters, and My cheeks to them that plucked off the hair: I hid not My face from shame and spitting. For the Lord God will help Me; therefore have I not been confounded: therefore have I set My face like a flint, and I know that I shall not be ashamed. He is near that justifieth Me" (Isa. 50:5–8).

For all others resurrection is a matter of pure grace. The Resurrection of Christ was His due. His sinlessness, a fact which even His bitterest enemies admitted, demanded it. The very terms of God's Law decreed it. Perfect obedience to its commands guaranteed the assurance of life: "He that doeth them shall live in them" (Lev. 18:5, quoted in Gal. 3:12). He was the only One who ever fulfilled absolutely the conditions laid down in the Law. "Tempted in all points like as we are," He was yet without sin. Tested in every way, He alone of all men since the Fall "was so born that He needed not to be born again." Yet, be it always remembered, the nature which He took in His Incarnation was that of true humanity, possessing all the essential properties of manhood. He identified Himself with humanity in everything but sin.

It is, therefore, of Christ that the psalmist says, "Thou wilt not leave My soul in Sheol, neither wilt Thou suffer Thine Holy One to see corruption. Thou wilt show Me the path of life," i.e., resurrection life (Ps. 16:9–11).

(b) His was

Priority in Resurrection

Others had been translated, or had been raised with bodies not entirely delivered from the power of death. He, first, was raised to die no more. "If we died with Christ, we believe that we shall also live with Him; knowing that Christ being raised from the dead dieth no more; death no more hath dominion over Him" (Rom. 6:8, 9). He Himself says, "I am . . . the Living One; and I was dead, and behold, I am alive forevermore" (Rev. 1:17, 18). He has been shown to be preeminent over creation (Col. 1:15), and in providence (v. 17), and now He is seen to be preeminent over the new creation as the first to rise from the dead. Here, again, the expression has reference to others, who would follow, and enter through Him the vast sphere of reconciliation.

The Founder of the Church

(c) What we have remarked above, with reference to the description of Christ in Revelation 3:14, as "the Beginning of the Creation of God" applies here. As "the beginning," He is the Originator of the Church. It owes its very existence to Him; firstly, by reason of the predetermining and eternal counsels of God in Him; secondly, by reason of His death and resurrection; thirdly by the mission of the Holy Spirit, sent forth by the Father and the Son at pentecost. Thereupon began the fulfillment of His Word to Peter, that on the ground of the truth of his confession concerning Himself as "the Christ, the Son of the Living God," He would build His Church (Matt. 16:16–18).

His Preeminence over the Church

(*d*) Because He is "the beginning, the Firstborn from the dead," He is related to the Church as the Head of the Body. All that is naturally set forth in this relationship is true of the spiritual union suggested. The Church is under His control and government, and derives its sustenance from Him. As He sustains the natural creation, so He does the spiritual. From Him "all the body fitly framed and knit together through that which every joint supplieth, according to the working in due measure of each several part, maketh the increase of the body unto the building up of itself in love" (Eph. 4:16), and again, "all the body, being supplied and knit together through the joints and bands, increaseth with the increase of God" (Col. 2:19). This constant care and nourishment relates to the present circumstances of believers on the earth; for it is here that Christ, as Head of the Church, gives gifts, "for the perfecting of the saints unto the work of ministering, unto the building up of the body of Christ" (Eph. 4:11–13). He will, however, always be the Head, the Source of all life and energy in His members throughout eternity.

The divine purpose in view is that "in all things [or, as the margin, "among all"] He might have the preeminence." Either rendering is possible. If we read "in all things," then the reference is both to the universe and the Church. If the rendering "among all" is adopted, then the reference is especially to the Church. The context indicates the rendering "in all things." For the apostle goes on to say that it was the divine good pleasure "through Him to reconcile all things unto Himself . . . whether things upon the earth, or things in the heavens."

III. CHRIST THE FIRSTBORN WITH REFERENCE TO HIS RESURRECTION (SECOND ASPECT)

There is another passage which speaks of Christ's position as the Firstborn in resurrection. In Revelation 1:5 He is called "The Firstborn of the dead." Now while in Colossians 1:18, as we have seen, He is spoken of as "The Firstborn *from* [*ek*, out from among] the dead," in Revelation 1:5 the Greek has no preposition, according to the best manuscripts. Each passage refers to His resurrection. The distinction is that Revelation 1:5 indicates more specially the fact that Christ had been dead, whereas Colossians 1:18 lays stress upon the fact that He arose "from the midst of the dead." In accordance with what is more particularly in view in Revelation 1:5, is the Lord's own statement in verse 18, "I was dead, and behold, I am alive forevermore." Here Christ calls attention to the fact that, while He is essentially the Living One, and is alive forevermore, He was dead.

It is as Son of man that He is seen in this chapter. The opening chapters of Genesis present to us the first man forfeiting everything God had placed in his hands, even life itself. But here in the closing book we have the second Man presented in all His victory over death and Hades and ready to take the kingdom. God's purpose in man is fulfilled through Him who is the second man and in whom all things in heaven and on earth are yet to be headed up in the ultimate triumph of God over evil. Only through death could Christ "bring to naught him that had the power of death." So that what before was the evidence of the enemy's power comes now, to the believer, the portal into unending bliss, the key of which is held by One who is Himself the Firstfruits of His own victory as "the last Adam," "the Firstborn of the dead."

IV. CHRIST THE FIRSTBORN AMONG HIS GLORIFIED SAINTS

Passing now chronologically from the above two passages, which refer to His resurrection, we are next directed to the consummation of the purposes of God in Christ for the Church at His Second Coming. In the eighth chapter of Romans the apostle refers again and again to this event. Indeed that chapter is divided by these references into five distinct sections. The first ends at verse 11, which speaks, not of the present reinvigoration of the bodies of believers, but of their transformation by the Lord at His Second Coming, the assurance of which is based upon the fact that His Spirit dwells in them. The second ends at verse 17, which speaks of their being glorified together with Christ as being joint-heirs with Him, and as those who have known what suffering with Him is. The third ends at verse 23, which speaks of "the adoption, to wit, the redemption of our body." The fourth is marked off at verse 30, where the apostle says, "For whom He foreknew, He also foreordained to be conformed to the image of His Son, that He might be the Firstborn among many brethren and whom He foreordained, them He also called: and whom He called, them He also justified: and whom He justified, them He also glorified." Here Paul is confirming his statement that "to them that love God all things work together [or "He worketh all things together"] for good, even to them that are called according to His purpose" (v. 28). The confirmation consists of an unfolding of the divine purposes of grace in the complete salvation of believers. The whole scheme rests upon the foreknowledge of God: "Whom He foreknew He also foreordained." God in His foreknowledge foresaw certain persons in whom He would fulfill His counsels of grace, with the grand purpose in view that they should be "conformed to the image of His Son, that He might be the Firstborn among many brethren"; the Firstborn being the Son by nature, His many brethren sons by adoption, yet conformed as kindred beings to the image—a moral and spiritual likeness now, and corporeal also hereafter—of God's Son.

The Future Glory of the Son

The divine determination that the Son of God should be glorified carries with it the full salvation of believers. Their assurance of coming glory is due to the certainty that God will fulfill His purposes toward His Son, and that their conformity to Him will enhance His glory in the highest possible manner. In being glorified with Him they will show forth His glory to a degree impossible by any other means. Conformity to the image of Christ is indeed a process now determined by God in the spiritual life of His children, but when the Church is complete, and the Lord comes with His shout to raise the saints that have fallen asleep and change the living, then will He Himself be seen in the midst as "the Firstborn among many brethren." Then will He have brought the "many sons" unto glory (Heb. 2:10). Then "He that sanctifieth and they that are sanctified" will be all together, all being "of one" (i.e., of one Father). It is for this cause that "He is not ashamed to call them brethren." Then will He say, "Behold, I and the children which God hath given Me." They will be an unbroken family, an undivided company, and His prayer will have been fulfilled, "Father, those whom Thou hast given Me, I will that where I am they also may be with Me, that they may behold My glory." Subsequently, at their revelation with Him in manifested glory, the world will see their perfect unity and will know "that the Father sent Him, and loved them as He loved the Son" (John 17:22–24).

The Church of the Firstborn (Ones)

The Church is associated with Christ in this title of the Firstborn in Hebrews 12:23, where the apostle calls them "the Church of the firstborn [ones] who are enrolled in Heaven." Israel is similarly described as "Israel, My son, My firstborn" (Exod. 4:22; cp. Jer. 31:9). In each case the thought is that of preeminence in relationship to God. In regard to Israel, other nations are to be brought into divine favor hereafter because of the relationship which God established between Himself and His chosen people. In this sense they are His firstborn. So also with the Church. Those who constitute it are brought into the closest possible relationship with God through the operation of the Holy Spirit. The privileges too of spiritual primogeniture are theirs. Theirs is the kingdom and the priesthood. First dying in their substitute they live to serve (cp. Exod. 13:13).

Firstfruits

We may compare the term "firstfruits," which signifies a special position as the outcome of the favor of God and His dealings of grace. "Two Hebrew words are thus translated, one meaning the chief or principal part (Num. 18:12; Prov. 3:9, etc.); the other the earliest ripe, of the crop or of the tree (Exod. 23:16; Neh. 10:35, etc.); they are found together in Exodus 23:19, etc., "the first of the firstfruits." The term is applied in things spiritual:

(a) To the presence of the Holy Spirit with the believer as the firstfruits of the full harvest of the Cross; "And not only so, but ourselves also, which have the firstfruits of the Spirit, even we ourselves groan within ourselves, waiting for our adoption, to wit, the redemption of our body" (Rom. 8:23).

(b) To Christ Himself in resurrection in relation to all who have fallen asleep believing in Him; "But now hath Christ been raised from the dead, the firstfruits of them that are asleep . . . But each in His own order: Christ the Firstfruits; then they that are Christ's at His coming" (1 Cor. 15:20–23).

(c) To the earliest believers in a country in relation to those of their countrymen who believe later: "Salute Epaenetus my beloved, who is the firstfruits of Asia unto Christ" (Rom. 16:5). "Ye know the house of Stephanas, that it is the firstfruits of Achaia, and that they have set themselves to minister unto the saints" (1 Cor. 16:15).

(d) To the believers of this age in relation to the whole of the redeemed here, and James 1:18: "Of His own will He brought us forth by the Word of truth, that we should be a kind of firstfruits of His creatures."[1]

Both Hebrew words occur in Leviticus 2. Verse 12 points to Him as the leader of those who will be like Him. Verse 14 points to Him as the captain made perfect through suffering, and preeminent as Firstborn from the dead. All others who are brought into divine favor are viewed in this term. Just as Christ as "the firstfruits," is the earnest and pledge of the future resurrection of saints, so believers, "a kind of firstfruits," are the earnest and pledge of the eventual restoration of creation.

Just as the whole land of Canaan was consecrated to God by the consecration of the firstfruits, so the whole nation of Israel was acknowledged as belonging to God by the setting apart of the firstborn (Exod. 13:12–16). Subsequently, the tribe of Levi was substituted for the firstborn of the families, to minister to the Lord (Num. 3:12, 45–50). Since, however, there were 273 more firstborn in Israel than there were male Levites, the 273 were redeemed at five shekels each. Notwithstanding, in order to mark the whole nation as consecrated to the Lord, the redemption money had to be paid for every firstborn (Num. 18:15).

Just so the Church is the peculiar possession of God. It is not His only possession, but as it is "the Church of the firstborn ones," they are, in their special relationship, a token that all else belongs to Him. Their union with Christ in His resurrection life, obtains for them this distinction over other members of the human race. The title identifies them immediately with Christ Himself.

The occasion when the Lord Jesus will be seen to be "the Firstborn among many brethren" is further indicated in the verse which follows in Romans 8, "Whom He justified, them He glorified." The past tense here is prophetic. Distinctions of time are not in view, the apostle's object being to present the work of divine grace in its finality.

V. CHRIST THE FIRSTBORN WITH REFERENCE TO HIS MANIFESTED GLORY

In point of time the last event in reference to which Christ is spoken of as the Firstborn, is His Second Advent, His return in glory to the earth to set up His kingdom. There are two passages in which the title occurs which speak of this, one in the epistle to the Hebrews and the other in the Psalms. The former is as

---

1 *An Exposition of the Epistles to the Thessalonians*, by Hogg and Vine.

follows: "And when He again bringeth in the Firstborn into the world, He saith, And let all the angels of God worship Him" (Heb. 1:6, r.v.).

It is important to notice the position and meaning of the word "again," here; it does not in this case serve simply to link a further statement to one preceding; it is to be taken with the word "bringeth." The time of which the apostle is speaking is not of the Incarnation, as we shall see from the passage in the Old Testament from which the quotation is taken. Besides this, there is nothing in Scripture to show that what is here said of the angels took place at the birth of Christ. Upon that occasion there was "a multitude of the heavenly host praising God" (Luke 2:13). The whole company of the glorious angels was not present. When He returns to earth in the day of His manifested glory, for the purpose of overthrowing the foes of God and establishing His kingdom, He will be accompanied by all His holy angels. As He Himself said, "For the Son of man shall come in the glory of His Father with His angels" (Matt. 16:27). Again, "But when the Son of man shall come in His glory, and all the angels with Him, then shall He sit on the Throne of His glory: and before Him shall be gathered all the nations" (25:31, 32). The Lord Jesus will be revealed from heaven "with the angels of His power in flaming fire, rendering vengeance to them that know not God, and to them that obey not the gospel of our Lord Jesus: who shall suffer punishment, even eternal destruction from the face of the Lord and from the glory of His might, when He shall come to be glorified in His saints, and to be marveled at in all them that believed" (2 Thess. 1:8–10). It will be as the Firstborn in relation to all creation, including the angels, that He will be brought into the world to receive the inheritance awaiting Him.

The Song of Moses

The words in Hebrews 1:6, "And let all the angels of God worship Him," are quoted from the Septuagint Version of Deuteronomy 32:35–43, at the close of the song of Moses, which consists of the history of the nation of Israel from its inception to the time yet future, when they shall be delivered from their enemies and become the praise of the Lord and the leading nation in the world. The end of the song speaks of the divine judgment upon the foes of Israel, the final deliverance of that nation, and the blessing of the Gentiles which will follow upon the restoration of God's earthly people at the beginning of the Millennium.

In order to get the connection it will be well to quote the passage in full as from the Septuagint Version: "For I will lift up My hand to heaven, and swear by My right hand, and I will say, I live forever, for I will sharpen My sword like lightning, and My hand shall take hold of Judgment; and I will render judgment to Mine enemies, and will recompense them that hate Me. I will make My weapons drunk with blood, and My sword shall devour flesh, from the blood of the wounded, and from captivity, from the head of the rulers of the enemies. Rejoice, ye heavens, with Him, and let all the angels of God worship Him. Rejoice, ye Gentiles, with His people, and let all the sons of God strengthen themselves in

Him; for He will avenge the blood of His sons, and He will render vengeance, and recompense justice to His enemies, and will reward them that hate Him; and the Lord shall thoroughly purge His people's land."

The poetic narrative regarding Israel's history begins at the eighth verse, which describes how the Lord, in primarily allotting the gentile nations their inheritance, set their geographical limits in relationship to the future population of Israel, Palestine thus being predetermined ethnologically as the center of the world. The song proceeds to declare the care bestowed by God upon His people, and then the apostasy and rebellion of the nation, in provoking Him to anger with their idolatry. Consequent judgment upon them is next predicted (v. 35). The cruel treatment meted out to them, however, at the hands of their gentile enemies, to whom they would be delivered, would in turn call for divine vengeance upon these nations. Their enemies must come under the wrath of God through their disregard of His claims and their hatred of His people.

The Doom of Antichrist

The close of the song thus brings into view the end of the present age, the time elsewhere called "the Day of the Lord," and falls into line with 2 Thessalonians 1:7-10, noticed above, and with many other Scriptures relating to the same period, such as Isaiah 63:3-6, for instance, which foretells the day of vengeance, and the year of God's redeemed. See also Joel 3:1-6, 12-17; Revelation 19:11-21, etc. All these speak of the climax of the warfare of Armageddon, the termination of the Great Tribulation. There is a very close connection between the latter passage and the one under consideration in Deuteronomy 32. The nineteenth chapter of Revelation describes the Beast and the kings of the earth under him, and their armies, gathered together to make war against Christ. The Beast is the same being as is spoken of in Revelation 13, who by that time, will have received worldwide worship, the political and social affairs of the world likewise being under his control. So also in chapter 17, which foretells that the rulers of the Ten-Kingdomed League will hand over their power and authority to him, and, with him will "war against the Lamb. And the Lamb shall overcome them, for He is Lord of lords and King of kings" (17:14).

The Consummation

Deuteronomy 32:42 gives perhaps the earliest intimation in Scripture of the overthrow of this great Antichrist and the kings of the earth and the consequent deliverance of Israel from their tyranny. The sword of the Lord is to begin its work with "the head of the rulers of the enemy," i.e., the Antichrist, the Beast of Revelation 19, who is to be taken and destroyed, and with him the False Prophet, while "the rest," that is the rulers of the earth and their armies, are to be killed "with the sword of Him that sat on the horse" (Rev. 19:20, 21). Immediately upon their overthrow the heavens are called to rejoice and "all the angels of God" are summoned to worship Christ. Thereupon, the tyrant oppressor of the Jews having been removed, the Gentiles are called to rejoice with His people. The land, now freed from its anti-Christian despots, will be thoroughly purged. For a more extended view of this see Ezekiel 39:12 to the end of the chapter.

"The King of Kings"

This is the time, then, to which Hebrews 1:6 refers. In this way God will bring His Firstborn into the world. Then will be fulfilled the prophecy of Psalm 89:27, "I also will make Him My Firstborn, the highest of the kings of the earth," a direct antithesis to the position held by the Beast under Satan, who, as the above passages show, will for a short time have ruled over the kings of the earth. But Christ is the "King of kings." The brief despotism of the Antichrist will yield place to the permanent dominion of the Christ of God.

Though the psalm immediately speaks of David, it refers prophetically to David's "greater Son," and to His enthronement as God's king "upon His holy hill of Zion." Then will the nations be given to Him "for His inheritance, and the uttermost parts of the earth for His possession" (Ps. 2:6–8).

The Doxology

This completes our brief and inadequate review of the glories of the Lord Jesus Christ as "the Only begotten" in relation to the Father, and as "the Firstborn" in relation to the old and new creations. Under these titles we see Him, in the one, in His eternal and unique relationship, and, in the other in His present exaltation and in the rapidly approaching consummation of this age, when, having received His Church to Himself in resurrection life and power, He will return to set up the kingdom which shall never be destroyed. May our contemplation of His glorious Person ever lead us to worship and adore Him, the Son of the Father, "the faithful Witness, the Firstborn of the dead, and the Ruler of the kings of the earth." "Unto Him that loveth us, and loosed us from our sins by His blood: and He made us to be a Kingdom, to be priests unto His God and Father: to Him be the glory and the dominion forever and ever. Amen."

THE ATONEMENT

Sin entered the world because of disobedience and a penalty was demanded. In order for sins to be atoned once-and-for-all, Jesus provided a sacrifice. He died in our place so that we could be reconciled with God. Christ's atonement is our redemption.

When God created man, He constituted him a fit subject for moral government, a being who could understand the character and will of His Maker, worship and hold communion with Him, and experience the joy of obedience to Him. Consistently with this, and for his own welfare, God imposed upon him a single prohibition. It was entirely within man's power to conform to this or to transgress. That was essentially a feature of his constitution. He was not a helpless mechanism.

Submitting to the adverse and subtle influence of God's enemy, man decided to transgress. This act of disobedience demanded a penalty. Not to exact it would have argued a defect in God's commandment, and therefore in His own character.

THE CHARACTER OF SIN

Sin is not a misfortune. It is not a mistake. Nor is it a disease. Nor again is it a necessary stage to higher things. It is not the mere product of circumstances, the result of heredity or environment. Sin is lawlessness (1 John 3:4). That being so, a righteous satisfaction was demanded. Pardon could be given only in a manner consistent with God's attributes and character, with the rectitude of His administration and His irreconcilability to evil.

THE CONDITIONS REQUIRED

The readjustment of the broken relationship was impossible to man. No act on his part could atone for his guilt.

Firstly, repentance could not effect it. Repentance would be unavailing to restore the broken relation.

Secondly, an amended life could not effect it. An amended life could not cancel previous guilt.

Thirdly, no fellow man could accomplish it. All men share in the guilt. "All have sinned, and fall short of the glory of God" (Rom. 3:23).

THE PERSON REQUIRED

We turn therefore to inquire who could accomplish what was necessary in order that God might pardon the sinner and clear the guilty?

Firstly, one was required who could entirely apprehend the attributes, the character, and the claims of God.

Secondly, this person must put himself into relationship with the sinner, come under the claims of divine righteousness, and stand its test without failure. To this end, being himself in complete acquaintance with the holy nature and righteous demands of God, he must become identified with human constitution and nature.

Thirdly, such a person must be free from guilt himself, and he must be tested and proved to be free from all taint of sin.

Fourthly, he must himself endure the penalty of sin, bear the curse of the broken Law. If he had any taint in himself he would suffer judgment on his own account and no advantage could accrue to the sinner. But, though sinless himself, it would be necessary for God to deal with him as He would deal with sin.

THE ONLY BEING POSSIBLE

Now there was only one being who could fulfill these conditions, and that was the Son of God Himself.

Firstly, He was one with the Father in Godhead. The prophecy that predicted accurately where He would be born declared at the same time that His "goings forth are from old, from everlasting" (Mic. 5:2). That is what in Psalm 90 is predicted of God, and could be predicted of no other: "From everlasting to everlasting Thou art God" (v. 2). He Himself said, "I and the Father are One" (John 10:30). Before His Incarnation He was "in the form of God" (Phil. 2:7). In that phrase, "being in the form of God," two points are to be noted: (1) the word rendered "being" is not the verb "to be," it signifies "existing originally," and its use indicates that what the person of whom it is said was before the event referred to, he continued to be after the event took place; (2) the "form" is not a mere resemblance, it expresses the real existence as such of what is described; the same passage says, for instance, that Christ took "the form of a servant." That He became so in reality is clear; as really, then, being in the form of God, He was God. Again, to the Son the Father saith, "Thy Throne, O God, is forever and ever" (Heb. 1:8).

Being, therefore, possessed of Deity, He knew absolutely the attributes, character, and claims of God.

Secondly, He put Himself into relationship with man who had sinned. Thus He became Incarnate. He partook of flesh and blood. He became real man, possessed of body, soul, and spirit. "When the fullness of the time came, God sent forth His Son, born of a woman, born under the Law" (Gal. 4:4).

Thirdly, He was tested and found to be sinless. He was "in all points tempted like as we are, yet without sin" (Heb. 4:15). His sinlessness was vindicated in every possible manner. His most ardent critics and His bitterest enemies have acknowledged it.

Fourthly, the great object for which He thus put Himself into connection with man by means of His Incarnation, was that He might die and thereby "might redeem" men (Gal. 4:4). He, and He alone, was born in order to die. He partook of flesh and blood "that through death He might bring to nought him that had the power of death, that is, the devil; and might deliver all them who through fear of death were all their lifetime subject to bondage" (Heb. 2:14). He did not come merely to teach men how to live, to set us an example, though this He did. The object of His Incarnation was that in His death He might become a curse for us, and endure the penalty due to our guilt.

Fifthly, in going to the Cross, He submitted Himself to be dealt with as God must deal with sin. This mode of His death, by the shedding of His blood, was necessary for atonement. And for the following reason. Sin had brought death. Death came through sin (Rom. 5:12). Sin thus involved the forfeiting of the life. Now "the life of the flesh is in the blood." If, then, there was to be an impartation of life to the sinner, it must be by a death caused by the shedding of that element which is the life of the flesh. Again the mode of execution must be by hanging on a tree. For God had declared, "Cursed is every one that hangeth on a tree." Thus would Christ become a curse for us. Accordingly He submitted Himself to the kind of execution that was in vogue under the Romans. National events had been overruled that thus should His death be accomplished.

THE MODE OF DEATH

The shedding of the blood, in the language of Scripture, involves the taking, or the giving, of the life. "The blood of Christ" signifies the death of Christ by His bloodshedding. "It is the blood that maketh atonement by reason of the life" (Lev. 17:11).

Inasmuch as Christ had no sins of His own to die for, it follows that His death was endured voluntarily and vicariously on behalf of those who were sinners. He gave Himself up to death. He presented Himself to be made sin and to become a curse for those who, having sinned, had thereby brought themselves under the curse. He laid down His life. He said, "I lay down My life . . . No one taketh it away from Me, but I lay it down of Myself. I have power to lay it down, and I have power to take it again. This commandment received I from my Father" (John 10:15, 18). In the Garden of Gethsemane He gave proof that no man had power to put Him to death. He submitted to be bound and led away. He could have called legions of angels to defend Him. Again, as to His crucifixion, it was unique. He died as no other crucified person ever died. In every other crucifixion the breathing of the last breath is followed by the helpless drooping of the head; the Lord Jesus first bowed (or rather "reclined") His head and then dismissed His spirit. He reversed the natural process. "He poured out His soul unto death" (Isa. 53:12). The word rendered "bowed" is that rendered "lay" in His statement, "The Son of God hath not anywhere to lay His head." He found His true rest in the fulfillment of the will of the Father and in becoming obedient "even unto death."

In His crucifixion God's divine justice smote Him. The sword of Jehovah was awakened to smite "the Man" who was "Jehovah's Fellow" (Zech. 13:7). "He was wounded for our transgressions, He was bruised for our iniquities; the chastisement of our peace was upon Him; and with His stripes [His bruise, *margin*] we are healed . . . It pleased Jehovah to bruise Him; He hath put Him to grief" (Isa. 53:5, 10). He made His soul "an offering for sin" (v. 10). "Him who knew no sin He made to be sin on our behalf" (2 Cor. 5:21). God dealt with Him, the sinless One, as He must deal with sin.

THE CONDITIONS FULFILLED

All the conditions required were fulfilled in the person and death of Christ. Thus it is, that, whereas "all have sinned," God can pardon, yea, justify the sinner on a perfectly righteous ground. We are "justified freely by His grace, through the redemption that is in Christ Jesus; whom God set forth to be a propitiation, through faith, by His blood" (Rom. 3:24, 25). The Authorized Version is incorrect here. It is not "through faith in His blood." The preposition is "by," not "in." Faith rests in the person. The comma after the word "faith" is important. Propitiation signifies that by which God shows mercy, and the ground of this is the blood of Christ.

AN OBJECTION

Various objections are raised against the atonement. It is said to be impossible because guilt is untransferable. Now blameworthiness is not transferable, but it is possible for one person to suffer for another's sins. This is frequent in human experience. The one distinction is that one sinner cannot make atonement to God for another sinner, and this we have pointed out. If, however, one person can suffer for another's sin, how much more could Christ the sinless voluntarily submit to suffer the condemnation due to our guilt!

A SECOND OBJECTION

Another objection raised is that it is immoral to smite the innocent for the guilty. Now that objection overlooks the fact that the person who judges and the surety for the sinner are one. God the Father and Christ His Son are one in the Godhead. It never was other than true, "I and the Father are One." There is not more than one God. The triune God is one God, Father, Son, and Holy Spirit. "God was in Christ reconciling the world unto Himself." No natural illustration can illustrate the work of Calvary. No human reasoning can analyze the work of the atonement.

That it was an act consistent with moral rectitude is witnessed by the effects. It has never produced immoral relationships. The sinner who comes under its effects is brought into relationship with God and goes on his way, a justified believer, rejoicing to serve his Redeemer. The atonement is the means of bringing him into union with Christ, a union of love and loyalty to Him.

A THIRD OBJECTION

Another objection raised is that it is inconceivable that God should demand an atonement when man forgives his fellow without demanding an atonement. Would God act on a lower scale than man? Could He not forgive sin without an atonement? This objection ignores the fact that the relation of God to men in the matter of trespass differs from the relation of one man to another. Even among men different relations make a difference in the consequence of an act. A Christian man, suffering from the maltreatment of a disturber of the peace, may express his willingness to forgive, but a policeman has something else to say, and there are police courts and magistrates. The interests of the state demand satisfaction. A man may forgive the murderer of his relative, but a murderer must be hanged. So God can justify only on a ground consistent with His attributes as the judge of mankind.

A FOURTH OBJECTION

Another objection charges God with vindictiveness in meting out punishment to Christ. That, however, ignores the fact that the Father never ceased to love the Son. This infinite unchanging love is quite consistent with the fact that "God so loved the world that He gave His only begotten Son," that "He spared Him not, but gave Him up for us all."

ATONEMENT NOT AT-ONE-MENT

What has been set forth above is perhaps sufficient to show that the English word "atonement," if understood to mean "at-one-ment," is utterly inadequate to express the truth of the doctrine. "At-one-ment" is the effect of the atoning sacrifice of Christ. The Hebrew word signifies "to cover." It is that used by David in the 32nd Psalm when he says, "Blessed is the man . . . whose sin is covered." It further suggests the removal of divine wrath. Christ did not die to reconcile God to man, but the effect of the death of Christ is to remove God's wrath from him who believes. The wrath of God still abides on the unbeliever (John 3:36). God gave His Son in order that, dealing with Him for our sin and guilt, executing His wrath upon Him against sin, the believing sinner might be delivered from deserved wrath and condemnation. The gospel is a ministry of reconciliation, "as though God," says the apostle Paul, "were entreating by us: we beseech on behalf of Christ, be ye reconciled to God" (2 Cor. 5:20).

GOD'S TRIBUNAL

Atonement is not merely the payment of a debt. It is much more. It is not just a commercial transaction. God is not simply a creditor, He is a judge. Every man must appear before Him as in that capacity. Christ in His death satisfied the claims of divine justice, and the guilty sinner may go free, with wrath removed, pardon granted, his sin cleansed by the precious blood of Christ. The death of Christ was not simply the payment of a debt, it was the clearing of sinners at the bar of God's Tribunal.

A SUBSTITUTIONARY SACRIFICE

The sacrifice of Calvary was offered to make provision for all men. The actual effects of Christ's atoning sacrifice are experienced only by those who accept the Savior. The death of Christ was substitutionary, but Christ is not the substitute of the unrepentant sinner. We dare not go to a rebellious, hardhearted man and tell him "Christ is your substitute." I may tell him that Christ died on his behalf, to deliver him from the consequences of sin, but if I tell a hardened sinner that Christ died in his stead it follows that he is no longer in the place of condemnation and death, whereas the contrary is the fact. Let him receive Christ by repentance and faith, and he passes from death to life, from condemnation to justification. Christ died on behalf of all men. He "gave Himself a ransom," a substitutionary ransom, "on behalf of [*huper*] all" (1 Tim. 2:6). He gave Himself a ransom "for [*anti*] many" (Mark 10:45). Note, "on behalf of all," "for many." The actual substitution is fulfilled for those who, receiving Christ by faith, are delivered from death present and future. All infants who have never come under the condemnation of trespass against God come under the atoning efficacy of the blood of Christ. But for all who have sinned there is justification through faith, and there is no condemnation to those who thereby are "in Christ Jesus."

How wonderful is the grace of God that He against whom man had sinned should Himself provide the atonement! How unsearchable is His mercy to the guilty that He did not spare His own Son, but freely gave Him up for us all, to bear our sins in His body on the tree! If only we recognize the heinousness of our guilt and the infinite grace of our Lord Jesus Christ in suffering the penalty for us, "the just for the unjust to bring us to God," we shall bow in acknowledgment and present ourselves unto Him in devoted service all our days.

> Great God of wonders! all Thy ways
>   Display Thine attributes divine!
> But the fair glories of Thy grace
>   Beyond Thine other wonders shine.
>
> Such deep transgressions to forgive!
>   Such guilty, daring worms to spare!
> This is Thine own prerogative,
>   And in that honor none shall share.
>
> Pardon—from an offended God!
> Pardon—for sins of deepest dye!
> Pardon—bestowed through Jesus' blood!
> Pardon—that brings the rebel nigh!
>
> *Who is a pardoning God like Thee!*
> *Or who has grace so rich and free!*

CHRIST IS LORD

Jesus' death brings all who believe the gift of eternal life. There is promised blessing to know Him as our Savior; surely not prosperity on this earth, but one of future blessing. Not only is Jesus called Savior, but He is also described as "Lord." There is connectivity to these two titles for Jesus—titles that are truly demonstrative of His character. To receive Jesus as Savior is to receive Him as Lord. We are no longer servants to sin, but servants of God.

It is important to bear in mind that the Gospel proclaims

CHRIST AS LORD

as well as Savior. A Savior He is indeed, but let us see how He was proclaimed according to the testimony of Scripture. The angelic message to the shepherds at the time of the birth of Christ announced that He who was born that day in the city of David was "a Savior, which is *Christ the Lord*" (Luke 2:11). In his proclamation of the Gospel on the day of Pentecost the apostle Peter declared that "God hath made Him *both Lord and Christ*, this Jesus whom ye crucified" (Acts 2:36). The testimony of the apostles before the Sanhedrin Council was, "Him did God exalt with His right hand to be a *Prince* and a Savior" (Acts 5:31).

Peter begins his message to Cornelius and his household by declaring that Jesus Christ is "*Lord of all*" (Acts 10:36). The apostle Paul says, "We preach . . . *Christ Jesus as Lord*" (2 Cor. 4:5). When he expounds the conditions upon which salvation is to be possessed, he stresses the necessity of acknowledging the Lordship of Christ: "If thou shalt confess with thy mouth *Jesus as Lord*, and shalt believe in thy heart that God raised Him from the dead, thou shalt be saved" (Rom. 10:9). "To this end Christ died and lived again, *that He might be Lord* of both the dead and the living" (Rom. 14:9). To Him every knee is to bow, and every tongue confess "that Jesus Christ is Lord to the glory of God the Father" (Phil. 2:10, 11). "The free gift of God is eternal life in Christ Jesus *our Lord* (Rom. 6:23).

Scripture does not endorse our inviting our hearers to receive Christ as simply their Savior. Let us consider the passage which speaks about receiving Him Who is it of whom it says, "But as many as received Him, to them gave He the right to become children of God, even to them that believe on His Name" (John 1:12). He is God (v. 1); He is the Creator (vv. 3 and 10); He is Life and Light (vv. 5 and 8); He is "the only begotten Son, which is in the bosom of the Father" (v. 16); He is One who has a claim upon men (v. 11). To receive Him as Savior is to receive Him as Lord.

A REQUIRED RECOGNITION

How needful therefore to make clear that regeneration, which comes by receiving the Son of God by faith, involves the recognition of His Lordship! It is blessed indeed to know Him as Savior, to be assured of the remission of sins, and to be saved from perdition; but the change of mind signified by repentance is a change of mind with regard to Christ and to the world and sin. Christ now becomes Lord of the life. This may not be fully apprehended at first; but it is important to give prominence to it.

He who believes on the Son of God and so receives Him is no longer a servant of sin but a servant of God. "Thanks be to God," says the apostle, "that, whereas ye were servants of sin, ye became obedient to that form of teaching whereunto ye were delivered: and being made free from sin, ye became servants of righteousness . . . now being made free from sin, and become servants to God, ye have your fruit unto sanctification, and the end eternal life" (Rom. 6:17–22).

"Ye serve the Lord Christ" (Col. 3:24). "Sanctify in your hearts," says the apostle Peter, "Christ as Lord" (1 Pet. 3:15). This is not an attainment to be reached by the Christian of mature experience, it is the joyous rule of life for every believer.

There are not a few who are attracted by Gospel messages to seek the way of salvation, but are still possessed of a craving for the world. How great the need of care lest by an inadequate presentation of the truths of the Gospel we deceive such into a professed conversion which lacks reality! Christ and the world cannot rule together. We cannot serve two masters. "If any man love the world, the love of the Father is not in him" (1 John 2:15). To receive Christ is to be sealed by the Holy Spirit, who immediately comes to indwell the believer. By this sealing he is set apart to Christ; he belongs to Him (Mark 9:41; 1 Cor. 3:23); he is "Christ's bondservant" (1 Cor. 7:22). The realization of this enables him to say with the apostle, "I have been crucified with Christ; yet I live; and yet no longer I, but Christ liveth in me: and that life which I now live in the flesh I live in faith, the faith which is in the Son of God, who loved me and gave Himself up for me" (Gal. 2:20).

CHRIST THE PROPITIATION

The necessity of recognizing the true character of sin in the sight of God is but preliminary to the adequate setting forth of the righteousness of God in the punishment of sin and the grace He has manifested toward the guilty. This is precisely the order adopted by the apostle in the epistle to the Romans, an order deeply significant and demanding careful attention. After the introductory declarations as to the person whom the Gospel proclaims, and the instruction concerning the universality and the heinousness of human guilt, he proceeds to vindicate the righteousness of God in His attitude toward sin and His mode of dealing with it. God's judgment is "according to truth" (Rom. 2:2); He will be "justified in His words, and will prevail when He comes into judgment" (3:3).

THE REQUISITE PERSON

One was required who could combine in Himself an absolute apprehension of the attributes, character and claims of God, and a complete understanding of human nature—One, that is to say, who, being possessed of Godhood, would put Himself into relationship with man, thus identifying Himself with human constitution and nature. Further, being thus truly man, coming under the claims of divine righteousness, and being tested in every respect, He would need to be attested as free from all taint of sin, and thus endure the penalty of sin, bearing the curse of the broken Law. Any taint of sin would involve the suffering of the penalty on His own account, and no advantage could accrue to those who were actually guilty.

THE APPOINTED MODE

Again, by divine decree, Atonement was to be by the shedding of blood. "Without shedding of blood there could be no remission." But this does not signify merely the pouring out of the physical element. The "blood" stands for a sacrificial "death" by the shedding of blood. "The life of the flesh is in the blood," and life had been forfeited by sin, for sin involved death; therefore life could only be imparted by means of the giving up of life through the shedding of that element in sacrifice. "It is the blood that maketh atonement by reason of the life" (Lev. 17:11, R.V.).

Only one Being could fulfill the required conditions, and that was the Son of God Himself, He who was "the effulgence of the Father's glory and the very image of His substance," He who "upheld all things by the Word of His power."[1] He it is "whose goings forth" were "of old, from everlasting" (Mic. 5:2). In keeping with this He himself said, "Before Abraham was, I am" (John 8:58), and again, "I and the Father are one" (John 10:30). Moreover, it was the Son of God who brought creation into being. "By Him were all things created" (Col. 1:16). He could not therefore Himself have been created. This sixteenth verse interprets the preceding statement descriptive of Him as "the Firstborn of all creation"; that is, as the Firstborn in unoriginated relationship with the Father, He gave creation its being. In this objective sense the verse in Revelation 1, "the beginning of the creation of God" is also to be understood.

Being thus

INALIENABLY POSSESSED OF DEITY

as the co-equal with the Father, He put Himself into relationship with man by becoming Incarnate, "partaking of flesh and blood." "When the fullness of the time came, God sent forth His Son, born of a woman, born under the Law" (Gal. 4:4). He did not dispossess Himself of Deity, but, as we have seen from Philippians 2:7, continued in the form of God. Thus combining in Himself absolute Deity and true humanity, He submitted to be tested in all points and was proved sinless. His sinlessness is stated in every variety of manner. "In Him is no sin" (1 John 3:5); "He did no sin" (1 Pet. 2:22); "He knew no sin" (2 Cor. 5:21). Tempted in all points like as we are He was "yet without sin" (Heb. 4:15). Thus, knowing absolutely the attributes, character, and claims of God, and the conditions of human nature, sin apart, as the spotless Lamb of God He was

---

1 Not as the Millennial Dawn teachings misinterpret the verse, "being now the brightness of His glory." The insertion of the word "now" is a perversion of the meaning, for clearly the first clause in verse 3 states His preexistence before He came to put away sins. The apostle Paul similarly predicates the preexistence of Christ when he says, He "being in the form of God, counted it not a thing to be grasped (R.V., margin) to be on equlity with God" (Phil. 2:6). The word translated "form" does not signify the mere resemblance, it expresses all that essentially characterizes God, and therefore the preexistence of Christ as God. Again, the word rendered "being" is not the word "to be," it signifies "existing originally," and its use indicates that what the person referred to was before the event mentioned, he continued so to be after the event took place.

entirely fitted to make Atonement for sin. On the Cross He endured the penalty of our guilt, becoming a curse for us, and in this manner "He is the propitiation for our sins," that is to say, in His own Person He is the ground upon which God shows mercy to the guilty sinner. "He made Him sin for us," that is to say, He dealt with Him as He must deal with sin. To all this the Lord Jesus voluntarily submitted, in perfect fulfillment of His Father's will. He said, "I lay down My life. No one taketh it away from Me, But I lay it down of Myself. I have power to lay it down, and I have power to take it again. This commandment received I of My Father" (John 10:15, 18).

The giving up of His life as a propitiation involved more than physical death. His soul was made an offering for sin. In this way judgment was meted out to Him in the righteousness of God, in a manner altogether hidden from human vision. It was this, that, under the stroke of divine judgment, led Him to cry in His anguish on the Tree, "My God, My God, why hast Thou forsaken Me?" In His crucifixion God's divine justice smote Him. The sword of Jehovah was awakened to smite "the Man who was His Fellow" (Zech. 13:7).

This was the grace of our Lord Jesus Christ. By this means the believing sinner is delivered from the curse. His sins are remitted. He stands justified in the sight of God, and is in possession of eternal life.

THE CROSS OF CHRIST

We preach the Cross, but what is meant by that phrase? It's not the iconic shape of a cross which is associated with Christianity, nor is it the suffering and death of Jesus. When the apostles speak of "the Cross," their thoughts are directed toward the Person of the Redeemer and what He accomplished there. The phrase "The word of the Cross" is interpreted in the apostle's statement "we preach Christ crucified"—not Christ on a cross, but "Jesus Christ, and Him crucified," that is to say, the living, exalted, glorified Christ, as the One who has been crucified.

"The preaching of the Cross!" What heights and depths of Gospel grace and truth lie enfolded in that phrase! "The word of the Cross," as the Revisers literally and rightly put it—that gives, in one terse expression, the sum and substance of the divine evangel.

When the apostles speak of "the Cross" they direct our thoughts, not to the material, nor to the particular shape of the Cross itself, but to that with which it is associated,[1] the Person of the Redeemer who hung and suffered there, and all that in the eternal counsels of God was thereby accomplished and set forth.

---

1 This is but one instance of an important principle in the use of phraseology, namely, that a word often stands for what is associated with it. We have observed, for instance, that "the blood of Christ" signifies, not the physical element itself but the death of Christ by the shedding of His blood in sacrifice. Again, the phrase "the Lord's Table" engages the thought, not with the substance of a table,

"The Word of the Cross" comprehends, then, all doctrine that bears upon the Crucifixion of Christ, the purpose, the mode, the meaning and the effect of His death, the nature and penalty of sin, the doom of the sinner and the salvation of the believer. So also in the verse preceding, where Paul says that Christ sent him to preach the Gospel, "not with wisdom of words, lest the Cross of Christ should be made void."

A DISTINCTION

Further, "the Cross of Christ" is not simply an alternative expression for "the death of Christ." It is of the utmost importance to bear this in mind. "The Cross of Christ" does far more than express the fact of the infinite love of God to man in the death of His Son; it exposes the enmity of the human heart against God, reveals the true nature of sin as in the sight of God, and makes known the impossibility of bridging, by any human effort, the chasm that separates unregenerate man from God.

This distinction has been strikingly set forth as follows: "'The preaching of the Cross.' Not the death of Christ merely, but 'the Cross' . . . 'The preaching of the Cross is foolishness to them that perish.' Not so the preaching of the death of Christ, apart from the truths which cluster round 'the Cross.' The whole fabric of apostate Christianity is based upon the fact of that death . . . The Savior's death is owned as part of the world's philosophy. It is a fact and a doctrine which human wisdom has adopted and rejoices in as the highest tribute to human worth. How great and wonderful must be the creature on whose behalf God has made so marvelous a sacrifice! And thus God is made [i.e., in human thought and teaching] to pander to man's pride of heart and sense of self-importance.

"And as with the world's philosophy, so also with the world's religion. The doctrine of the *death* of Christ, if separated from 'the Cross,' leaves human nature still a standing ground. It is consistent with creature claims and class privileges. . . . But the preaching of the Cross is 'the axe laid to the root of the tree,' the deathblow to human nature on every ground and in every guise . . . It has measured out the moral distance between God and man, and has left them as far asunder as the throne of heaven and the gate of hell."[1]

The phrase "The word of the Cross" is interpreted in the apostle's statement "we preach Christ crucified"—not Christ on a cross, but "Jesus Christ, and Him crucified," that is to say, the living, exalted, glorified Christ, as the One who has been crucified.

---

but with what is on it and the truth associated with it. Compare, "Let their table be made a snare" (Rom. 11:9).

1 "The Gospel and its Ministry," by Sir Robert Anderson.

THE VICARIOUS SACRIFICE OF CHRIST

The Bible never says that God has determined that all people will be saved. In fact, there are passages that teach the contrary. While the debate will never end in this lifetime, what we know for certain is this: God has been gracious in spite of human sinfulness against Him. And the means of grace is the vicarious sacrifice of Christ. Read below to get a detailed visual on what this theological phrase—vicarious sacrifice—means in practical and everyday terms.

In one of that series of statements of foundation truths of the faith which are interspersed throughout the first epistle to Timothy, the apostle declares that God "willeth that all men should be saved and come to the knowledge of the truth. For there is one God, one Mediator also between God and man, Himself man, Christ Jesus, who gave Himself a ransom for all; the testimony to be borne in its own times" (1 Tim. 2:4–6, R.V.). "Willeth" is the right rendering, as expressive of goodwill rather than of determination. There is no Scripture which intimates that God has determined that all men should be saved. There are passages, indeed, which teach the contrary, and nowhere does Scripture contradict its own teachings. What is set forth, then, is God's gracious will toward men in spite of their universal sin. To determine that all men should be saved, whether they persisted in evil or not, would be inconsistent with the divine attributes of righteousness and holiness and with the fact that, being God, He is the Judge of all.

THE MEANS GOD HAS CHOSEN

for the manifestation of His grace are set forth in verses 5 and 6. The former describes the Person through whom it is manifested, the latter the work He has undertaken for its fulfillment. As to His Person, He is the only Mediator between God and man, uniquely combining in Himself, as He has done, true manhood with His essential Godhood. He thus possesses all that is requisite for His mediatorial office and work. He knows absolutely all the divine claims upon man, for He is essentially one in Deity with God the Father. He knows all the circumstances constituting man's condition as God created him, for He Himself has become man, and is still possessed, in His resurrection glory and power, of true and full manhood, spirit, soul, and body.[1]

It was in this unique combination of manhood with Godhood, so entirely suited for the purposes of divine grace, that He undertook the work of redemption. The preposition here is *huper*, which signifies "on behalf of." This expresses

---

1 He is not merely a spirit, as the International Bible Students' Association teaches. Neither did He divest Himself of Deity at His Incarnation, nor has He ever divested Himself of His full powers and qualities of manhood since His Resurrection.

the universal provision God has made to meet men's need, and is in line with the statement in verse 4 that He willeth that all men should be saved.

A NOTICEABLE DISTINCTION

The vicarious nature of the Sacrifice of Christ is taught in similar language, but with a distinct point of difference, in the Lord's words in Matthew 20:28, and the corresponding passage in Mark 10:45, "the Son of man came not to be ministered unto, but to minister, and to give His life a ransom for many." Here the preposition rendered "for" is *anti*, which signifies, not "on behalf of," but what is given as an equivalent for, or in place of, something else. It expresses more definitely the substitutionary character of the sacrifice of Christ. Noticeable, too, is the significant distinction that the Lord does not say that He came to give His life a ransom for all, but for many. The "many" comprises those who by faith avail themselves of the efficacy of His death, thereby obtaining remission of sins and passing from death unto life. They are delivered from their former condition. Formerly unbelievers, abiding under the wrath of God, they are now freed from condemnation (John 3:36 with Rom. 8:1, R.V.).

It is true that the word rendered "ransom" in 1 Timothy 2:6 is *antilutron*, whereas in the passages in the Gospels the word is *lutron*; and *anti* in combination simply expresses the vicarious nature of the ransom, and the statement there is, as we have pointed out, that the ransom was given "on behalf of" all men. Vicarious in itself it is available for all. Its effects are only realized by those who, through its instrumentality, are delivered from the doom and penalty of sin.

REDEMPTION

Two different Greek words are translated as "redemption" in our English Bibles, and each carries its own nuance of meaning. Understanding the distinction expands our understanding of what Christ's redemption means for believers.

In the New Testament there are two distinct words each translated "redeem." Our English word therefore represents two different ideas. The first is *agorazō*, which, with its longer form *exagorazō*, signifies "to buy," the latter being especially used of the purchase of a slave with the object of securing his freedom; the shorter form points particularly to the payment of the price; the longer also points to the purpose in view.

The other word is *lutroō*, which signifies "to set free," "to deliver," corresponding to this are the nouns *lutrōsis*, and its strengthened form *apolutrōsis*, which denote "freeing," "deliverance." (Compare *lutron* which, as mentioned in our last chapter, signifies the ransom price.)

A TWOFOLD SIGNIFICANCE

The distinction between the two sets of terms with regard to redemption is obvious. First there is the payment of the price, and then the actual liberation. In other words, redemption is first by purchase, and then by liberating power.

We will notice the various passages where these words occur with reference to the redemptive work of the Cross. The apostle Paul twice reminds the saints at Corinth that they were bought (*agorazō*) with a price (1 Cor. 6:20; 7:23); the death of Christ was the price paid that they might belong to God and glorify Him in their body, and that they might become the bondservants of Christ and not the bondservants of men.

Again, the apostle Peter warns his readers against false teachers who would privily bring in destructive heresies, "denying even the Master that bought them," and "bringing upon themselves swift destruction" (2 Pet. 2:1). The difference between this word "bought" (*agorazō*) and the word *lutroō* is particularly important here. It could not be said that these men were redeemed, for they denied the Lord's rights of purchase. Christ paid the price for them, as for all men, but only believers are actually redeemed. Redemption, in the full sense of the term, goes further than purchase, as a reference to Ephesians 1:14 shows.

There are

THREE PLACES IN THE APOCALYPSE

where *agorazō* is used of the work of divine grace; in each case the Revised Version rightly translates by "purchase." They are as follows: "Worthy art Thou to take the book and to open the seals thereof: for Thou wast slain, and didst purchase unto God with Thy blood men out of every tribe, and tongue, and people, and nation" (v. 9). The hundred and forty-four thousand who are seen standing on Mount Zion, are said to have been "purchased out of the earth" (14:3); they were "purchased from among men, to be the firstfruits unto God and unto the Lamb" (v. 4). Everywhere else the word is rendered "buy," "buyeth," "bought."

The longer form (*exagorazō*) is used

FOUR TIMES IN THE NEW TESTAMENT,

twice with reference to the redeeming work of Christ (Gal. 3:13 and 4:5), and twice of "buying up the opportunities" (Eph. 5:16; Col. 4:5). The two passages in Galatians refers to the deliverance of believing Jews from the Law and its curse. "Christ redeemed us (Jewish believers) from the curse of the Law, having become a curse for us." The reference is to His sacrifice on the Cross as the means of effecting the redemption. There it was, and there alone, that He became a curse. At no time in His life previous to His Crucifixion did He make expiation for sin. He bare our sins "in His body upon the tree" (1 Pet. 2:24)—not 'unto the tree' as some would translate it. Nowhere does Scripture state that Christ became the Sin-Bearer at any time previous to His Crucifixion. In His life He had satisfied the requirements of the Law by undeviating obedience to all its demands. In His death He satisfied the claims of the Law in the curse pronounced upon failure to fulfill it. Therefore He did so, not on His own account, but on behalf of all who were under the curse. Thus was redemption provided. He who knew no sin was "made sin for us" (2 Cor. 5:21).

This was the object for which He became Incarnate. He was "born under the Law, that He might redeem them which were under the Law" (4:4, 5). Neither did His Incarnation nor did His obedience prior to the Cross avail to effect redemption. They were preparatory to it. His redeeming work began and ended on the Cross. As we have pointed out in a preceding chapter, the "one act of righteousness" in Romans 5:15 was the sacrifice of Christ on the Cross (the A.V. rendering "the righteousness of One" is both inaccurate and misleading). So in verse 19, "the obedience of One" is not His obedient life, but the same act of obedience to the Father's will, in the death of the Cross. By that act of redeeming grace freedom, both from the curse and from bondage to the Law, is secured for the believer.

We will now consider the passages which contain

THE OTHER WORDS

all of which direct our thoughts to the actual liberation, i.e., redemption by power, the fulfillment of that for which the purchase price was paid. "We hoped that it was He which should redeem (*lutroō*) Israel," said the two disciples on the way to Emmaus, referring to the deliverance of their nation from Roman tyranny (Luke 24:21). Christ gave Himself for us, "that He might redeem us from all iniquity (lit., lawlessness)," that is, that He might set us free from the power of all that is contrary to the will of God (Titus 2:14). "Ye were redeemed, not with corruptible things, with silver or gold, from your vain manner of life handed down from your fathers, but with precious blood, as of a lamb without blemish and without spot, even the blood of Christ" (1 Pet. 1:18); that is, they were liberated, at the price of the precious blood of Christ, from servitude to tradition.

Three passages contain the corresponding noun *lutrōsis*, "redemption." Zacharias begins his hymn of praise with "Blessed be the Lord, the God of Israel; for He hath visited and wrought redemption for His people" (Luke 1:68). Anna "spake of Him to all them that were looking for the redemption of Jerusalem" (2:38). In each case Christ is spoken of as the Liberator of the nation. The third passage is Hebrews 9:11, 12: "Christ having come a High Priest of the good things to come . . . through His own blood, entered in once for all into the holy place, having obtained eternal redemption," that is to say, eternal deliverance from the guilt and power of sin.

Of the nine places where the strengthened form *apolutrōsis* is used with regard to redemption, four refer to

DELIVERANCE FROM THE GUILT OF SIN

Believers are "justified freely by His grace through the redemption that is in Christ Jesus" (Rom. 3:24); the power by which they are freed from guilt is in Christ, and is exercised through His death. Twice redemption is defined as forgiveness. In Him "we have our redemption through His blood, the forgiveness of our trespasses, according to the riches of His grace" (Eph. 1:7; so in Col. 1:14). Fourthly, Hebrews 9:15 sets forth the death of Christ as the basis, while the actual redemption consists in the removal of transgressions: "He is the Mediator of the new covenant . . . a death having taken place for the redemption of the transgressions that were under the first covenant."

Inasmuch as believers themselves are the subjects of God's redeeming grace, their redemption consists of far more than their deliverance from guilt, it is to extend to their whole being, body as well as soul and spirit, and of this complete redemption *apolutrōsis* is used four times. The deliverance of their bodies from bondage to corruption will bring deliverance also from the very presence of sin, and is to take place at the Coming of the Lord Jesus. This redemption of the body is the object of their expectation, and is spoken of as "the adoption," or sonship (Rom. 8:23); for the sonship which believers enjoy in their union with the Son of God, and which secures their inalienable relationship with God the Father, constituting them "heirs of God" (v. 17), will be consummated when Christ comes "to fashion anew the body of their humiliation, that it may be conformed to the body of His glory." They will then enjoy the full felicity of sonship and will enter upon their promised inheritance. Unto that "day of redemption" believers have been sealed by the Holy Spirit (Eph. 4:30). He is "the earnest of our inheritance until the redemption of the purchased possession" (1:14). It is in this full sense of the term that the apostle speaks of Christ as being "made unto us wisdom from God, and righteousness and sanctification and redemption" (1 Cor. 1:30).

THE NATURE OF THE REDEEMER

No effort on the part of man could effect redemption. He who could accomplish it must be possessed of both Godhood and manhood, and in this combined nature the Lord Jesus, the Son of God, paid the price and accomplished the work.

The distinction between the ransom price paid in the blood of Christ and the actual redemption by God's liberating power, is illustrated and foreshadowed by the provision made by God for Israel in Egypt in the blood of the lamb, directions for the shedding and the application of which are recorded in Exodus 12:3, 7, and by the actual deliverance of the people, recorded in the same chapter, and in chapter 15:13. For further teaching on the subject, see Numbers 3:44–51 and Leviticus 25:23, 24, 47, 54.

The question has often been raised as to whom the ransom price was paid. Scripture does not specify this. It certainly was not to Satan. Speculative reasoning on the subject is profitless and vain. While the claims of divine righteousness were satisfied in the death of Christ, our attention is drawn to and fixed upon the Person Himself and His atoning Sacrifice and God's redeeming grace in and through Him.

THE PROLOGUE OF THE GOSPEL

Much can be learned by reading a book's introduction; it establishes the author's presuppositions and purposes for writing. The opening statements in the books of the New Testament carry profound truths about God—His person and His purposes. The prologue to the Gospel of John invites us to discover a "revelation of Jesus Christ the Son of God." However, John does not fully state his purpose until he closes the book. In his conclusion, he declares that everything has been done and written for their sake. "These are written, that ye may believe." He invites those who have learned of Christ and His work to come to faith in Him.

The great subject of this Gospel is clear from the very first statements. Christ is at once presented to us in the grandeur of His eternal Deity, His distinct personality in the Godhead, His essential oneness with the Father, and His power as Creator and as the Giver of life. The Gospel is verily a "revelation of Jesus Christ the Son of God." It depicts His glory and His grace. The marvels of His grace are enhanced by the unveiling of His glory. The sublime glories of His Deity and His power bring out the more strikingly the grace of His condescension and love toward man. No profounder truths concerning the Son of God are to be found in the contents of the Sacred Volume than those which are given in the first few verses of this Gospel.

All this, however, is soon seen to be preparatory to a series of revelations concerning Him which expand the theme of His glories and His grace. Each item in this series has its own special setting and its own immediate purpose. The details of the series are to a considerable extent briefly intimated, as we shall see, in the first chapter. Throughout the Gospel the doings and teachings of the Lord Jesus pass before us in a divinely arranged order.

THE PURPOSE STATED

It is not, however, until we come almost to the close of the Gospel that the object for which it is written is definitely stated. This stands in remarkable contrast to the ordinary method of writing a book. The purpose of a book is customarily set forth in a preface or introduction, and in most of the writings of men this is necessary. Not so in this Gospel. That the mention of the reason why it was written should come near the end is entirely appropriate. "Many other signs therefore," says the apostle, "did Jesus in the presence of the disciples, which are not written in this book: but these are written, that ye may believe Jesus is the Christ, the Son of God; and that believing ye may have life in His name" (20:30, 31).

A reader to whom the Gospel story was new, carefully reading this short book straight through, would, by reason of the revelation thus given of Christ and His work, at least feel the tremendous force of this statement of the purpose of the book as applicable to his own case, if indeed, he had not, through the power of the Spirit of God, already accepted Christ as his Savior. The Gospel was written, then, for the purpose of bringing men into life by faith in the Son of God.

A FURTHER PURPOSE

While the exercise of faith in Christ is the object for which the Gospel was written, the presentation of the Son of God in the way indicated above has another purpose. This, though not expressed by the author in so many words, becomes clear on careful perusal of the record. The various aspects of glory and power, of grace and love, in which the Lord is seen, have in almost every case a special bearing on the life and service of believers. Each revelation of Christ is connected with some particular purpose of God for His children. The teachings of the Lord given to His disciples, either directly in His private conversation with them, or indirectly in public testimony, constitute a development of truth as to the will of God for us, all being based upon the foundation truths relating to Christ.

It is our purpose to look somewhat closely into this development, as its order is not a little striking. Speaking broadly, the earlier presentations of Christ are preparatory to the later ones. The object in view is evidently efficiency in service, and the teachings concerning service (which occupy the latter portion of the Gospel) are preceded by a number of revelations and truths which bring home to the heart the glory and power of the Lord in a way that is calculated to establish and strengthen the faith of His servants.

THE PAST ETERNITY OF THE SON OF GOD

We will consider first the way in which Christ is presented to us in the opening portion of the book as the initial declarations concerning Him bear very largely upon all that follows. Each truth stated at the beginning is unfolded in the course of the Gospel record. Each is like a bud opening out in fuller beauty under the sunlight of the Holy Spirit's revelations.

The initial words, "In the beginning," speak of the past eternity of the Son of God. This is expanded in His teachings as recorded subsequently. Thus, for instance, as expressive of the eternity of His Deity, He uses again and again the Jehovah title "I AM." When the Jews call into question His preexistence, He says, "Before Abraham was I am" (8:58). Again, He says to them, "Except ye believe that I am, ye shall die in your sins"; and further, "When ye have lifted up the Son of Man, then ye shall know that I am" (8:24, 28). Later on, when He is instructing His disciples in the upper room, after having washed their feet, He says, "From henceforth I tell you before it come to pass, that, when it is come to pass, ye may believe that I am" (13:19). The great truth of His eternity is finally told out in another and fuller way when He says in prayer to the Father, "And now, O Father, glorify Thou Me with Thine own self with the glory which I had with Thee before the world was"; and, "Thou lovedst Me before the foundation of the world." That is only a way of amplifying the words, "In the beginning." But the teaching is now expanded into the themes of His eternal glory and the eternal love with which the Father loved Him. How striking is the Holy Spirit's development of the first truth of the Gospel!

CHRIST AS "THE WORD"

Let us now take the full statement, "In the beginning was the Word." A word is the expression of a thought. The mind of God is told out in and through Christ. This truth is developed almost immediately in this first chapter. "The only begotten Son which is in the bosom of the Father, He hath declared Him" (John 1:18). The Son of God, as the Word of God, has made known the Father. But it is as One in the very center of the affections of the Father that He has declared Him. Christ is "the heart of God revealed."

This title, "the Word of God," again receives a series of comments which run through the Gospel. John speaks of Him thus, "He whom God has sent speaketh the words of God" (3:34). Christ Himself opens up the theme as follows: He says to Nicodemus, "I tell you heavenly things" (3:12). Again, He says that hearing His Word and believing on Him that sent Him are conditions upon which life is granted (5:24). His Word, then, reveals the Father, and this leads to faith in the Father. By His word (who is the Word) He opens up to us the heart of the Father for our faith. His teaching was not His, but the Father's who sent Him. He spoke not from Himself (7:16–18). Again, He says, "The things which I heard from Him, these speak I unto the world. . . . As the Father taught Me, I speak these things. . . . I speak the things which I have seen with My Father" (8:26, 28, 38). And again, "The Father which sent Me, He hath given Me commandment, what I should say and what I should speak" (12:49). Further, to the disciples, "The words that I say unto you I speak not from Myself, but the Father abiding in Me doeth His works" (14:10).

There is clearly an advance in this truth as given to His disciples, beyond what He gave to the Jews. He declares now that the Father was in Him, expressing Himself by word and work. His works were at the same time teachings. Continuing the theme, He says, "The word which ye heard is not Mine, but the Father's who sent Me; . . . all things that I heard from My Father I have made known unto you" (14:24; 15:15). The subject of Christ as the Word of God is finally brought out in His prayer in the seventeenth chapter, when He says, "The words which Thou gavest Me I have given unto them. . . . I have given them Thy Word" (17:8, 14). Thus throughout the course of the Gospel the first introductory declaration is unfolded. The passages we have quoted are the amplification by the Spirit of God of the great truth, "In the beginning was the Word." They serve to emphasize the truth with increasing beauty and power, just as each touch of the painter's brush sets out in greater grandeur the central figure of a picture.

The words "In the beginning" convey no suggestion of a commencement of the existence of Christ. The apostle's meaning is, firstly, that Christ, as the Word of God, was coexistent with God, for He was God; and, secondly, that at whatsoever time any order of creatures came into being, Christ was preexistent to them, for "all things were made by Him." In the beginning of all else He was existent. The evangelist's statement is similar to what Wisdom utters in Proverbs 8:23, "The Lord possessed Me in the beginning of His way before His works of old." Wisdom is an unoriginated, attribute of God. So Christ is His unoriginated Son, one with Him in the Godhead.

"THE WORD"

We will now consider the second statement, **"The Word was with God."** This declares, firstly, the distinct personality of Christ in the Godhead, and, secondly, the eternal and unbroken fellowship existing between the Father and the Son. Thus the truth of His preexistence is here also implied. The Word was not, as early errorists taught, an eternal emanation proceeding from God. The Son had a proper personality, eternal, as was that of the Father. The preposition *pros*, rendered "with," is not the one which merely denotes the presence of one person with another. Its underlying idea is "toward." This may be illustrated by its use in 1 John 2:1, "We have an Advocate with (*pros*) the Father." It suggests attitude toward, and intimate intercourse with, the Father, as well as presence with Him.[1]

Let us now see how this truth is continued and expanded in John's Gospel. First it is repeated in verse 2, **"The same was in the beginning with God."** This is not a mere repetition of the words in verse 1. Firstly, it combines the truth of the first two statements of that verse, and then it forms, in its twofold doctrine, the basis of what is to follow as to the work of creation. **"All things were made by Him."** The creation could be effected only by One who was eternally existent, and actually was effected by the conjoint operation of the Father and the Son. **"Without Him** [apart from Him] **was not anything made that has been made."** Thus in creation "The Word was with God."

"THE ONLY BEGOTTEN"

Further on in the prologue to the Gospel this truth is conveyed with the additional ideas of intimate communion and affection. These are contained in the title, "The Only Begotten." **"We beheld His glory,"** says the writer, **"glory as of the only begotten from the Father"** (v. 14).

The term "only begotten" implies, firstly, the eternal relation of the Son with the Father, and, secondly, the Father's delight in the Son. Both these ideas are likewise contained in the similar title "Firstborn," as used of Christ.[2]

This subject is still further developed in verse 18, and here the idea of affection receives special emphasis. Christ is now called "The only begotten Son,

---

1 While we think of His distinct personality as the Son of God, we must remember the absolute oneness of the Father and the Son in the Godhead. This is made clear in the next statement.

2 See Romans 8:29; Colossians 1:15, 18; Hebrews 1:6; Revelation 1:5; Psalm 89:27. The distinction between the two titles is that "Only Begotten" refers absolutely to His Divine relationship; "Firstborn" is used in reference to created beings, but distinguishes Him absolutely from all creatures, and relatively from those who are, or will be made, children of God by the grace.

which is in the bosom of the Father." The Son, ever abiding in the seat of the Father's affection, was "daily His delight, rejoicing always before Him." Even while Christ was on earth in the days of His flesh, He did not cease to be in the bosom of the Father. Again, one of the keynotes of this Gospel is that the Father sent the Son into the world. The Lord constantly asserted it, and this implies that before He came He was "with God." The very term "Father" involves Sonship. If there was a Father who sent, there was a Son to send. If the Father was eternal, His Son must have been eternal too.

The continuance of the oneness and fellowship of the Father with the Son in the days of His flesh is really a further development of the subject. Christ says to the Jews, "My Father worketh even until now, and I work" (5:17). Three times He states that the Father is with Him, twice to the Jews and once to His disciples. To the former He says, "I am not alone, but I and the Father that sent Me" (8:16); and again, "He that sent Me is with Me; He hath not left Me alone" (8:29). And to the latter, "Behold, the hour cometh, yea, is come, that ye shall be scattered, every man to his own, and shall leave Me alone: and yet I am not alone, because the Father is with Me" (16:32).

To each of these three statements of the presence of the Father with the Son a special idea is attached. The first relates to the thoughts and words of Christ, the second to His deeds, and the third to His experiences.

The truth of the eternal presence of the Son with the Father before the Incarnation is further expanded in the Lord's prayer in the seventeenth chapter. He says, "And now, O Father, glorify Thou Me with Thine own self with the glory which I had with Thee before the world was" (17:5), and again, "Thou lovedst Me before the foundation of the world" (v. 24). Thus the themes of glory and love embodied in the teachings of the prologue concerning this second declaration stand out in their full light in these two utterances of the Lord in the closing portion of the Gospel.

"THE WORD—GOD"

The third statement is, **"The Word was God."** The Deity of Christ constitutes the great foundation doctrine of this Gospel. As in other parts of Scripture, the doctrine is sometimes directly expressed and sometimes implied. The latter cases are very numerous, and demand careful and reverent attention. In our present consideration of the subject we shall not sharply distinguish the two.

The Deity of Christ is at once implied in the third verse of the prologue, which declares that "all things were made by Him," and again in verse 10, "the world was made by Him." The Creator of all things must Himself be God. The same is true in reference to the statement in verse 12, "As many as received Him, to them gave He the right to become the children of God, even to them that believe on His Name." Only by God could such a right be bestowed. Again, His Deity is to be inferred from the title "The Only Begotten Son." Limitations of space prevent a full enumeration of the passages in the Gospel in which the Deity of the Lord is implied. Nathanael confessed it when he said, "Rabbi, Thou art the Son of God, the King of Israel" (1:49). Christ Himself directly declared it when He said, "My Father worketh even until now, and I work." In the opinion of the foes by whom He was confronted this was a claim to Deity. This it was that led them to seek the more to kill Him. To them His language was unambiguous—"He called God His own Father, making Himself equal with God." Their opposition to this truth, and their hardness of heart, drew from Him still stronger affirmations of His Deity.

"ONE WITH THE FATHER"

The Lord proceeded to claim that equal honor was due to the Son and to the Father, and further stated that the Father had committed all judgment to Him (5:21–29). His essential Deity, implied in the truth of His oneness with the Father, forms the central teaching of His testimony to the Jews, and is continued in His subsequent discourse to the disciples, and again in His closing prayer. Thus He says to the Jews, "I and the Father are One." This claim to Deity they met by an attempt to stone Him, and when He further said, "The Father is in Me, and I in Him," they endeavored to seize Him (10:30, 31, 38). To the disciples He says, "If ye had known Me, ye would have known My Father also. From henceforth ye know Him, and have seen Him." And when Philip requests that He will show them the Father, He says, "Have I been so long time with you, and hast thou not known Me, Philip? He that hath seen Me hath seen the Father, . . . I am in the Father, and the Father in Me; . . . the Father abiding in Me doeth His works. Believe Me that I am in the Father, and the Father in Me: or else believe Me for the very works' sake" (14:7–11). Finally, in His prayer following that discourse He says, "Thou, Father, art in Me, and I in Thee; . . . we are One" (17:21, 22). Thus the truth of the opening declaration, "The Word was God," stands out in every part of the Gospel as its great leading theme.

CHRIST AS THE LIGHT

In the prologue to the Gospel of John, Jesus is introduced as the Life and the Light of men. Some of the characteristics of Jesus what we will read here is that of being placed in opposition to the darkness of Satan and the power of death. Faith in Christ is said to bring light to man, and so everyone has the opportunity to step out of the darkness and into eternal life.

The first verses of the Gospel consist of statements concerning the Deity of Christ as the Word of God, His eternal oneness with the Father, and His power as Creator. We have shown how each of these themes is developed throughout the Gospel. In *verses 4 and 5* the subject of His relationship with mankind is introduced, and in this respect Christ is represented as Life and Light. "In Him was life, and the life was the light of men." This subject of eternal life in and through the Son of God is a special feature of this Gospel. We shall now endeavor to show how, as in the case of the preceding statements, this theme is expanded.

LIGHT SHINING INTO DARKNESS

In the first chapter of Genesis the mention of God's work of Creation is followed by a description of the darkness which existed therein, and the introduction of light into the scene. So here in the first chapter of John the fact of the creative power of the Son of God is followed by the mention of the world's darkness. Into this His life-giving light shone, and the darkness apprehended it not. There is more in this than a failure to "comprehend" the light, as the word is rendered in the Authorized Version. It most frequently means "to lay hold of," and implies an effort on the part of an opposing power to seize the light so as to hinder its benign effects (see margin of R.V., "overcome").

Unsuccessful Opposition

When Christ was born Satan, acting through Herod, sought to destroy Him. The darkness was endeavoring to overpower the light. Satan failed. He failed again in the wilderness. He failed again at the Cross. Never did the darkness apprehend the Light. Never will it do so. The light is now shining through the Church. The gates of Hades shall not prevail against it. Satan's power is yet to reach its climax in this world, yet the darkness will not prevail. Nay, the light of the Lord's Second Advent will overpower it, Satan will be hurled into the abyss. Yet another effort at the close of the Millennium on the part of this great power of darkness, and he will be confined to the lake of fire. Never again will the darkness be able even to make an attempt to apprehend the light.

THE LIGHT AS THE LIFE

Continuing the subject as indicated in the prologue, we must notice the fundamental truth of this Gospel, that faith in Christ is the means of the possession of life. Through faith His life is imparted to us. So the aim of the ministry of John the Baptist was "that all men might believe" (*v. 7*). That is at once the beginning of the development of the theme "the life was the light of men." The Light shone, but could not produce life unless men exercised faith. Without that the darkness continues. Yet the Light shone, and still shines. It shines for every man.

Now that is just the point of the much misinterpreted *verse 9*. By the omission of a comma after "man" the Authorized Version has proved very misleading. The verse has been taken to mean that there is an inner light from God in every infant that is born into the world, and that thus there is the essence of eternal life in every man by natural birth. This of course is not the meaning of the verse at all. The Revisers rightly inserted a comma after the word "man"; the remaining part of the verse, "coming into the world," goes with the "light" and not with "man." Thus the verse rightly reads, "There was the true Light, even the Light which, coming into the world, lighteth every man." That is to say, the Light shines provisionally for every man; but only because it came into the world; otherwise man must have remained in spiritual darkness. That Christ came into the world forms one of the outstanding truths of the Gospel of John. Verse 9 gives the first definite mention of it, and here the Person is represented figuratively as the Light.

How Does Life Come?

The metaphor of the light served to introduce the subject of life, and the latter theme is now developed in association with that of faith. We are shown how the life is produced. "As many as received Him, to them gave He the right to become children[1] of God, even to them that believe on His Name; which were born, not of blood, nor of the will of the flesh, nor of the will of man, but of God" (*vv. 12, 13*). Spiritual birth involves spiritual life. But the birth is effected by faith. Those who "believe on the Name" of Christ become "children of God." Life comes through faith.

THE NECESSITY OF THE NEW BIRTH

In John's Gospel, the theme of life and light is picked up in the discussion between Jesus and Nicodemus. The Lord declares that new life is necessary in order to enter the kingdom of God, and that new life can only begin with a new birth. A choice stands before every individual—life or death. Those who love light find salvation, and those who love darkness reject the love of God and remain in darkness. Without faith in Jesus, the only thing left is wrath.

The theme of Christ as the life is introduced in the first chapter of John. It is resumed in the third. The first chapter reveals the *means* of life, the third reveals the *necessity* for it. This phase of the theme has its setting in the narrative of the dialogue between the Lord and the inquirer Nicodemus. "The same came to Jesus by night." Thus in the physical sense the light was to shine in the darkness. The darkness within the soul of the ruler of the Jews had its counterpart in the darkness without. The Light shone at once with its life-giving power. The ruler's initial statement was met with the unexpected rejoinder, "Verily, verily, I say unto thee, except a man be born anew, he cannot see the Kingdom of God." This aroused inquiries, and the light flashed forth again, "Verily, verily, I say unto thee, Except a man be born of water and of the spirit, he cannot enter into the Kingdom of God." Literal water is not here in view. The new birth does not come by baptism. In whatever way the metaphor of the water is applied, whether to the Spirit ("and" being "even") or to the Word of God, the application is spiritual. This is clearly so elsewhere in the Gospel (see chaps. 4:10, 14; 7:38, 39). In the

---

1 Not "sons" as in Authorized Version. In John's writings the word "children" not "sons," is always used to describe those who are born of God. The title "Son" is reserved by him for the Son of God.

sixth verse the Lord confines the subject to the Spirit, "That which is born of the flesh is flesh; and that which is born of the Spirit is spirit." How this life was to come about He proceeds to show. If the Spirit's operation is essential the heart too must be receptive. Moreover, the life can come only by the death of Christ. "As Moses lifted up the serpent in the wilderness, even so must the Son of Man be lifted up: that whosoever believeth may in Him have eternal life."

THE CONSEQUENCE OF REFUSAL

Yea, there must be faith in Himself and the only alternative to this is to perish. Moreover, it must be faith in Christ as the Son of God, "For God so loved the world, that He gave His only begotten Son, that whosoever believeth on Him should not perish, but have eternal life." But more, to perish is to perish under the judgment of God. "He that believeth not hath been judged already, because he hath not believed on the Name of the only begotten Son of God." God's provision in Christ is the very infinitude of mercy, the highest height of love. Here, where love is brought in, the theme of light is reintroduced. The light has revealed God's love. Only willful love of darkness could account for the rejection of such love. Love of darkness means hatred of light: and hatred of light can only be accounted for by the practice of evil (see v. 20, R.V., margin). Accordingly, "This is the judgment, that the light is come into the world, and men loved the darkness rather than the light, for their works were evil." God loved men; men loved darkness. How vast the depth to which man has fallen! Yet God's love, God's light, God's life, remain for all who will accept them. "He that believeth on the Son hath eternal life." "Verily, verily, I say unto you, he that heareth My word, and believeth on Him that sent Me, hath everlasting life, and shall not come into condemnation; but is passed from death unto life" (John 5:24). Refusal is disobedience to the Son. In that case sentence of judgment has been passed already, and wrath abides. "He that obeyeth not the Son shall not see life (let the universalist take note!); but the wrath of God abideth on him" (3:36).

THE EVIDENCE OF LIFE

There is a further expansion of the theme in this section of the Gospel. If light brings life, the life is evidenced in the doing of the truth. "He that doeth the truth cometh to the light"—not the initial coming for the acceptance of salvation, but "that his works may be made manifest, that they have been wrought in God" (3:21). Thus the first three chapters of this Gospel give us (1) the *provision* of life through the coming of the Light; (2) the *means* of life through the acceptance of the Light; (3) the *necessity* for the life in contrast to the rejection of the Light; and (4) the *evidence* of the life in coming to the Light.

CHRIST AS THE LIFE

When Jesus spoke to Nicodemus, He said that eternal life is a gift of faith. To the Samaritan woman, Jesus goes a step further by revealing the character and the effect of that gift. Jesus is Life, and He describes Himself as the Water of Life and the Bread of Life. The very words He speaks are spirit and life, capable of feeding those who hear, giving them life.

In the fourth chapter [of John] the coming of the Samaritan woman to fill her pitcher at the well becomes the occasion for the teaching of the Lord that He Himself is the Fountain of living water. The water that He gives becomes in the recipient a well of water springing up into eternal life. This is an advance on His teaching to Nicodemus. To him He made known that eternal life is a gift conditional upon faith; "Whosoever believeth in Him should not perish, but have eternal life" (3:16; cp. v. 36). To the woman of Samaria He reveals something more than the fact of the gift of life. He declares the character and the effect of the gift. The water of life will act as a springing fountain within the believer—a joyous refreshment, an energizing power.

Passing from that scene the Gospel now proceeds to show us how it is that Christ is the Life, and what further effects are derived from Him in this respect. In His discourse with the Jews, as mentioned in chapter five, He declares that the power to give life lies with Himself and that this power rests upon the fact that what belongs to the Father belongs likewise to Himself in essential union with the Father: "As the Father hath life in Himself, even so gave He to the Son also to have life in Himself" (5:26). Accordingly

THE BLESSING OF LIFE

formerly offered to the Jews on condition of keeping the law, must, in view of their failure, come to them only from Himself. They searched the Scriptures thinking that in them they had eternal life. But these very Scriptures bore witness to Him. He must, therefore, be the Fountain of life, a life incommunicable save through Himself. They would not come to Him that they might have life, and therefore they remained without it (v. 40). Further, God the Father had confirmed the fact that the power for life rested in the Son. This is what underlies the statement, "Him the Father, even God, hath sealed" (6:27). For Christ states this as a proof that eternal life can be given them only by the Son of Man. Again, He shows that He is the Life by describing Himself as "The Living Bread" which, having come down from Heaven, is the necessary means of the sustenance of spiritual life for men. This sublime truth was elicited by the reference on the part of His critics to the manna provided for their fathers by God (6:30–35). Twice He declares "I am the Bread of Life" (vv. 35 and 48), and in the latter case He points out that their fathers, even though they ate manna, died, whereas, on the contrary, to partake of Himself is to live forever (v. 51). That He is

THE EMBODIMENT OF LIFE

equally with the Father is declared further in His words, "I live because of the Father" (v. 57).

Again, the words He speaks are spirit and life (v. 63). They are part of His being, and therefore they communicate life. When we feed upon His words we are feeding upon Himself. Our spiritual life is maintained thereby. Peter at once began to apprehend this when, immediately after the discussion now referred to, he said to Christ, "Lord, to whom shall we go? Thou hast words of eternal life" (v. 68, margin). On our part the sustenance of our spiritual life depends upon the exercise of faith.

LIFE-GIVING OVERFLOW

What we receive from Christ sustains our spiritual life then overflows to those around us. This is done in part through the Holy Spirit as well. When these "rivers of living water" flow from believers, they bring glory to Jesus. Giving glory to the Lord, then, entails living life from one's spiritual overflow.

The seventh chapter [of John] develops this truth in this way, that, in addition to the fact that Christ and His words are the sustaining element of our spiritual life, this life in us is

TO OVERFLOW IN LIFEGIVING

enrichment to others. Jesus said, "He that believeth on Me, as the Scripture hath said, out of his belly shall flow rivers of living water. But this spake He of the Spirit, which they that believe on Him were to receive" (7:38, 39). The Holy Spirit is described by the apostle Paul as "the Spirit of life in Christ Jesus." Now Christ taught the disciples that the Spirit's work in and through the life of the believer could not be carried on until He Himself had been glorified. For, firstly, the Spirit would be sent forth by the Son of God as well as by the Father (16:7). Secondly, He would take of Christ's and declare it unto them, and this in order to glorify Him (16:14). Accordingly the flowing forth of the rivers of living water in the lives of believers is the glorifying of Christ by the Spirit in and through them.

THE RESURRECTION, AND THE LIFE

When Jesus raised Lazarus from the dead, His enemies determined once and for all that He must die. This miracle stood as stunning proof that He was the Lifegiver. The incredible attributes and qualities of Jesus Christ are memorable; verses and passages in this section are worthy of being memorized. Indeed, He is the Resurrection and the Life.

The crowning point in the Lord's teaching concerning Himself as the means of life, was His statement to Martha, "I am

THE RESURRECTION, AND THE LIFE

he that believeth on Me, though he die, yet shall He live; and whosoever liveth and believeth on Me shall never die" (John 11:25, 26). The resurrection of Lazarus from the dead was the crisis of the Lord's dealings with the Jews. They had ignored all His other works. Would they accept this greatest evidence of His power, and so acknowledge His claim to be the Son of God? They refused even this evidence. Nay, more, they took counsel together to put Him to death. From that time, therefore, the Lord ceased to deal with them, and left them to their darkness (11:53, 54). The resurrection of Lazarus, the greatest manifestation of His Deity up to that time, was, however, the occasion of the most comprehensive declaration of His power as the Lifegiver. He declared nothing less than that resurrection and life were embodied in His own Person, and that spiritual life, imparted through faith in Him, excluded the possibility of death. In contrast to the rejection of His testimony by the Jews, even after the proof He gave of His power to raise the dead, stands the unquestioning acceptance by Martha of His tremendous claim, even before the event of her brother's resurrection. His declaration to her was an advance upon His preceding teaching concerning His power of resurrection. He had previously stated that He would quicken the dead, that they would hear His voice and live (5:21, 25); that He would raise up at the last day those who believe in Him (6:40, 44). But now He gathers up all this power into His own Person and says, "I am the Resurrection, and the Life."

THIS TRANSCENDENT CLAIM

is the climax of the teaching of the Gospel, regarding the initial and foundation truth of the introduction: "In Him was life" (1:4). After gathering His disciples around Him in the upper room prior to His crucifixion, He takes up the same theme with them, and declares that He is "the Way, the Truth, and the Life," and that in order to come to the Father it is necessary to come through Him (14:6). He tells them further that because He lives they shall live also (v. 19). Thus in two distinct statements He makes known to them what he had combined in His words to Martha, "I am the Resurrection and the Life."

THE RECIPIENTS OF LIFE

The Lord is the source of life; He is life itself. He died to provide this life to those who would believe. Eternal life is defined anew in John 17, where He declares, "This is the life eternal, that they should know Thee the only true God, and Him whom thou didst send, even Jesus Christ." Only through His death could we receive eternal life.

In His prayer in [John] chapter seventeen the theme of Christ as the source of life is further expounded. Not only has the Father given to the Son to have life in Himself, but He has given Him authority over all flesh, that He should give eternal life to all whom the Father has given Him. This specifies

THE RECIPIENTS OF LIFE

in a way not mentioned before. They are not simply those who believe, they were the gift of the Father to the Son from eternity. Moreover, the life which is derived from Christ is here defined as personal acquaintance with the Father and the Son. "This is the life eternal, that they should know Thee the only true God, and Him whom thou didst send, even Jesus Christ" (17:3). This is a new definition of life. Spiritual vitality is not merely endless existence, it consists of the knowledge of God, a knowledge which molds character and determines action.

As the subject is brought to a close toward the end of the Gospel the apostle specifies the object for which it is written, and in doing so sums up the subject of Christ as the Life. He says, "These are written that ye may believe that Jesus is the Christ, the Son of God; and that believing ye may have life in His Name" (20:31). In the phrase "In His Name" are included all the preceding teachings of this Gospel which are developed from the statement "In Him was life." For His Name expresses what He is. It represents His character and attributes. It suggests that among other things He is the embodiment and the fountain of life. The exercise of faith in Him brings His life into the soul. That life is therefore the light of men.

"IN HIM WAS LIFE"

Yet He died. He yielded up His life. Only through His death could His life be communicated to man. A vicarious death it must be, too. For man was dead through sin. But since "in Him was life," death "could not hold or bind Him." He is "the resurrection, and the life." His life out of death brings life to us in our death. We have life out of His death. And because He lives we shall live also—a deathless life like His. May we know increasingly here, and now, the power of His resurrection!

CHRIST THE SENT ONE

Jesus was sent by the Father to fulfill His purposes. Vine provides a clear and concise summation of Christ's role as seen in the Gospel of John—His purpose, His character, His identification with the Father, and the witnesses that verified His claims. All of these things work together to proclaim that Jesus Christ is the Son of God, and in Him we can find salvation.

A leading theme of this Gospel is that Christ came into the world as the One sent from the Father. This basic truth of the faith is stated in almost every chapter, and frequently in most of the chapters. The statement, as recorded by John, was constantly upon the Savior's lips. Its importance lies in this, that it implies His preexistence, and that it signalizes His coming into the world as distinct from that of every other being, and especially in this respect, that coming as the preexistent Son of God He was "of the full Deity possessed."

THE ONLY-BEGOTTEN FROM THE FATHER

Moreover, He came as "the only begotten from the Father" (1:14), a title indicating eternal relationship. God was eternally the Father, therefore the Son was eternal with the Father. Further, having come, He was still "in the bosom of the Father" (1:18); He was one with Him in the Godhead. He declared, "I and the Father are One" (10:30). His having been sent by the Father is a direct testimony to His distinct personality. Yet when He says to Philip, "He that hath seen Me hath seen the Father" (14:9), He declares His oneness with the Father in the Godhead.

His preexistence with the Father was constantly stated by Christ Himself. He described Himself as "the One who descended out of Heaven" (3:13), and again, as the One who is "from God" (6:46). He says further, "I am from above; . . . I am come forth, and am come from God" (8:23, 42). Again, in making acknowledgment to the disciples of their belief of this fact, and in assuring them that the Father loves them because of this belief, He repeats, "I came forth from the Father, . . . and am come into the world" (16:27, 28). His satisfaction with their belief comes out again in His closing prayer when He says, "They knew of a truth that I came forth from Thee, and they believed that Thou didst sent (*a*) Me" (17:8).[1] He states His preexistence in other ways. Putting it negatively He says, "I am not come of Myself but He . . . send (*a*) Me" (7:29 and 8:42).

---

1 Two distinct words are used in John's Gospel for the verb "send," *pempō*, which is used 24 times, and *apostellō* 17 times. They are sometimes used interchangeably. Any distinction lies in this, that *pempō* is a general term, without any special idea being necessarily attached to the relation between the sender and the one sent; *apostellō*, from which the English word "apostle" is derived, expresses this relation, and suggests an official, authoritative sending. We shall indicate which word is used in the various passages by the letters (*p*) and (*a*). *Apostellō*, not *pempō*, is always used when Christ is addressing the Father concerning His having sent Him. It is also noticeable that in direct statements, when "God," or the "Father," or the personal pronoun "He," is the immediate subject of the verb "to send," *apostellō* is used. When, on the contrary, the statement is not thus directly made, but is introduced by a relative pronoun, *pempō* is used. The use of the subordinate relative clause, that is, one introduced by a relative pronoun, comprises all the occurrences of the verb *pempō* in reference to Christ as the sent One, while, on the other hand, no relative clause, introduced by a relative pronoun, contains the word *apostellō*. Now a relative clause (*e.g.*, "He that sent Me") necessarily gives much less stress in the expression of an idea than the direct statement of a principal clause (*e.g.*, "He sent Me"); in this latter the mission is the main thought, whereas in "He that sent Me is true," e.g., the main thought is not that of the mission. The above facts therefore serve to confirm the distinction already pointed out, and to show that *apostellō* is the more expressive word of the two.

SANCTIFIED BEFORE SENT

The Father had sanctified Him before He sent (*a*) Him into the world (10:36). He was thus set apart for His mission before His incarnation. Again, He says that the Father who sent (*p*) Him gave Him commandment what He should say and speak (12:49). Further, His acts were done in the consciousness that He came forth from God and was going back to God (13:3). The fact of His return to the Father from whom He had come finds frequent mention in this Gospel, and is another link in the testimony both to His preexistence and to His Deity. For of no other could such statements be true. He says to the Jews, "Yet a little while am I with you, and I go unto Him that sent (*p*) Me" (7:33). This He repeats to the disciples, "Now I go unto Him that sent (*p*) Me; . . . I leave the world and go unto the Father" (16:5; cp. v. 28).

John's Gospel does not state the actual details of the manner of His coming. The record of that is found in the first and third Gospels. The omission of the facts relating to His birth is entirely appropriate to the character of this Gospel, the object of which is to present Christ as the eternal Son of God. In the paper under the heading of "Christ as the Light" we drew attention to the ninth verse of the first chapter, which states that Christ is a light for every man because He came into the world. This is the first direct mention of the truth of our present theme. The place to which He came is next mentioned. "He came unto His own things [Palestine, the land of God's choice] and they that were His own [the Jews, the people of God's choice] received Him not" (1:11). Then follows a statement of the mode of His coming, "The Word became flesh, and dwelt among us" (1:14). Thus in a threefold way the introduction to this Gospel presents the truth of the first Advent.

The first teaching given by the Lord Himself on the subject is in His conversation with Nicodemus, when He says, "God so loved the world that He gave His only begotten Son . . ."; this, with a statement of the purpose of the gift, He amplifies by saying that "God sent (*a*) not His Son into the world to judge the world; but that the world should be saved through Him." Here is given the first definite statement that the Father sent the Son. This great truth is stated over forty times in the Gospel. Its teaching upon the subject may be further set forth under the following heads: (I.) the purpose for which He came; (II.) the character He manifested; (III.) His identification with the Father; (IV.) the witness borne to Him.

I. The following are

The Purposes for Which He Came

(1) That the world might be saved through Him (3:17[*a*]). (2) To do not His own will, the will of Him that sent (*p*) Him (6:38). In this connection He declares that He seeks the glory of Him that sent (*p*) Him (7:18), and that He works the works of Him that sent (*p*) Him (9:4). (3) That He might give life unto the world (6:33). (4) That a man might eat of Him as the Living Bread, and not die (6:50); compare verses 51 and 58. (5) For judgment—not, that is to say, to judge the world,

but—"that they which see not may see; and that they which see may become blind" (9:39). (6) That His sheep might have life, and have it abundantly (10:10). (7) That whosoever believeth in Him may not abide in the darkness (12:46). (8) That He might bear witness of the truth (18:37).

II. Associated with the fact of His being sent is

The Character He Manifested

This may be set forth in three ways, as to (1) His life, (2) His acts, (3) His words.

(1) The most notable feature in His character as the sent One is His perfect representation of the Father. This was the outcome of His entire obedience to His will. At the same time the Father manifested Himself in and through Him. He says "The living Father sent (*a*) Me, and I live because of the Father (6:57). Again He says "He that sent (*p*) Me is with Me" (8:29).

(2) Of His deeds He says, "My meat is to do the will of Him that sent (*p*) Me, and to accomplish His work" (4:34); "I seek not Mine own will, but the will of Him that sent (*p*) Me" (5:30); "I do always the things that are pleasing to Him" (8:29); "I must work the works of Him that sent (*p*) Me" (9:4). He was thus Himself the fulfillment of the promise of Jehovah to Israel that He would raise up from among them a prophet to whom they must hearken; for He would put His words in His mouth, and would speak all that He commanded (Deut. 18:15–18). That He did nothing of Himself is further shown in His statement that no one could come to Him except the Father that sent Him drew him (6:44[*p*]).

(3) Of His words He says, "He whom God hath sent (*a*) speaketh the words of God" (3:34); "My teaching is not Mine, but His that sent (*p*) Me" (7:16); "He that sent (*p*) Me is true; and the things which I heard from Him, these speak I unto the world" (8:26). To the disciples He says, "The word which ye hear is not Mine, but the Father's who sent (*p*) Me" (14:24).

Thus His whole life bore testimony to the initial truth of the Gospel: "The only begotten Son, which is in the bosom of The Father, He hath declared Him." Men could never have learned the true character of God save through Him.

III. The following texts show

The Identification with the Father

as the One who sent Him: "He that honoreth not the Son honoreth not the Father which sent (*p*) Him" (5:23); (2) "He that believeth on Me, believeth not on Me, but on Him that sent (*p*) Me" (12:44); (3) "He that beholdeth Me beholdeth Him that sent (*p*) Me" (12:45); (4) "He that receiveth Me receiveth Him that sent Me" (13:20); (5) "This is life eternal, that they should know Thee the only true God, and Him whom Thou didst send (*a*), even Jesus Christ," (17:3).

IV. Concerning

The Witness Borne to Him

He says: (1) "The very *works* that I do, bear witness of Me, that the Father hath sent (*a*) Me" (5:36); (2) "The *Father* that sent (*p*) Me beareth witness of Me" (8:18); (3) *Christ Himself* likewise bore this witness. It was not only the burden of His whole testimony, but He occasionally made certain statements in the hearing of men for the very purpose that they might believe that the Father had sent (*a*) Him (11:42). Though His testimony was generally rejected, and is still rejected, yet the world is to be convinced that the Father sent (*a* in each verse) Him by the unity of all believers in Him (17:21 and 23). Amidst the cold refusal of the world to acknowledge His mission He expresses His delight in the fact that His followers believed in the truth of it (17:3, 25—*a* in each verse).

THE CONCLUSION

The last statement in this Gospel in connection with this subject is the Lord's word to the disciples on the evening of the day of His Resurrection, when, having shown them His hands and His side, and thus rejoicing their hearts, He said, "Peace be unto you; as the Father hath sent (*a*) Me, even so send (*p*) I you (20:21).[1] A few evenings before He had said, "As Thou didst send (*a*) Me into the world, even so sent (*a*) I them into the world" (17:18). Now He confirms the words of His prayer. This statement He accompanied by breathing on them, and saying, "Receive ye the Holy Ghost (or, perhaps, holy breath): whose soever sins ye forgive, they are forgiven unto them; whose soever sins ye retain, they are retained" (20:21–23). That is to say, in their mission the Gospel they preached would be the means of forgiveness in the case of those who received it; it would be a savor of life unto life. On the other hand, the unbeliever, rejecting the Gospel, would remain in His sins, and it would thus be to him a savor of death unto death. Inasmuch as His sending us into the world bears a resemblance to His own mission from the Father, we have much to learn from the teaching of this Gospel on this subject as to what should be the character of our life and our work here. As it was His chief pleasure to do the will of Him who sent Him and worthily to represent Him, so may we unceasingly enter into the responsibility and privilege of doing the will of God and living to give a faithful witness for Him in this dark world of sin!

---

1 In view of the precision with which the choice between *pempō* and *apostellō* is made throughout the Gospel, it cannot be gathered that the two words are used simply interchangeably in this verse. Even though in the corresponding statement in 17:18, the word *apostellō* is used in both parts of the verse, yet the use of the two different verbs in 20:21, suggests the significance pointed out in the footnote referred to on pg. 128. Certainly, whatever distinction there is between the two words, the Lord does not observe the distinction when addressing the Father, but He does so when speaking to the disciples, suggesting perhaps, not a difference in the mode of sending but a difference in the relation between Himself and the Father on the one hand, and Himself and the disciples on the other.

WITNESSES TO CHRIST

The Gospels exist as a testimony to the life and words of Jesus, bearing witness to Him so that everyone has the opportunity to hear and believe. These testimonies of ordinary people whose lives were transformed by the person and work of Jesus have borne witness to the amazing power of God. In John's writings, we see these testimonies in two clear ways. First, people have borne witness to the fact that Jesus is the Son of God. Second, we see that in Him we can find eternal life. This is an overview, then, of the Book of John focusing specifically on the witnesses to Jesus Christ.

The reader of the Gospel of John cannot fail to be struck with the constant reference therein to the subject of the witness born to Christ. Testimony to Christ is, of course, the very *raison d'etre* of all the Gospels, but with John the specific mention of the fact forms a characteristic feature of his Gospel. The same is true of his first Epistle. He there says, "If we receive the witness of men, the witness of God is greater" (1 John 5:9). Possibly he means by "the witness of men" the testimony of himself and his fellow apostles, though more probably he is stating as a general fact that men receive human witness on good evidence, and that therefore the witness of God is much more to be received. Even from the human standpoint the testimony to Christ is cumulatively of such a character that to reject it savors either of willful ignorance or blind antagonism.

Now John's testimony is very definite. It is twofold, and consists of proofs, firstly, that Christ is the Son of God, the sent One of the Father; and, secondly, that eternal life for men is in Him. This is stated pointedly in the Epistle: "The witness of God is this, that He hath borne witness concerning His Son; . . . that God gave unto us eternal life and this life is in His Son" (1 John 5:9–11).

It will perhaps be useful to go through the records of the Gospel on the subject, as we have done in the case of other leading themes.

The first witness is

JOHN THE BAPTIST

The earlier part of the Gospel is largely occupied with his testimony. In the introduction he is mentioned as the one who came "for a witness, that he might bear witness of the Light that all might believe through him" (1:7). Obviously the record of the Baptist's testimony is designedly introductory to the whole theme of the witness to Christ. The apostle emphasizes the fact that the Baptist was not himself the Light, but "came that he might bear witness of the Light" (v. 8).

Next comes a preliminary record of his actual testimony. "John beareth witness of Him, and crieth, saying, This was He of whom I said, He that cometh after me has become before me: for He was before me" (v. 15). The next three sections of the first chapter (vv. 19–42) give a detailed report of the Baptist's witness and its effects. Verse 19 is a heading to the subject. "And this is the witness of John, when the Jews sent unto him from Jerusalem priests and Levites to ask him, Who art thou?" John the Baptist's testimony increases in definiteness; it is like a light which glows the more as it is turned on.

1. He denies that he is the Christ (v. 20).
2. He is preparing His way (v. 23).
3. One is in their midst who is incomparably superior to him (vv. 26, 27).
4. He is "the Lamb of God, which taketh away the sin of the world" (v. 29).
5. John has seen the Spirit descending upon Him, and He abides upon Him (v. 32).
6. He will baptize with the Holy Spirit (v. 33).
7. This Person is the Son of God (v. 34).

To show that this is the climax of his testimony he says, "And I have seen and have borne witness that this is the Son of God."

The increasing definiteness of all this is noticeable:

1. His first statement is purely negative.
2. The second shows John's relationship toward Christ.
3. The third signalizes Him, but indefinitely.
4. The fourth specifies him definitely, but symbolically.
5. The fifth declares the Divine testimony to His Godhead.
6. The sixth states His Divine power.
7. The seventh declares specifically that He is the Son of God.

There are two further references to John the Baptist's witness, one when, in reply to the remark of his disciples that all men were coming to Christ, he declared that since he himself was not the Christ, but was sent before Him, Christ must increase while he must decrease (3:26). The other is Christ's declaration of John, that he had borne witness unto the truth, as a burning and shining lamp, but that there was a still greater witness than that of John. The Lord's statement, "the witness which I receive is not from men" (v. 34), meant primarily that the witness of John the Baptist was not simply John's testimony, but that it came from God through him. The Authorized Version, "I receive not testimony from man," is a mistranslation, and does not convey the Lord's meaning.

A SERIES OF WITNESSES—THE FATHER

He is here engaged in controversy with the opposing Jews, and now mentions one after another of those who have borne witness to Him. He declares that the testimony which he has given Himself is not His alone. He says, "If I bear witness of Myself, My witness is not true." Later on He says, "I am He that beareth witness of Myself and the Father that sent Me beareth witness of Me." Thus there are Two bearing witness, and, as he reminds the Pharisees from their law, the witness of two men is true. Here in the fifth chapter He lays stress upon the Father's witness: "It is another that beareth witness for Me; and I know that the witness which He witnesseth of Me is true . . . The Father which sent Me, He hath borne witness of Me" (5:31, 32, 37). The Lord was perhaps referring partly to the voice uttered by the Father on the occasion of His baptism, "Thou art My beloved Son: in Thee I am well pleased." But there seems to have been more in view than this. For He has just said that His works bore witness of Him, and that these were given Him to do by the Father (v. 36), and subsequently He declared that the Father Himself dwelling in Him did the works (14:10). Accordingly the Father was bearing witness to Him by the works He wrought.

HIS WORKS

His works constitute the third of the witnesses of which the Lord speaks in this discourse. By His works He does not mean merely His miracles. Everything He did bore witness both to His Deity and His character, and to His mission as the One sent of the Father. "The very works that I do," He says, "bear witness of Me, that the Father hath sent Me" (v. 36). He tells the Jews that they had neither heard His voice at any time nor seen His form. There is perhaps here an intimation that they had never understood the messages God had given to the nation, and that now they completely misunderstood the Person who was now before them, in their refusal to recognize Him as His Son, and so neither did they understand the nature and significance of His works.

His works are called "signs." The word *sēmeion*, "sign," is more than a mere miracle. A miracle is that which excites wonder, but a sign is a significant appeal to the heart of man, used in this case by God to produce an acknowledgment of His existence, power, or character. So the miracles wrought by Christ were testimonies to the fact that He was the Son of God. Three in John's Gospel are recorded in a way which shows that they were specially wrought with a view to convince the Jews of the Lord's Divine Sonship and mission. The first of these three was that of the lame man by the pool of Bethesda. It was that miracle that led to the discussion now under consideration, in which the Lord spoke so much of the witness borne to Him. The second was the healing of the blind man, which led to the discussion as to whether Jesus had come from God or not, and which was followed by His declaration, in answer to their request that He would tell them plainly whether He was the Christ, "I told you, and ye believed not: the works that I do in My Father's Name, these bear witness of Me" (10:25). The third is the resurrection of Lazarus. That was, as we have already seen, His last testimony to them by this special means.

THE SCRIPTURES

The next witness mentioned by the Lord is the Scriptures. He says, "Ye search the Scriptures, for in them ye think ye have eternal life; and these are they which bear witness of Me" (5:39). The Jews looked to the law of Moses as a means of life, and prided themselves in the exclusive privileges God had given to them; but they read the sacred page with spiritually blinded eyes. Their table had become a snare, and the proof of their blindness was that they failed to see any correspondence between the One who was in their midst and the Scriptures which foretold of Him. Hence they would not come to Him that they might have life. It was a stupendous claim to make that the inspired records committed to the nation concentrated their testimony from beginning to end on a Person who had grown up in a humble, unobtrusive path of life in the nation, and had but recently come forth from a cottage home, the home of a laboring man. Yet all the circumstances of His life and ministry thus far only vindicated His claim. The various witnesses mentioned by Him in these discourses, the witness, that is to say, of the Father and of John the Baptist, of the Lord's own works and the Scriptures, blend together to form a light that shines with intense power, revealing to our worshiping hearts the glories of the Son of God.

PAST, PRESENT AND FUTURE

So far the witnesses to which the Gospel of John refers were either past or present. When we pass to the latter part of the Gospel the reference is to the future, that is, to testimony which was to be given after the Lord had ascended. This change in the subject is appropriate to the circumstances of the Lord's life on earth. For it was when He had ceased His public ministry and had gathered His disciples around Him, just before His crucifixion, that He told them of the witness that was yet to be borne to Him. It would be twofold.

THE HOLY SPIRIT

The Holy Spirit would bear witness, and, as a result of His operation, the Lord's followers would do so. He says, "When the Comforter is come, whom I will send unto you from the Father, He shall bear witness of Me; and ye also bear witness, because ye have been with Me from the beginning" (15:26, 27). It is the one object of the Holy Spirit in all His operations to glorify Christ. With that in view, those who are really yielded to God, so that the Holy Spirit can use them, will be led by Him to make it the great and constant object of their lives also to glorify Christ.

HIS DISCIPLES

That was characteristic of His apostles. They had had proof positive in all their associations with Him in the days of His flesh, and subsequently after His resurrection, that He was the Son of God, the One sent of the Father, the Messiah of the nation, and the Lord of His people. They were Spirit-filled men, and the Holy Spirit was able to use them in bearing witness to Him. It was given to them to bear witness, not only by oral testimony, but by continuing and completing the Scriptures of truth, the Word of God. All the witness that believers have given since, both individually and collectively in the Churches, while it is due to the work of the Spirit of God in their hearts, is at the same time the outcome of the witness which was given by the first disciples of the Lord. When the Church is complete and removed at the Rapture, that particular testimony will cease, and the Holy Spirit will bear witness in another way.

THE SEVENTH WITNESS

Thus far in this Gospel we have read of six witnesses to Christ: the Father, John the Baptist, the works of the Lord Himself, the Scriptures, the Holy Spirit, and the disciples. There is yet another. It is that of the writer of this Gospel. He records the supernatural circumstances in the death of Christ in that he saw blood and water coming out of the smitten side of the Crucified. He says, "And he that hath seen hath borne witness, and his witness is true; and he knoweth that He saith true, that ye also may believe" (19:35). This flowing of the water and the blood was not an evidence of mere physical suffering, it was a Divine and supernatural testimony to the fact of the impartation of life eternal. Concerning it John says: "This is He that came by water and blood, even Jesus Christ, not with the water only, but with the water and the blood. . . . There are three who bear witness: the Spirit, and the water, and the blood; and the three agree in one, . . . and the witness is this, that God gave unto us eternal life, and this life is in His Son" (1 John 5:6–11).

"YE ARE MY WITNESSES"

Finally, the apostle concludes his Gospel by a statement characteristic of his references therein to himself. It forms a kind of climax to his testimony. He says, "This is the disciple which beareth witness of those things, and wrote these things; and we know that His witness is true" (21:24). His Gospel is itself a wonderful fulfillment of the promise of the Lord on the day of His ascension, "Ye shall be My witnesses." May it be ours by sound doctrine and godliness of life to continue the witness!

DIVINE LOVE

John, "the disciple whom Jesus loved," took great care to write about God's love in his Gospel. He understood the greatness of Jesus' love for him, and he appreciated it. More than any of the other Gospel writers, John gives testimony of his personal experiences of the love of Christ. The following section traces the theme of love through the book of John.

That the apostle John should write about Divine love to a greater extent than any other writer of Scripture is what we might expect on reading his testimony of his personal experiences of the love of Christ to him. This disciple seems to have enjoyed the manifestation of His love in a special manner, he delights to call himself "the disciple whom Jesus loved" (13:23; 19:26; 20:2; 21:20). Not that there is any hint of favoritism in this. The Lord did not bestow His love upon John at the expense of His love to the other disciples. On the contrary, John himself says that Christ "loved His own which were in the world," and "He loved them unto the end" (13:1). Christ's affections went out indeed especially to him, but not so that the others were losers by it. If the beloved disciple was loved the more, they were not loved the less.

And yet, the love of the Lord Jesus was not a kind of indiscriminate benevolence, smiling on all alike, nor could it have been the outcome merely of a sovereign will. There was no doubt something in John that drew it forth in a special way. However that may have been the case, John himself apprehended the fact that Jesus loved him, and he appreciated it.

Nor, again, does his testimony concerning the love of Christ toward him savor of boastfulness in the slightest degree. Nay, verily, it breathes a tone of childlike humility. There is a complete lack of self-consciousness about his assertions—not a breath of protestation that he was unworthy of the love, nor any such disclaimer of merit. What he says is just the spontaneous expression of his enjoyment of the fact. This then is the disciple whom the Spirit of God used to write preeminently on the greatest of all themes.

ITS PLACE IN THE GOSPEL

We have observed in the case of other subjects in this Gospel that there is a somewhat different treatment in the first half, which gives our Lord's public ministry; from that in the latter part, which gives His private instructions to His disciples, and so it is with the present subject. It naturally occupies a more prominent place in the latter part of the Gospel than the former. In the latter part the theme is almost continuous. Not so in the first half, the first ten chapters, though the love of God to men is recorded, contain no statement concerning the love of Christ. From the eleventh chapter onward the Gospel is full of it. And here in His private intimacy with His disciples He unlocks the treasures of the Father's heart toward them. Here love is not spoken of as the love of God; save where Christ's own love is mentioned, the love is always that of the Father.

THE FIRST MENTION

Nothing could be more appropriate than that the theme should be introduced by the sublime testimony, "God so loved the world, that He gave His only begotten Son, that whosoever believeth on Him should not perish, but have eternal life" (3:16). That this should be the first mention is suggestive; we must learn of the love of God toward ourselves as sinners before we begin to learn of His love as our Father. It is fitting, too, that the next should consist of a statement of the love of the Father to the Son; it occurs in the same chapter, and, like the first statement, it is associated with believing "The Father loveth the Son, and hath given all things into His hand. He that believeth on the Son hath eternal life" (3:35, 36). "God so loved the world," and the evidence is that He gave His Son: "The Father loveth the Son," that suggests the value of His gift, and the evidence is that "He hath given all things into His hand."

TWO SYNONYMS

The statement, "the Father loveth the Son," occurs again in chapter 5:20, in the Lord's controversy with the Jews. But here a different word, *phileō*, is used for "loveth"; it was *agapaō* in chapter 3:35. These two words are nowhere used simply interchangeably; each is used upon occasion to convey the thought of deep affection, but *phileō* suggests a still more emotional love than *agapaō* The change of the word in chapter 5:20 is significant.[1]

In chapter 3:35 the Father's love to the Son is predicted in connection with His committal of all things into His hand. The similar statement in chapter 5:20 is the Lord's own testimony, not the writer's, and here He is speaking about the constant communion between Himself and His Father. The Son does what He sees the Father doing; the Father shows the Son what He Himself does. The word of deeper emotion is therefore entirely appropriate here.

THE ELEVENTH CHAPTER

There is not much more about the love of God in this section of the Gospel, for the Lord is holding a controversy with His enemies. He says to them, "Ye have not the love of God in yourselves" (5:42); and again, "If God were your Father, ye would love Me" (8:42). Their attitude toward Him shows that God is not their Father. We pass now to the latter part of the Gospel. The eleventh chapter is transitional; it records Christ's final witness to the Jews in the resurrection of Lazarus, and also the first of a series of private conversations with His followers. In regard to the latter, this chapter contains a touching testimony about the love of Christ in connection with the death of Lazarus. The message of the sisters is, "Lord, Behold he whom Thou lovest (*phileō*) is sick" (11:3). Then comes the

---

1 The two words are used in the same connection in three or four instances in this Gospel. The case which has received most notice is in the conversation between the Lord and Peter in chapter 21:15–17. The note in the Expositor's Green Testament is to the effect that here at all events there can be no distinction between the words, as it could not be said, if there were, that Peter was grieved because Jesus *the third time* said, "Lovest (*phileō*) thou Me," when in the same question just before He used the other word *agapaō*; and that therefore the words are identical in meaning, and are "interchanged for the sake of euphony." This supposition is entirely unfounded. Firstly, it may not be concluded that the two words could not have a different meaning, because the same question was asked three times. The question would be practically the same een though the word "lovest" in the third expressed a more emotional feeling. Secondly, there is good reason to think that Christ did not address Peter in Greek. John's Greek was an inspired translation of original utterances. Thirdly, the idea about euphony must be ruled out; anyone who reads the Greek text through can see that there would be more euphony in verse 16 if *phileō* were used instead of *agapaō*. Fourthly, the commentator quotes a sentence from a nonbiblical writer to show the identity in meaning, which shows the very contrary. Moreover, Greek writers themselves point to the difference in meaning. Thus Dio Cassius says of the loyalty of the people to Caesar, "ye had affection (*phileō*) for him *as a father* and ye loved (*agapaō*) as a benefactor" (44:48). Aristotle plainly states that there is a distinction (Rhet. 1, 11, 17). The distinction must be observed in every case in John's Gospel.

testimony of John, the writer: "Now Jesus loved (*agapaō*) Martha, and her sister, and Lazarus." Bearing in mind that each word speaks of deep affection, it is again quite suitable that the more emotional word should be used by the sisters. So, too, when the Jews, seeing the intensity of the Lord's feelings, say, "Behold how He loved him!" they use the same word, *phileō* (v. 36). The writer is not changing the verb simply for the sake of variety or euphony.

THE UPPER ROOM

When we come to the Lord's conversation with the disciples in the upper room, the subject of Divine love becomes the prominent theme. This river, running through the Gospel record, here broadens out. The narrative begins with the statement of the love of Christ for His followers in all its sufficiency and permanency. "Jesus knowing that His hour was come that He should depart out of this world unto the Father, having loved His own which were in the world, He loved them unto the end" (13:1). This is the special love of which John delights to speak. The reader cannot fail to be struck with the way in which the Lord unfolds to His disciples the Father's love toward them and His own association with Him in it. He uses the Father's love toward Himself as a comparison of His own love to the disciples. He says, "He that hath My commandments, and keepeth them, he it is that loveth Me: and he that loveth Me shall be loved of My Father, and I will love him, and will manifest Myself unto him." And again, "If a man love Me, he will keep My words: and My Father will love him, and we will come unto him, and make our abode with him" (14:21, 23). Following this assurance of the united love of the Father and the Son for those who fulfill His will, there comes the still more wonderful statement: "Even as the Father hath loved Me, I also have loved you: abide ye in My love. If ye keep My commandments, ye shall abide in My love; even as I have kept My Father's commandments, and abide in His love" (15:9, 10). This expresses the immeasurable degree of the love He is unfolding to them; it is the infinite love of the Father for the Son Himself. And this is the standard for our love to one another, for He gives it as His "commandment" that we love one another even as He has loved us (v. 12). Toward the close of His discourse to the disciples the Lord uses the more emotional word to express the Father's love, as being a response to the love they had shown to Him. He says, "The Father Himself loveth (*phileō*) you, because ye have loved Me, and have believed that I came forth from the Father" (16:27).

THE LORD'S PRAYER

In His prayer which follows He renews the comparison of the Father's love to Him and His own love to them, only reversing the order. Previously He had said, "Even as the Father hath loved Me, I also have loved you"; now He says, "Thou lovedst them even as Thou lovedst Me" (17:23). But this love is to be realized in their experience. The close of this prayer is to the effect that the love wherewith the Father loved Him is to be in them and Christ Himself is to be in them. This then is to be the practical effect of that love. This, the closing utterance of His prayer, is also the close of this section of the Gospel. It begins and ends with the same theme of divine love, the unfailing love of Christ (13:1), and the abiding love of the Father and the Son (17:26). There can be no higher expression of divine love toward God's children than that He loves them as He loves His own Son. Thus the theme of the Father's love to the Son gradually expands in the Gospel from the introductory statement in chapter 3:35 to the closing testimony in the seventeenth chapter.

THE LAST CHAPTER

As we consider this great subject the questions must arise, What response has this infinite love in our hearts and lives? Do we really love the Lord with that deep-rooted affection which will mold our very life and shape our conduct according to His own character? Is our path the path of the ardent follower? Are our acts impelled by a burning devotion that gives Christ the uppermost place in our lives, and makes it our one great purpose and ambition to be well-pleasing to Him in all things? These indeed are the questions suggested by the closing narrative of that Gospel. Peter had avowed to his Master that though all would forsake Him, yet would not he. Then came his time of temptation and his faithlessness, the time, too, of his restoration by the One whose look had already melted his heart, and after this the morning scene on the shore of the lake. "Simon, son of John," says the Lord, "lovest (*agapaō*) thou Me more than these?"—that is, more than the other disciples. Peter replies by using the other and still more tender word, *phileō*, to declare his love. The second time Christ asks the question with the same word He had already used. Again Peter insists. The third time the Lord touchingly uses Peter's word. This elicits a still stronger declaration in which the disciple naturally adheres to his same expression. The Master's work in His follower's heart is done, and done as He only could do it. The love that He gladly recognized in that heart is to manifest itself increasingly for others that belong to Him—the lambs and sheep of the flock.

THE LESSON

This is the lesson for us all, enforced upon our own hearts as we come to the end of this Gospel. Christ must have the preeminent place if our lives are to be happy and useful, and only thus shall we be His instruments in blessing to others.

THE DEATH OF CHRIST

In the Gospel of John, we learn of Jesus' upcoming death in the very first chapter. There is no surprise in this outcome; it is foretold as a part of God's plan and purpose. He is the Lamb of God who will take away the sins of the world. This section traces the theme of Christ's death through the book of John.

In the first three Gospels the reader goes through several chapters before direct reference is made to the death of Christ. Not so in the fourth Gospel. The very first chapter, which so definitely describes the glories of His Deity, His creative power, and the grace of His incarnation, foretells His death. This is given in the testimony of John the Baptist at the river Jordan. Here, where the Lord came to be baptized, and so, in obedience to the last command to Israel under the law, to identify Himself with the nation in this respect, His herald gave the first public announcement of His death, pointing Him out to the people as

"THE LAMB OF GOD"

This first mention is figurative. The phraseology would be familiar to the people, but how startling the personal application! Still more so the declaration that He was the One "who taketh away the sin of the world."

We cannot but be struck with the contrast in the titles ascribed to the Lord in this chapter. He who is declared to be the Word of God is also the Lamb of God. He is at once the Father's eternal Coequal and the voluntary Victim for the sin of the world.

The similar announcement made next day, "Behold the Lamb of God," had the effect of causing two of John's disciples to follow Jesus. They at least grasped something of the significance of the message. To point to Christ as the Lamb of God is the way to win men to be His followers.

"DESTROY THIS TEMPLE"

The next reference to His death is in connection with the cleansing of the Temple, recorded in the second chapter. Having drastically put a stop to the traffic of those who were defiling the house of God with their merchandise, He was asked by the Jews for a sign of the authority for His action. His reply contained a purposely veiled reference to His death. "Destroy this Temple," He said, "and in three days I will raise it up." They naturally took Him to mean the building in which His power had just been displayed. In reality His utterance was prophetic of the blind selfwill which would yet lead them to desecrate the still more sacred Temple of His Body.

"AS MOSES LIFTED UP THE SERPENT"

In John's Gospel, then, the first mention of Christ's death is in the language of the Passover, the second is on the first occasion of the Passover feast itself after the inception of His public testimony. In each of the first two cases the language is symbolical. The third is a direct statement, associated with the Lord's conversation with Nicodemus. There was something in the well-known narrative of the brazen serpent which lay beyond the ken even of the ruler of the synagogue, at least if we take the paragraphing of the Revised Version, according to which the statement, "As Moses lifted up the serpent in the wilderness, even so must the

Son of Man be lifted up," is part of what the Lord said to Nicodemus. Here the manner of His death is foretold, and though the actual mode is not named, yet probably Nicodemus would connect it with the Roman method of execution.[1]

"THE BREAD WHICH I WILL GIVE"

The next reference to His death occurs in the Lord's second discussion with the Jews, which resulted from the feeding of the five thousand. The conversation turns upon His statement that He is the Living Bread which came down from Heaven. The Jews had already begun to reject His testimony concerning His relationship with the Father (5:18), and the continuation of His witness met with still more determined opposition. The first part of this Gospel is largely a history of this controversy. One of its great lessons is that willful rejection of the truth leads to the impossibility of receiving it. The hardening of the heart is God's retributive answer to refusal to listen to His Word. This lies behind the increasing difficulty of the Lord's utterances to the Jews. Having declared that He is the Bread of Life which came down from Heaven (6:33; 6:35–41), He goes on to say that the bread which He will give is "His flesh for the life of the world" (v. 51). This is the first mention of His death in His conversations with them. The idea of His giving His flesh to eat was utterly impossible to them and created strife among them. "How," they said, "can this Man give us His flesh to eat"; "My flesh is meat indeed."

And now a still more difficult statement: "Verily, verily, I say unto you, Except ye eat the flesh of the Son of Man, and drink His blood, ye have not life in yourselves. He that eaten My flesh, and drinketh My blood, hath eternal life; and I will raise him up at the last day. For My flesh is meat indeed, and My blood is drink indeed. He that eateth My flesh, and drinketh My blood, abideth in Me, and I in him" (6:53–56). The Jews were expecting that their Messiah would simply liberate the nation from bondage to the Gentile yoke and establish the Kingdom of God in their midst. But Christ had come to tell them that salvation could be theirs only through His death, that the blessings which God had to give could be enjoyed only through spiritual life. Salvation for the Jews, and for all men, must be by regeneration, and this must be by means of His atoning death. They must eat the flesh and drink the blood of the Son of Man or they could have no life. His words, so difficult for their hardened hearts to grasp, meant that He Himself must die if they were to live. What could be more opposed to their religious scruples than to drink blood? Had not God's own Law strictly prohibited it? Yet "His flesh is meat indeed, and His blood is drink indeed."

LIFE THROUGH HIS DEATH

His words, so difficult to His enemies, are clear in the light of the completed Scriptures. The words "flesh" and "blood" point to the fact of His death. Life

---

1 Quite possibly the record of the Lord's conversation with Nicodemus ends at verse 12. We need not discuss the point here.

is given by God to the sinner by means of it. To receive Christ as Savior is to acknowledge that the death sentence, due on account of one's sins, was carried out in the Person of Christ on the Cross. In this acknowledgment by faith we eat the flesh and drink the blood of Christ, and live unto God in Christ. Eating His flesh, coming to Him, believing on Him, all issue in eternal life. Not only is that life imparted by His death (v. 53), it is also sustained through it (v. 56). True it is that the constant nourishment we receive, and the spiritual life we live, are derived from the living Christ by the power of the Holy Spirit, but the maintenance of the spiritual life is nevertheless the result of constant feeding on the flesh and drinking of the blood of Christ. Spiritual life is maintained in communion with God by faith, and Christ is Himself our life, but this is because He died for us, and we must own His death as our death before we can enjoy His life as our life. "He that eateth My flesh, and drinketh My blood," He says, "abideth in Me, and I in him." The one who believes on Him is brought into permanent union with Him, and it is as we constantly realize the value and efficacy of His death that we really experience what abiding in Him is and He in us.

The tenses in verse 53 for "eat" and "drink" are different from those in the following verses. In verse 53 the words "eat" and "drink" are in the aorist or momentary tense, indicating the necessity of obtaining life once and for all on the ground of the death of Christ. In the following verses the tenses are continuous, showing that the one who has passed from death to life appropriates by constant experience as a believer the effects of His death, effects which are ministered by the Spirit of God. There is also a change in the verb. The word for "eat" in verse 53 is *phagein*, the ordinary word with that meaning; in the verses which follow it is *trōgein*, which denotes "to chew." The change of word suggests that in Aramaic the Lord expressed with similar emphasis to His opponents the necessity of their obtaining life through His death.

"THE BLOOD IS THE LIFE"

Our Lord's word as to "eating" His flesh and drinking His blood no doubt had direct reference to the Passover; the blood of the Lamb being the divinely appointed means of the deliverance of the nation from the doom of Egypt. The shedding of the blood involved the taking of the life of the animal, and, the blood having been sprinkled in the manner ordained of God, the Israelites fed on the flesh of the lamb roasted in the fire. So again, in subsequent sacrifices, they were to offer the flesh and blood of their burnt offerings upon the altar. The blood was to be poured out thereon, and they were to eat the flesh (Deut. 12:27). They were not allowed to eat the blood, "for the blood is the life," and they were not to eat "the life with the flesh" (v. 23). How difficult, then, and purposely so, for the hardened Jews to receive the Lord's teaching! How blessed for us to enjoy the fullness of the reality which the Mosaic injunctions but dimly foreshadowed!

Christ's words to the Jews are to be distinguished from the teaching of the Lord's Supper. Both converge to the same point; both direct our hearts to the Cross; but we may not say when we are partaking of the bread and of the cup at the Lord's Table that we are thereby eating the flesh and drinking the blood of Christ. For by means of eating His flesh and drinking blood we have life, but we do not obtain life by partaking of the Lord's Supper. We proclaim His death, we declare that He died for us, we partake of that which is communion of His body and His blood; but that is not the same thing as what the Lord taught the Jews.

"HIS HOUR HAD NOT YET COME"

The next reference in the Gospel occurs in the fourth discussion with the Jews (chap. 8). The Lord's renewed testimony—now given in the Temple—to His unity with the Father, again aroused their animosity, and would have led to His immediate arrest, but no man took Him, because "His hour had not yet come"; that is to say, the appointed hour in which He would offer Himself in sacrifice. There may be a similar reference in the preceding chapter, where He says, "My time is not yet come" (7:6, 8). But probably all that He meant there was that, while in the case of His brethren their arrangements were carried out according to their own inclinations, His were under the direction of His Father. Here again, in this fourth stage of the controversy, He intimates the mode of His death. "When ye have lifted up the Son of Man," He says, "then shall ye know that I am He, and that I do nothing of Myself but as the Father taught Me, I speak these things" (8:28). That Messiah should die was not in all their thoughts. Yet now He declared that His identity will be disclosed to them after they have put Him to death.

"THE GOOD SHEPHERD"

In the fifth and last discussion with the Jews, resulting from the healing of the blind man, the Lord takes occasion to tell them of the parable of the Good Shepherd, basing His teaching on the fact that the man He had healed had become one of His own sheep. This is how He now speaks of His death: "I am the Good Shepherd: the Good Shepherd layeth down His life for the sheep." Again, He tells His critics, but now in a different way, that life must come by His death. Here His thoughts are occupied with His followers. He had come that they might have life, and might have it abundantly. But more, the laying down of His life for this purpose was to be the outcome of the most intimate communion with the Father. So when He says again, "I lay down My life for the sheep" (10:15), it is not a mere repetition of His word in verse 11. There He simply said that He had come to give them life through His death. Now He bases His statement on the fact that He knows His own and His own know Him, even as the Father knows Him and He knows the Father. And further, the Father's love is combined with the Father's omniscience, and He loves the Son because His death is a means to an end. "Therefore doth the Father love Me, because I lay down My life, that I may take it again. No one taketh it away from Me, but I lay it down of Myself. I have power to lay it down, and I have power to take it again. This commandment

144

received I from My Father" (vv. 17, 18). He had given the Jews to understand that they would accomplish His death. It was they who would lift up the Son of Man (8:28); but now He shows that they had no power to do this at all except by His permission. He gave them signal proof of their inability at the close of this discussion, in that though they sought again to take Him "He went forth out of their hand" (v. 39).

THE COUNSEL OF CAIAPHAS

Now comes the climax of the controversy. The raising of Lazarus was His last public testimony to His divine claims, His last offer to His critics to acknowledge Him. Instead the chief priests gather a council to decide what was to be done with Him, and this provides the occasion of the next statement concerning His death. It is the prophecy uttered by Caiaphas. His advice to the council, "It is expedient for you that one man should die for the people, and that the whole nation perish not," was, from his own point of view, simply an argument for getting rid of Christ. National ruin could be averted by His death. Political expediency was a pretext serving the purposes of the high priest's personal animosity against Him. Yet there was a higher Power controlling his utterance. "This he said not of himself." His personal motives were subservient to the counsels of God, who makes the wrath of man to praise Him. Upon occasion God compelled His foes to prophesy. The position of Caiaphas lent itself to this. He was in line of succession of the priests who had communicated divine messages from God by the Urim and Thummim. "Being high priest that year he prophesied that Jesus should die for the nation, and not for the nation only, but that He might also gather together into one the children of God that are scattered abroad." Probably, too, the fact that He was the high priest, the religious leader of the people, accounted to some extent for the divine influence over his utterances. Mark the immediate effects: "From that day forth they took counsel that they might put Him to death." No effort on their part could attain to success until His hour had come; but that hour was drawing near.

"THE DAY OF MY BURYING"

The Gospel now gives us several intimations by the Lord that His death was at hand. The first of these is at the supper at Bethany, where Mary anointed the feet of Jesus. The remonstrances of Judas at the waste of the ointment called forth the Lord's answer, "Suffer her to keep it against the day of My burying." The disciples knew well by this time that death was to be His lot. When He had decided to go to Jerusalem owing to the death of Lazarus, Thomas had said: "Let us also go that we may die with Him." The indications were becoming more numerous that the end was near.

"IT BEARETH MUCH FRUIT"

His second utterance recorded in this chapter regarding His death is contained in His reply to those who told Him of the desire of the Greeks to see Him. Apparently their wish was not granted. The Lord was not there to gratify curiosity. The incident, however, drew forth some remarks which showed that He was thinking of that vast multitude of Gentiles which would be drawn to Him through His death. "The hour is come," He says, "that the Son of man should be glorified. Verily, verily, I say unto you, Except a grain of wheat fall into the earth and die, it abideth by itself alone; but if it die, it beareth much fruit" (12:24). The seed must die to produce the harvest. This is the law in both the physical and spiritual realms. In the latter it is a law of self-renunciation. Its fulfillment in the case of the Lord Jesus Christ stands alone, yet He lays it down as a law of life for His followers. "He that loveth his life loseth it; and he that hateth his life in this world shall keep it unto life eternal" (v. 25). The thought of "the hour," and all that it meant for Him was burdening His soul. Yet His "now is My soul troubled" was not a mere outburst of sorrow. His utterance had in view a testimony to His devotion to the Father. The burden was real and heavy, and He did not conceal it, but His one engrossing desire was the Father's glory. Hence His prayer, "Father, save Me from this hour," is followed by the confession, so full of redemptive truth, "but for this cause came I unto this hour," and by the prayer, so indicative of absolute submission to the Father's will, "Father, glorify Thy Name."

The Father's voice out of Heaven, the immediate answer to the prayer, was a witness to the people of His infinite approval of His Son, and of the unbroken union between them.

The Lord now shows to the people standing by that His death is to be the great crisis of the world's history.

The twelfth chapter of this Gospel gives us a series of momentous utterances by the Lord concerning His death. Firstly, there is the prediction of His burial (v. 7); secondly, the comparison of His death to the falling of a grain of corn into the earth to die, that it may bring forth fruit (v. 24); thirdly, the announcement that the hour was at hand for which He had come to glorify the Father (vv. 27, 28); fourthly, His declaration that His death would involve the world's judgment, that it would effect the casting out of Satan, and be the means of bringing all men within the scope of His own attractive power (vv. 31–33). The first three of these we considered in our last paper. Now as to the fourth, and with that we come to a parting of the ways as to the Lord's testimony.

"I, IF I BE LIFTED UP"

The Father's response from Heaven to the prayer of Christ, "Father, glorify Thy Name," came, He said, for the sake of the multitude that stood by. As the actual response was not revealed to them, the Lord explains the occurrence by saying, "Now is the judgment of this world; now shall the prince of this world be cast out. And I, if I be lifted up from the earth, will draw all men unto Myself." The word rendered "judgment" is *krisis*, which gives us our word "crisis." That may possibly be its meaning here, but only so because the death of Christ would, on the one hand, involve the condemnation of the world for its rejection of the Son of God, while on the other hand it would provide a means of deliverance from condemnation on the fulfillment of God's conditions. This would also involve deliverance from the world's spiritual tyrant: "Now shall the prince of this world be cast out." The death of Christ would judicially and potentially be the destruction of "him that had the power of death," and the annihilation of all his claims to authority over the world. Satan's claims were the outcome of man's rejection of the claims of God upon him. The death of Christ has abrogated the claims of Satan and opened the way for men to be drawn to the Savior: "I, if I be lifted up from the earth," He says, "will draw all men unto Myself." What a note of triumph sounds in the Redeemer's "I!" He sets Himself antithetically, and with strong emphasis, as the Conqueror of Satan and the Deliverer of men, and this by His own death.

Three times, as recorded in this Gospel, the Lord uses the term "lifted up," first at the beginning of His public career, when speaking to Nicodemus (3:14); then about halfway through it, when addressing the Jews who opposed Him (8:28); and now just as the end was drawing near, when addressing the multitude for the last time (12:32). Does not this itself reveal how continually the Cross occupied His mind?

The Lord points, then, to His death as the ground upon which He will exercise His attractive power. The multitude understood what was meant by His being "lifted up," but found it impossible to harmonize His Messianic claims with the fact that their Messiah would abide forever. How could the Son of man be lifted up? and who was this Son of man? Christ does not satisfy their inquiries. He simply warns them to make use of the light while it is with them.

THE UPPER ROOM

The crises had come. His public testimony must now cease. He will confine His attention from henceforth to His disciples.

John's preface to the discourse in the upper room views the Lord's approaching death and departure to the Father in the light of His infinite love: "Jesus, knowing that His hour was come that He should depart out of this world, having loved His own which were in the world, He loved them unto the end." These are the thoughts which pervade the discourse in what has been called "The Holy of holies" of the New Testament. Our consideration will here be limited to the references to His death.

Again and again in the course of His remarks He reminds them that He is about to leave them and go to the Father. True, He does not say in so many words that this is to be by way of the Cross, yet that is implied. His journey to the Cross was His pathway back to the Father. This we may see more forcibly by putting together some of His utterances to His disciples at this time. He says, "Yet a little while I am with you" (13:33); "Wither I go thou canst not follow Me now; but thou shalt follow afterwards"—plainly a direct reference to his death (v. 36); "I go to prepare a place for you" (14:2)—we can scarcely take this as referring merely to a preparation in Heaven itself after He had ascended there. The great preparation for our reception into the Father's house hereafter lay in the work of the Cross. This is confirmed by the statement of the writer to the Hebrews when he says that it was necessary that the heavenly things should be cleansed with better sacrifices than those of the earthly tabernacle, the plural standing for the one Sacrifice in its various aspects. Our entrance there, now by faith, and eventually at the Lord's Coming, depends on the atoning work of the Cross. Moreover, the Lord reminded the disciples that they knew the way He was going, for He told them clearly about His death (v. 4). Again, He says, "Now I go unto him that sent Me" (16:5); "a little while, and ye behold Me no more . . . because I go to the Father" (vv. 16:17); "I leave the world and go unto the Father" (v. 28). Similarly in His prayer that follows He says, "I am no more in the world . . . I go to the Father" (17:11–13).

These utterances constitute most of His references in the upper room to His death. The four other utterances present

A STRIKING CONTRAST

when put together. After Judas had gone out, Jesus said, "Now is the Son of man glorified, and God is glorified in Him." What calm and majestic dignity there is in this remark concerning the deed which the traitor was just about to perpetrate, and its effect! The Lord was viewing His death in the light of its issues. His obedience to the Father and His redemption of sinners thereby would bring undying glory to His own Name, and thus also His Father would be glorified. With the same thoughts in His mind He says, at the beginning of His prayer, "Father, the hour is come; glorify Thy Son, that the Son may glorify Thee" (17:1); and, anticipating the accomplishment of what He was about to do, "I glorified Thee on the earth, having accomplished the work which Thou hast given Me to do" (v. 4).

Now contrast this with His remarks about His great spiritual foe. Still looking on the Cross, He says, "The prince of this world cometh: and He hath nothing in Me." There was nothing in Christ that responded to the Devil's temptations or claims. Never could the evil one achieve success by His efforts against the Lord. On the other hand, there was everything in Him that responded to the Father. His very meat, the sustenance of His life, was to do the will of the Father, and so His death would yield nothing to Satan. Nay, rather, by it the world would know that He loved the Father. It is particularly His death He has in view when He says, "And as the Father gave Me commandments, even so I do." That was His heart's desire, and the thought of its accomplishment leads Him to say, "Arise, let us go hence." His heart was fixed, His step was steadfast. It was as if He was ready to go immediately through the dread sufferings that were awaiting Him. How great is the contrast between those two utterances, "Now is the Son of man glorified, and God is glorified in Him," and, "The prince of the world hath nothing in Me!" The world, which was lying under his tyrannical sway, would learn to know that, by very reason of the Devil's effort against Him, He would deliver it from his grasp, and so display His love to the Father.

"GREATER LOVE"

There is one more reference to His death in this upper room conversation, and this bears specially upon His followers, and their attitude one toward another. "This is My commandment," He says, "that ye love one another, even as I have loved you. Greater love hath no man than this, that a man lay down His life for His friends." His was the "greater love," and, in laying down His life for us as the great expression of His love, He puts before us His standard of our love one toward another. How far short have we come!

JOHN'S NARRATIVE OF THE DEATH

Two things stand out prominently in regard to John's narrative of the death of Christ. Firstly, he writes as one who was an eyewitness of all that happened. This, indeed, he himself states (19:35). There is more detail given by John than in any other Gospel. Secondly, those facts which John gives, and which are not supplied by the three Synoptists, contribute very largely to that testimony which is a characteristic feature of this Gospel, namely, that Jesus is the Son of God. For instance, it is John who mentions the reply of the Jews to Pilate, that death was the rightful penalty for Jesus, according to their law, because He made Himself the Son of God (19:4–7). In the details throughout the narrative there is a tone of dignity and exaltation consistent with His relationship to God as His Son. We notice this in His witness before Pontius Pilate, and again in such incidents of His actual crucifixion as His commendation of His mother to John (vv. 25–27); the statement that "knowing that all things were now finished, that the Scripture might be accomplished, He saith, I thirst"; His closing utterance, "It is finished"; the fact that He bowed (or reclined) His head before giving up His spirit—self-determined acts expressive of His submission to the Father's will; the fact that His legs were not broken; the flowing forth of the blood and water after the piercing of His side by the soldier, a further testimony to the supernatural character of His death, and significant of the fact that Christ by His death has become the Source not only of cleansing, but also of the impartation of life.

We may mention here, for reference, other details which are also supplied by John alone in connection with the death of Christ, namely, Pilate's "Behold the Man" (19:5); his "Behold your King" (19:14); Christ's bearing His own Cross (19:17); the part of the superscription "Jesus of Nazareth," and the fact that Pilate wrote it (19:19); the vessel of vinegar and hyssop (19:29); the quotation, "A bone of Him shall not be broken" and "They shall look on Him whom they have pierced" (19:37); the presence of Nicodemus at the burial and the part he took in it (19:39).

"THE WATER AND THE BLOOD"

The closing testimony regarding the death of Christ, *i.e*, as to the flowing of blood and water from His pierced side, is explained in the writer's first Epistle. "There are three who bear witness, the Spirit, and the water, and the blood: and the three agree in one . . . and the witness is this, that God gave unto us eternal life, and this life is in His Son" (1 John 5:8, 11, R.V.).

Putting now together the first and the last references in God's Gospel to the death of Christ, we see that each bears testimony to the means of eternal life. The first was the Lord's statement to Nicodemus that "the Son of man must be lifted up that whosoever believeth may in Him have eternal life." The last is the record by John that blood and water flowed from the Savior's side, symbolic of the cleansing and life provided for us through His death. John immediately says that the testimony of what he saw is given that we might believe (19:35). Life comes with faith, and comes by reason of His death. This is the sublime message of this great theme that runs through the fourth Gospel.

SECTION

2

THE LIFE OF CHRIST

THE CHOOSING OF DISCIPLES

Many followed Jesus, but He singled out twelve men to be His closest com-
panions. Their understanding of who He was increased gradually over time.
It is important to not only understand the attributes and qualities of our
Savior, but it is important to see the flow of His life lived out on earth, giving
us clear examples of how we too should live.

The two disciples who **"followed Jesus"** were Andrew and, no doubt, John (the writer). From the conversation that ensued (vv. 38, 39) two things arise. Firstly, just as the disciples' knowledge of Christ only gradually increased (they knew Him just as the Messiah, v. 41), so he who receives Christ by faith receives Him in the fullness of His person, but the perception of His excellences, His power and glory is gradual. Secondly, Christ's knowledge of them and His direction of their lives give intimation of His authority and headship. **"And Jesus turned, and beheld them following and saith unto them, What seek ye?"** He did not ask, "Whom seek ye?" That they were seeking Him was evident. He asked them what they sought in Him. His invitation and their acceptance, resulting in their abiding with Him for that day, must have meant a wonderful unfolding by Him of the truth relating to Him.

That third day produces three, if not four, disciples, Andrew, John, Peter, and perhaps James. Peter was not the first to become one. Cephas (v. 43) is the Aramaic name. *Petros*, Peter, denotes, not a mass of rock, but a detached stone or boulder (easily thrown or moved); in Matthew 16:18 the word *Petra*, a mass of rock, is used of Christ, figuratively of a sure foundation, not of Peter, who is spoken of as *Petros*.

On the fourth day a new circumstance arises; for the Lord Himself goes to seek a disciple. Hitherto they had come or had been brought to Him. Now **"He was minded** [or as the word *thelō* commonly means, He willed] **to go forth into Galilee."** He finds Philip, who was of the same city as Andrew and Peter and bids him follow Him. Philip finds Nathanael (a name meaning gift of God) and gives a special testimony to Christ, firstly, as the subject of the Law and the Prophets, secondly as to His coming from Nazareth, thirdly as to the belief about His being the son of Joseph.

NATHANAEL'S CONFESSION

To say the least, Galileans were the objects of contempt owing to their lack of culture, their rude dialect and their association with Gentiles. Hence Nathanael's surprised question, **"Can any good come out of Nazareth?"** Philip does not stop to argue but bids him come and see. At the interview the Lord immediately reveals His divine powers of knowledge, which at once elicits the confession, **"Rabbi, Thou art the Son of God; Thou art King of Israel."** The absence of the definite article before "King," while grammatically serving to stress His kingship, perhaps indicates Nathanael's hope of an earthly king.

The fig tree under which he was is doubtless figurative of the nation of Israel, fruitless under the old covenant, though Nathanael himself is representative of the godly remnant in the nation. In this connection the promise that he and other believers would see the **"Heaven opened, and the angels of God ascending and descending upon the Son of man,"** points to the coming day when Christ will come in His glory and manifest Himself as the King of Israel in a far higher sphere than was in the mind of Nathanael. The Lord was thinking of Millennial scenes.

THE WEDDING IN CANA

Jesus' "signs and wonders" are begun in Cana of Galilee. It was not a grand display of supernatural power, but a quiet miracle in an obscure little town. Few noticed when the water was turned into wine, but the disciples saw and their faith was established.

The **"third day"** (2:1) was the third day of His stay in Galilee, making a week altogether (1:29, 35, 43). There is much in the details of the marriage feast in Cana that is indicative of things beyond the actual circumstances. The third day is suggestive of the coming period of resurrection life and millennial glory. In a special sense in the future celebration on earth of the spiritual and heavenly marriage between Christ and His saints, the water of purification for Israel (i.e., the godly remnant of the nation) will be turned into the wine of joy. Then indeed the nation will say **"Thou hast kept the good wine until now."**

Again, the word to His mother, **"Woman what have I to do with thee? Mine hour is not yet come,"** can only be rightly understood in the way it points to His relation to Israel. His mother was the natural connection with the nation under the law. His relation with Israel will in a coming day be a matter of grace. But that could be brought about only through His sacrificial and atoning death. To that He referred when He said "Mine hour is not yet come." That "hour" would and will be the means of bringing about the new relationship of grace. Figuratively and anticipatively therefore He indicates that which will be greater and more blessed than the natural tie of kinship.

HIS SIGNS

That all this, and more, is indicated, is set forth in the statement, **"This beginning of His signs did Jesus . . . and manifested His glory"** (v. 11). The word *sēmeion* is rightly rendered "sign"; it is more than a miracle; it is a miracle with a significance. Christ's signs were (1) evidences of His combined Godhood and manhood, (2) evidences of the character of His mission, (3) symbolical of spiritual truths. Eight are recorded by John. This at Cana was the first, and being a

153

sign, its details conveyed the spiritual teachings above mentioned. In this, too, He manifested His **"glory."** The glory of the Lord is the shining forth of His character and His power, the presentation of His nature and His actings. The manifestation of His glory was at the same time the manifestation of the glory of His Father.

He graces our gatherings with His presence spiritually, not only at the marriage of two of God's children, but wherever any are gathered in His Name. He never fails to fulfill His promise to be "in the midst." His sanctifying presence imparts the utmost blessedness at every such gathering.

He gives His best to the lowly. They were a humble folk at the Cana feast. There was no outstanding display. Cana itself was an obscure village. It was in the rustic home that the Lord displayed the glory of His power. He "came to minister." He loves "to revive the spirit of the humble" (Isa. 57:15).

A FULL SUPPLY

He is ready to meet our needs. The need was great. To run short of wine, to be unable to provide adequate entertainment, was a grievous predicament. Our lives are largely made up of needs. He knows them all. They are designed to cast us upon Him. Nothing is too hard for the Lord.

He gives a full supply. **"Fill the waterpots with water." "They filled them up to the brim."** That was what He intended. There would be enough for all. If our hearts and lives are empty of self, His fullness will fill us.

He transmutes natural things, making them ministers of joy and gladness. He makes water become wine. Our daily routine of work, so often dull and even dreary in our poor estimate, our round of labor, our "common task," can all become radiant with joy and gladness if we live in the light of His countenance and enjoy true fellowship with Him.

He uses home circumstances as a means of blessing to others. The closing statement of the narrative is, **"His disciples believed on Him"** (v. 11). They were guests at the wedding. What the Lord had wrought had marked effect on them. It established their faith in Him. Thus the union of the married pair was made by Him a means of blessing to others than those of the family circle.

THE CLEANSING OF THE TEMPLE

Jesus demonstrated His power and authority in a very public way at Jerusalem during the Passover feast. The temple that had been established as a place of prayer was filled with the stench and noise of greedy merchants and money-changers. Christ's righteous indignation overflows; no one stands in His way as He casts out the sordid businessmen, cleansing the center of worship from the evidence of moral impurities.

154

This was the public display of Christ's authority and power. His glory had been exhibited privately at the marriage at Cana. Now He came forth in official manifestation to the place where God had set His Name in the nation, the place where He would dwell among them, where shone the glory of His own uncreated light. At Cana He had manifested His grace; now He was about to manifest His truth.

THE OCCASION

The occasion was **"the Passover of the Jews"** (v. 13). Three times the apostle (and he alone of the Gospel writers) designates the Passover feast thus (see 6:4 and 11:55, and cp. 5:1 and 7:2), a plain reflection upon the deplorable condition of the people and their religious rulers. What was by His own declaration "the Lord's Passover" (Exod. 12:11), had become by national departure and the desecration of the temple, "the Passover of the Jews."

Pilgrims had assembled in Jerusalem in immense numbers for their great national feast. On the eve of the occasion the head of every family had assiduously collected all the leaven in the house and given the dwelling place a general cleansing. How vastly different was the condition of God's house at this time! Again, the divinely appointed half-shekel atonement money would be paid into the temple treasury. The payment sealed to each his status as a member of the divinely chosen nation, and religious fervor reached its height. But now the offering was desecrated by the jingling of the coins of the money changer swindlers. The glory of the temple had been robbed of its spiritual significance and power. How could a man bring his lamb to God amidst the hindrances of such unholy confusion? Commerce, supported by the priests, robbed the poor of their privileges.

This kind of corruption has been reproduced in Christendom. Priestcraft, perhaps commercially the most paying concern in the world, has perverted the cause of the humble believer, by striding across the path of his free access to God through the one mediator on the ground of His expiatory sacrifice.

THE STARTLING INTERPOSITION

Now the Lord suddenly comes to His temple. He finds in the temple those that sold oxen and sheep and doves and the changers of money sitting. The place of prayer for all nations resounds with the noisy traffic of a cattle market, with all its filth and stench. The covetous hearts of the dealers in small change gloat over their ill-gotten gains. What a sickening sight for the devoted pilgrim as he entered the court of the temple! How he must have longed for the time when the promise would be fulfilled, "there shall be no more a Canaanite (a trafficker) in the House of the Lord of Host" (Zech. 14:21)! How much greater was the holy indignation of Him who thus beheld the unutterable desecration of His Father's house!

In the midst of all the desecration He appears whose "eyes are as a flame of fire," and whose heart burned with zeal for the glory of His Father's house. He makes a scourge the instrument of the exercise of His authority. Was it emblematic of a greater scourge destined to chastise rulers and people, when the Romans would destroy both temple and city? Certainly the paramount significance of this cleansing process, this divine attack upon the vested interests of the evildoers, was the vindication of the Name of God and the honors of His house, His hatred and condemnation of sin. And on this account the Lord's act was the presage and pledge of God's mercy to men in the eventual freedom of access into His presence on His conditions of grace in and through Christ. While the actual cleansing was not that of the inner sanctuary (the *naos*) but of the precincts, the outer court, yet it stood for the reconsecration of the entire building for the holy purposes designed of God.

EVIDENCE OF HIS DIVINE POWER

But there was a deeper significance in this supernatural act; for such it was. The expulsion by a single person of the hosts of avaricious traffickers and their belongings, the overthrow of the tables and scattering of their money piles, notwithstanding the fact that their sordid business had the sanction and support of those who had legal possession of the whole place, was proof of His divine power; this indeed was tacitly acknowledged by the surprised religious authorities in their question recorded in verse 18. And the deeper significance is this, that whatsoever is consecrated to God for His service is to be freed from mere worldly profit. The veneer of religion is often but a covering to hide the selfish interests of those who promote it. Personal advantage can only act as a defiling influence in any church or assembly. The sheep, the oxen and the doves were sold for sacrificial purposes, but the motive and methods of the business were an abomination in the eyes of the Lord. Mere conformity to religious rites and ceremonies may make their appeal to the natural, the religious, the sentimental mind, but human motives and ambitions are doomed to meet the exposure and judgment of Him who searches the hearts.

A church is a temple of God, the dwelling place of His Spirit (1 Cor. 3:16), and he who mars it will be marred of its owner (v. 17). "For the temple of God is holy, which temple ye are."

THE EFFECT OF THE SIGN

The temple authorities dared not question the moral rectitude of the Lord's action in cleansing it. Taken by surprise at the display of His power and authority, they decided to ask Him for a sign in confirmation thereof. For them the value of a sign would consist in its being simply indicative of the triumph and greatness of the chosen nation.

Their blindness, consequent upon their hardness of heart, is evinced in their failure to recognize that He was, by the very character of His dealings, the greatest possible sign Himself. According to their request (He absolutely refused it later when their persistent refusal to recognize His claims had reached its height,

Matt. 16:1–4), He gives them a sign, but not in accordance with their expectations: **"Destroy this temple, and in three days I will raise it up"** (*naos* is the word here, the inner sanctuary, not *hieron*, the entire building), and this was appropriate to His reference to **"the temple of His body."** And such His body was. In it shone the abiding Shekinah, the glory of the Lord. "In Him dwelleth all the fullness of the Godhead bodily."

Voluntarily He would hand over this holy temple for them to "destroy" (*luo*, to loosen, was sometimes used with reference to a structure; cp. Eph. 2:14, where it is used of the breaking down of a wall). How constantly His impending death and what it involved formed the subject of His utterances! Here also He mentions "the glory that would follow," foretelling withal His own part in His Resurrection. This, too, was a clear indication, for those to whom the fact would be revealed, of His oneness with the Father in Godhood. For in the act of His resurrection the Father and the Son were, as ever, inseparable. The Jews eagerly laid hold of what they considered a discrepancy in His utterance. Conviction, however, eventually was borne in upon them. That is recorded by Matthew (27:63).

THE EFFECT UPON THE DISCIPLES

The significance of His act of cleansing the temple was realized by the disciples immediately. They remembered that it was written, **"The zeal of Thine House shall eat Me up"** (R.V.). The significance of His reply to the Jews was realized after His resurrection. The disciples then remembered His utterance **"and they believed the Scripture, and the word which Jesus had said."** As for the people, many believed on Him, but with a shallow if sincere credence.

Here, then, we observe the contrasting effects which so constantly marked the Lord's public ministry of work and word, and still mark those of His faithful witnesses, namely, rejection and reception. If by grace we have received Him, let us on our part follow the path He trod.

There were more signs wrought by Him at that time in Jerusalem, purposively unrecorded in this Gospel, and these caused many to believe on His Name, by way of sincere conviction, a natural recognition of facts; but this did not alter their spiritual condition, and **"Jesus did not trust Himself to them."** **"He knew all men"** and **"He Himself knew what was in man."** The same emphasis "He Himself" should be expressed in both statements. The Lord knew the state and character of every man. He knew man's moral nature.

NICODEMUS

In John 3, Jesus speaks with a man who stands as an exception. Nicodemus comes to Christ with questions, and the Lord helps the man shift his perspective from natural things to spiritual ones. As they talk long into the night, Nicodemus learns about new birth and new life.

"**B**ut there was a man" who was an exception. Chapter three continues the last paragraph of chapter two by this contrast. The connecting word should be "But," not "Now," as in the R.V. (it should not be omitted as the A.V. does). "Now" suggests a completely new subject.

The contrast was twofold. Nicodemus was not a case of mere acknowledgment of the facts about Christ because of the signs He wrought. His conscience was reached; he felt his soul's need. And Christ on His part, in response to this need, opened His heart to meet it, trusting Himself in this way to His inquirer.

Nicodemus begins by expressing an assurance concerning Jesus, based upon the signs He did (v. 2). This utterance was an evidence of exercise of heart which he dared not disclose to his fellows. It is "night" with us when we fail to witness for fear of the world. The Lord goes at once to the root of the matter. He did not stop to give mere mental instruction to him. How can anyone be spiritually blessed by patching up the "old man"? The old is carnal and cannot discern spiritual things. Nicodemus doubtless thought the Lord's signs were indication of the approaching earthly kingdom. Hence the reply, **"Except a man be born anew, he cannot see the kingdom of God."** The word *anothen* may mean "from above" (R.V. margin), as in 19:11; James 1:17; 3:15, 17 (a very probable meaning here), or "again," anew, as in Galatians 4:9.

THE NATURAL AND THE SPIRITUAL

The thoughts of Nicodemus are occupied with the natural (v. 4). The Lord points to the spiritual: **"Except a man be born of water and the Spirit, he cannot enter the kingdom of God."** He first said **"cannot see,"** for Nicodemus was occupied with the visible. Now He goes deeper. Water is a means of cleansing. Cleansing is by the Word of God. "Ye are clean," says the Lord, "through the word which I have spoken unto you." Christ sanctifies the Church by cleansing it "through the washing of water by the Word." The Spirit of God applies the Word of God to the heart. There is another possible interpretation. The *kai*, "and," may mean "even," as it does sometimes. The effect of regeneration by the Holy Spirit is to produce a corresponding spiritual life. What God creates may be material; but what He begets partakes of His spiritual nature and likeness. **"That which is born of the Spirit is spirit."** The origin determines the nature. Accordingly baptism cannot produce the new birth and beget a child of God. Baptism is first a sign of death. The Lord gives the illustration of the wind (the R.V. and A.V. renderings are doubtless right).

How could **"the teacher** [the representative of such] **of Israel"** grasp **heavenly things**, if notwithstanding his reading of the prophets, he did not understand **earthly things**? Christ and those associated with Him spoke what they knew (the "we" is not the plural of majesty); they bore witness of that which they had seen— a witness rejected. The origin was heavenly. No one had ascended into heaven to receive these heavenly things and bear witness of them. The only One possible was He who **"descended out of Heaven,"** and who while still on the earth, was "**the Son of Man, which is in Heaven.**" He was the very embodiment of the heavenly and in His combined Godhood and manhood was the manifestation of the heavenly to men. Therefore to understand these things Nicodemus must be related to Christ by the new birth, and that would involve a share in the witness.

THE MEANS OF LIFE

But the Lord has a further and still more explicit word to say about the new life (imparted in the new birth), and gives "the teacher of Israel" a fact from the Old Testament (which he had often read without getting any further than the earthly circumstance), in order that he may perceive the great foundation application and realize its eternal importance: "**And as Moses lifted up the serpent in the wilderness, even so must the Son of Man be lifted up: that whosoever believeth may in Him have eternal life**" (vv. 14, 15). There is something necessary then before the new birth can take place. Truly the new birth brings life eternal, and this comes by faith. But this can be brought about only by the remission of sin. There could be no life without that. For that purpose this very person, the Son of man, whom Nicodemus had sought, "**must be lifted up.**" He must be made sin to take sin away. He must become a curse, the very antitype of the serpent in the wilderness. For this purpose He had come down from heaven. Whosoever rejected Him, for such there could be no remission of sins, no removal of the curse, no new birth, no eternal life, no entrance into the kingdom. The Son of God, the Son of man, alone knew the character and requirements of God against whom man had sinned and from whom he was alienated.

The great fact of the means for this is immediately stated in another way.[1] To accomplish this, and meet the need of the new birth for Nicodemus and for all who are brought to realize their need, "**God so loved the world, that He gave His only begotten Son, that whosoever believeth on Him should not perish, but have eternal life.**" Man's sinful condition and God's holy character and requirement, and His infinite love, all meet at the Cross.

All this goes beyond the limits of His dealing with the Jewish people: God sent His Son into the world "**not to judge the world; but that the world should be saved through Him**" (v. 17).

The purpose of Christ's coming was not to pass sentence but to bring salvation. As for the believer no sentence can be passed on him; as for the unbeliever, he stands self-condemned, for he has refused to accept the self-revelation, the Name, "**of the only begotten Son of God.**" His Name is the expression of His very person (v. 18).

---

1 The present writer regards the passage from verse 16 to verse 21 as a continuation of the Lord's discourse to Nicodemus, rather than remarks made by John the writer of this Gospel.

THE CAUSE OF REFUSAL

But it is more than a case of refusal to accept the Divine testimony; **"men loved the darkness rather than the light"**; that is to say, they hated the light; and that because their works were evil (*ponēra*, a word which combines the ideas of base and baneful; *ponēros* describes the character of Satan as "the evil one," 17:15; 1 John 2:13, 14; 3:12; 5:18, 19). **"For every one that doeth** [*prasso* means to practice, to do a thing by way of constant activity] **ill** [here the word is *phaula*, which signifies worthless things, good-for-nothing] **hateth the light, and cometh not to the light** [a hatred exhibited in a deliberate refusal to come], **lest his deeds** [his works] **should be reproved** [or rather, convicted, i.e., of being what they actually are, by being exposed in their true character and so meeting with condemnation]."

The contrary is the case with the true believer. As to the nature of his activity, he **"doeth the truth"** (the truth in its moral aspect). As to the character of his walk, he **"cometh to the light"** (he loves the presence and fellowship of Him who is the Light). As to the purpose of his coming, **"that his deeds may be made manifest** [he is attracted to that which marks the character of his doings], **that they have been wrought in God,"** that is, in fellowship with, in the presence of, and by the power of, God.

THE BAPTIST'S FURTHER TESTIMONY

John the Baptist served as Jesus' forerunner. His example guides our attitude when it comes to the Lord—satisfied to decrease so that He may increase. He lived to bring glory to Christ, pointing others to the Savior.

The next part of the chapter gives a beautiful picture of John the Baptist, by reason of his faithfulness and devotion to Christ, his delight in Christ's superiority in antecedence, in position, and in purpose, and his joy in the privilege appointed to him of being as near to Him as he was. To him Jesus was everything; His exaltation and His interests were his consuming object. When a question arose between John's disciples and a Jew about purifying, and they reported that Christ was attracting everybody, he presented with true humility and with manifest satisfaction (1) the truth as to the source of any revelation, verse 27; (2) the facts of his past witness, verse 28, and its present fulfillment, verse 29; (3) the contrast in position: he was simply a forerunner, sent before the Messiah Himself; (4) the contrast in relationship: Christ was the Bridegroom, John was but the friend of the Bridegroom, His devoted attendant and listener, (5) his joy of heart in every word spoken by the Bridegroom, verse 29; (6) the increase of the One for whose sake he testified, (7) his own decrease in the very path of his devotedness, verse 30.

In this lowliness and satisfaction John the Baptist is an example to us. The intimacy of our relationship to the Bridegroom is no doubt greater positionally than his. It should be so with us as it was with him, the only thing that should matter should be that Christ is glorified by us and in all our ways and circumstances. That Christ may be magnified in our bodies—if that dominates our desires, aims and ambitions, all will be well with us, no matter how greatly we may be despised, no matter how great may be our suffering and trial.

THE WOMAN OF SAMARIA

In Samaria, a woman beside a well is presented with a clear declaration of who Jesus is. He tells her that He has living water, and then He reveals that He is Messiah. By the end of this chapter, she calls Christ the Savior of the world.

Everything was by divine counsel and appointing, each fact the Son's fulfillment of the Father's will: the weariness, the thirst, the locality (the plot of land bought by Abraham, given by Jacob to Joseph, and Joseph's burying place, Gen. 33:19; 48:22; Josh. 24:32). Christ's ministry of grace there was a particular fulfillment of Genesis 49:22, "a fruitful bough by a well" and a branch running "over the wall," i.e., of Judaism. The side of the well, the time of day, everything was ready for the one who now becomes the object of God's grace and mercy.

THE OPENING OF THE DIALOGUE

The beginning of the flowing forth of the fountain of grace was by way of a request, **"Give Me to drink."** The blessed Savior had a spiritual thirst as well as the physical. His request had more than a natural significance. How satisfying to the spirit is the salvation of a soul!

There is no discrepancy between the statement that **"Jews have no dealings with Samaritans"** (there are no definite articles in the original) and the fact that the disciples had gone into Samaria to buy food. Even the Pharisees allowed fruit, vegetables, etc., to come from Samaria. Moreover, Galileans were less strict.

The surprise of the Samaritan woman meets with the response, **"If thou knewest the gift of God, and who it is** (not who I am) **that saith to thee, Give me to drink; thou wouldest have asked of Him, and He would have given thee living water."** This combines the glory of His Godhood with the evidences of the reality of His manhood, and the lowliness of His stoop in that respect. The combination enhances the grace by which the Lord seeks to meet her spiritual need. For the "living water" see Genesis 26:19 (R.V., margin); Leviticus 14:5 (margin); Jeremiah 2:13; 17:13; Zechariah 14:8.

DIFFERENT WATERS

Her thoughts are occupied solely with her natural circumstances and surroundings. "The natural man understandeth not the things of the Spirit." That Jacob gave the well, as she said, was a Samaritan tradition. In her opinion the well was good enough for him and his; could this tired person provide a better one? **"Art Thou greater . . . ?"** The "Thou" is very emphatic. He does not answer her question concerning comparative greatness, He develops His subject, pressing home the contrast between the natural and the spiritual, between that which provides no permanent satisfaction and that which involves the placing of the spiritual well within a person himself. **"Every one that drinketh of this water shall thirst again: but whosoever drinketh of the water that I shall give him shall never thirst, but the water that I shall give him shall become in him a well of water springing up unto eternal life."** There is a noticeable change of tense: **"every one that drinketh"** (v. 13) is in the present tense, drinketh habitually; but the verb in the original **"whosoever drinketh"** (v. 14) is in the perfect tense, "whosoever hath drunk," an act with an abiding result. The negative in **"—shall never thirst"** is very strong, and the rendering might well be *"shall certainly not thirst forever."*

This would surely take her mind off the natural. But no! Whatever it is He can provide let it provide an antidote to thirst and put an end to her daily toil and weariness, so that she does not **"come all the way hither to draw"** (R.V.).

A TURN IN THE CONVERSATION

Now begins the second stage of His dealings. He will now deal with her conscience. One word, and it leads to the tremendous disclosure that her whole life lies open to His eye. Her limited recognition, that He was a prophet, makes clear that she realized that she had come face to face with a messenger from God. Yet she shrinks from anything further along this line and turns to the subject of the right place for worship.

The Samaritans claimed that on Mount Gerizim Abraham offered up Isaac and here he met Melchizedek. The Lord speaks no more of her sinful life, but leads her thoughts again, and in another way, to the spiritual realm, taking up the question to which she had turned. This was grace indeed, and wisdom, too, for He would lead her to the realities of His own person, and it is this great revelation which brings the blessings of salvation. Sufficient had been said to bring home the sinfulness of her life. The Lord would not probe that further.

He shows that it is not a question whether Jerusalem or Gerizim is the appointed spot for worship. The Samaritans were ignorant even of the person to be worshiped. It was not so with the Jews; for **"salvation is from the Jews."** They were God's people, and salvation comes from them by reason of promises to Abraham and Isaac. True worship must accord with the nature of Him who is to be worshiped. **"God is Spirit"** and must be approached by means of that part of our being which is spirit. There are no limitations of space and locality with Him. He must be worshiped in truth, not in ignorance, superstition, and sectarianism. There must be submission of thought, feeling and desire to His will; **"spirit and truth"** present two aspects of the one fact. **"For such** [an emphatic word] **doth the Father seek to be His worshipers,"** that is to say, true worship must answer to the nature of His being. And how this is to be brought about has been made known by grace in the person and work of His Son.

It was not in any spirit of contradiction to the Lord's words **"ye know not"** (v. 22) that the woman now said **"I know."** She was thoroughly arrested in her ideas by the great truth which Christ had just uttered. She was sure that all this and more would be declared by the Messiah when He came. This instruction concerning worship would be confirmed by Him and everything else would be made clear.

THE GREAT REVELATION

Now comes the climax: For this the Lord had been preparing. It is when Christ is revealed to the needy soul that the work of grace accomplishes its end. So it had been in other ways with John the Baptist, with Nathanael and other disciples, and with Nicodemus. So it was now with the woman. **"Jesus saith unto her, I that speak unto thee am He."** There are immediate evidences that His saving work was done. The water of life had been poured into her soul. She forgot her water pot and the temporal requirements. The customary toil gave place to a quick step back to the city. She becomes a messenger to others. An invitation had not long since been given to a very different person, "Come and see." **"Come, see,"** she says, **"a man, which told me all things that ever I did. Can this be the Christ?"** (the R.V. is correct). Her heart was occupied with Him and He became her satisfying portion. She confessed Him with her mouth and thus confirmed her faith. She attracted the men of the city to Him.

SPIRITUAL HARVEST

While they **"were coming to Him"** (v. 30), the disciples, who had come upon the scene marveling, were begging Him to allay His hunger. He found His nourishment from another source. His food consisted in doing the will of Him who sent Him and accomplishing His work. They were occupied with mundane matters. Firstly, they wondered whether, while they had come with food which they had gone to Samaria to buy, someone else had supplied Him. Secondly, they were discussing the time of the year and the prospect of harvest. They must wait four months before bread became cheaper (perhaps they had paid a good price for what they had brought from the city).

But there was reaping to be done that day, for the spiritual fields were **"white unto harvest."** There were wages for laborers and **"fruit unto life eternal."** Those who had prepared by sowing and those who enjoyed the counterpart by reaping could **"rejoice together."** The Baptist had sown, Christ had sown, and now the woman had sown. The disciples could join in the reaping. That was better than buying food. It is one thing to trade with folks, and quite proper withal, but another thing to win their souls to Christ.

The woman's testimony produced abundant fruit. Many believed on Christ (there must have been a large crowd from the city). They asked Him to go back with them and stay, and He stayed two days. More reaping was done. Many more believed, rejoicing in having the witness of the woman confirmed by hearing Him themselves, and acknowledging Him as, more than the Messiah, **"the Savior of the world"** (v. 42).

THE SECOND SIGN

When Jesus returns to Galilee, He is approached by a Roman officer whose son is ill. The Lord refuses to accompany the man to his home but accepts his faith. "Go thy way, thy son liveth." In the healing of the nobleman's son, we discover the power of Jesus' words. He needed only to speak, and the boy was healed.

After the two days He goes to Galilee, where the people received Him because they had seen the things He did in Jerusalem. It did not mean that they honored Him. He knew they would not (v. 44), but He did not go there to get that, He went to bear witness. And He bore witness by another sign.

The "second sign" which Christ did in Galilee, the healing of the "nobleman's" son, has at least this significance, that it marks a striking difference between the ground upon which faith was now exercised and that which created faith in the heart of the Samaritan woman and her fellow townsfolk. This nobleman (or rather, king's officer, R.V., margin, an official under Herod Antipas, a tetrarch who held his father's title of king) urged Him to come and heal his dying son. His faith rested upon the signs and wonders wrought by Christ, news of which had reached him from Judaea (v. 47). That this was so is clear from the Lord's remonstrance, **"Except ye see signs and wonders ye will not believe."** A faith based on miracles was not of such value as that manifested by the woman, which was the result, not of news of His wonder workings in Judaea, but of His own testimony and teaching. She and the other Samaritans believed because of the truth He spoke; the officer rested his hopes upon Christ's miraculous acts. The Lord would not reject his faith, but He found less pleasure in that which rested on His power to deliver from calamity than in that which rested in His own person, and was established by His character and teaching.

Christ did not go to the sickbed to accomplish the healing and receive acknowledgment as acting in the capacity of a healer. He simply said, **"Go thy way, thy son liveth,"** and the man departed believing.

The different words used to describe the sick lad are characteristic: the father speaks of him as his *paidion* (v. 49), a term of endearment; the servants use the word *pais*, a boy, a term of ordinary familiarity (v. 51); the Lord and the writer John call him *huios*, "son," a term of dignity.

THE CHIEF FACTOR

The important point in the discovery that the healing was coincidental with the Lord's utterance, is the power of His word. That which caused the man and his household to believe was not so much the fact of the supernatural deed, but the personal word of the Lord. The person Himself is ever greater than the deeds wrought by Him.

The two signs wrought in Galilee represent the twofold way in which the Lord manifested His delivering power and grace when on earth, and will yet manifest them in the restoration of His earthly people. The one was by intervention in circumstances of difficulty, the other by healing. The Jews will yet find in Him the One who can remove their natural difficulties and can give them spiritual recovery.

THE HEALING OF THE IMPOTENT MAN

In healing the man beside the pool of Bethesda, Christ invites the invalid to demonstrate his faith. The miracle causes amazement and scandal, for Jesus commanded the man to bear a burden on the Sabbath. In the dialogue that follows, Christ is established as Lord, even of the Sabbath.

The occasion the Lord chose for this sign was **"a feast of the Jews."** Various suggestions have been made as to which feast it was. It could scarcely have been that of Purim, as there was no Sabbath connected with that feast. That of Pentecost, "the feast of weeks" (Deut. 16:10–16), seems not unlikely, especially if the Lord used in turn the three greatest feasts in the year for the fulfillment of the witness which Moses bore to Him. The first was the Passover (2:13); the third was the Feast of Tabernacles (7:2).

The apostle John, however, does not specify the time, simply mentioning it as "a feast of the Jews," their religious functions being observed with punctilious exactitude, as if all was right with God. Yet their ways were not His ways, nor their thoughts His thoughts.

"THE GLORY THAT EXCELLETH"

Perhaps they considered that the miraculous powers of the pool of Bethesda in their city were a token of their enjoyment of the divine favor. Thither accordingly the Lord goes to give a sign that a different kind of healing was necessary for "the daughter of Zion" from that which the Bethesda waters indicated. The pool is to be disregarded. The healer Himself was in their midst. Their sabbath-keeping would avail nothing for their salvation. As has been well said, "The poverty of the pool is exposed. It is seen to be nothing but a beggarly element. It has no glory by reason of the glory that excelleth . . . Jesus is there standing . . . in contrast with all that system of ordinances and observances which had gone before, and He exposes them in all their impotency and poverty."

There among the multitude of the diseased and infirm in the five porches or colonnades, He singles out the man who shall be both the object of His compassion and the means of His witness. He is touched with the feeling of his infirmity. He knew all about his past and his constant disappointments. There is no entreaty on the man's part. Christ takes the initiative. He asks him **"Wouldst thou be made whole?"** He knew what the answer would be, knew that the invalid's thoughts would still be concentrated on the pool. It is futile expectancy that looks for other resources than the Lord.

FAITH EXPRESSED IN ACTION

Most frequently Christ made some remark concerning the requisite of faith. In this case He immediately bids him **"Arise, take up thy bed, and walk."** Faith was indeed necessary, and faith was there. The word was with power, power to heal, power likewise to elicit the obedience of faith. **"And straightway the man was made whole, and took up his bed and walked."** Here was faith without wavering, faith that turned from the pool to the person.

The carrying of his mat was a testimony to his miraculous restoration. More than this, it declared the boldness of a faith that ignored the startling spectacle of a Jew carrying a "burden" on a Sabbath! It bore eloquent testimony to his sense of indebtedness to his healer.

THE LORD OF THE SABBATH

The Sabbath day! The Jews at once seized upon the breach of the Law. It was enough for him that His healer had bidden him carry his mat. The healer was in his eyes greater than the law of the sabbath, and the healer Himself testified on another occasion that He, the Son of man, was "Lord of the Sabbath," a repudiation of the punctilious observances of their traditional exactitudes, regarding the letter of the law to the neglect of the spirit of it (Matt. 12:8). They do not ask the man as to who cured him, but as to who told him to break the Sabbath.

That this miracle was wrought on a Sabbath day roused the fierce hostility of the Jews. They were "up in arms to defend their favorite piece of legalism." **"For this cause did the Jews persecute** [imperfect tense, continued to persecute] **Jesus, because He did these things on the sabbath."** Their religious zeal utterly outweighed any consideration of the marvelous deliverance granted to the cripple and his joy and comfort in his healing. Religion is the greatest persecuting force in the world. From the days of Cain onward it is in religion that the innate enmity of the natural mind toward God is particularly manifested, and as each sign disclosed something of what God is in the person of His Son there was a rising tide of opposition to the One thus revealed and the great incomprehensible depths of mercy and grace of God.

CHRIST'S REPLY TO HIS PERSECUTORS

With sublime dignity and calm the Lord, in response to their antagonism, begins to disclose His great prerogatives as the Son of God, His perfect oneness with the Father, the love of the Father for Him, the uninterrupted communion existing between them, and His entire and delighted submission to the Father's will.

He here makes no comment on the sabbath law, as on other occasions. He had something more important to deal with, and His testimony constitutes an essential feature of the fabric of this Gospel. **"My Father,"** He says, **"worketh even until now, and I work"** (v. 17). This reveals the character of the sign just accomplished. It was one instance of the co-work of the Father and the Son. That God should break the sabbath law was impossible. In censuring the Son they were censuring the Father. The work of the Son was as indispensable as that of the Father, and was the Father's work. The declaration exposed at once the untenable character of their position.

LAW AND GRACE

But more than the one incident was involved. The co-work was "even until now." God could not find rest where sin existed, save by the atoning sacrifice of His Son. Had it not been so the race must have perished entirely. Ever since sin entered, God had anticipatively wrought in grace. Of this the miracle of healing just wrought was an instance. So the work of the Son was the work of the Father with Him. The obligation regarding the Sabbath under the law did not nullify the actings of grace. Nay, the law, by its inability to justify men and give them true rest, served to enhance the power of grace. The Jews' method of keeping the Sabbath must be exposed and set aside, to reveal the mercy of God in Christ and the true nature of the mercy in the joint operation of the Father and the Son.

The claim made in His statement is at once clear to them. It intensifies their antagonism. They cannot deny the miracle. Ignoring its significance, they resort to the additional charge of blasphemy and endeavor to act accordingly. **"For this cause the Jews sought the more to kill Him, because He not only brake the sabbath, but also called God His own Father, making Himself equal with God."**

THE FIVE THOUSAND

The Lord meets the needs of those who depend upon Him, often in miraculous ways. In John 6, Jesus shows that He is the Bread of Life and the God Who Provides. Thousands are fed and taught and continue to follow their compassionate Savior. What Christ demonstrated in the feeding of the five thousand, He confirms in the calming of the storm. The Creator of the bread is also the Creator of the waters; in His presence, we find both provision and protection.

In [John] chapter six [the Lord] is seen as the supporter of life, and that by reason of His relation to the believer. In this chapter there is again, as in chapter five, first a sign, or miracle, and then a discourse arising from it, but now the results of the discourse are narrated. In addition to the sign given in public, that of the feeding of the five thousand, there is a sign privately to the disciples, that of His walking on the water.

Now it seems evident from verse 1 that the Lord had gone away to get rest and quiet, and to pray. When, however, He saw the multitude toiling up the hill, whither He had gone with His disciples, His heart, instead of being disturbed by the interruption, was moved with compassion. He had known everything beforehand and His many signs were wrought so as to lead up to this great act with all its spiritual significance.

DEPENDENCE ON CHRIST

But the Lord had His eye on the disciples, and especially now upon Philip. So He asks him, **"Whence are we to buy loaves that these may eat?"** the object being to test his faith and turn his mind from mere material resources to Himself as the great personal means of meeting every need, and so lead him to be occupied more with Himself, His power and grace, than with circumstances. That is just what we all need. The heart must realize its dependence upon Christ Himself and be occupied with Him more than with difficulties and exigencies. He desired to make Philip and his fellow disciples grasp the fact that, though they had neither loaves nor money adequate for the occasion, they had the Lord Himself.

Philip remarked that even about a year's wages[1] would not buy enough loaves for all that multitude. Andrew, like Philip, is occupied with material things and their insufficiency. How meager are such thoughts! And what a majestic contrast is presented by the Lord as He says, **"Make the people sit down"** (v. 10)! The word *anthrōpous* is rightly rendered "people," for it includes both sexes, whereas in the latter part of the verse the word is *andres*, men. That was His one preparation for the manifestation of His powers of godhood, and of His grace and mercy.

DIVINE ECONOMY

As the people, now in orderly groups, witnessed how He gave thanks and how their need was more than supplied, they were preparing to make Him their messianic king, regarding Him as the promised prophet, foretold in Deuteronomy 18:15. There was one thing that must have impressed the disciples especially, if not the people themselves, in that, while He could minister bountifully, it was not a case of mere lavishness, this was economy: nor a case of mere wonder-work, every detail had divine significance. The fragments must be gathered up "that

---

1 Publisher's note: The original says, "£8."

nothing be lost." What need was there for this, considering that the Lord could multiply food at His will? There was the lesson to be learnt, that there must be no waste. No idea must be entertained that, considering what was possible as to further acts of bounty, there must be no disregard for what might naturally be considered as superfluous. For everything had a significance; no act was without its meaning. The provision of such supplies of bread was introductory to spiritual teaching of the utmost importance concerning the Bread of Life.

In this connection John purposely omits reference to the fragments of fish (whereas Mark mentions them, Mark 6:43), for the spiritual application to follow is a matter of that life of the nourishment of which the bread was symbolical.

THE HIGH PRIEST OF HIS DISCIPLES

And now the great provider has to withdraw from all this popular excitement regarding Him. Instead of becoming the people's king, and that in a way contrary to the Father's will and to Scripture testimony, He takes a position which sets Him forth as the high priest of His people. He goes up into the mountain, from whence He can consider the needs of His followers, pray for them, and come to their assistance in a time of danger (v. 15).

Evening had come on; it had become dark; the disciples had entered a boat and were well on their way across the sea to go to Capernaum.

THE PURPOSE OF THE STORM

So now, having become the object of their faith in the matter of providing food, He makes Himself the object of their faith amidst peril. The creator of bread was likewise the creator of the waters, and whether they were too tempestuous or calm His power was to be in evidence in each respect. The trust of His followers must be amplified.

He stills their fears with His **"It is I; be not afraid,"** and stills the storm. His will to pass them by (Mark 6:8), to deepen their confidence in Him, issues in their will to receive Him into their boat. **"They were willing"** to do so (R.V.). But there is an additional act in the sign given to them. The boat immediately arrives at its destination. Distance is nullified by His powers. His presence is both protection and deliverance. So He bringeth them at once "to their desired haven."

There follows the incident of the efforts of the multitude to seek for Jesus. They had remained in the locality where the Lord had provided the bread, and next day, finding that He and the disciples had gone, the people took boats and came to Capernaum, astonished to find that He was there already. All this, and their question as to when He came across, is both the sequel to what had taken place on the mountain slope, and introductory to His discourse concerning Himself as the means of life.

CHRIST AND THE TWELVE

Thousands of people followed Jesus in order to hear His teachings and see His miraculous works. From among them, Jesus chooses the Twelve. We see that they stay with Christ throughout His earthly ministry—yes, many listen to Jesus, but few follow Him.

In [John 6] verses 67 to 71 there is a distinction between the Twelve and those disciples who ceased to walk with Christ. This is the first mention of the Twelve as such. Here Peter's fidelity becomes conspicuous. When the Lord says "Would ye also go away?" (not "will ye?" as if a future possibility), He means "Surely ye also do not desire to go." He knew their loyalty. The whole passage marks His omniscience.

Peter's answer has three reasons why they cannot leave Him, and these in designed order: (1) His uniqueness as the master, (2) His fullness as the teacher, (3) His divine personality: (1) **"to whom shall we go?"** (no teacher remained since the Baptist had gone); (2) **"Thou hast (the) words of eternal life";** He is sufficient to meet all need; (3) **"And we have believed and know** [have come to know, *ginōskō*] **that Thou art the Holy One of God";** He fulfilled His messiahship completely. Christ's answer is to them all (v. 70): **"Did not I choose you, the twelve?"** Both pronouns are emphatic. The question mark should come here. He then reveals His divine knowledge of the character and course of Judas, by which he identified himself with the arch-spiritual foe. The apostle adds a striking confirmatory testimony, marking him as **"one of the twelve."**

THE WOMAN TAKEN IN ADULTERY

In John 8, the scribes and the Pharisees concoct a devious plan to trap Jesus. A woman caught in the very act of adultery is brought before Him, and they put Him on the spot. According to Moses, she should die. If He condemns her, there is a lack of grace. If He lets her go, He fails to uphold the Law.

As to the narrative concerning the woman brought by the scribes and Pharisees to the Lord because of adultery, whatever may be said about the MSS. and versions, the narrative bears its own witness to the likelihood of the facts. The criticisms against its validity are plainly futile. The enemies of the Lord were not bringing her before Him as a judge to try a case involving the presence of witnesses; their appeal was to one regarded as a prophet, who should know the mind of God and speak accordingly. They were filled with madness against Him. They had just failed to have Him seized openly (7:32–40). They therefore contrived an ingenious plan by which He either would, by condemning the woman, give evidence of lack of grace and failure to act as a Savior the "Friend of publicans and sinners," and thus bring condemnation upon Himself in this respect, or, by letting her go, fail to uphold the Law. The people must choose Moses or Him, and they would cling to Moses. If His foes entangled Him they could have a pretext for bringing Him before the Sanhedrin.

They little knew that they were dealing with One who Himself searches the heart, and who knew the secret history of their own lives. The Lord makes no oral answer at first, thereby the more forcibly to bring them to commit themselves. They could not have considered Him embarrassed; at first they gave the appearance of misunderstanding Him, and kept plying their question. Can they have discerned what He wrote on the ground? If so they must have hardened their hearts against His testimony.

A TEACHER, NOT A JUDGE

He lifts Himself up (not standing erect) therefore and addresses them. He does not nullify the edict of the Law of Moses; let it be obeyed, but those who execute it must have unstained hands and pure hearts. **"He that is without sin among you, let him first cast a stone at her."** This is the voice of a teacher, not a judge. Moreover a judge has to deal with the accused, not with the executioner. This teacher deals with the accusers. He finds them out, and uses the Law to do it. And as for the manifestation of grace, about which they sought to expose Him, they were the very ones who needed it.

Again He stoops down and writes on the dust of the floor, the very dust being a veritable suggestion of their physical doom. Conviction is designed to lead to repentance. But their hearts know nothing of this. They flee from the light, it is too much for them. "The wicked shall be silenced in darkness." The elder ones go out first, they would be the older in sin; the younger follow. The Lord is left alone and the woman by Him where they had brought her. He says to her, **"Woman where are they? did no man condemn thee? And she said, No man, Lord."** And Jesus said, **"Neither do I condemn thee: go thy way; from henceforth sin no more."**

Here then was a notable example of His fullness of *"grace and truth"*; *truth* in that instead of counteracting the Law He maintained it: *grace* in that in the rights of His own prerogative He did not condemn the woman but bade her sin no more.

THE LIGHT OF THE WORLD

Clearly, then, this passage is seen to be an integral part of this Gospel. It is essentially connected both with what precedes and with what follows. As to the former, it was the Pharisees who had failed in their open attack upon Him (7:44–49), and it was the Pharisees who, changing their tactics, adopted the subtle method of attack. They failed again, and that because His holy light had shone into their seared consciences, and into the woman's soul. In contrast therefore to the darkness of His foes, who were under the Law, and breakers of it, He immediately says to the people, **"I am the light of the world: he that**

followeth Me shall not walk in the darkness, but shall have the light of life"
(8:12). This constituted a direct claim to be the Messiah.

BLIND FROM BIRTH

In John 9, Jesus spits upon the ground and daubs mud on the eyes of a man who was blind from birth. In His act of compassion, the Lord conveys a lesson about the reason for his lifelong affliction—"that the works of God should be made manifest in him." Obedience to Christ's call to come for cleansing, life, and light, leads to personal acquaintance and relationship with Him. After healing the man, Jesus later seeks him out and speaks with him, revealing Himself as the Lord and inviting him to have faith.

The opening words of chapter nine show that the healing of the man who had been blind from his birth took place immediately after the Lord's controversy with the Jews in the temple, as recorded in the preceding chapter, and therefore at the close of the Feast of the Tabernacles. His opponents had been just about to stone Him. But He **"hid Himself, and went out of the Temple."** This was a judicial blindness inflicted upon them, and indicative of their spiritual blindness, which refused to recognize His claims and the evidences He gave of their validity.

VERSES 1 TO 41

He had claimed to be the Light of the World (8:12). They had refused this testimony, and accordingly the Lord, seeing a blind man as He passed by, decided to use his case both as illustrative of the condition of the Jews and as a means of vindicating His claim. This would confirm the faith of the many who had believed and might be the means of carrying home the truth to the heart of skeptics.

A Curious Question and Its Answer

Previous to the act of healing, the disciples asked Him who had sinned, as the cause of his blindness. Repudiating the thought that the man's condition was the outcome of some special sin, the Lord reveals the divine purpose of it all, namely, **"that the works of God should be made manifest in him."**

There is a lesson for us in this. There may be a lurking tendency to seek to find some reprehensible cause for another person's suffering, to say nothing of the possibility of a natural feeling of self-satisfaction with the case. The Lord's reply is a rebuke to all that kind of thing, and points the way to finding a means of dealing effectually with sorrow and misery.

The Time Appointed for Service

There is something suggestive in this connection in the Lord's remark, as rendered in the R.V., **"We must work the works of Him that sent Me."** The most authentic texts have the plural of the pronoun (not infrequently the more difficult reading has the better MS. evidence). While He here refrains from identifying His disciples with His mission from the Father, He does associate them (and ourselves too) with Himself in fulfilling the works of God. He was sent by the Father, but He himself sent His disciples (20:21). There lay the distinction.

The work must be done **"while it is day,"** not merely the natural period as distinct from the night, but the period of opportunity afforded during the lifetime. The Lord applies this to Himself in regard to His life here in the days of His flesh, and connects it with the immediate act He was about to perform, in relation to the great subject of His testimony to Himself as the Light: **"When** [different from "while" or "so long as," as in v. 4] **I am in the world, I am the light of the world."** The absence of the emphatic personal pronoun in the original stresses the fact and effects of His presence in the world rather than His person.

Significance of the Lord's Acts

The facts that the Lord, instead of restoring the man's sight by a word, spat on the ground, and made clay of the spittle, and anointed the man's eyes with the clay, telling him to go and wash in the Pool of Siloam, have a special significance. Doubtless all would help the man's faith. At the same time the process adopted by the Lord suggests the character of the spiritual condition of the Jews, to whom light must come by a process, granted that they were willing even yet to receive His testimony. The man must needs grope his way to get to the pool, a circumstance illustrative of the darkness that blinded the eyes of the Jews. Moreover, that the meaning of the name Siloam (sent) is given in the Gospel narrative, is undoubtedly purposive. The meaning is evidently to be connected with Christ's valid claim to be the sent one.

Again, as to the man himself, the method the Lord chose to use must have brought home to his heart his need of cleansing, as he went on his way to the water. Here then were the great requisites for salvation, a Savior to save, the realization of need, and the obedience of faith. The sequel introduces us to the next great controversy between Christ and the Pharisees. The Lord had given a practical demonstration of His power to heal, and with it a vivid parable of His power to give the light of life to men, as well as a testimony to His authority as Lord of the Sabbath.

The Controversy

The curiosity, not to say perplexity, of the neighbors is aroused. Their question is twofold. How was the healing done? and where was the healer? The man can answer the first but not the second. So now he is brought to the Pharisees. The consequent discussion is full of interest. They first affirm that a sabbath-breaker cannot be from God. Some of them argue, however, that the accomplishment of such signs was impossible on the part of a sinner. Hence a division among them. And this is by no means unique. The person and work of Christ have constantly been matters of controversy and of divided opinions. Happy are those who have the confidence of faith and the experience of Christ's power to deliver, and are able to bear such a courageous testimony as was given by this subject of the Lord's healing mercy.

The man's parents did not share that courage, fearing excommunication by their religious leaders. Their son shall answer for himself. So the man is called again, and receives a command and a confident statement about his healer: **"Give glory to God. We know that this man is a sinner."** The man knew better than to give glory to God by agreeing to this. Regardless of scorn, and altogether independent of the opinions of his examiners, he meets their bullyings with trenchant argument and even sarcasm. The facts of his healing were incontrovertible. How futile and foolish to deny them! Yet the only answer of these "blind leaders of the blind" was to denounce him as **"altogether born in sins"** (as if forsooth their own state was quite otherwise), and scornfully to repudiate the very idea of his teaching them. Accordingly they excommunicate him from all attendance in the temple and synagogues, and from participation in all religious privileges.

The Spiritual Healing and Its Lesson

The Lord makes a special point of finding him after this, so as to reveal to him more fully who He Himself was. He would more than make up to him for what he had lost. To know Him is life eternal, and to enjoy the secret of His friendship outweighs everything else that the natural mind deems valuable.

This spiritual opening of his eyes made him at once a worshiper, and upon this the Lord issues a declaration in the very hearing of the Pharisees who were present, which introduces the discourse recorded in chapter ten. **"For judgment,"** He says, **"came I into this world, that they which see not may see; and that they which see may become blind"** (v. 39). These are the two companies formed by contact with Christ, the seeing and the blind. Christ is the great divider as well as the great uniter. This is the twofold effect of testimony concerning Him. The self-satisfied, whether religious or otherwise, confident in their complacent imaginings that they have true sight, remain in their blindness; the humble souls who realize their actual spiritual condition and, exercising their simple faith, become His followers, have their eyes opened.

Four Lessons

Obedience to Christ's call to come for cleansing, life and light, leads to personal acquaintance and relationship with Him. Refusal to accept the call means death and darkness. That is the first great lesson of the miracle. Mere religion and the traditions of men blind their adherents to true spiritual conception. Mere ritualistic ordinances are as futile as the clay on the blind man's eyes would have been if he had never washed. That is the next great lesson. Thirdly, we cannot but marvel at the gracious desire and loving care shown by the Lord to beget faith in the heart. His patience, forbearance and longsuffering render the state of the impenitent all the more terrible. Fourthly, the design of the grace that enlightens the soul is to make the recipient a simple but effective witness to Christ. Such a one finds no place or time for discussions with rationalistic quibblers. He has no place for the wisdom of words as a means of dealing with skeptics. Christ is made to him "wisdom from God, and righteousness and sanctification and redemption."

THE RAISING OF LAZARUS

The raising of Lazarus is the pinnacle of the signs that are recorded in the Gospel of John, standing as a final testimony to Jesus' deity as the Son of God. This narrative shows both Jesus' tender compassion and His almighty power, evidences of His godhood and manhood.

FAITH'S TESTING

This crown of His miracles was both a witness to His critics and a means of establishing the faith of His followers. True faith is tested faith. Hearing that Lazarus was sick, Jesus **"abode at that time two days in the place where he was"** (R.V.). The Lord's testings are always proofs of His love. **"Jesus loved Martha, and her sister, and Lazarus . . . Therefore He abode . . . where He was."** But beyond His love for them He honored them by putting them in the furnace of affliction for the completion of His final witness to the people.

The case with His disciples was different. Upon His decision to go, they would have stayed Him so as to deliver Him from danger. The Lord uses their devoted representations to give them a lesson concerning the highest motive of service. To be faithful to God is to walk in the light. To be governed by mere expediency is to walk in the darkness and to stumble.

THE HIGHEST MOTIVE

But everything must be the outcome of faith and, as with the sisters, that was the immediate need of the disciples. So, after an explanation of the actual meaning of His statement, **"Our friend Lazarus is fallen asleep,"** He says, **"I am glad for your sakes that I was not there, to the intent ye may believe."** Thomas was anxious to believe. His, **"Let us also go, that we may die with Him,"** evoked by Christ's decision to go, was not a case of melancholy foreboding, but of downright and cheerful loyalty. Jesus was more to him than life itself. What a lesson for us! Activity in His cause is valueless if it is not subordinated to love for Christ Himself. Let the preciousness of His person ever be the dominating motive of our service for Him.

"Jesus Wept"

This intense attachment to Him is touchingly evinced in both Martha and Mary. The one goes to meet Him, the other stays to receive Him. Martha's attitude is that of reverent confidence and entire submission. She combines the recognition of His power with that of His love: **"And even now I know that whatsoever Thou wilt ask of God, God will give it Thee."** His question, **"Where have ye laid him?"** betokened, not a lack of knowledge, but a kindly design to kindle their expectations. **"They say unto Him, Lord, come and see"**—a combination of expectancy and earnest desire, but withal a natural ignorance of the actual power possessed by Him. **"Jesus wept."** There was more than the sight of human sorrow in this, more even than sympathy with the sorrowing. Sympathy there was indeed. He knew the feelings and emotions of every heart in the company, but He knew more than this. He knew all the circumstances of fallen humanity that brought about death and all its woe. The sin and ignorance of all were laid open to His infinite mind. The touching detail, so briefly told, discloses His combined deity and humanity.

The Jews regarded His tears merely as the evidence of His love for Lazarus. Others were skeptical. One who had given sight to a man born blind could surely have prevented Lazarus from death. Since He let him die, how could He really love him so much? **"Jesus therefore again groaning in Himself** [a preferable rendering to the R.V. margin] **cometh to the tomb."**

"The Glory of God"

His command to take away the stone would have two different effects. It would encourage faith, for it was clear that something was about to be done. At the same time, to touch a grave would be running the risk of defilement, so faith might be tested. Yet the act of obedience indicated that He had drawn them into harmony with His will.

Martha's shrinking from the effects draws forth His gentle rebuke to her unbelief: **"Said I not unto thee that, if thou believedst, thou shouldst see the glory of God?"** This gathers up what He had said in the course of His conversation, concerning the glory of God (v. 4) and of the assurance of resurrection (vv. 25, 26). To know that they were going to see the act which would exhibit the glory of God, must have banished all misgivings.

The stone having been removed, the Lord lifts up His eyes and says, **"Father, I thank Thee that Thou hast heard Me, and I** [with special stress on the pronoun] **knew that Thou hearest Me always; but because of the multitude which standeth around I said it, that they may believe that Thou** [with stress also] **didst send Me."** By this the Lord intended that all around should know that what He was about to do was combined work of the Father and Himself, and that the impending event was of such importance, that it would finally substantiate His claims for the acceptance of faith. He had never preceded a miracle by any such utterance.

THE GREATEST OF HIS SIGNS

And now the mighty deed is done. He cries with a loud voice, **"Lazarus, come forth."** The spirit returns to the body. The resurrected brother comes forth, the gravecloths still around him. This and the command to loose him were designed to give directions and force to the testimony. That he was still bound with the cloths was convincing proof to any skeptical and hostile Jews that he had actually been dead. He is to be "let go," suggesting his retirement from immediate and idle curiosity.

The miracle foreshadowed the death and resurrection of Christ, which would effect both the present spiritual resurrection of believers with their loosening from the binding power of sin, and their coming physical resurrection, when with His mighty shout He brings all together to meet Him in the air.

But the immediate effect was decisive. It was the crisis which finally gave rise to the greatest crime in the nation's history. Many of the Jews believed on Him. But some went their way to report it all to the Pharisees. Thus did Christ become, as He has ever been, the dividing line among men.

JESUS WASHES THE DISCIPLES' FEET

During the Last Supper Jesus takes on the role of a servant and washes the feet of His disciples. The basin and the towel offer an object lesson, teaching the need for cleansing from sin and for humility in service. Once the physical washing was done, another kind of purification took place. The spiritual atmosphere had to be cleansed before the Lord's Supper could be instituted. Judas was sent out, and Jesus prepared the eleven for the ministry for which they were to be sent into the world.

[Jesus'] thoughts center, not in His impending sufferings, but in the Father and "His own." This latter phrase refers to different objects from "His own" in 1:11; there it spoke of His natural property and kin, here it speaks of those who were the Father's spiritual gift to Him. The great key word here is "love."

As to the immediate circumstances, the A.V., "supper being ended" does not represent the original. There are only two possible renderings, either "when supper was come" or "when supper was taking place." The R.V. **"during supper,"** is probably right. The indication is that it was the early part of the meal. The opening words of the chapter point to the supper as being that of the paschal feast. The scene is full of preparations. The Lord, who knew all that was coming upon Him, and who had, only a day or two before, told the disciples that in this Passover period He would be delivered up to be crucified (Matt. 26:1), had prepared all the arrangements for this Upper Room occasion. Satan had been preparing. He had already put it into the heart of Judas Iscariot to betray Him. Other human agents of the evil one were busy making preparations, and holding a council of death.

"JESUS, KNOWING"

What is said about the devil and Judas is followed by a statement for the second time as to the Lord's knowledge, and the two very different subjects are combined as an introduction to the washing of the disciples' feet; **"Jesus, knowing that the Father had given all things into His hands, and that He came forth from God, and goeth unto God, riseth from supper, and layeth aside His garments; and He took a towel, and girded Himself."** This was another preparation, a preparation, first by act and then by teaching, for the life the Eleven were to live after He had gone, and the testimony they were to give in their service after the coming of the Holy Spirit at Pentecost. Hence the three statements as to the Lord's knowledge.

The vivid present tense is used, almost entirely, to depict the circumstances. Every act had its special significance. His laying aside His garments spoke of the fact that He who ever was "in the form of God" took "the form of a servant" (Phil. 2:6, 7). It does not seem to have entered the minds of the disciples that they might wash one another's feet. Indeed they do not appear to have been in a mood for it (see Luke 22:24). If, as Edersheim thinks, Judas, as the manager for the company, took the first place, the Lord may have washed his feet first. In any case here was malice met with kindness. Here was long-suffering manifested with grace and dignity. It has been well remarked, "Jesus at the feet of the traitor—what a picture! What lessons for us!"

CLEANSED TO RENDER SERVICE

The feet-washing was designed to teach two distinct things in the Christian life, first the need of cleansing from sin, second the need of serving one another with humility. The first is brought out by Peter's exclamatory question, **"Lord, dost Thou wash my feet?"** by his impetuous remonstrance, **"Thou shalt never wash my feet"**; and (on hearing that without this he can have no part with Him) by his impulsive desire, **"Lord, not my feet only, but also my hands and my head."**

In answer to the question, the Lord says, **"What I do thou knowest not now; but thou shalt understand hereafter."** The "I" and the "thou" are emphatic. The R.V. brings out the distinction between the verbs, *oida*, to perceive intuitively, and *ginōskō*, to understand by learning. In the reply to the remonstrance the Lord reveals the deep significance of the washing. To have no part with Him means the lack of more than the external washing of the feet. The answer to the impulsive desire makes clear the difference between the initial removal of the defilement of sin at the time of the new birth, and the need of renewed cleansing consequent upon the committal of an act.

The Lord immediately distinguishes between the condition of the Eleven, who had all been bathed and were thus **"clean every whit,"** and the one who, because his heart was defiled, had not been bathed. So, knowing who would betray Him, He said **"Ye are not all clean"** (v. 11). After resuming His place at the table He gives the second explanation of His act. **"Ye call Me,"** He says, **"Master** [teacher, a term of respect and recognition of instruction] **and Lord** [a term of honor and recognition of authority]." If He, with all that these titles meant, did what He had now done, there rests upon them, as upon us all, a sacred obligation, consequent both upon His example and upon the claims of nature common to all **("one another")**.

TRUE BLESSEDNESS

The apostle Peter recalls this scene, when he says, "Yea, all of you, gird yourselves with humility to serve one another" (1 Pet. 5:5). It speaks of freedom from high-mindedness, of self-forgetting love, of submitting to one another in the fear of God, of putting on "a heart of compassion, kindness, humbleness of mind, meekness, long-suffering." For a servant is not greater than his lord, nor one that is sent greater than he that sent him. **"If ye know these things,"** He says (and they did, and we do), **"blessed are ye** [a better rendering than "happy," as it conveys not mere joy but the sense of divine favor that carries its reward] **if ye do them."**

THE DISCLOSURES OF THE BETRAYAL

It cost the Lord much to make the disclosure as to who would be the instrument of His betrayal: **"He was troubled in spirit** [in 11:33, in seeing the sorrows of others, "He troubled Himself"], **and testified, and said, Verily, verily, I say unto you, that one of you shall betray Me."** The statement evinces His sorrow more than the guilt of the act. More than this, it shows the voluntary nature of His suffering. He could have suggested a way of escape, or some mode of prevention or resistance; but there is nothing of all this. It was part of the predetermined path toward the accomplishment of that for which He came into the world.

The disciples are stirred to sorrowful and bewildered anxiety (an emotion absent from Judas) as to which of them would be the cause. Peter makes a sign to John (who was leaning on the bosom of the Lord) to find out, and says **"Tell us who it is of whom He speaketh."** So John, **"leaning back** [a different word from that in v. 23, "reclining"], **as he was on Jesus' breast** [the R.V. "as he was" represents the single word, *houtos*, "thus," which the A.V. omits, but this adverb would rather indicate that John, having paid attention to Peter's request, did what he wished (the "thus" referring to his so doing as Peter had desired), and, leaning back again (the change in the tense, to the aorist, points to this)] **saith unto Him, Lord, who is it?"**

"Jesus therefore answereth [and the narratives in Matthew and Mark show that the answer was not given privately to John alone], **He it is, for whom I shall dip the sop, and give it to him."** The definite article "the" is to be noticed. It specifies the regular act at the Feast of the Passover (the A.V. "a sop" misses this, and gives the idea of a passing act). According to custom, the sop, prepared by the head of the household, was delivered at the proper moment to the person chosen by him. Apparently Judas had dipped his hand in the dish (Matt 26:23, r.v.). The Lord dips the sop and hands it to him. Quite possibly Judas had chosen the chief couch for himself and acted accordingly.

"THAT THOU DOEST"

Thereupon Satan enters into him. He had prepared himself for this climax. The Lord was fully cognizant of this act on the part of the spiritual foe: **"Jesus therefore** [i.e., because of Satan's entry] **said unto him, That thou doest, do quickly."** All that was required for the removal of the traitor was said; nothing more, nothing less. All is known between Christ and Judas. Judas sees both that the master is not deceived and that he himself is discovered. Yes, discovered, but not exposed; he has admonition, but freedom to act; separation, but not expulsion. Much was prevented which would have deprived the disciples of that ministry which they were about to receive. Self-humbled, they are not roused to animosity against the culprit. He allows their ideas to be mistaken (vv. 28, 29).

What an example (an additional example) the Lord set us! What self-restraint, what forbearance, what freedom from severity of judgment and strong judicial action! Much would never have happened in the past, much would not be taking place now, if the spirit the Lord manifested had characterized believers.

The language of the original in Christ's command "That thou doest, do quickly" is striking. Firstly, there is a change of tenses in the verb: the first is the present continuous, i.e., "What thou art doing" (what thou art engaged in doing); the second is the aorist tense, the tense of definite act, i.e., "go and do it." The first views the doing, the process of betrayal, as a whole; the second views it as a single deed. Again, the word "quickly" is in the comparative degree (lit., "more quickly"), suggesting the possibility of interruptions or hindrances, which might arise from Christ's intervention. But He will not so interfere. He is the controller of the whole situation.

"IT WAS NIGHT"

Judas, **"having received the sop went out straightway: and it was night"**— nature's night around him, moral and spiritual, night in his soul, the precursor of a darker night to follow, and all to do with the darkest and greatest crime in human history.

And now the atmosphere is cleansed. The immediate burden is lightened. The reserve, hitherto necessary, can yield place to the outflow of affection, to the unfolding of the deepest truths, and, almost at the beginning of it all, the institution of that love-feast, "the Lord's Supper."

The opening statements disclose the highest truths, truths that are basic to all that follows to the end of the seventeenth chapter: **"Now is the Son of man glorified, and God is glorified in Him."** In the original the verbs are in the aorist tense, which gives the literal rendering "Now was the Son of man glorified, and God was glorified in Him" (see the r.v. margin). But they are not simply statements of past events. What is indicated is that the events that are to follow, both the immediate events in connection with the Cross, and the succeeding events in both the near and the distant future are regarded and spoken of as assured and accomplished facts. The Lord was looking through all that was then actually in course of preparation for His death, and the circumstances and effects of His death. And having used this comprehensive form of expression, He proceeds to a direct statement of the future: **"and God shall glorify Him in Himself, and straightway shall he glorify Him."** In all that the Father is essentially, in His own being, the Son will ever be glorified in perfect oneness with Him. He straightway glorified Him in that "He raised Him from the dead and gave Him glory."

GETHSEMANE

It was in a garden where God had walked with man in perfect communion that man treacherously handed over the springs of his being to the spiritual foe and was at enmity with God. It was again in a garden, where Christ had held communion with His disciples, that one of them, having treacherously handed over his being to the human foe, manifested his enmity against the Son of God and betrayed Him.

THE TRAITOR'S PRECAUTIONS

Judas had had experience of the power of Christ in various ways. Determined therefore to make sure of the carrying out of his object, he obtained **"a band of soldiers,"** a Roman cohort together with officers, or the temple guard, from the chief priests (Luke includes some of the latter themselves) and Pharisees, and guided this large company, carrying lanterns and torches, to the familiar spot. These elaborate preparations were perhaps made because of the possibility that Jesus might do as He had done before, and hide Himself and escape. There was no need for all this precaution: **"Jesus . . . knowing all the things that were coming upon Him, went forth, and saith unto them. Whom seek ye? They answered Him, Jesus of Nazareth. Jesus saith unto them, I am He."**

Three facts stand out conspicuously in these circumstances. The form of the verb rendered "betrayed" in verses 2 and 5 indicates the whole process of the treachery of Judas. It is, literally, "the one betraying Him," and while it is almost equivalent to a title, it indicates the whole course of his procedure.

THE EFFECT OF THE JEHOVAH NAME

Secondly, that Jesus went forth to meet the company indicates the voluntary character of His sacrifice. The hour had come for the great fulfillment of His becoming obedient even unto death. Hence the significance of His word to Peter, **"Put up the sword into the sheath; the cup which the Father hath given Me, shall I not drink it?"** (v. 11).

Thirdly, there is the striking effect of the Lord's reply to His foes, who stated that they were seeking Jesus of Nazareth. The words *egō eimi*, "I am," were to

Jewish ears the equivalent of the name Jehovah. That the company went backward and fell to the ground, was the effect, not of guilt confronted with innocence, but of the majesty and power of His utterance. The fact that He permitted them to rise again and seize Him serves to confirm the voluntary character of His giving Himself up to death.

And now He shows His loving care for, and His power to defend, His followers, as a shepherd cares for his sheep: He says, **"if therefore ye seek Me, let these go their way,"** thus fulfilling His own word in 17:12, with a change from "not one of them perished" to "I lost not one," which brings out forcibly the Lord's own act in intervening on their behalf.

THE ECCLESIASTICAL TRIBUNALS

The Lord is seized by the cohort ("the band") under their commander, the military tribune, "the chief captain," as well as the Jewish officials, and taken before Annas. He was the most influential member of the hierarchy. He secured the high priesthood for Caiaphas, his son-in-law, and for five of his own sons, the last of whom, also named Annas, put James to death. There were several deposed high priests in the Sanhedrin, Annas was the acting president. The attitude Caiaphas would adopt was clear from his statement in 11:50, an unconscious prophecy, doubtless too an advice that if Jesus were put to death the Romans would postpone their enslavement of the nation and devastation of the land.

The court into which Christ was taken, and into which the disciple mentioned in verse 15 (almost certainly John) entered was quadrangular, and around it the high priest's house was built. There was a passage running from the street through the front part of the house. This was closed at the street end by a gate with a wicket, which on this occasion was kept by a maid. The rooms round the court were open in front; in one of these Jesus was being examined, and the Lord could see and hear Peter. John had seen Peter following at a distance and went to the maid with a request to let him in. She, knowing that the one was a disciple, naturally greets Peter with the question, **"Art thou also one of this man's disciples?"** In confusion at being confronted by such a hostile crowd, and remembering the blow he had struck in the garden, Peter denies any such connection. One denial prepared for more.

THE EFFECT OF IMPULSE

The impetuous act of using the sword in the garden was no inconsiderable factor in bringing about the terrible circumstances of these denials. We need to be on our guard against acting by sudden impulse on any occasion. One act of mistaken zeal in the energy of the flesh may have a bearing upon ensuing circumstances which are fraught with dire consequences.

Had Peter been void of self-confidence, and had he heeded the Lord's warning, he might have acted otherwise than remaining in the company of the servants and officers warming himself with them by the fire. That was a position full of danger. The repetition of the fact in the record is very suggestive: **"Peter also was with them, standing and warming himself"** (v. 18), and again, after an interval, **"Now Simon Peter was standing and warming himself"** (v. 25).

In the conversation his Galilean accent was readily detected. **"They said therefore unto him, Art thou also one of His disciples?"** That produced a second denial. In the groups was a servant of the high priest, a relative of the man whose ear Peter had cut off. **"Did not I see thee,"** he says, **"in the garden with Him?" Peter therefore denied again: and straightway the cock** [rather, "a cock"] **crew."** This, Luke tells us, was about an hour after the second denial. Then it was that the Lord turned and looked on Peter, either from the room looking out into the court, or as He was being led across the court. That brought Peter to himself and he went out and wept bitterly. The tenderness of the look brought home the terrible nature of the guilt, and saved him from blank despair.

This is all written for our admonition, a warning against self-confidence, against planning our own steps, against associating with the world even with a good motive, and a strong reminder that, should we fail to take heed to ourselves and fall, He who went to the Cross for our sakes, yearns for our restoration and has provided the means for it.

JEWISH ILLEGALITIES

The record of the trial before Annas and Caiaphas is brief. Nothing could be done until Pilate's ratification. Every detail of the trial was illegal to hold it at night at all. The high priest asked Jesus both about His disciples and about His teaching. He answers nothing concerning them, shielding them from the unscrupulous ways of these foes. Concerning Himself His statements as to the openness of His teaching stand in contrast to their secret method. **"Why askest thou Me?"** He says. **"Ask them that heard Me"** (not the disciples, but witnesses present). Witnesses for the defense should be heard first.

The act of the attendant officer who struck Jesus with the palm of his hand (not with a rod, as R.V. margin) was particularly noted by John. The meek yet firm reply of the Lord was sufficient to finish that part of the proceedings. **"Annas therefore sent Him bound unto Caiaphas."**

PILATE AND THE JEWS

When the Jews hauled Jesus to the Praetorium, they demanded a death sentence from the Roman official, but Pontius Pilate decides to question Jesus personally. His interview of Jesus is recorded in the Gospel of John. He asks, "Art Thou the King of the Jews?" and "What is truth?" In the end, he resignedly declares, "Behold, the man!" and finally, "Behold, your king!" The question remains for all of us: what is your response to the claims of Jesus?

John describes this scene at some length. He records what is elsewhere omitted, the conference between Pilate and the Jews (18:28–32) and the two private examinations by Pilate (18:33–38 and 19:8–11).

Caiaphas had passed sentence of death on Christ, and now they led Him into the Praetorium, the official residence of the procurator. The circumstances which follow are partly outside this place, partly inside: in verses 28–32 Pilate deals with the Jews, the accusers outside; in 33–37 he deals with Christ inside; in 38–40, with the accusers outside; in 19:1–3, with Christ inside (now the scourging and cruelty take place); in 4–7 outside with the accusers; in 8–11 with Christ inside (when the Lord's testimony produces a climax); in 12–16 with the Jews outside.

The significance of the statement in verse 28, **"and it was early,"** is as follows. A Roman court could be held after sunrise. The occasion being critical, Pilate would be ready to open the court, say, between 4:00 and 5:00 A.M. The Sanhedrin officials were in a difficulty, as a whole day must intervene between their sentence and execution. Hence they go at once to Pilate. If he agrees to execute he can fix the time. So they transferred the breach of their law from themselves to him.

Their supercilious adherence to the Law prevented their entering a polluted house, uncleansed from leaven (Exod. 12:15). **"Pilate therefore went out unto them,"** lit., "went out . . . outside unto them," with emphasis on the verb "went out," marking his concession to their religiousness and his anxiety to avoid disturbance.

PILATE'S INTERVIEW

His question as to the accusation (v. 29) has an air of judicial formality. At the same time the prisoner looked very unlike a criminal. On their refusing to name their charge, and with a combination of contempt and irritation, he tells them to judge Him by their law. Upon this they raised an accusation with regard to the Roman power, that He forbade to give tribute to Caesar and claimed to be a king. Could they not have stoned Him otherwise? However that may be viewed, the point is that Christ had foretold by what manner of death He would die. They said it was not lawful for them to do the execution. He had said He must be "lifted up."

The private interview inside the Praetorium therefore takes place, and Pilate puts the question **"Art Thou the King of the Jews?"** There is stress on "Thou," and the question indicates surprise. Christ demands that the responsibility of making the charge should be put upon the right persons (v. 34). Pilate says, **"Am I a Jew?"** (with stress on the "I"), brusquely repudiating the idea that he has any interest in Jewish affairs. So he emphatically says, **"Thine own nation** [the nation that is thine] **and the chief priests delivered Thee unto me. What hast Thou done?"**

Three times over in His reply the Lord says, with similar emphasis, **"The Kingdom that is Mine,"** and likewise, **"The servants** [or officers] **that are Mine,"** setting Himself and His affairs in direct contrast to the world. The "now" in verse 26 indicates that there is to be a kingdom hereafter. He shows therefore that His kingdom could not engage in conflict with the kingdom represented by Pilate. The latter scornfully asks **"Art Thou a king, then?"** with stress on the "Thou." If he had any lurking fear of some secret society, it is removed by Christ's reply, that a king He is, that He had been born for this, and has come into the world also to bear witness to the truth. There is special emphasis upon the "I" in the statement **"I have been born to this end."** Moreover, He has authority, His voice has power, everyone who is of the truth (the characteristic of His kingdom) is subject to Him, listens to His voice.

PILATE'S INJUSTICE

All this is essentially different from what Pilate had expected. There is nothing but innocence in such statements. And as for truth, that sort of thing has no place in the Roman procurator's mind. With a sort of combination of impatience and pity, and not in jest or serious inquiry, he says **"What is truth?"** Upon this he goes out again to the Jews, declaring the innocence of the prisoner and suggesting His release, according to custom at the Passover. To pronounce the accused guiltless and then to try and propitiate the savage accusers was the extreme of weakness. Injustice removed the one means of resisting their bloodthirstiness.

BARABBAS

Barabbas was popular, he was a bandit (*lēstēs*), a man of violence (not a thief). He rose against the Romans, that which Christ refused to do. The accusation by the Jews was that Jesus was dangerous to the Roman government; in reality one great reason for their antagonism was that He was not against the government.

According to Luke 23, Pilate had sent Christ to Herod before this, and Herod, with his troops, maltreated Him and sent Him back to Pilate. Pilate "took Jesus, and scourged Him." This was not the immediate preliminary to execution. He doubtless hoped that this might somehow satisfy the fury of the Jews. This form of Roman scourging (not that of the lictors' rods; Pilate had no lictors) was barbarously cruel. The heavy things were loaded with metal, and bone was woven into them, a piece of metal being fastened at the tip. Every cut tore the flesh from the bones, chest and back (see Ps. 22:17). Eusebius tells how he saw martyrs sinking down in death under the lashes of this kind of scourging.

BRUTAL MOCKERY BY TROOPS

Upon this followed the cruelty of the soldiers, who **"plaited a crown of thorns, and put it on His head, and arrayed Him in a purple garment"** (a military cloak), and saluting Him in mockery as a king, put, as Matthew says, a reed (a stout rod, as a scepter) in His right hand, spat upon Him, and taking the reed, one after another, from His hand, smote Him on the head (imperfect tense in the Greek, *i.e.*, they kept on doing it). See Isaiah 50:6. All was intentionally a cruel caricature of Jewish hopes of a king.

ECCE HOMO

Pilate now brought Him out, still arrayed (previously he had left Him inside), and declared again His guiltlessness. With pity rather than contempt he says **"Behold the man."** The chief priests and the Sanhedrin officers, perhaps fearing some signs of compassion among the people, begin at once to shout **"Crucify, crucify."** Pilate, goaded into taunting them, tells them to do it themselves, a thing he knew they dared not do. They were clever enough to advance a new accusation, held in reserve, which might appeal to his fears. When therefore, they brought the accusation that He made Himself the Son of God, and so broke their law, fear laid hold of Pilate, by very reason of this word (*logos*, not a mere saying, *rhēma*). There was the combination of his wife's message, the awesomeness of Christ's demeanor throughout, the possibility that, even according to Roman religion, he had been dealing with the offspring of a god. Apprehensive about it all he took Jesus into the Praetorium again and said **"Whence art Thou?"**

To this Christ gave no answer. For one thing, the information would have been useless in Pilate's case. For another, the injustice of his actions could now have only one issue: no explanation would have altered what was a foregone conclusion. In the next question, **"Speakest Thou not unto me?"** the special emphasis is on "me." The Roman governor could naturally claim power to release or to crucify. And now, in Christ's last word to him, He shows His judge that He is Himself the judge. Any exercise of power by Pilate depended on the permissive will of a power **"from above."** And his prisoner could pronounce and measure guilt. The sin of Caiaphas was declared to be greater than Pilate's.

THE FINAL ARGUMENT

Going again outside he made efforts (more than one, as the imperfect tense shows) to release Him. At this the accusers played their last card. To release the prisoner would endanger the governor's position. A report would go to a suspicious emperor (his fear of the emperor was real). The political argument succeeded. Pilate brought Christ out and prepared to pass sentence; it must be passed in public. He sat down on the judgment seat (probably a temporary one; there is no definite article, as everywhere else in the N.T. with *bēma*), on a tessellated pavement, called in Aramaic Gabbatha (or raised). His **"Behold, your king!"** was uttered in bitter irony. They shouted in one loud cry (aorist or definite tense), **"Away with *Him*, away with *Him*, crucify, crucify."**

In declaring that their only king is the heathen emperor, the chief priests, the official exponents of Israel's religion, with blasphemous callousness renounce the faith of their nation. If Pilate was guilty of judicial murder, they were guilty of suicide. In his delivering Christ **"unto them to be crucified"** (v. 16), the actual execution would be done by soldiers.

THE DEATH OF CHRIST

They crucified Jesus at Golgotha, "the place of the skull." Four soldiers show their disregard for Jesus' suffering by gambling for his robes, and four women stand by, showing their devotion for their Lord to the bitter end.

"**T**hey took Jesus (*paralambanō*, to receive, is used in 1:11 of not receiving the Father's gift of His Son; here, of receiving Him from Pilate; in 14:3, of His coming to receive His own to Himself); and He went out, bearing the cross [*stauros*, a single beam, a stake, a tree trunk, not a two-pieced cross, a thing of later arrangement from pagan sources], for Himself," R.V. (the A.V. misses this point), that is to say, like the vilest felon. Yet there is in this an underlying intimation of His voluntariness.

JESUS IN THE MIDST

The name Golgotha, **"The place of a skull,"** refers to the configuration and markings of the place. At the same time it suggests the emptiness of all mere human ideas, methods, aims and schemes. John describes more fully than the Synoptists the fact that the cross of Christ was the central one: **"They crucified Him, and with Him two others, on either side one, and Jesus in the midst"** (v. 18). The position assigned may have been a Roman mockery. Yet it serves to make prominent both the contrasting sinlessness of Christ, and His actual bearing of our sins, His being "made sin" for us. But further, it indicates the eternal separation between repentant, saved sinners, as represented by the converted robber on the one side, and unrepentant, unsaved sinners, represented by the other on the other side.

Pilate carried on further mockery, writing a title in Hebrew, Latin and Greek, for the cosmopolitan crowd to read, and putting it on the cross: **"Jesus of Nazareth, the King of the Jews."** The Septuagint in Psalm 96:10 has that "the Lord reigned from the tree." Pilate's contemptuous reply to the objection raised by **"the chief priests of the Jews"** (a phrase here only in the N.T.) shows that, now that his personal interests were not at stake, he could be obstinate instead of vacillating.

THE SEAMLESS ROBE

Four soldiers (a small force was sufficient, as there was no more danger of an outbreak of the mob) divided Christ's garments. These were the legal perquisites of soldiers who carried out executions. In casting lots for the seamless tunic they fulfilled Psalm 22:18. As the high priest's robe was seamless (Exod. 28:6–8), the detailed mention of this by the apostle John would suggest that this garment of Christ was symbolic of His high priesthood (Heb. 8:3).

In the Greek in the closing statement of verse 24 and the first statement of verse 25, there are two particles setting in marked contrast the callous doings of the four soldiers and the devoted attitude of the four women standing by the cross. This is partly expressed by the "But." That John here again calls himself the disciple whom Jesus loved is definitely connected with the Lord's loving commital of His mother to him. It was a mark of Christ's love for His disciple, that He should thus give him a mother and her a son. John takes her at once to his own home, sparing her from seeing the end.

"I THIRST"

One prophecy remained to be fulfilled. True, He experienced in terrible measure the physical anguish of thirst. Spiritually, too, he felt the drought of the condition of being forsaken of God. What, however, John mentions is that He said **"I thirst, knowing that all things are now finished** (or rather have been completed), **that the Scripture might be accomplished."**

The stupefying draft mentioned in Matthew 27:34 He refused. He did not refuse the vinegar or hyssop. Hyssop was appointed in connection with the Passover lamb (Exod. 12:22). Thereupon He said **"It is finished";** all the will of the Father, all the types and prophecies, all the redemptive work, He declared to have been fulfilled; **"and He bowed His head,"** He reclined (*klinō*) His head, putting it into a position of rest, with face turned heavenward, indicative of the rest He found in the fulfillment of the will of His Father, **"and gave up His spirit,"** a voluntary act, committing His spirit to the Father. No other crucified person ever died thus. In every other case the head dropped forward helplessly on the chest. He had said of His life, "No one taketh it from Me, but I lay it down of Myself" (10:18).

The request of the Jews, in their scrupulosity as to the sabbath, had been forestalled in the case of Christ by Psalm 34:20; Exodus 12:46; Numbers 9:12. But a soldier pierced His side with a spear, **"and straightway there came out blood and water."** God, overruling the act of human enmity, testified to the efficacy of the death of Christ. The blood speaks of redemption, and cleansing, the water speaks of the new birth and separation. Both tell of life, life bestowed through the giving up of His life in propitiatory sacrifice; "it is the blood that maketh atonement by reason of the life" (Lev. 17:11, R.V.), and life is bestowed by the water or regeneration (Titus 3:5). Accordingly the apostle lays special stress on his own evidence: **"his witness is true** [*alethine*, not simply truthful, but real, genuine, fulfilling the conditions of valid evidence], **and he knoweth that he saith true** [*alethe*, true things], **that ye also may believe"** (v. 35).

THE BURIAL

Joseph of Arimathaea and Nicodemus, of whom we hear nothing afterwards, are representatives of a future remnant of repentant Israel. Nicodemus would now certainly understand the significance of the brazen serpent (3:14). The tomb was "new" (*kainos*, fresh, not newly hewn out), no body ever having been laid in it. Matthew speaks of its newness, Luke of its freshness.

EVIDENCES OF THE RESURRECTION

Jesus Christ died before many witnesses and He was buried. Three days later, He defied death's hold, fulfilling prophecy with His return. Doubt and disbelief were scattered as He appeared to those who loved Him. Can the impossible be proven? Here are five evidences for the Resurrection.

THE FIRST EVIDENCE OF THE RESURRECTION

The first day of the week, the third from the burial, was the day on which Abraham typically received his son as from the dead; it was also the day of Jonah's deliverance, and is the day of Israel's future revival (Hos. 6:2). Mary Magdalene knew Christ as yet only "after the flesh." Hence her message to Peter. What he saw on entering the tomb was the evidence, in the very condition of the clothes, of resurrection. There had not been a tidying of the wrappings. They had not been disturbed, any more than the tomb and the stone, when the Lord arose. His body, possessed of supranatural resurrection power, left the wrappings, not in a heap, but in the shape in which they had been. Every detail gave proof of resurrection. That revealed the fact to both Peter and John (vv. 6–8). What they failed to learn and understand from the Scripture they realized from what they saw. There was no need to stay and make inquiry: so they went home.

THE SECOND EVIDENCE OF THE RESURRECTION

The outstanding fact about Mary Magdalene is the utter absorption of her mind and heart in the person of Christ, whom she regards as dead and whose lifeless body she wants. She **"continued standing,"** after the others had gone. Even the appearance of the two angels in the tomb did not startle her, nor did their question to her distract her from her preoccupation. Even though she was thinking only of the body, the lifeless form was still to her **"my Lord."** Turning herself and thinking that the person who asked her the same question as did the angels, was the gardener (Christ's risen body was so changed that He was not recognized by those who had known Him), she wanted to know, should he have taken the body out, where he had put it (she says "Him") and she would take Him away, the wrappings and the hundred pounds weight of spices and all. **"Jesus saith unto her, Mary."** That awakened the ecstasy of her heart. "He calleth His own sheep by name." She turned again (she had evidently turned away while thinking she was talking to the gardener), addressed Him as **"Rabboni,"** in the language used by the Lord and His followers, and reached out to hold Him. His command, rendered **"Touch Me not,"** is used in the present continuous tense and is to be understood with the meaning "Do not hold Me" (or "Do not be clinging to Me").

"For I am not yet ascended," He says, **"unto the Father."** The former intermittent intercourse is to be replaced by the new and continuous intercourse, but this cannot be till He is with the Father.

He was going to place them in the same position as His own, of relationship with His Father and His God. Hence He sends this devoted soul as His first messenger to His **"brethren,"** to say **"I ascend unto My Father and your Father, and My God and your God."** Heavenly, eternal and infinitely intimate relationship, with all the joy of the love of the Father and the power of God realized and enjoyed in Christ.

THE THIRD EVIDENCE OF THE RESURRECTION

The **"therefore"** in verse 19 indicates that it was owing to her testimony that the disciples assembled. If the news reached the authorities it would excite their hostility. They gathered **"for fear of the Jews."** It was **"evening,"** late in the day; it was **"that day,"** the memorable day, but it was still **"the first day of the week"** (not the second, though the second had begun in the evening by Jewish reckoning). A new week-period had begun; it was the Resurrection day, not the sabbath, there was beginning a perpetual sabbath-keeping of rest in Christ (Heb. 4:9). **"The doors were shut"**; that marks two things, a protection against the Jews and the supernatural entrance of the Lord. **"Jesus came and stood in the midst, and saith unto them, Peace be unto you."** Peace was His last message to them before He went with them to Gethsemane; it was His first word to them after His resurrection.

He then showed them **"His hands and His side,"** and Luke says His feet (24:39). Whatever other scars there had been were obliterated at His resurrection, but not these marks of His crucifixion and the significant wound in the side. Their sorrow is turned into joy. He repeats to them what they had heard Him say to the Father (vv. 17, 18, 21). Thereupon **"He breathed on them."** The same word (here only in the N.T.) is used in the Septuagint in Genesis 2:7; that was more than natural life, it was spiritual life as well.

His word **"Receive ye the Holy Spirit"** (R.V. margin) referred not merely to His own breath, it was symbolic of the Holy Spirit as about to be sent at Pentecost. It was connected with their being sent into the world, and with the effect of their ministry of the gospel in the forgiveness of sins by the Spirit's power, or the retention of sins by the rejection of the message (vv. 23, 24). It was a prophetic act as well as symbolic.

THE FOURTH EVIDENCE OF THE RESURRECTION

When Thomas, who had been absent, rejoined his brethren, they repeatedly told him (imperfect tense, *elegon*, they kept telling him) that they had seen the Lord. He had only one reply to make (aorist tense; *eipen*), it was decisive. Doubtless they told him that Christ had bidden them handle Him and see. Hence his persistent asseveration, **"Except I shall see in His hands the print of the nails, and**

190

put my finger into the print of the nails, and put my hand into His side, I will not (a strong negative, I will in no wise) **believe."**

A week later, the next first day of the week, Thomas being present, the Lord appears again in the midst, and shows him, by quoting his words, that He had heard the condition he laid down. This draws forth immediately the acknowledgment of the authority of Christ as his Lord and of His deity as God. Christ accepts both titles (just as He accepted the charge of the Jews in 5:18, that He made Himself equal with God), and proclaims the blessedness of the multitudes of those who, not having seen, have yet believed.

Here the apostle looks back over the whole book he has been writing, recording the fact that the Lord did many other signs (a miracle was a sign) in the presence of His disciples. What he wrote was not a history of Christ, or the life of Christ, but just those facts which would enable readers throughout this period to believe **"that Jesus is the Christ, the Son of God** [the outstanding fact and feature of this Gospel]; **and that believing ye may have life in His Name."** Were He not the Son of God, He would not be the Christ, the Messiah. Jehovah's anointed must be very God as well as very man. "In His Name" indicates that the gift of life comes by reason of His character, His attributes and His dealings.

THE FIFTH EVIDENCE OF THE RESURRECTION

The narrative (miscalled an epilogue) continues the proofs of the reality of Christ's resurrection. The manner in which the Lord manifested Himself at the Sea of Tiberias after His resurrection, forms the closing act, as recorded in [the Gospel of John], of the preparation of His disciples for their service. On this occasion there were seven of them. What memories the lakeside had for them. There they had listened to His teaching. There they had seen wonders of His glory. Thither their boat had been safely and suddenly brought from out of the storm that threatened to overwhelm them.

Deciding to pursue their former occupation they had gone **"a fishing,"** had toiled all night, and taken nothing (cp. Luke 5:5). Natural skill and persistent effort avail nothing apart from the will and power of the Lord. God brings us to an end of ourselves that He may give us to see His all-sufficiency to meet our need. "Man's extremity is God's opportunity."

JESUS APPEARS TO HIS DISCIPLES

The disciples returned to Galilee, and there the Lord appeared to them. After a long night of unsuccessful fishing, Jesus calls to them from the water's edge. They join Him for breakfast, and Peter is commissioned— or better stated, "re-commissioned" due to his unfaithful denial of Jesus before His death.

THE WITHHOLDING AND THE REVEALING

"But when day was now breaking, Jesus stood on the beach: howbeit the disciples knew not that it was Jesus" (v. 4, R.V.). As He had dealt with Mary Magdalene at the tomb and with the two on the road to Emmaus, so now with these seven. In each case the initial withholding of His identity had the design of imparting the greater assurance, in the immediately succeeding manifestation, of the fact of His resurrection. The brightness of a light is rendered more vivid by an antecedent darkness. As the natural dawn that morning shone out upon the darkness of the weary night, so He first veiled the reality of His person that the power of the disclosure might be the more effective.

Accordingly, permitting them to regard Him as an ordinary bystander, He addresses them in the customary and familiar manner of such. Our English versions render His question **"Children have ye aught to eat?"** (A.v., any meat). The word *paidion*, translated "children," was used variously, e.g., of a newborn infant, a more advanced child, a son. In affectionate, colloquial address, as in the present instance, our term "lads" would almost represent it.

In response to their somewhat cheerless **"No."** He says, **"Cast the net on the right side of the boat, and ye shall find."** There was still nothing in that to make His identity known, nothing more than the natural interest any stranger might take in a fishing enterprise.

A READY RECOGNITION

But now the surprising and magnificent haul, rendering it impossible to draw the net into the boat, immediately effects in **"that disciple . . . whom Jesus loved"** the recognition characteristic of strong and intimate attachment. John's frequent mention of himself in this way was not, as some have suggested, indicative of the soft character of a weakling. How could it be so? Was he not described by his Master as "a son of thunder"? Nor was it a vaunt of superiority over his fellow disciples. He does seem to have had a readier, if not fuller, grasp of spiritual verities. **"It is the Lord,"** he says to Peter. Ardent, impetuous Peter, first at the sepulcher, and now first to make for the Lord, girds his coat about him and casts himself into the water. He had cast himself before into the waters of the same lake to reach Him in very different circumstances. Acts reveal character. The impulse which made him leave all behind to go to his Master was the eagerness of love. This was a renewal, with the added attractiveness of the risen Christ, of that former renunciation of all things for Him, concerning which he had afterwards said, "Lo, we have left our own, and followed Thee" (Luke 18:28, R.V.).

PROVISION AND COOPERATION

Leaving the larger boat in which they had spent the night, the other disciples come **"in the little boat . . . dragging the net full of fishes."** Getting out upon the land, with the net and its catch left for the moment in the water, they see **"a fire** of coals . . . and fish [less in size than the "great" fish of their catch] **laid thereon, and bread.**" Their guide becomes their host.

Nothing is said as to how the Lord provided the repast, and surmisings are fruitless. There is no indication of the miraculous in this respect. That He bade them bring of the fish which they had taken would remove feelings of mere awe and prevent any misgivings. This token of fellowship on His part added to the homely intimacy of the feast. Besides this, the kindly gesture serves to remind us how the Lord delights to use our cooperation in His ministrations, the more fully to reveal Himself to us in His grace and love.

LESSONS OF DEPENDENCE ON THE LORD

Then there were the lessons of their entire dependence upon Himself in all that lay before them, and of His sufficiency to meet their needs in all the details of their life and service. That is what the Lord would likewise have us learn. How futile are our own schemes for bettering ourselves! How constant and ready are the provisions of our great El Shaddai!

The details were so vividly impressed on the mind of the apostle John that some sixty years later he could remember the precise number of fish caught. Speculations as to the significance of the number tend to obscure the true force and meaning of the facts. The very simplicity of the narrative, the brevity in the recounting of the details, the freedom from undue enlargement upon the miraculous, give eloquent evidence of the reality of His risen person. That was the Lord's design in all that He did, besides the confirmation of their faith in Him and in His power to meet their need.

REASSURANCE OF HIS RESURRECTION

After the counting, the customary thing with the fishers upon occasion, the Lord bids them **"Come and break your fast."** The homeliness of the welcome, given in the same gracious tone with which they were familiar in days gone by, at once leads to the statement, **"And none of the disciples durst inquire of Him, Who art Thou? knowing that it was the Lord."** There might have been some ground for the question. The Lord's body was not the former natural body, though still real, corporeal, and tangible. But the character of His utterances and His acts, His ministration of the bread and the fish, together with the marks of His identity, dispelled all possible misgivings, and the way was now opened for further and different ministry.

"We walk by faith, not by sight." "Blessed are they that have not seen and yet have believed." It is ours not only to believe in the fact of the resurrection of Christ, but to experience the joy and power of His presence, as the apostles did of old when, after His ascension, His promise was fulfilled for them, as it is for us, "Lo, I am with you all the days even unto the end of the age." Let us lay hold of the significance for us of this post-resurrection sign. Let us learn day by day our entire dependence upon Him both for our temporal needs and for all that is involved in our occupations as His followers and servants. May we realize that the same loving heart that planned for the disciples, cared for them with tender affection, taught and disciplined them and attached them to His own glorious person, does the same for us if we, as they did, follow Him with Spirit-filled devotion.

CHRIST AND PETER

Peter's relation to his Master had been established. He is now to be reinstated in view of his responsibility as an apostle and as one who could strengthen his brethren, his self-confidence having been banished. Three times he had denied his Lord. Three times the Lord says **"Lovest Thou Me."** The first time he says **"Lovest thou Me more than these?"** Grammatically the "these" might refer either to persons, fellow disciples, or to things. But (1) Peter had boasted that he was a more ardent disciple than the others: they might deny their Master, but he would not, (2) to speak of loving the matters connected with fishing does not give a sufficient application to the meaning; (3) would the Lord be likely to ask the question with this in mind, considering that the moment Peter saw it was the Lord he left the boat and the nets and swam ashore to be with his Master?

AGAPAŌ AND PHILEŌ

As to the change of verb in Peter's reply to the Lord's question, "Lovest thou Me?" Christ uses *agapaō* in His first two questions; Peter uses *phileō* in all three answers. *Phileō* expresses a natural affection, and in this Peter is perfectly sure of himself and is keenly desirous of stating his affection, particularly after his denials. This the Lord fully appreciates; but He is thinking of the practical manifestations and effects as well, as is evident from His commands And the verb *agapaō* combines the two meanings: it expresses a real affection, but likewise raises it to the thought of an active and devoted exercise of it on behalf of others. Accordingly He first says **"Feed My lambs"** (showing that the love is the expression of mind in action). So again, when Peter adheres to *phileō*, Christ replies, **"Tend My sheep."** Shepherd work (all that is involved in tending sheep) must exhibit the love. The commands show how fully reinstated Peter was.

The third time the Lord adopts Peter's word, and this grieved him. It was not that Christ had asked three times, but that now the third time, in using Peter's word, He should even seem to question the deeply felt, genuine affection he felt for Him. This is confirmed by the statement Peter makes, **"Thou knowest all things** ["Thou knowest intuitively," *oida*]; **Thou knowest** [*ginōskō*, "Thou dost recognize"] **that I love Thee** [*phileō*].

THE CALL TO FOLLOW

In what the Lord now says He takes up both the aspects of love, the practical and the deep-seated, affectionate and emotional love. First He adheres to the practical: **"Feed My sheep."** Then He foretells how Peter will manifest his affection in laying down his life after all for his Master's sake. Thus it would be given him to do what he had in self-confidence boasted he would do. And it was devotion to his Master that made him say it. The being girded and carried **"whither thou wouldest not"** did not imply unwillingness to die, but a natural shrinking from a cruel death, especially crucifixion as a criminal.

That the Lord said to him **"Follow Me"** (v. 19) may have had a literal meaning, as the same word in the next verse has, but it certainly had a figurative sense; it was a call to follow in the path of testimony and suffering (see 13:36). The apostle now clearly discloses his identity. In telling how, as the Lord moved away and Peter after Him, John himself followed, intimating his own devotion, he recalls how he leaned on Christ's breast at the supper, and asked as to who would betray Him.

FELLOW APOSTLES

In John's record concerning Peter and the Lord's reply to his question regarding himself we cannot but note the continued and special intimacy between these two disciples, an intimacy which would be seen in the earliest apostolic testimony. Noticeable also are the Lord's combined foreknowledge of, and authority over, the future lives of His servants. He not only foretells Peter's martyrdom, but says that the length of John's life depends upon what He wills (vv. 22, 23). In verse 22, the "he" and the "thou" are emphatic and set in contrast: "whatever concerning *him* My will may be, *thou* must follow Me." In the last utterance of Christ recorded in this Gospel He speaks of His coming, and the Lord holds out to us the possibility that it may take place during our lifetime.

As to the statement in verse 24, the mode of expressing his identity is characteristic of John. The **"these things"** probably refers to all the contents of this Gospel. The change of tense from **"beareth witness"** to **"wrote,"** shows that though the writing was finished, the witness was continuing. The use of the plural "we" in **"we know"** is quite in keeping with John's style (cp. 1 John 5:18–20); as there so here, he includes all the believers of his time.

The last verse expresses a note of appreciation and admiration regarding all that Christ wrought during the whole course of His life here including the period after His resurrection, and an overwhelming sense of the infinitude of His person and His activities.

THE TEACHINGS OF CHRIST

THE FIRST PUBLIC DISCOURSE IN JOHN'S GOSPEL

In John 5, Jesus begins to teach the multitudes, openly declaring Himself as the Son of God and teaching about the reasons He was sent by the Father. This is recognized as Christ's first public discourse. It contains twelve great subjects: (1) The essential relation between the Father and the Son (vv. 19–21); (2) The commission, authority and dignity of the Son (vv. 22, 23); (3) The everlasting blessings of those who believe (v. 24); (4) Spiritual resurrection (v. 25); (5) Christ the lawgiver (v. 26); (6) Christ the judge (v. 27); (7) Universal physical resurrection (vv. 28, 29); (8) The infallible judgment of Christ (v. 30); (9) Witness to Christ, by the Father, John the Baptist, Christ's works, the Scriptures (vv. 31, 39); (10) Man's perverse will and consequent ruin (vv. 38, 40–43); (11) The love of man's praise as the cause of unbelief (v. 44); (12) The importance, claims and object of the writings of Moses (vv. 45, 46).

THE ONENESS OF THE FATHER AND THE SON

The first part, (A), is characterized by a threefold **"Verily, verily"** (vv. 19, 24, 25). This is a translation of the Hebrew word "Amen," which signifies "truth." The repeated word (used by the Lord twenty-five times as recorded in this Gospel and not found thus elsewhere in the New Testament) always introduces a solemn pronouncement demanding the utmost attention.

The first of the three in this discourse is followed by declarations which govern all that follows. They are foundation truths predicating (1) the impossibility of His acting independently of the Father: **"the Son can do nothing of Himself,"** (2) the intimacy and unbroken continuity of their communion—**"but what He seeth the Father doing,"** (3) the coincidence and coextension of Their work **"for what things soever He doeth, these the Son doeth in like manner,"** (4) the love of the Father for the Son as the causative element characterizing this unity, communion, and cooperation: **"For the Father loveth the Son** [note the connecting word, "For," gathering up the preceding truths into the underlying cause]**, and sheweth Him all things that Himself doeth"**: as the Son does nothing without the Father, so the Father keeps nothing secret from the Son; this, coupled with the earlier statement as to the preexistent cooperation, **"My Father worketh even until now, and I work,"** clearly establishes the eternal preexistence of the relationship; (5) the increasing nature of the work as further revealing the intimacy now made known, and challenging the acknowledgment of the beholders: **"and greater works than these will He show Him, that ye may marvel."** These "greater works" are mentioned in what follows.

RESURRECTION, SPIRITUAL AND PHYSICAL

Having made known that what He did represented the joint work of the Father with Himself (as exemplified in the healing of the impotent man on the Sabbath), and that the great feature of this divine cooperation was the love of the Father for Him, a love which involved the unbroken and most intimate communication to Him of all that the Father did (5:19, 20), the Lord now confirms all this, for the attention of His critics, by instancing the most transcendent operations of God, those, namely, of resurrection, spiritual, and physical; these He describes as "greater works" (i.e., than those of healing the sick). This is dealt with in the first part of the discourse (vv. 21–29), first as to spiritual resurrection (vv. 21–27), then as to the physical (vv. 28, 29).

"For as the Father raiseth the dead and quickeneth them, even so the Son also quickeneth whom He will." This at once constitutes a positive and explicit claim to deity. Not only are the Father and the Son conjointly engaged in the salvation of the souls of men and the impartation to them of spiritual life from their dead condition, but this impartation is the effect of the will of the Son, not apart from the Father, but determined in equality of mind and counsel with Him. This is the significance also in His "whom He will," that there is no limit to His life-bestowing power to those who accept the condition of faith in Him, a condition which He is just about to state.

HOW TO OBTAIN ETERNAL LIFE

As the quickening involves the raising, there is a definite connection between His power as the imparter of life and His capacity as judge, as is obvious from the "For" introducing verse 22: **"For neither doth the Father judge any man, but He hath given all judgment unto the Son."** And the connection surely lies in this, that, as the bestowment of spiritual life depends upon the will and act of the Son, His knowledge as to who is to receive life from Him and who is to remain without it, constitutes Him an infallible judge in determining the destiny of all. Hence He says (though without a prior and very important declaration, v. 23), **"Verily, verily I say unto you, He that heareth My Word, and believeth Him that sent Me, hath eternal life, and cometh not into judgment, but hath passed out of death into life"** (v. 24, R.V.). Note that it is not "believed on Him," as in the A.V., but "believeth Him," that is to say, "believeth God's Word respecting His Son."

Now this makes clear that the "whom He will" in verse 21 is not a matter of arbitrary selection. Each one is responsible to decide whether he will believe and thus receive life, or not. This is open to all who hear. God's interposition in and through His Son has alone made it possible. The case of the impotent man was illustrative of this. His condition was the outcome of sin and was hopeless, but for Christ's intervention. His "Wilt thou be made whole?" is typical of the human responsibility to accept. Nevertheless salvation must be the effect of His

Word. The obligation rested with His hearers to see the significance, and to place themselves among the recipients of life from Him.

THE SON'S EQUALITY OF HONOR

The Lord precedes this glorious truth of the Gospel by a statement as to the great reason why the Father has committed all judgment to Him. It is not simply that He may act as the judge of men, nor that He may give eternal life to all who believe, but **"that all may honor the Son, even as they honor the Father,"** and this He substantiates by the declaration, **"He that honoreth not the Son honoreth not the Father which sent Him"** (v. 23). This is of paramount importance in view of the variety of tenets, arguments, and propaganda which detract from the honor of the Son. He it is against whom the arch-spiritual foe exerts his fiercest and unremitting antagonism.

"The obligation of honoring the Son is defined to be just as stringent as the obligation of honoring the Father. Whatever form that honor may take, be it thought, or language, or outward act, or devotion of the affections or submission of the will, or that union of thought and heart and will into one complex act of self-prostration before finite greatness, which we of the present day usually mean by the term adoration, such honor is due to the Son no less than to the Father. How fearful is such a claim if the Son be only human! how natural, how moderate, how just, if He is in very deed Divine!" (Liddon).

Since the Father does nothing apart from the Son, and the Son nothing apart from the Father (vv. 19, 20), this unity of operation demands equality of honor. To this honor of the Son all will be inevitably constrained, either in full and gladsome recognition by those who have eternal life, or compulsorily in the case of all rejectors, human and spiritual. It is the unthwartable determination of God that every tongue shall "confess that Jesus Christ is Lord to the glory of God the Father" (Phil. 2:11).

THE LIFEGIVER AND JUDGE

The hour of verse 25 is already 1,900 years long. The authority of **"the voice of the Son of God"** in the bestowment of life on dead souls rests upon two great facts, (1) that **"as the Father hath life in Himself, even so gave He to the Son also to have life in Himself,"** (2) that **"He gave Him authority to execute judgment, because He is the Son of Man"** (vv. 26, 27). The first does not imply that the Father had imparted life to the Son, it declares that as the Father is the source of life, so the Son in incarnation is the source, by reason of the appointment of the Father. Life stands here for the vivifying power. The life, the Divine counsels and operations, everything centers in Christ, and by reason of this and of His incarnation and what results from it, spiritual life becomes communicable only through Him.

The second statement, that His authority to act as the judge of all men is based upon the fact that He is **"the Son of Man"** (not here indicating His messiahship but His humanity) receives especial stress from the absence of the article in the original before both "Son" and "Man." He will judge as being in full understanding experimentally of human conditions, sin apart, and thus as sharing the nature of those He judges. Being Son of God He knows what only God knows, the possibilities of man (Matt. 11:21). He who is judge must be God and man.

THE TWO RESURRECTIONS

The astonishment of the Jews at such claims met with a still more startling proclamation. **"Marvel not at this,"** He says, **"for the hour cometh, in which all that are in the tombs shall hear His voice, and shall come forth; they that have done** [*poieō*] **good, unto the** [**"a"**] **resurrection of life; and they that have done** [*prassō*, have practiced] **ill, unto** ["a"] **resurrection of judgment."** The two resurrections, distinct in character (stressed by the absence of the article in each case), are shown in other Scriptures to be separated in time, *e.g.*, Revelation 20:4–6. What the Lord had already taught governs the statements as to doing good and ill. Doing good (plural) is that which marks the lives of those who have believed and so have passed from death unto life (v. 24); doing evil (plural) is that which characterizes unbelievers, the unregenerate (Rom. 3:9; Gal. 3:10). The distinction between "have done" (*poieō*) and "have practiced" (*prassō*) lies in this, that *poieō* denotes an act complete in itself, while *prassō* denotes a habit (cp. 3:20, 21, where the same distinction is made).

Having declared His authority to execute judgment upon all men, the Lord repudiates any idea that this is a matter simply of His own will and doing, reiterating what He had said in verse 19. There, however, He said, "What I see the Father doing I do"; now He says, **"As I hear, I judge."** This is an additional attestation of the essential unity of the Father and Himself. Nevertheless He was here in entire and delighted subjection to the Father's will, which in itself was the guarantee of the infallible equity of His judgment: **"and My judgment,"** He says, **"is righteous; because I seek not Mine own will, but the will of Him that sent Me"** (v. 30). The judgment passed by the Jews was perverted because they sought their own will. The accuracy of our judgment in anything depends upon our entire subservience to the will of God.

In the latter part of this discourse (vv. 31–47) the Lord pointedly rebukes the unbelief of the Jews. The great force of His rebuke lies, however, in the continuation of His claims to His oneness with the Father, still answering the charge that He had made Himself equal with God.

The chief point in this vindication is

THE WITNESS GIVEN HIM BY THE FATHER

"If I bear witness of Myself, My witness is not true. It is Another that beareth witness of Me: and I know that the witness which He witnesseth of Me is true" (vv. 31, 32). As to the question who this "other" is, the answer is provided in verse 37. He designedly postpones the actual mention of the person, so that it may come the more forcefully by reason of the contrast to human witness, particularly that of John the Baptist, concerning whom they had sent making special inquiries (1:19). Moreover, the immediate necessity was to rebut any imputation that He was the sole source of His testimony. In that case, while the testimony would be true, it would be invalid. So for the moment He speaks of "Another," and proceeds with "and I know (*oida*, I have perfect knowledge) that the witness which He witnesseth of Me is true." The essence of His knowledge consisted in His unity with Him to whose voice He listened and whose will was His unremitting delight.

THE SOURCE OF THE BAPTIST'S LIGHT

He valued, as He alone could, and far more than they did, the witness of the Baptist; **"he hath borne witness** [perfect tense, expressing the enduring effect] **unto the truth." "He was the lamp** [*luchnos*, not a torch, but a portable lamp] **that burneth and shineth"** (v. 35). Christ Himself is the Light. From Him John, the human lamp, derived his light. Their rejoicing in John's witness was ephemeral and unproductive. If only they would realize and recognize that the source of his light was now testifying to them! **"I say these things that ye may be saved."** How wonderfully this exhibits the tender compassion of His heart, even toward the hardhearted and antagonistic! Verily these are words of One who was "full of grace and truth."

And now the Lord leads up to the definite statement as to the witness borne to Him by the Father, by speaking of the witness of His works. They are not simply His own doing **"the works which the Father hath given Me to accomplish, the very works that I do bear witness of Me that the Father hath sent Me."** This recalls verse 20, and, in the light of that, the works clearly are comprehensive not only of those of healing and similar signs but of the impartation of life, affecting the character and conduct of His followers, works accomplished by His teaching (as in the case of the conversion of the Samaritan woman, see 4:34). In His prayer in chapter 17 He sums up all, including the sacrifice of the Cross, in the phrase "the work" ("the work which Thou hast given Me to do," 17:4).

The comprehensive character of His reference to His works here is intimated in His statement that they are those "which the Father hath given Me to accomplish," lit., "in order that I may accomplish." This being so, the way is now open for Him to make clear to whom He had referred when He said, "It is another that beareth witness of Me" (v. 32). **"And the Father which sent Me, He hath borne witness of Me."** There is the strongest emphasis both upon "the Father" and upon "He."

This is

THE KEYSTONE OF HIS DECLARATIONS

as to the various kinds of witness borne to Him. It manifests His keen pleasure in glorifying the Father. The witness of the Father was given not simply by the works which He wrought through Christ, it was especially borne, for instance, on the occasion of His baptism, when **"a voice came out of heaven, Thou art My beloved Son; in Thee I am well pleased"** (Luke 3:22).

Now, in His capacity as their judge, He proceeds to pronounce His judgment upon them. His remonstrances follow in solemn sequence. **"Ye have neither heard His voice at any time, nor seen His form. And ye have not His word abiding in you: for whom He sent Him ye believe not"** (vv. 37, 38). This is all closely connected. That they had neither heard the Father's voice nor seen His form, is reminiscent of God's words concerning Moses in Numbers 12:8, Moses combining in himself the promulgation of the Law and the function of the prophet. The Jews, who had neither understood nor heeded the voice of God to their nation, and especially that of Moses, on whom they had set their hope (v. 45), failed now to apprehend that the Father was speaking to them in and through the Son (cp. Heb. 1:2), and that the Son, whom they were refusing, was Himself the manifestation of the Father (*eidos*, the visible form or representation).

The connection between the voice and the form is repeated in what follows. As to the voice, "*Ye have not His word abiding in you*," as to the person, **"whom the Father sent ye believe not."**

The Lord had spoken to His critical and unbelieving audience of three kinds of witness which had been borne to Him, that of John the Baptist, that of the Father, and that of His works. John's witness they simply made the subject of an inquiry. To the witness of the Father their unbelief blinded them. The witness of the works of Christ met with their criticism of His person and His claims, a criticism fostered by the misconceptions and prejudices of human tradition.

AN ERRONEOUS USE OF SCRIPTURE

There was a further witness to Him, one with which they had been longer and more intimately acquainted than those already mentioned. To this He now draws attention. **"Ye search the Scriptures,"** He says, **"because ye** [emphatic] **think that in them** [emphatic] **ye have eternal life; and these** [emphatic—the objects of your search] **are they which bear witness of Me; and ye will not** [ye are not willing to] **come to Me, that ye may have life"** (vv. 39, 40). Whether the opening verb be regarded as indicative, "Ye search," or imperative, "Search" (and either is possible), the great point is that, while the Scriptures were theirs for their guidance, they were so out of touch with the mind of God therein revealed, that they failed to grasp their purport, that, namely of witnessing to Christ. They imagined that they had life simply by their possession of the Word of God, by their devotion to the letter of the Law, and by a formal perusal of the Scriptures, the real and divine purpose of which is to lead the reader to the life-giver. In this lies the connection between His statements **"these are they which bear witness of Me,"** and **"ye will not come to Me that ye may have life."** The revelation and ministry of Christ to the soul are ever the paramount objects and power of the sacred page.

THE TRUE SOURCE OF GLORY

The Lord follows this with the statement, **"I receive not glory from men."** As to the bearing of this upon the course of His remarks, the preposition *para*, "from," in this construction, indicates the source or origin. This at once suggests that the source of glory He received was not human; it was divine, it came from God (v. 44). Even the Scriptures, the import of which the Jews grievously missed in not finding them a means of coming to Him to obtain eternal life, were not of human origin.

Now the true recognition of this and the consequent apprehension and application of the Scriptures as pointing to Christ, would produce the love of God in the heart, as they ever do when so applied. In all this His hearers utterly failed. **"But I know you,"** He says, **"that ye have not the love of God in yourselves"** (v. 42). It was all very well to boast in the Scriptures, but what did their use of them avail when they had not the love of God and refused to receive His Son, to whom the Scriptures bore witness? He had come in His Father's Name (as the personal presentation of, and with the authority of, the Father), and they received Him not.

But there was more than this in His declaration that He received not glory from men. That was just where the Jews erred. And their error lay at the root of their unbelief. **"How can ye believe,"** He says, **"which receive glory one of another, and the glory that cometh from the only God ye seek not?"** It was not want of proof that hindered faith on their part, it was pride, vanity and earthly desires, alienating their heart from God. Their rejection of Christ nationally would ultimately put them under the delusive power of the Antichrist: **"If another shall come in His own name, him ye will receive."** While that points on to the future national reception of the man of sin, the evil principle was working in their own hearts, and they were forerunners of the nation's final apostasy. To come in one's own name is to attract honor to oneself and seek human applause, and that is the very negation of the love of God. Christ had come to manifest the Father and to do nothing but His will. Hence the Father's glory ever shone transcendently in Him. With them there was neither the love of God nor the faith which worketh by love (v. 44). There is no neutral ground. Men must either receive Christ or suffer the blinding delusions of the powers of darkness and stand on the side of His foes.

THE GREAT SUBJECT OF THE PENTATEUCH

At the close of His discourse the Lord knocks away the very foundation of their false confidence. He increases the force of His blow by preceding it with the negative statement that He will not Himself act as their accuser to the Father (v. 45). Nay, His immediate object was their salvation (v. 34). Their accuser was Moses, on whom they had "set their hope." They imagined that in accusing Christ of breaking the sabbath they were defending the Law of Moses, which, however, condemned them (cp. Deut. 31:21, 26; 32:28). Their rejection of Christ was, in point of fact, a rejection of Moses. **"For if,"** He says, **"ye believed Moses, ye would believe Me; for he wrote of Me."**

In this He states the outstanding subject of the whole Pentateuch, testifying at the same time to its authorship, authority and divine inspiration. The emphasis may be brought out by the rendering "It was of Me that he wrote." His statement (which recalls His words as to all the Scriptures, v. 39) affords us the great guide to a right understanding of the much-criticized and misunderstood Pentateuch. Happy is he who, assured of a response, breathes the prayer.

> Teach me to love the sacred page
> And view my Savior there.

With what solemn abruptness the Lord closes His discourse! "For if ye believe not his writings how shall ye believe My words?" It is virtually an exclamatory protest, and in it He puts the writings of Moses in the same divine category as His own words. He demands the acceptance of each as a matter of faith. Refusal means the loss of valid hope of salvation.

THE SECOND PUBLIC DISCOURSE IN JOHN'S GOSPEL

In John 6, we find this Gospel's record of Christ's second public discourse. These teachings are divided into two parts: the first (John 6:26–40) answers the application of the multitude to Him because of the miracle that He had wrought; the second (verses 43–59) is a reply to the murmuring of the Jews. Each part contains the same two leading truths, (1) that Christ is the Bread of Life, (2) that as such He came from Heaven to earth to give life to men.

"VERILY, VERILY"

He begins with a "Verily, verily," lit., "Amen, Amen," a mode of arresting attention which was frequently upon His lips. It introduces a subject of pressing urgency by reason of its essential importance, and usually because it runs counter to, or exceeds, the ideas in the minds of His hearers.

"Verily, verily, I say unto you. Ye seek Me," He says, **"not because ye saw signs, but because ye ate of the loaves, and were filled. Work not for the meat which perisheth, but for the meat which abideth unto eternal life, which the Son of Man shall give unto you: for Him the Father, even God, hath sealed"** (vv. 26, 27). His "work not" has a comparative force: the spiritual nourishment is a matter of far greater concern than the material. And what toil they had given themselves in endeavoring to find Him! With a view doubtless to obtaining more bread! His injunction was certainly not against earning their living; the R.V. rightly has "work" instead of "labor," as the same word is used by His hearers in the next verse. Let their pursuits be directed to obtaining the spiritual food. It abides. A hint perhaps against their idea of getting continual supplies of material bread from Him! The spiritual bread abides unto eternal life: it sustains forever. And there it was for the having. Let them do the real seeking and they shall find. The Son of man gives it. He is the provider of the vastly more important spiritual sustenance.

THE SEALING OF THE BREAD OF LIFE

The sealing here signifies the authentication, the commissioning with authority, by God, of the Son of man as the sole giver of eternal life. The allusion may be to the impress of a mark by bakers upon their loaves, or, with a typical reference, to the testing and sealing of lambs for sacrifice, foreshadowing Christ as the Passover Lamb (other suggestions seem less satisfactory).

The Lord's admonition to the Jews to **"work . . . for the meat which abideth unto eternal life,"** elicited from them the apparently acquiescent inquiry (earnest enough, we may suppose), **"What must we do that we may work the works of God?"** They perceived that His remarks had a moral implication in contrast to their materialistic conceptions. How then should they act so as to do works pleasing to God and then obtain the imperishable spiritual bread?

"AND THAT NOT OF YOURSELVES"

His reply strikes immediately at the idea, so innate in the hearts of men, that the favor and mercy of God are conditional upon human merit and self-effort. Man's fallen condition should of itself suffice to demolish such expectations. But that is just what men fail to recognize. Man must be ruled out; God alone can meet the need. And God has met it, and that in the person and work of His Son, His sent One. But this requires a divine revelation. God has given it. He has "spoken unto us in His Son." But this again requires faith. And God who bestowed upon man the faculty of faith, has given "assurance unto all men (this word *pistis* in Acts 17:31, which ordinarily denotes faith, here signifies a ground for faith), in that He hath raised Him from the dead."

Accordingly, the Lord states directly and specifically that **"This is the work of God, that ye believe on Him whom He hath sent"** (v. 29). The reply is anticipative of the great doctrine for which the apostle Paul contends in Romans and Galatians, justification by faith, in contrast to the futility of works. It is not "do" but "trust."

The Jews, like many others, could not look upon things that way. They must have tangible evidence, something for the natural vision. Seeing is believing. Such is blind unbelief. **"What then,"** they say, **"doest Thou for a sign, that we may see, and believe Thee? What workest Thou?"** Moreover, had not their fathers been granted through Moses something for the natural sight, and bread for the natural man? If then the One who addressed them was the Messiah and therein greater than Moses, would He not demonstrate this by a confirmatory sign?

"THE TRUE BREAD"

Again, the Lord repudiates their ideas with a **"Verily, verily, I say unto you,"** and with a denial and a contrast: **"It was not Moses that gave you the bread out of Heaven: but My Father giveth you the true bread out of Heaven."** The word *alēthinos* denotes true, not in the sense of actual, or true to fact (*alēthēs*), but of that which is ideal, as well as genuine; it is also used of Christ in 1:9; 15:1; 1 John 2:8; 5:20 (thrice); Revelation 3:7, 14; 19:11. Just as to the Samaritan woman He had contrasted the "living water" with that of the well sacred to the name of Jacob, so now He contrasts Himself as the true bread, with that which they attributed to the provision made by Moses.

Reserving for the moment the specific identification of Himself as this "true Bread," He confirms its character as follows: **"For the bread of God is that which cometh down out of heaven, and giveth life unto the world"** (v. 33). Two contrasts stand out in this: (1) whereas the manna is spoken of as "bread from Heaven" (Ps. 78:24), and "the bread of Heaven" (Ps. 105:40), the Lord stresses His "coming down out of Heaven" attesting the fact of His descent to earth by His incarnation as the Son of man and as the One sent by the Father (vv. 27, 29); (2) whereas the manna could not prevent their "fathers" from dying ("their carcasses fell in the wilderness"), the true bread imparts an imperishable life; and whereas the manna was the exclusive privilege of Israel, the true bread ministers life to the world, that is to all who partake of it, racial distinctions being ruled out.

AN EARNEST REQUEST AND THE GREAT DISCLOSURE

This elicits from them the request **"Lord,** (why was it not rendered "Sir," as in the utterance of the Samaritan woman in 4:15? They were not addressing Him as humble followers in willing submission to His authority), **evermore give us this bread."** The request was sincere enough; they believed in His power, though they disbelieved His mission.

The Lord answers this by a climax of stupendous disclosures concerning Himself which constitute the remainder of the first part of this discourse. As, again, to the Samaritan woman, He had turned upon Himself the full light of His revelations, when He said, "I that speak unto thee am He," so now He says to the people, **"I am the bread of life: he that cometh to Me shall not hunger, and he that believeth on Me shall never thirst."** This claim, so unambiguous, so authoritative, so imperative, could have but one of two effects upon His hearers. Life abundant, unendingly sustained, would be theirs upon believing on Him by coming to Him. Refusal, with its evidence of lack of appetite for the bread He gives, involved the spiritual death of separation from Him. Their choice is made clear in the rest of the chapter. The alternatives still remain for all to whom the offer comes.

COMING AND BELIEVING

The Lord's two statements are in the couplet form of Hebrew parallelisms. In the original each contains the same strong double negative (*ou mē*, "by no means"), and the combined declarations close with the strongly stressed "never" (*pōpote*), which, standing in its emphatic position at the end, governs both, as if to say, "He that cometh to Me shall by no means hunger, and he that believeth on Me shall by no means thirst, no never." As hungering and thirsting express what can be met conjointly by natural supplies, so coming to Christ and believing on Him are the indissociable means of the supply of spiritual need.

The figure He uses is of paramount significance. Bread means nourishment, sustenance, strength, the building up of the very tissues of life. And this, spiritually, is what Christ becomes to the believer. Communicating His life to us He becomes part of our very selves, the strength of our soul. He is the adequate supply of every spiritual need, the full satisfaction of every spiritual desire. We cannot live the natural life without bread. We cannot live the spiritual life without Christ. He who is thus sustained by Him can say with the apostle, "Christ liveth in me." And what possibilities this holds for one who knows the joy and power of this holy union of life and love! Such can truly say, "I can do all things in Him that strengtheneth me."

The promises, conditional upon coming to Christ, of never hungering or thirsting, were hindered of fulfillment in the case of the Jews by their persistent unbelief. This He forcibly brought home to them by His contrasting statement, **"But I said unto you, that ye have seen Me, and yet believe not"** (6:36), the reference probably being to their having seen Him as the miraculous provider of bread, without their having entered into any relation with Him by faith (vv. 26–29). Their hearts, naked and open to Him, entirely lacked any appreciation of the real character of His person, His acts, and His ways. How many hear of Him and get no farther than they did!

DIVINE ELECTION AND HUMAN FREE WILL

His next words make clear, however, that their unbelief did not argue any frustration of His mission: **"All that which the Father giveth Me shall come to Me: and him that cometh to Me I will in no wise cast out"** (v. 37). This sublime utterance conveys two fundamental facts regarding God and man, (1) the eternal foreknowledge and electing purpose of God in salvation, (2) the exercise of human free will to accept God's conditions or to reject them. Human experience confirms both verities. There is no inconsistency therein. The twofold operation is expressed in the well-known words, "the grace of God by Christ preventing us, that we may have a good will, and working with us, when we have that good will."

Note the change from "all that which" to "him that." The former, expressed in the neuter, views the whole body of believers as an entity and unity foreseen and predetermined by the Father, stressing this apart from the offer made to, and accepted or refused by, individuals (see also v. 39, and cp. the same use of the neuter in 17:2, "whatsoever," and 17:24, "that which Thou hast given Me"). Then follows the masculine, speaking of each individual who, exercising his will to accept the offer, decides to come to Christ (cp. again the same change to the personal in 17:2 and 24).

There is a change also in the verbs rendered "shall come" and "cometh." The former (*hekō*) stresses the arrival and the being present, and here from the Father's point of view; the latter (*erchomai*) presents the act of coming and marks the voluntary decision of the comer.

The strong negative "in no wise" suggests that, so far from casting out a believer, the Lord will embrace and protect him; it conveys something more than the promise to receive, it carries with it the assurance of eternal security, and intimates the delight of the Lord in this grace toward what is given Him by the Father (for the confirmation of the irreversible and unending security of the believer, see also 11:25, 26).

THE WILL OF THE FATHER

All this, with His assurances of resurrection, He now bases upon (1) the fact of His having come from heaven to do the Father's will, (2) the design of His will. He says, **"For I am come down from Heaven, not to do Mine own will, but the will of Him that sent Me. And this is the will of Him that sent Me, that I should lose nothing, but should raise it up at the last day. For this is the will of My Father, that every one that beholdeth the Son and believeth on Him, should have eternal life; and I will raise him up at the last day"** (vv. 38–40).

The significance of the connecting "For" lies in this, that His having come from heaven to carry out the will of the Father in the eternal salvation of those who come to Him, rules out the possibility of His casting out one such. Four times the Lord speaks of His coming down from heaven, here and verses 50, 51, 58. He thus precludes the idea that He is expressing simply His own opinion or speaking for Himself.

Again the neuter is used, signifying the complete company of believers viewed as an entity. That He will not lose any implies His guarding care (cp. 17:12; 18:9). This negative is followed by the positive declaration of His consummating act in their resurrection, an act which confirms the assurance of their eternal security.

The statement as to resurrection is repeated, with the same change as has been noted above. When He says, firstly, that it is the Father's will that He should raise up at the last day all that which He has given Him (the entire company), He is declaring the salvation of believers from the Father's point of view. When He repeats His assurance, and says "I will raise him [the individual believer] up at the last day," He is regarding the matter from the point of view of the believer himself as one that "beholdeth the Son and believeth on Him." In the first pronouncement He gives the assurance that He will lose nothing, all is the gift of the Father; in the second each one has eternal life, as the result of his faith.

NO OUTER DARKNESS FOR ANY BELIEVER

This pledge that everyone will be raised, as the result of having been given Him irrevocably, utterly refutes the erroneous doctrine that certain believers will be cast into the outer darkness during the millennium on account of their state of unwatchfulness at the time of His Second Coming.

The verb rendered "beholdeth" is *theōreō* (not the simple verb *horaō*, to see, as in the A.V.); it indicates a close contemplation or careful perusal, and the meaning is, "everyone who contemplates the Son with the effect of believing on Him." It was not so with the Jews. They had seen Him (*horaō*) and did not believe. A person cannot believe in the Lord Jesus Christ and be saved without that measure of consideration of His person and work of redeeming grace which results in faith in Him. No mere passing consideration is sufficient.

As to the phrase "at the last day," the word is used to mark the time in which all who have part in the first resurrection will be raised, both those at the Rapture (1 Thess. 4:16) and those who, having suffered death during "the time of Jacob's trouble" or "the great tribulation," will be raised subsequently (Rev. 20:4–6). The Lord did not disclose such details to the Jews. Nor would they have received it. And though He revealed the subject more fully to His disciples later in the Upper Room, the full revelation was reserved for apostolic ministry after churches had been formed. This gradual process of the unfolding of prophetic truth at different times in the course of divine revelation demands consideration in order for a right perspective of the purposes of God.

The interruption in the Lord's remarks, by the murmuring of the Jews, is suggestive of their dissatisfaction with His exposure of the condition of their hearts. The immediate reason was His claim involving their deprivation of eternal life through their refusal to accept Him. They evidently felt this. As a matter of fact, His guarantee of resurrection to life is the crowning point of the truth that He is the Bread of Life.

UNBELIEF'S EXCUSES

Unbelief is ever ready to make excuses. Accordingly, ignoring the implication of His assurances of life eternal and resurrection for those whom He contrasted with their own guilty attitude, they support their self-complacency by the mutterings of their presumed acquaintance with the circumstances of His birth: **"Is not this Jesus, the Son of Joseph, whose father and mother we know? How doth He now say, I am come down out of Heaven?"** Their plausible questioning, virtually impugning His veracity, was simply an evasion of the chief point of His testimony.

A LESSON FOR THE PREACHER

While briefly rebuking their grumbling, He does not answer their objections, nor does He convey the facts of His birth, or repudiate the calumnies of the Jews concerning it. To do so would have but plunged them deeper into their darkness. The matters of immediate and paramount importance are their own spiritual need and danger, not the mode of His coming into the world, but the means of their coming to Him. What a lesson for the preacher of the gospel when confronted with skeptical arguments on side issues of theology!

"**Murmur not among yourselves,**" He says. "**No man can come to Me, except the Father draw him.**" This necessity of the drawing power of the Father presses home again the sovereignty of God, while what follows enforces the responsibility of man to come to, that is, to believe on, His Son (vv. 45–51), just as the same two facts were combined in verse 37. The power of the Father to draw is available for those who are willing to come.

Then, for the third time, stressing the tremendous importance of the fact for His hearers, He declares that He will raise up at the last day him who comes. The divine attracting begins the work of salvation; resurrection will complete it.

HOW THE LORD APPEALED TO SCRIPTURE

He now directs them to the Scriptures, with a deeply significant connection with, and continuance of, the subject of coming to Him; "**It is written in the prophets, And they shall all be taught of God. Everyone that hath heard from the Father, and hath learned, cometh unto Me**" (v. 45). Here the Lord uses the prophecy of Isaiah 54:13 (a passage foretelling millennial blessing) to show that God draws men by teaching, not by legal statutes, nor by outward vision, nor by mere action on the emotions, but by gracious instruction, and that His teaching has Christ Himself as its object. His quotation does not imply that the Scripture provides Him with His doctrine; nay, He confirms His doctrine by appealing to the Scripture.

THE NECESSITY OF COMING TO THE SON

Later on to the disciples He says, "**No one cometh unto the Father but by Me**" (14:6). Now He says, No one cometh unto Me but by the Father (v. 44). Yet it remains the responsibility of men to hear and learn, and so, by the Father's instruction, to come to the Son, in whom all the counsels of grace and glory center.

But why does He now say, "**Not that any man hath seen the Father, save He which is from God; He hath seen the Father**"? Firstly, to prevent any idea that the Son is to be dissociated from the Father. Their unity He stresses in a subsequent discourse (10:30). Secondly, to show that the revelation of the Father is by the Son: "The only begotten Son, which is in the bosom of the Father, He hath declared Him" (1:18): "He that hath seen Me hath seen the Father" (14:9). Thirdly, to show that any access to the Father is to be distinguished absolutely from that open, immediate and uninterrupted vision enjoyed alone by the Son. He thus puts Himself above Moses, whom the Lord knew only "face to face" (Deut. 34:10). Fourthly, to enforce upon His hearers not only the fact of His deity as the Son, but the necessity of coming to the Son as the One who, in virtue of this, can alone be the means of spiritual life and subsistence.

The preposition *para*, "from," in the phrase "He which is from God," signifies "from beside," "from (being) with"; it indicates source of origin (cp. 15:26, of the Holy Spirit). While pondering over such phraseology, we need to bear in mind the unity of the Three in One Godhead. As has been well said, They are "neither three Gods, nor three parts of God. Rather they are God threefoldly, God tri-personally. The personal distinction in the Godhead is a distinction within, and of, unity, not a distinction which qualifies unity, or usurps the place of it, or destroys it." All this remained true and in continuity throughout the life of Christ on earth.

In verse 47 we come to the Lord's third "Verily, verily," each being, as we have noticed, designed to arrest the attention of His hearers in a particular way. In what follows He declares still more explicitly certain facts which He had before stated. Albeit His teaching leads up to a point (concerning His "flesh") which, owing to their unbelief and hardness of heart, becomes judicially more difficult and unacceptable to their prejudiced minds. And this, as we shall see, increases as He proceeds further toward the close of His discourse. Persistent unbelief makes truth all the harder to grasp.

THE LIVING BREAD: THE PROVISION AND PURPOSE

"**Verily, verily, I say unto you, He that believeth hath eternal life. I am the bread of life.**" The first statement recalls more definitely what He said in verse 40. It is now not "should have" but "hath." His second statement reiterates what He said in verse 35. The repetition is due to the fact that this was the special point of their murmuring (v. 41). He then refers again to the subject of the manna. When they had remarked that their fathers "**ate the manna in the wilderness,**" His reply presented the subject from the point of view of gifts from God, both the manna and Himself, the true bread as the gift of the Father. Now He states the contrast in regard to the receivers. Their fathers ate the manna and "died." Even the manna, the typical bread, did not suffice to maintain physical life in perpetuity. He, the Antitype, is "**the bread which cometh down out of Heaven, that a man** [anyone] **may eat thereof and not die** [the divine purpose, and the unbounded provision]." "**I am,**" He says, "**the living Bread which came down out of Heaven**" (vv. 50, 51). It is important to notice the difference between the present tense, "cometh down," and the aorist, the past definite, "came down." The former does not signify a continual coming down, it indicates the inherent characteristic of the bread, defining (as the article with the present participle does) that which is essential to its nature and to the circumstances indicated. The past tense denotes the historic fact of the descent, the act by which He became incarnate (cp. v. 33). In verse 38 the perfect tense is used, "I have come down," expressing the fact with stress upon the abiding effects.

Again, in each part of this discourse the Lord couples with the fact that the Father sent Him His own voluntary act in coming, in delighted fulfillment of the Father's will. He **"sent Me"** (v. 44); **"I . . . came down"** (v. 51). We must note, too, the change from **"I am the bread"** (v. 48) to **"This is the bread"** (v. 50), and the change from that again to "I am" in verse 51. The "This is" suggests a demonstrative reference to their ignorant reasoning, **"Is not this Jesus, the son of Joseph?"** (v. 42).

THE SENDING AND THE COMING

Further, He had hitherto said **"I am the bread of life"** (vv. 35, 48). Now He says **"I am the living Bread,"** with special stress on "living." There is a difference. The former statement stresses the impartation of life by reason of the characteristic nature and productive power of His person: the latter stresses the essential principle and quality of life which is inherent in Himself.

What a contrast to the lifeless manna, which, under certain conditions, went to corruption! It sustained life just for the day. For those who by faith receive Christ, the living bread, He becomes in them a veritable principle of imperishable life, causing them to live forever.

This confirms positively the preceding negative, **"that a man may live and not die."** So that more than spiritual life is therein assured. To live forever involves the resurrection life hereafter, the eternal life of the whole person, body, soul and spirit. With this in view He had given the assurance, **"I will raise him up at the last day"** (v. 40).

A CLIMAX AND A PARALLEL

His teaching now reaches a climax, in statements more difficult of apprehension for His incredulous hearers than anything He had said hitherto. And the difficulty increases as He proceeds after their interruption. He says, **"Yea, and the bread which I will give is My flesh, for the life of the world."** His "flesh"! In this addition lay a staggering difficulty for them, and they are not alone in experiencing it.

The statement, coupled with what follows, is exhaustive and forms the subject of the next chapter. We may now notice the parallelism between verses 48 to 50 and 51.

(a) **"I am the bread of life"** (v. 48):
(b) **"I am the living bread"** (v. 51).

(a) **"Your fathers did eat manna and died"** (v. 49):
(b) **"If any man eat of this Bread, he shall live forever"** (v. 51).

(a) **"which cometh down out of Heaven"** (v. 50):

(b) **"which came down out of Heaven"** (v. 51).

(a) **"that a man may eat thereof and not die"** (v. 50):
(b) **"the bread which I will give is My flesh, for the life of the world"** (v. 51).

FEASTING ON THE LIVING BREAD

How fully He is able to supply our spiritual needs! What an infinite wealth of provision resides in Him for our growth and development, our strength and refreshment, enabling us to "grow up into Him," becoming conformed to His image (Rom. 8:29)! And all the outcome of His going down into death that we, having been identified with Him therein, and "becoming conformed unto His death," might here and now, in the power of His resurrection, walk in newness of life. May we ever feast upon the living bread. Only so can we in any measure here and now "attain unto the resurrection from the dead" (Phil. 3:11).

A SUMMING UP

The Lord now sums up His discourse by reaffirming, with three reminders, the main facts of His discourse: (1) He is **"the bread which came down from Heaven,"** (2) their fathers ate manna and yet died, (3) **"He that eateth this bread** [Himself "the true Bread," v. 32, "the living bread," v. 51] **shall live forever."** He thus makes a closing appeal for faith in Him.

All this was said in the Capernaum synagogue. The congregation included a considerable number of disciples (many more than the twelve), not a few of whom regarded His speech (*logos* would seem to include the discourse as a whole), as "hard," *i.e.*, difficult to accept, an obstacle to their faith; who could listen to it? They were talking to one another in a low tone.

"But Jesus, knowing in Himself [intuitively perceiving] **that His disciples murmured at this, said unto them, Doth this cause you to stumble? What then if ye should behold the Son of Man ascending where He was before?"** He refers to His ascension. He does not say that they would see it. His rhetorical question did, however, apply to those in the company who actually witnessed it.

His question carries with it the implication of His resurrection and the certainty of His ascension. That event would be the complete vindication and ratification of all His testimony.

Having conveyed the fact of the spiritual and vital import of what He had stated regarding Himself as the Bread of Life and His flesh and blood as the means of life, He reveals the separative effect of His message, separative because of the faith of some and the unbelief of others: **"But there are some of you that believe not."** He **"knew from the beginning who they were that believed not, and,"** among them, in contradistinction to the eleven of His inner circle of disciples, **"who it was that should betray Him."** He knew in precise detail the way in which His death would be accomplished. The shadow of Calvary ever lay across His soul!

APOSTASY OR FIDELITY?

The separative power of His ministry is seen in regard not only to believers but to professed followers. For, following upon His repeated declaration that no one could come to Him **"except it be given of the Father** [all who believe are known to God as such before and to those it is given to come], **many of His disciples went back and walked no more with Him."** Defection or devotion? The choice lies with us in our day.

So it has ever been. The gospel is either the word of life to those who accept it, or a ministry of death to those who refuse: it is "the power of God" to those "who are being saved," but "foolishness" to "them that are perishing."

When the Lord said to His unbelieving hearers **"the bread which I will give is My flesh,"** He knew that this would meet with a stronger objection on their part than anything He had said previously. Their unbelief retributively made the unfolding of the mystery of His person and purpose for which He had come into the world the more difficult for them to understand. And the difficulty was enhanced when, after their altercation with one another and the skeptical nature of their question, **"How can this man give His flesh to eat?"** He went further and said, **"Verily, verily, I say unto you, except ye eat the flesh of the Son of Man and drink His blood, ye have not life in yourselves. He that eateth My flesh and drinketh My blood hath eternal life; and I will raise him up at the last day. For My flesh is meat indeed, and My blood is drink indeed,"** an astonishing statement to Jews in view of Leviticus 17:10–16!

What was a stumbling block to them, and has been the subject of much misinterpretation in Christendom, receives its true interpretation, not from the bias of ecclesiastical tradition, but from the Scriptures themselves, and indeed from the Lord's subsequent remarks to His disciples. The Jews persistently took His statements to refer to literal blood and flesh and to the physical acts of eating and drinking. This erroneous view He repudiated in the explanation, **"It is the spirit that quickeneth; the flesh profiteth nothing: the words that I have spoken unto you are spirit, and are life. But there are some of you that believe not."**

HIS FLESH AND HIS BLOOD

His "flesh" stands here, not simply for His bodily frame, but for the entire manhood, spirit, soul and body of the Son of man, Who, by giving Himself up to the death of the cross, provided Himself thereby as the means of eternal life and sustenance. His "blood" represents, not simply the physical element, but the giving up of His life by atoning sacrifice, in the shedding of His blood. The blood is essential to life. "For the life of the flesh is in the blood . . . for it is the blood that maketh atonement by reason of life" (Lev. 17:11, R.V.). Thus the saving efficacy of the death of Christ depends upon the fact that by the shedding of His blood He gave His life (Matt. 20:28), that "He gave Himself up" (Gal. 2:20).

NOT THE LORD'S SUPPER: A DISTINCTION

What He says in this sixth chapter has no reference to the Lord's Supper. And for the following reasons: (a) Had the Supper been in view, to eat of the bread of the Supper would constitute the participant a partaker of eternal life apart from the condition of faith in Christ; (b) the paramount subject in this part of the discourse is eternal life: that subject is never mentioned in connection with the Lord's Supper; (c) to take His teaching to refer to that, is to give a literal application, whereas He plainly indicates that His words concerning His flesh and blood were not so intended; (d) He says that the giving of His flesh is "for the life of the world"; the Lord's Supper was instituted not for the world but for His disciples; (e) in His instruction concerning the Supper He speaks of His body, whereas here He speaks of His flesh.

FIVE RESULTING BENEFITS

The solemn warning in verse 53 of the consequences of not partaking of His flesh and blood is followed by a series of gracious assurances as to the blessedness of doing so:

1. To eat His flesh and drink His blood, that is, to appropriate to oneself the saving efficacy of His death, is to be in *possession of eternal life*. In verse 54 the word for eating is changed from the general term *phagō*, which was used previously, to *trōgō*, which is used in the rest of the discourse. This verb, primarily signifying to chew, lays stress upon the process of eating; it is thus more intensive than *phagō*, and the change marks an increase in the difficulty of His language for His skeptical audience.

2. He will *raise him up at the last day*. For the third time, and with evident joy in the repetition and in the assured prospect of His mighty act, the Lord looks on to His final victory over death.

3. **"For My flesh is meat indeed, and My blood is drink indeed"**—or, closely to the original, "*true food*" and "*true drink*" (see R.V. margin; cp. v. 32).

4. **"He that eateth My flesh, and drinketh My blood, abideth in Me, and I in him,"** *a mutual indwelling* of which the Lord speaks more fully to the disciples later in the Upper Room, a permanent oneness of life and the deepest intimacy of communion. The believer finds his life in Christ, and Christ imparts His to the believer.

5. **"As the living Father sent Me, and I live because of the Father; so he that eateth Me, he also shall live because of Me."** The phrase "the living Father" implies His self-existence and describes Him as the One in whom life, unoriginated, resides essentially. He is therefore also the center and source of life. So with the Son, Who is one with the Father (10:30). Here He testifies that, as the Son, the sent one, who had become man, He lives **"because of** [or by reason of, not "by," as in the A.V.] the Father" (see 5:26). And since the Son communicates life to the one who by faith appropriates Him to himself the believer lives and ever will live by reason of Him.

THE THIRD PUBLIC DISCOURSE IN JOHN'S GOSPEL

During the Feast of Tabernacles, Jesus returns to Jerusalem, and He addresses some of those who have crowded the city. There are really four public discourses in John chapter seven, the first in reply to the Jews (vv. 14–24), the second in reply to some of the people in Jerusalem (vv. 25–31), the third after the officials from the Sanhedrin had come to take Him (vv. 32–36), the fourth, on the last day of the feast (vv. 37–39).

In [John] chapter seven the scene of Christ's controversy with the Jews shifts from Galilee to Jerusalem. The crisis grows in intensity. The circumstances are now connected with the Feast of Tabernacles, with its immense concourse of the people, and the Jewish feasts in the Gospel of John in connection with the Lord's testimony seem to occur in their chronological order. While in Galilee, His brethren, who, in their worldly wisdom, did not believe on Him, had bidden Him go into Judea, that He might give an exhibition of His works to His followers, manifest Himself to the world, and so restore the national glory of Israel. To this He pointedly replied that their ideas and ways were contrary to His. They were yet on the side of the world (though that attitude was not to continue indefinitely). He bade them go to the feast; He Himself would be absent from its beginning. After they had gone He went up Himself **"not publicly, but as it were in secret,"** fully cognizant of the trend which the renewed controversy would take, and purposely ordering His movements with the eventual issues in view leading to His death. He knew that the Jews would be seeking Him at the feast, and so they did (v. 11).

THE SOURCE OF TRUTH AND LIGHT

To the crowds, and particularly those who had come up from Galilee, He was the subject of much discussion and of very divergent ideas. There was **"much murmuring among them."** Some regarded Him as **"a good man,"** but they had to keep their discussions quiet through fear of the religious leaders and their "Gestapo" agents. Others declaimed Him as a deceiver and dangerous. The close of this part of the controversy issues in an actual attempt, instigated by the hierarchy through the said agents, to seize Him, an attempt in which some of the multitude themselves were ready to take part (vv. 30, 32, 44, 45). At the appointed time, the midst of the feast, the Lord goes right up into the temple and begins to preach. In what follows in this and the next few chapters the Lord reveals Himself as the source of truth and light, just as in the preceding discourse He had revealed Himself as the source and support of life.

There are really four public discourses in chapter seven, the first in reply to the Jews (vv. 14–24), the second in reply to some of the people in Jerusalem

(vv. 25–31), the third after the officials from the Sanhedrin had come to take Him (vv. 32–36), the fourth, on the last day of the feast (vv. 37–39).

"I DELIGHT TO DO THY WILL"

The teaching He gave in the temple aroused the astonishment of the Jews: **"How knoweth this man letters,"** they said, **"having never learned?"** "This man" was contemptuous, as in 6:42. Their astonishment lay in the fact that He had manifested such learning without having attended the rabbinical schools, to receive the usual instruction from the recognized representatives of traditional religion. The Lord, ever delighting to glorify the Father (see 17:4), at once replies, **"My teaching is not Mine, but His that sent Me"** (cp. 5:19, as to His deeds; 5:30, as to His judgment; 6:38, as to His will; 6:57, as to His life; 8:26, 28, 38, as to His words).

How insignificant was the rabbinical instruction compared with this! Here was a source unique; for it lay in the absolute and unbroken oneness of the Son with Him who had sent Him. Both the evidence of His teaching and His own testimony concerning it should have silenced all cavils.

THE WILL TO DO GOD'S WILL

He proceeds at once to bring home to them the responsibility to receive His teaching and the condition upon which that responsibility can be discharged: **"If any man** (anyone) **willeth** (not simply the future "will," but the exercise of the human will, the definite intention) **to do His will, he shall know of the teaching, whether it be of God, or whether I speak from Myself"** (v. 17). To know that He spoke from God was to realize that His teaching was the voice of God to men. His teaching and our doing are to be conjoint. And the condition for this lies in our willingness. The doing of God's will is not merely a matter of faith, but of a heart in harmony with Himself: It is neither mechanical nor compulsory, but intelligent and voluntary. This was not to be obtained simply in the rabbinical schools; nor is it acquired merely by courses of theological study.

The Lord now states the motival evidence of the source of His teaching. The test of its validity lay in its motive. **"He that speaketh from** (not "of," in the sense of "concerning") **himself seeketh his own glory: but He that seeketh the glory of Him that sent Him, the same is true, and no unrighteousness is in Him."** This was true only of Christ. Human teachers who are possessors of the highest motives are not thereby free from error. Any ambassador who seeks the glory of his master is "true," and carries out his commission righteously. But the Lord alone perfectly fulfilled the criterion. His, and His only, was undeviatingly selfless obedience to the Father.

In the next verse He does not pass to a different subject, He illustrates what He has just said by the utter contrast in their case. They gloried in the Law as being distinctively their national possession, and had they sought the glory of God they would have been possessed of a will to fulfill His commandments.

With them it was otherwise. **"Did not Moses give you the Law, and yet none of you doeth the Law? Why seek ye to kill Me?"** (cp. Acts 7:53).

Once in seven years, at the Feast of Tabernacles, the whole Law was publicly read daily (Deut. 31:10–13). Whether that took place on this occasion or not (though it is quite possible), there was doubtless a reference to it in the charge He made. The first part of the Law as customarily read, namely, Deuteronomy 1:1–6:3, contained the command, "Thou shalt not kill," an injunction they were breaking in their intention concerning Him.

"THE MEEKNESS AND GENTLENESS OF CHRIST"

At this, the multitude, whether ignorant of the fact, or under the influence of their religious leaders, broke in with the insulting rejoinder of His being demon-possessed. With what dignified meekness He meets it! Meekness under insult is the most potent weapon to bring home the guilt of the offense. He simply recalls their attitude on the occasion of His healing of the impotent man at the pool of Bethesda, and their accusation against Him of sabbath-breaking. **"I did one work,"** He says, **"and ye all marvel. For this cause** (the text is to be preferred to the R.V. margin) **hath Moses given you circumcision (not that it is of Moses, but of the fathers;)** perhaps a reference to the rabbinical technicalities of interpretation; the rabbis had a saying that "Circumcision gives away the sabbath"; **and on the sabbath ye circumcise a man. If a man receiveth circumcision on the sabbath, that the Law of Moses may not be broken, are ye wroth with Me, because I made a man every whit whole on the sabbath? Judge not according to appearance, but judge righteous judgment"** (vv. 21–24).

If the Sabbath yielded place to a ceremonial ordinance, how much more a deed of mercy! (The word *cholao*, here only in the New Testament, signifies to be bitterly resentful; cp. English "choler.") His gracious act was a breach of the Sabbath only in outward appearance. Their view of the deed was the negation of righteous judgment.

The Lord's vindication of Himself and His work of healing (7:21–24) was again interrupted by a questioning on the part of some of the Jerusalem residents (perhaps proud of their local connection, in contrast to the numerous visitors) as to why the rulers (the hierarchy) had not taken measures against Him. Surely they could not "have come to know" (*ginōskō*) that He was the Messiah (v. 26). **"Howbeit,"** they say, **"we know** (*oida*, we are perfectly aware of) **this man whence He is, but when the Christ cometh, no one knoweth whence He is."** In their opinion that was a sufficient answer to their question. They may have referred to His parentage. The belief had been disseminated among the Jews that since the Messiah would appear in the manner foretold, e.g., in Daniel 7:13 and Malachi 3:1, His origin would be unknown.

A SERIOUS LACK OF KNOWLEDGE

Taking up the words of their objection the Lord concedes to them their knowledge as to the external facts concerning Himself, but they lack the all-important knowledge, the higher truths of His being. **"Ye both know Me, and know whence I am; and** [here a word of contrast, as often in John's writings] **I am not come to Myself, but He that sent Me is true** [i.e., He has fulfilled His Word in sending Me], **whom ye know not. I know Him** [*oida*, I have absolute knowledge of Him], **because I am from Him and He sent Me"** (cp. vv. 16, 17).

A CLIMAX IN HIS TESTIMONY

He declares His complete consciousness of His eternal Sonship, His unoriginated preexistence with the Father, and His combined deity and humanity as the Father's sent one.

This aroused an intense enmity against Him on the part of the fanatical Jews, who would have seized Him there and then, and were only just not bold enough to do so, through force of circumstances. Their action was impossible because **"His hour was not yet come."** The attitude of the multitude was different. Many had been favorably impressed and **"believed on Him,"** admitting, that is to say, His claim to be the Messiah (v. 31). This was too much for the hierarchy. Christ's influence was clearly in the ascendant. Accordingly they issued a warrant for His arrest and sent temple officers to seize Him (the chief priests are here mentioned for the first time by John). This He calmly and boldly met with a declaration anticipative of His death, at the same time continuing His testimony as to the Father and intimating the terrible doom of His opponents: **"Yet a little while am I with you, and I go unto Him that sent Me. Ye shall seek Me, and shall not find Me; and where I am ye cannot come."** An impassable barrier would be placed between Him and them, both as to any purpose or desire regarding Him, whether hostile or otherwise, and as to any possibility of their ever being in His presence in His Father's glory (cp. 8:21; 13:33; and Luke 17:26).

A SCOFF WITH AN UNINTENTIONAL REALITY

This met with scorn. Where would **"this man"** (a scoffing epithet) go? Would He go to their Hellenistic fellow-nationals scattered among gentile peoples? Would He, forsooth, even teach the Gentiles? How ignorantly their sarcasm anticipated the very thing He would do by the mission of the Spirit through His gospel messengers after His ascension!

The controversy died down till the last day, **"the great day of the Feast,"** the Hosanna Rabba. The eighth day was, like the first, observed as a Sabbath (Lev. 23:39); special sacrifices were offered (Num. 29:36–38). During the seven days preceding, pilgrims, leaving their booths, marched in procession seven times round the city, shouting "Hosanna." Crowds followed the priests and Levites daily bearing the golden vessels to the brook of Siloam to carry the water thereof up to the temple, where it would be poured into a silver vessel on the eastern side of the altar of burnt offering, and all to the chanting of Isaiah's words, **"Ho, every one that thirsteth, come ye to the waters,"** and **"With joy shall ye draw water out of the wells of salvation."**

This ritual was apparently not observed on the eighth day, for whereas the preceding ritual symbolized the water from the rock in the wilderness, the eighth day commemorated their entrance into the **"land of springs of water."**

"Rivers of Living Water"

This day therefore provided the occasion for the giver of the water of life to interpose His invitation to the spiritually needy. Standing before the crowds with a solemn and authoritative dignity, and with a kindly summons that rang out over the whole scene, He cried, **"If any man thirst, let Him come unto Me, and drink. He that believeth on Me, as the Scripture hath said, out of his belly shall flow the rivers of living water"** (v. 38).

The Lord thus promises a twofold source of refreshment and satisfaction: He Himself satisfies the thirsty soul, and by the indwelling Holy Spirit the believer is to be the means of satisfying others. To the Samaritan woman He had spoken of the water bestowed by Him as becoming in the recipient "a well of water springing up unto eternal life"; now He enlarges the promise: the believer is to be a channel of the fullness of life-giving ministry and enrichment to needy souls. He does not say "a river of living water," but "rivers." What a contrast to the ewer of water poured out each day of the feast!

How great the possibilities of a Spirit-filled life! How important that we should permit nothing to clog the channel! This being "filled with the Spirit" is not an attainment securing a condition of permanent freedom from any defect on our part, it necessitates recourse to the efficacy of the cleansing blood of Christ (1 John 1:7), and the renewing of our mind (Rom. 12:2). The purpose of the Spirit is to glorify Christ (John 16:14) and this ministry He fulfills in and through the believer who, seeking to refrain from grieving the Spirit, presents his body to God as a living sacrifice.

So let us thirst, come, be filled, and be a channel of supply. The "living waters" were figurative of the Holy Spirit (v. 38) and the Lord was promising what would, and did, take place at Pentecost, and from that time onward. The Spirit would not be given thus till the Lord Jesus was glorified. There is no mention here of the Church; only the individual believer is in view. Further, what is here mentioned is not the Spirit's work of regeneration. He was to be a gift to those who were already believers when Christ was on earth. What takes place since Pentecost is that when we believe and are born of the Spirit, He indwells us and becomes a river flowing through us in blessing to others.

DIVISION OWING TO HIS TEACHING

The reasonings and discussions which follow concerning Christ on the part of the multitude (vv. 40–44) are only samples of what has occurred ever since. The world by its wisdom, religious or otherwise, knows Him not.

The "multitude" are to be distinguished from "the Jews." The latter desired to take His life. Some of the people would have arrested Him. In respect the effects of His testimony upon the people afforded a sample of what has ever taken place since: **"there arose a division because of Him."** Such divisions have been numerous. Just as failure to understand His teaching produced such divisive results, so failure to understand and accept the Scriptures concerning Him have produced the numerous sects and parties of Christendom.

The officers sent by the chief priests and Pharisees to arrest Him failed in their purpose, apparently through timidity. His testimony was such as to prevent His being taken before the divinely appointed time. **"Never man so spake."** True it was, and ever has been. His words have ever had differing but decisive effects, either winning the heart or hardening it.

The religious leaders, the Sanhedrin, condemned all who dared to differ from them or who rejected their authority, a great characteristic of the potentates of traditional ecclesiastical systems. The multitude, regarded as ignorant of the law, were accounted "accursed." Even Nicodemus, who could speak from a position of equality and pointed out that while they were pleading for "the law" they were themselves breaking it (v. 51), became the object of their scorn. Was he, forsooth, of Galilee? No prophet, they said, arose from Galilee. But Jonah came from Galilee, and probably Hosea and Nahum, to say nothing of others.

THE FOURTH PUBLIC DISCOURSE IN JOHN'S GOSPEL

The fourth public discourse in the Gospel of John is a series of declarations and interruptions as controversy arises between Jesus and the Pharisees. The dialogue took place in a very public setting, so the whole crowd overheard His claims. Christ was speaking "in the Treasury," one of the most frequented parts of the temple. Close by, the Sanhedrin was in session planning His arrest, for they believed He spoke blasphemy.

In contrast therefore to the darkness of His foes, who were under the Law, and breakers of it, [Jesus] immediately says to the people, **"I am the light of the world: he that followeth Me shall not walk in the darkness, but shall have the light of life"** (8:12). This consituted a direct claim to be the Messiah.

Not improbably this statement in verse 12 had reference to another ceremony of the Feast of Tabernacles, just as His proclamation concerning the "living water" had reference to the carrying of water from the pool of Siloam. On the evenings of the Feast, except the last, the Court of the Women was brilliantly illuminated, in commemoration of the pillar of fire which guided Israel in the trackless desert, and the night was given up to dancing and festivity. Christ had appropriated to Himself the type of the rock; now He does the same with the pillar of fire. The city shone in the glow of the ceremonial light; He declares Himself to be "the Light of the world." The fiery pillar was Israel's guide for night journeying, to be a follower of Jesus is to have "the light of life."

LIGHT AND LIFE

Day by day, step by step, he who "follows His steps" (1 Pet. 2:21) will "see light in His light." Yea more, since Christ is Himself the light of life, the light that dispenses life, he who lives in Him and partakes of His life, himself becomes light, "light in the Lord," walking as a "child of light" (Eph. 5:8). And this is to love even as He loves. "He that loveth his brother abideth in the light, and there is none occasion of stumbling in him." Christ taught, then, that He was the Bread of Life, for nourishment; the Water of Life, for the thirsty, the Light of Life, for His followers.

"THE FAITHFUL AND TRUE WITNESS"

And now there follows a whole series of interruptions in His discourse. The controversy becomes keener. The claim to be the Light of the World, and to minister the Light of Life, aroused a fierce objection on the part of the Pharisees: **"Thou bearest witness of Thyself; Thy witness is not true."** They were doubtless recalling His words, **"If I bear witness of Myself, My witness is not true"** (5:31). With that His present reply, **"Even if I** [the pronoun is emphatic] **bear witness of Myself, My witness is true,"** is perfectly consistent. In 5:31 He had referred to their law of evidence, and had declared His fulfillment of its requirements.

The evidence of one may be perfectly true, but is not valid without corroboration which is afforded in the fuller way. The Lord's testimony was never single: **"I am One that beareth witness of Myself,"** He says, **"and the Father that sent Me beareth witness."** He shows that His evidence is true, because of the unique character of His being and destiny. In 5:31 He appealed to the dual witness of His Father and His own. Now, when He precedes the reaffirmation of this by saying that even if he does bear witness of Himself His witness is true, He shows that in the very essentials of His being the knowledge of His critics is deficient. For His own testimony is the outcome of His divine preexistence, His divine consciousness and futurity. Of all this they were entirely ignorant. About it only He Himself could bear witness. **"My witness is true,"** He says, **"for I know whence I came, and whither I go; but ye know not whence I come, or whither I go."** The change of tense from "I came" to "I come" is to be noted. As to His own knowledge He refers to His preexistence and His incarnation. In regard to their ignorance He speaks of His coming as in the present. Accordingly, though they could not know the former, they could recognize the present evidences and acknowledge the authority of the One who had sent Him.

They judged **"after the flesh,"** treating Him as a mere man and so rejecting His witness as invalid. **"I judge no man,"** He says. He had come not to judge but to save. **"Yea, and if I judge, My judgment is true; for I am not alone, but I and the Father that sent Me."** The requirement as to the twofold witness was therefore fulfilled. But why does He say "your law," and not "the Law," in the matter of the validity of the witness of "two men"? (Deut. 19:15). He was in no way repudiating the Law; the point of the "your" law in this, that they were professed expounders of it and charged Him with failure to fulfill it.

EQUAL HONOR TO THE FATHER AND THE SON

Christ's constant testimony to the fact that the Father had sent Him elicits, in 8:19, the scornful question, **"Where is Thy Father?"** as if to suggest "Granted, then, that you are one witness; let us see the other, Him of whom you speak as your Father. Thus you will evidentially fulfill the requirements of the Law!" This is an instance of the use of the Word of God to support erroneous ideas and prejudices! How very differently, on a later occasion, one of His disciples made the request "Show us the Father" (14:8)!

The Lord replies, **"Ye know neither Me, nor My Father; if ye knew Me, ye would know My Father also."** Their ideas of the dual witness to which He had referred were utterly awry. His statement conveys a vital truth. To ignore Him in the reality of His person and work is to be ignorant of God the Father. It is through the Son that the Father reveals Himself. The Son is the one and only means of knowing the Father. To claim God as Father while neglecting the Son is fatal blindness. Men are largely ready to talk about God, and to appeal to God, while failing to recognize and acknowledge His Son, Jesus Christ, and His demand that all men should "honor the Son, even as they honor the Father" (5:23).

DYING IN SIN

The dialogue was in public. The crowd could hear it. Christ was speaking "in the Treasury," called so because of the bronze chests placed for the reception of gifts in the Court of the Women, one of the most frequented parts of the temple. Close by, the Sanhedrin was in session planning His arrest. Their object failed **"because His hour was not yet come"** (v. 20).

Accordingly He continues His teaching, and now with solemn denunciation of His detractors. **"I go away,"** He says, **"and ye shall seek Me, and shall die in your sin: whither I go, ye cannot come."** "Away" is the right rendering; there is no pronoun representing "My" in the original. There is special stress on the "I," however. The feast was drawing to its close. Considerable numbers of the people would be leaving for various destinations. So, in the hearing of the crowd, He says to His critics, "I [I too] am going away," not that He was leaving there and then. His words had another significance, as is clear from His solemn declaration that whither He was going they could not come.

They would die in their sin: the singular, the right rendering of the original, points to the state of sin, not here to the acts, as in verse 24. The singular is used again in verse 34 and presents sin as a unity in essence though the effects are manifold.

They ignore His warning as to their sin, and ask, with malicious scorn, indicative of increasing hardness of heart, **"Will He kill Himself, that He saith, Whither I go, ye cannot come?"** The implication in this was that by suicide He would utterly perish, and therefore of course they, as Abraham's descendants bound for paradise, could certainly not go where He was going.

THE "I AM"

The Lord showed at once that He knew their hearts, and says **"Ye are from beneath; I am from above: ye are of this world; I am not of this world."** These statements are not parallel, as if "from beneath" is the same as "of this world." The first contrast presents extreme opposites, and is to be understood in the light of His words, **"Ye are of your father the devil"** (v. 44). Here in verse 23 the Lord passes, for the moment, from the more solemn declaration of their evil spiritual connection, to their identification with the world as alienated from God. And having thus patiently met their scornful remark, He impugns their refusal to believe, as the reason why they would suffer eternal doom: **"I said therefore unto you, that ye shall die in your sins** [plural now, expressing, not a condition, as in verse 21, but details of the life which mark conduct]; **for except ye believe that I am He, ye shall die in your sins."**

There is no word in the Greek representing "He." We must therefore take the "I am" as it stands; and while there is perhaps a connection with His word "I am from above," there is more in it than this. He is disclosing the essential nature of His being, as in the Name Jehovah, the "I am" of Exodus 3:14. It conveys the thought, "I am what I am," and carries with it the truth of His unoriginated pre-existence and immutability. See verse 58 and the sequel. This acceptance of the fact of His deity is essential to salvation.

THE EMBODIMENT OF HIS TEACHING

The declaration is so stupendous that they ask, with malicious violence, and with great emphasis on the "Thou," **"Who art Thou?"** or, more expressively, "Thou, who art Thou?" Their ignorance was their death. To know Him is "Life eternal" (17:3).

His reply is rendered in the A.V., "Even the same that I said unto you from the beginning," and in the R.V., **"Even that which I have spoken unto you from the beginning."** Certainly He did not mean that He was what He had told them at first. In the clause, "Even that which I have spoken unto you," the tense is not the perfect but the present, and the meaning, thus far, is that He is the embodiment, the personal expression, of what He speaks. His doctrine is Himself, it is insepa-rable from His being, His attributes and character. He says "I am that which I speak." Now as to the phrase rendered "from the beginning," in the clause in the original there is nothing representing "from." The Lord is not referring to what He had said from a special beginning, but to the essential character of what He speaks to them. The phrase has the meaning "absolutely" or "altogether."

Accordingly the meaning is "I am essentially and undeviatingly what I speak to you." It stood in direct contrast to the character of their religious leaders and to all with whom principles are one thing and practice another, to anyone who has the effrontery to intimate to his hearers that they must do as he says but not as he does. But of Christ alone could it be true that altogether what He spoke was the expression of what He was. This is in keeping with the main trend of all His testimony in these discourses (see especially the immediately following vv. 26, 28, 29), and with His later declaration, "I am the truth."

THE COMING JUDGE

Had it not been for their hardness of heart, Christ might have enlarged upon the matter of discipleship and explained more fully the nature of His being. Instead of this He has matters about which to speak concerning themselves. Hence the apparent break in the connection. They wanted to find out something by which they could judge Him. He shows that there are things in their own life which He has to reveal, and upon which He has to pronounce judgment: **"I have many things to speak and to judge concerning you"** (v. 26). Let the critic of Christ and the denier of His deity beware. Such will yet find Him to be their judge.

The time for His judicial dealings with the Pharisees had not come. His immediate object was to continue bearing witness concerning the Father and His unity with Him. Accordingly He proceeds with declarations to this end: **"howbeit He that sent Me is true and the things which I heard from Him, these speak I unto the world."** What they needed was a right understanding of His ministry and of its source. Had they apprehended this it would have adjusted their views in conformity with the teaching of the Old Testament Scriptures. But just here they failed, as many have done since: **"They perceived not that He spake to them of the Father"** (v. 27). Their hearts were so hardened that His words produced no awakening of their conscience.

Accordingly He at once points to the consummating act of their iniquity, and its effects, declaring at the same time His power to reveal the future: **"Jesus therefore said, When ye have lifted up the Son of Man, then shall ye know that I am, and that I do nothing of Myself, but as the Father taught Me, I speak these things."** His Crucifixion (cp. 3:14; 12:32, 34) would issue in the manifest vindication of the truth relating to His person ("I am") and therefore to His mes-siahship as the One sent of the Father. It would issue, too, in their recognition of what He had taught concerning His relationship with the Father in regard both to His works ("I do") and His words ("I speak"). All this was fulfilled at

Pentecost and subsequently, and will have its final accomplishment hereafter in the restored nation.

A FURTHER CLAIM

To confirm it all He declares that He who had sent Him was with Him, a fact utterly incomprehensible to minds occupied with merely mundane expectations. Yet it expressed His own consolation and His joy in the love of the Father amidst the sorrow of His pathway to Calvary: **"The Father hath not left Me alone** (the aorist is perfective in meaning, and should not be rendered "did not leave"); **for I do always the things that are pleasing to Him."** Here are two coextensive and simultaneous conditions, undeviating fulfillment of the Father's will, and consequently uninterrupted enjoyment of His presence. And the principle holds good for those who are Christ's followers, though we come far short of His perfect standard. Our realization and enjoyment of the presence of the Lord is conditioned by our devoted obedience to Him. Let us then make it our aim ever "to be well-pleasing unto Him" (2 Cor. 5:9).

THE EFFECTS

The ministry of Christ had widely different effects, as has ever since been the case with testimony concerning Him. A difference is noted by the apostle as he makes a break in the record of the discourse in chapter eight. This is brought out in the R.V. of verses 30, 31. What Christ had said caused many to believe "on Him." It is otherwise with those Jews mentioned in verse 31; they had merely "believed Him." The former had full faith in Him; the latter were simply disposed to believe what He said.

To these the Lord applies a test designed to raise their credence to a higher level. One crucial point, one essential condition, and their credence collapsed: **"If ye abide in My word,"** He says, **"then are ye truly My disciples."** Faith that saves produces discipleship. Discipleship depends upon the permanent application of His teaching to oneself. Passing impulses do not make disciples. The first "ye" and the first "My" have special emphasis: "If you on your part abide in the word that is Mine. . . ."

THE LIBERTY OF SUBJECT WILL

Now comes that part of the test that disclosed the actual state of their hearts: **"and ye shall know the truth, and the truth shall make you free."** How true it is! Acceptance of, and adherence to, the Word of God shake off the shackles not only of sin, but of human tradition, ecclesiastical bondage, and mere religion. Every truth received prepares for the unfolding of more truth, and each brings its own liberating power. Behind the acceptance is the will to accept. Let the will be unfettered, and we shall enjoy the liberty of devoted subjection to His will.

The idea of being made free was too much for their pride. They answered Him, **"We be Abraham's seed, and have never yet been in bondage to any man: how sayest Thou** [emphatic], **Ye shall be made free?"** Pride blinds the mind to facts. What about their times of oppression, their captivity, and their then-present subjugation to the Roman yoke? The Lord, however, goes deeper than all this. The needs of the soul outweigh material considerations: **"Jesus answered them, Verily, verily, I say unto you, Everyone that committeth sin is the bondservant of sin. And the bondservant abideth not in the house forever: the Son abideth forever"** (vv. 34, 35).

The tense of the verb rendered "committeth" signifies not the committal of an act, but a course of sin; the better rendering would be, "everyone who continueth to do sin." That is what constitutes slavery to sin (so in 1 John 3:4, 6, 7, 9, which should be read in the R.V.). True it is that the willful committal of a sinful act indicates a condition of heart which involves slavery to sin, but that differs from being overtaken by temptation and the committal of an unpremeditated act. Such bondage was the condition of His hearers, despite their high national ancestry.

Just as a slave is not a member of a family and has no claim to be in the house, so they, Jews though they were, were outside God's spiritual family. To be sons of God we must be spiritually related and united to the Son of God by faith. Thus it is that the Son makes us free from bondage to sin. Whosoever is begotten of God does not continue the practice of sin (1 John 3:9). If a person practices sin, whatever his profession may be, he has not been born again.

Identification with the ever-abiding Son gives us ever-abiding freedom. Hence He says, **"If therefore the Son shall make you free, ye shall be free indeed,"** in reality (v. 36). It is "the law (or invigorating principle) of the Spirit of life in Christ Jesus" that makes us "free from the law of sin and death" (Rom. 8:2).

Accordingly, the Lord exposes to them the entire inconsistence of their illusory appeal to Abraham with their determination to kill Him. And the secret of it all was that His word had **"no free course"** in them (v. 37, R.V.).

A TREMENDOUS CONTRAST

He then applies a further test to them: **"I speak the things which I** (emphatic: I on My part) **have seen with My Father,"** and reveals their actual and appalling spiritual parentage: **"and ye** (emphatic: you on your part) **also do the things which ye heard from your father."** Though the definite article is used for the possessive pronoun in each part in the original, the English Versions are right in supplying the possessive pronouns, as they are really involved in the emphatic words "I" and "ye." The "also" is likewise to be noted. It stresses the parallel in the principle involved in the relationships. Yet how great are the contrasts! He, in the infinitely blessed, ineffable, and eternal union as Son with the Father, representing Him here and delighting in fulfilling with unclouded vision His will: they, in a relationship consequent upon their sinful state and their willful persistence in evil, characterizing themselves, in their murderous intent, with the characteristics of the evil one!

The change of the tense is to be noted: "I have seen" (perfect tense), indicating divine counsels in the timeless past, carried into permanent effect in His teachings: "ye heard" (aorist or point tense), a communication proceeding from the devil, made when they became the bondslaves of sin, and issuing in the foul act they were ready to carry out and eventually accomplished!

They repeat their claim in respect of Abraham (v. 39), and then make the higher claim of having **"one Father, even God"** (v. 41). This indicates that their statement **"We were not born of fornication"** had a spiritual reference to idolatry, with perhaps a hint as to the Samaritans (cp. v. 48). He repudiates both claims. They did not the works of Abraham. The principle of like father like son had no application in that respect. And as to the greater claim, He says: **"If God were your Father, ye would love Me for I came forth and am come from God: for neither have I come of Myself, but He sent Me"** (v. 42).

OF WHOM IS GOD THE FATHER?

What a proof this gives of the falsity of the doctrine of the universal fatherhood of God! What a rebuke to the rationalist who professes belief in the fatherhood of God and yet sets Christ aside! Such belief is pure assumption, void of any foundation of fact. The relationship is dependent upon faith in Christ (Gal. 3:26), and is evidentially established by devotion to Him, not in mere sentiment but in true discipleship. To miss the object for which the Father sent Him, and to fail in the response of love to Him, is to be void of any claim to have God as one's Father. True children of God necessarily love Him who is the Son of God.

The Lord's statement, **"I came forth and am come from God,"** is anticipative of His similar and still more comprehensive words later to His disciples, **"I came forth from the Father. I came out from the Father, and am come into the world"** (16:27, 28). The two passages show that He was in eternally preexistent relationship as the Son with the Father, and that this relationship did not take inception at His Birth.

His necessarily stern denunciation of these opposing Jews reveals more even than previously their terrible spiritual condition. They could not hear His word (*logos*, the matter or substance of His speech), and hence could not understand His speech (*lalia*, the manner of language of His speech), verse 43. Refusal to listen to the voice of the Lord dulls the intelligence. "They were of their father the Devil, and the lusts of their father it was their will to do" (R.V.; cp. 1 John 3:8, 10, which perhaps recalls Christ's words). Their resemblance to the evil one as his spiritual offspring was twofold: **"He was a murderer from the beginning** [i.e., from the time of his jealous attack upon the human soul at the Fall, and permanently since], **and stood not in the truth"**; the true reading is probably "standeth not," as in the R.V. margin, which is confirmed by the next statement, **"because there is no truth in him."** That is to say, he continues to be what he was at the beginning referred to. **"When he speaketh a lie** [not that he ever speaks the truth, for, as the Lord has just stated, it is not in him], **he speaketh of his own** [the fallen nature and qualities which are characteristically his]; **for he is a liar** [e.g., Gen. 3:4] **and the father thereof"** (or, rather, as it may be rendered, "of him," i.e., of the liar—that with which the Lord was charging them).

A DOUBLE GUILT EXPOSED

Of these two sins, then, they were guilty: they were murderers because of their determination to do away with Him; they were liars because they said God was their Father (see vv. 54, 55, where He marks this as their lie). "But," He says, "because I say [*legō*, referring to all His teaching] the truth, ye believe Me not" (v. 45). The "I" is very strongly emphatic, as the order in the original brings out— "But I [or, as for Me], because I say the truth." Just as the devil does not stand in the truth through his natural dissociation from it, so they, by reason of their relationship to him, refused to accept the truth from Christ's lips.

The absolute truth of His teaching was the effect of His sinlessness. His sinless life gave proof of the truth of His doctrine. Accordingly, untruthfulness being sin, He issues the challenge, **"Which of you convicteth Me of sin?"** (not simply the sin of falsehood) and waits (so we may gather) for an answer. Only Christ, the sinless one, could utter such a challenge. And with what sublime majesty and dignified patience He does so! What grace and humility to submit such a question to such men!

No answer on their part is recorded. Accordingly He proceeds with the cogent question, **"If I say truth, why do ye** [emphatic] **not believe Me."** Since He was free from sin, He was free from falsehood. What then was the reason for their unbelief? His question was not so much an appeal for their faith as a preparation for the consummating proof that they were not God's children: **"He that is of God heareth the words of God: for this cause ye hear them not, because ye are not of God"** (v. 47).

Instead of yielding to the gracious, though firm, humility by which the Lord resisted their pride, they proceed further in evil and vilify and blaspheme, charging Him with being **"a Samaritan"** (ignorant, that is to say, of the God of Israel and apostate from the faith), and with being demon-possessed.

THE MEEKNESS OF CHRIST

His reply was the essence of meekness and forbearance. He first simply denies their foul second vilification and then passes to the vindication of the Father's honor, and to words of warning and virtual appeal. He does not reply to the accusation of being a Samaritan; He refrains from any denial which would endorse their contempt of the Samaritans. Had He not Himself carried on a lifegiving ministry among them (chap. 4)? We will quote His words, and then Peter's comment upon His meekness. And let us seek to carry home to our hearts the lesson of His example. He says **"I have not a demon; but I honor My Father, and ye**

dishonor Me [i.e., "you dishonor My Father in dishonoring Me"]. **But I seek not Mine own glory** [i.e., "My saying that you dishonor Me does not imply that I am seeking My own glory"]: **there is One that seeketh and judgeth** [that is to say, "He it is who seeks glory for Me and pronounces judgment on you"]. **Verily, verily, I say unto you, If a man keep my word, he shall never see death."** This last, which was still addressed to them, graciously held out an offer of mercy.

Such a reply is one outstanding illustration of the testimony afterwards borne by Peter to Him, in that "when He was reviled, reviled not again; when He suffered He threatened not" (1 Pet. 2:23). In this the apostle exhorts us to "follow His steps," that the example He left us may have its character-shaping effects upon us.

THE DEATHLESSNESS OF THE BELIEVER

To keep His word is not merely to bear it in mind, but to pay such regard to it as diligently to obey and fulfill it. The combined phrases in the original, rendered "never," are very strong and the statement more fully rendered would be "shall certainly not see death forever," *i.e.*, shall not know the experience of death. The negation is a way of expressing the positive assurance of eternal life. For in 11:26 the Lord makes clear that it is solely conditional upon believing upon Him (cp. 5:24 and 6:40). He who thus receives Christ enters upon a life which is essentially characterized by keeping His word. This was what He now held out to His hearers. He referred, not to physical death, but to a life in which physical death, so far from causing a cessation, issues immediately in a fuller realization of life.

The Jews construed His words as if they signified physical death, and exaggerated His language accordingly, changing His "see" into "taste of." Then, repeating their blasphemous calumny, they charged Him with vainglory. This He repudiates, declaring its worthlessness, and the fact that it is the Father who glorifies Him, whom they claimed as their God (v. 54). The Father glorified His Son by His double testimony, at His baptism and His transfiguration, "This is My beloved Son, in whom I am well pleased" (Matt. 3:17 and 17:5), and by the signs and wonders which He wrought (Acts 2:22), and by His resurrection and exaltation (1 Pet. 1:21).

A DIFFERENCE IN KNOWLEDGE

In His next statement there is a noticeable difference in the verbs rendered to know, a difference which makes an immeasurable distance between Him and them. He says **"and ye have not known Him** [*ginōskō*, to get to know: they had not even begun to know Him]: **but I know Him** [*oida*, here, of Christ, to have full knowledge; cp. 6:6, 64; i.e., "I know Him absolutely"; a knowledge not progressive but essential]." To deny this (and it made Him greater than Abraham and the prophets) would, He says, have made Him, like them, a liar. So He says again **"but I know Him,"** and adds **"and keep His word,"** the very condition (perfectly fulfilled in Him) which He had laid down as essential for the relation of His followers to Himself.

And as to Abraham, he exulted (that is the force of the word rendered **"rejoiced"**) in the anticipation of the coming of the Christ (**"My Day,"** the day when Christ in person would fulfill in both His advents the promises made by God). That was the goal toward which Abraham's life was set (cp. Heb. 11:10).

THE GOOD SHEPHERD

In John 10, Jesus sets forth an allegory about the relationship between Himself and His followers. This parable uses the metaphor of a shepherd and his sheep. He expresses His delight in having them as His own and in what He becomes to them. In the end, this is about a close-knit relationship with Jesus, something that this beautiful analogy brings to light.

THE GOOD SHEPHERD AND THE BAD SHEPHERDS

In His collision with His critics, whom He has just charged with abiding in a state of sin (the very thing that they had imputed to the man to whom the Lord had given sight, 9:34), the Lord introduces His allegory by a clear intimation that spiritually they belong to the class of the thief and the robber. He begins with His characteristic **"Verily, verily, I say unto you."** The Pharisees were bad shepherds; the blind man had found the Good Shepherd. They had not entered by the door into the fold of the sheep, but, like the thief and the robber, had climbed up some other way.

The Lord applies two details in the allegory to Himself in unfolding its meaning. He first says, **"I am the door"** (vv. 7, 9), and then **"I am the good Shepherd"** (vv. 11–14). If it is necessary to obtain an interpretation as to the porter (v. 3), it seems best to regard the figure as signifying the Holy Spirit, for it is His work to introduce sheep into the fold. In the East the intimacy between a shepherd and his sheep is very close, and the practice of the naming of the sheep is quite ancient. With the Lord's word, **"He calleth His own sheep by name,"** we may compare Isaiah 43:1; 45:3; 49:1; and Revelation 3:5.

Two words are used to express the act of the Shepherd in regard to the going forth of the sheep. **"He leadeth them out"** (v. 3) by going before them, but he first **"putteth them forth"** (v. 4). There is a striking significance in the latter expression. The verb in the original is the same as that rendered "they cast him out" (9:34, 35). False shepherds put them out to lighten the burden of caring for them; true shepherds put them forth to see that they are well fed. The intimacy just referred to is beautifully set forth further, first, by the fact that the shepherd goes before the sheep and they follow him (just as Paul, the faithful undershepherd, could say "Be ye imitators of me even as I am of Christ," 1 Cor. 11:1; cp. Phil. 3:17; 1 Thess. 1:6; 2 Thess. 3:7–9); secondly, in that they know the voice of their shepherd in contrast to that of strangers, from whom they flee. A Scottish traveler once changed clothes with a Jerusalem shepherd and endeavored to lead the sheep; they refused however to follow the shepherd's clothes on the stranger, in spite of all that he did to draw them; but they readily followed the voice of their own shepherd, in spite of the change of his garment.

THIEVES AND ROBBERS

The Pharisees failed to understand what the Lord had been talking about (v. 6). Their treatment of the man whose sight was restored made clear that their characteristics were entirely foreign to those of true shepherds. Accordingly the Lord now repeats the allegory, unfolding the special details and applying them to Himself. **"Jesus therefore said unto them again, Verily, verily; I say unto you, I am the door of the sheep."** The "I" bears special emphasis, just as in 4:26; 6:35, 41, 48, 51, etc. In each case what the Lord implies is, "I and no other." Here He declares that He is the one and only door through which both sheep and shepherds enter. His next statement, **"All that came before Me are thieves and robbers,"** refers not, of course, to those who had previously been sent of God, but to those who had misled the people, serving their own ends instead of God and His truth, false prophets who had come in sheep's clothing, but inwardly were ravening wolves (Matt. 7:15), men who had shut the kingdom of heaven, neither entering themselves, nor suffering others to enter (23:13), who took away the key of knowledge and hindered people from possessing it (Luke 11:52). The present tense, "are," indicates that they were the men of the time when He was upon earth; compare however Ezekiel 34, **"But the sheep did not hear them."** There were many who listened to them, but His own followers, the remnant in Israel, found nothing to benefit in what these ecclesiastical authorities taught.

THE HAPPINESS OF ENTERING

Now He states the blessedness of those who do enter in, and precedes it with an emphatic repetition of the fact that He is the one and only door. **"By Me,"** He says, **"if any man enter in, he shall be saved, and shall go in and go out, and find pasture."** He does not say "If any man enter in by Me," but puts the "by Me" first, placing the greatest stress upon the uniqueness and absoluteness of His own Person. How comprehensive is His word, "If any man [or, rather, anyone]!" His mind goes beyond Jews to Gentiles. There are not limitations either of sex or nationality.

He who enters in "shall be saved." This is more than being delivered from perdition; it points to the state of salvation consequent upon the step of entering. To go in and to go out is suggestive both of security and liberty. The double expression is used frequently in the Old Testament for describing the free activity of daily life (see, *e.g.*, Deut. 28:6, 19; 31:2; 1 Sam. 18:16; Ps. 121:8; Jer. 37:4). The same Hebraistic phrase is used in Acts 1:21; 9:28. The finding of pasture is descriptive of the feeding upon Christ, both by means of the Scriptures and in the daily appropriation of Christ in the life of communion with Him. The benefits are threefold: deliverance, freedom, and nourishment.

RADICAL DIFFERENCES

All this is followed by one of the most striking contrasts in Scripture. It lies between the motives and acts of the thief and those of the Good Shepherd. The former are described by way of a climax of selfish cruelty—stealing, killing, destroying—selfishness, bloodlust, brutality. The killing is not for sacrificial purposes, as some suggest, but for murderous intent. The destroying is more than the killing, it means the utter ruin of the flock.

The twofold motive of the Good Shepherd is in inverse antithesis to all that. He came (1) that they might have life; that stands in contrast to the killing and destroying; He does not take life, He gives it; (2) that they might have it **"abundantly"** (not "more abundantly," as in the A.V.: the word "more" has no MS. authority: it is not a matter of greater instead of less, but of a full supply of all that sustains life); instead of stealing He imparts abundance.

But there are two more contrasts. There is that of the emphatic "I," purposely set in contrast to "the thief." Then there are the different tenses. The thief **"cometh"**; he pays his visits, whensoever he finds possibility of attempting his fell design; **"I came,"** says the Good Shepherd; He had come by one great voluntary act of grace and compassionate love.

"I am the good Shepherd." The word *kalos*, "good," conveys all the attributes and characteristics of what is ideal, or of what is well adapted to its purposes because it is intrinsically good. Christ is the "good" Shepherd in each respect. His character is manifested, and His purpose fulfilled, in laying down His life for the sheep. His description of Himself as more fully rendered, is strikingly expressive: "I am the Shepherd, the good one"; this stands out in contrast to the hireling.

At the same time it breathes His delight in, and tender thought and care for, His flock. They are "His own," as intimated in His negative descriptions of the hireling who is **"not a shepherd"** and **"whose own the sheep are not."**

THE HIRELING

The hireling acts simply in his own interests. He saves his life by leaving the sheep to their destroyer. The Good Shepherd lays down His life that His sheep may not perish. The one saves himself by sacrificing his charge; the other sacrifices Himself to save His charge. Just there lay the difference between the religious authorities and Christ, in their respective treatment of the blind man.

A TWOFOLD MUTUAL INTIMACY

In verse 14 He repeats His statement, **"I am the good Shepherd,"** but now to introduce the subject of the intimacy between Himself and His sheep. There should be no break between verses 14 and 15, the one runs on into the other:

"I know Mine own, and Mine own know Me, even as the Father knoweth Me, and I know the Father." The mutual "knowing" is thus twofold, and the former has its source in the latter. The mutual intimacy between Christ and His followers is but the overflow and extension of the unoriginated and infinite mutual intimacy between the Father and the Son.

The verb in each of the four statements is *ginōskō*, expressing knowledge existent through constant experience (and here involving mutual appreciation), as distinct from *oida*, which conveys the idea of complete or absolute knowledge. As the Father delights in the full recognition and appreciation of all that the Son is to Him, and the Son in all that the Father is to Him, so the Son, as the Good Shepherd, delights in the full recognition and appreciation of all that His sheep are to Him, and the sheep in their recognition and appreciation of what He is to them. This latter mutuality finds its basis in the great sacrificial act of the Shepherd, and for this reason He says again, "I lay down My life for the sheep."

THE "OTHER SHEEP" AND THE "ONE FLOCK"

In view of His death His thoughts and tender affections go out to those "**other sheep**," other than Jewish believers. They were already His own though they had not come into being. They had been given to Him by the Father (17:7). Hence He says "**Other sheep I have**" (cp. Acts 18:10; 28:28). The Jews had derisively asked, "Will He go . . . and teach the Greeks?" (7:35). He affirms that there are His own among the despised Gentiles. As Bengel remarks, "He does not say, who are out of or in another fold." And in His statement "**which are not of this fold**," the emphasis is upon "fold," not upon "this" (which readers frequently stress). There is not a Gentile fold.

"**Them also**," He says, "**I must bring** [or rather, "lead"], **and they shall hear My voice** [see v. 3], **and they shall become one flock, one Shepherd**." Not "one fold," but "one flock." The oneness is not to be brought about by an external union of the sects and systems of Christendom (described in mistaken religious parlance as The Church). Scripture never speaks of "the Church on earth," consisting of all the believers in the world. The phrase "the Church on earth" is utterly unscriptural and is responsible for many a mistaken idea. The Church has never been on earth; heaven is its destiny and dwelling place. For its true unity and destination, see 17:22–24. This is the will of the "One Shepherd," that "**where I am, they also may be with Me; that they may behold My glory**." That is the destiny.

HIS RAISING OF THE TEMPLE OF HIS BODY

Therefore, in repeating the fact of the laying down of His life, He adds that of His resurrection, and that by His own power: "**That I may take it again**," assigning this as a special reason for the Father's love: "**Therefore doth the Father love me, because I lay down My life, that I may take it again**." Speaking of the temple of His body He had said, "**Destroy this temple, and in three days I will** raise it up" (2:19, 21). This power in His resurrection He shares with the Father: "No one taketh it away from Me, but I [with special emphasis] lay it down of Myself. I have power [or authority] to lay it down, and I have power to take it again. This commandment received I from My Father." His resurrection was therefore an essential act in fulfillment of the Father's will, which He had come to accomplish (6:38).

For this reason He is "the Good Shepherd," "the Great Shepherd," "the Chief Shepherd," and will be the "One Shepherd," with His one complete "flock."

NEVER PERISH

So in the next statement, "My sheep ["the sheep which are Mine"] hear My voice [cp. 10:4] and I know them, and they follow Me and I give unto them eternal life." Not "I will give," as if the bestowment of life was a promise conditional upon following Him. That interpretation has been put forward by some, but it is contradictory to 5:24, where the Lord declared that eternal life was imparted upon hearing His word and believing. The present tense indicates the possession of life already enjoyed. The enjoyment of life hereafter is a continuation of present spiritual life: "And they shall never perish, and no one shall snatch them out of My hand." The negative is very emphatic: "they shall never by any means perish" (so in 8:51 and 11:26).

There are, in two respects,

THREE SUCCESSIVE FACTS

As to the sheep: (a) they hear His voice, (b) they follow Him, (c) they shall never perish; and as to the Shepherd: (a) He knows them, (b) He gives them eternal life, (c) He holds them securely in His hand.

Then, as usual, the Lord leads up to teaching concerning the Father, whom He ever glorified: "My Father, which hath given them unto Me, is greater than all"; not here with reference to the Son (as in 14:28), for see the next verse, but as having complete control over all adverse powers. That His sheep are the gift of the Father ensures their eternal safety. Note the perfect tense, "hath given," denoting an accomplished act with permanent results.

"And no one is able to snatch them out of the Father's hand. I and the Father are one" (vv. 29–30). Those who are in the hands of the Son, having been given to Him by the Father, remain likewise in the hands of the Father, and this is a potent demonstration of the unity of the two. The Father and the Son, being one in godhood, are therein one in the infinitude of power, a power exerted against all adversaries. As Liddon says, "a unity like this must be a dynamic unity, as distinct from any mere moral and intellectual union, such as might exist in a real sense between a creature and its God. Deny this dynamic unity, and you destroy the internal connection of the passage. Admit this dynamic unity, and you admit, by necessary implication, a unity of essence. The power of the Son, which shields the redeemed from the foes of their salvation is the very power of the Father: and this identity of power is itself the outflow and the manifestation of a oneness of nature."

THE FIFTH PUBLIC DISCOURSE IN JOHN'S GOSPEL

Though they prided themselves on knowing the Scripture, the Jews did not expect Messiah to be deity. During "the feast of the dedication" in December, Jesus speaks out, refuting the charge of blasphemy with divine wisdom. Pointing them to the Psalms, he says, "If He [God] called them gods, unto whom the Word of God came (and the Scripture cannot be broken), say ye of Him whom the Father sanctified and sent into the world, Thou blasphemest; because I said, I am the Son of God?"

It was now **"the feast of the dedication,"** a feast observed to commemorate the purification and restoration of the temple after its defilement by Antiochus Epiphanes. It lasted eight days, from December 20th. The mention of its being winter (v. 23) seems to be connected with the fact that **"Jesus was walking in Solomon's porch,"** a cloister on the east side of the temple.

WHAT CHARACTERIZES THE TRUE SHEEP

He now resumes the subject about which He had spoken to them before concerning His sheep. . . . **"But ye** [with stress on the word] **believe not, because ye are not of My sheep,"** an emphatic phrase, more literally, "the sheep which are Mine."

There are no persons so obdurate as religious fanatics. The Jews prepare to stone Him. To this He replies, with calm dignity: **"Many good works have I showed you from the Father: for which of these works do ye stone Me?"** They base their act on what they regard as His one claim to deity. The Lord knew all their arguments. They failed to discern that His works were part and parcel of His divine nature itself and were not the acts of a kindly man. They were essentially a witness to His deity. To prove the validity of their charge they ought to have prepared to stone Him on the ground of His works as much as on the ground of His statement.

He has one word more for them before leaving them. The manner in which He absolutely rebuts the charge of blasphemy evinces His divine wisdom. He refers them to Psalm 82:6, speaking of the quotation as part of **"your law."** They prided themselves in their knowledge of Scripture. How little they really apprehended its truth! From their own principles and from the Scriptures they were wrong: **"If He** [God] **called them gods, unto whom the Word of God came (and the Scripture cannot be broken), say ye of Him whom the Father sanctified and sent into the world, Thou blasphemest; because I said, I am the Son** of God?" It is abundantly clear that the Jews did not expect the Messiah to be possessed of deity. The whole controversy between Christ and them shows that.

Accordingly, the Lord, in closing, makes His claim as clear as it could be made: **"If I do not the works of My Father, believe Me not. But if I do them, though ye believe not Me, believe the works: that ye may know and understand, that the Father is in Me, and I in the Father."** That statement brought the matter to a climax. It was both retrospective and anticipative: retrospective regarding all His "signs," and especially that of giving the blind man sight: anticipative regarding the next and last sign, the raising of a man from the tomb (see 11:42).

They made one more effort to take Him, but it was true for some days that His "time had not yet come." Escaping therefore from their grasp, He went beyond Jordan, where John had baptized, and abode there. Many came to Him and believed on Him.

THE PRELUDE TO THE SACRIFICE

While in Jerusalem, some Greeks wished to make Christ's acquaintance, and their inquiry led to Jesus' last two public testimonies, both of which contain constant references to His impending death. Gentile wise men from the east came to Christ's cradle; gentile men from the west came to His cross.

GREEK ASPIRATIONS

There were certain Greeks who had come to worship in Jerusalem. They were proselytes, Gentiles by birth, and had adopted the Jewish religion. They wanted to see Jesus, not simply to get a view of Him, that was easy enough, but to have an interview with Him, probably as to whether He could satisfy their aspirations. Now Philip had a Greek name, and being "of Bethsaida, of Galilee" ("Galilee of the nations"), he knew their language well, so they approached him; he saw the meaning of their request sufficiently to associate Andrew with himself in applying to Christ. Moreover, would the Lord be willing, considering that on a recent occasion He had bidden His disciples not to go among Gentiles?

Gentile wise men from the east came to Christ's cradle; gentile men from the west came to His cross. His reply to Philip and Andrew was not a refusal. The cross was occupying His heart. It was the only means of securing for Gentiles far greater benefits than these Greeks were seeking, the blessings of their salvation; and to secure this would be His very glory. Accordingly He immediately says, **"The hour is come, that the Son of Man should be glorified. Verily, verily, I say unto you, except a grain of wheat fall into the earth and die, it abideth alone; but if it die, it beareth much fruit."** The inquiring Greeks would get to know Him, and to realize His power, and thus would have the fulfillment of more than their aspirations, and that not by His miracles but by His death.

The Lord gives two lessons in His reply. His death provides the productive power of the life that is in Him, risen and exalted. That is His first lesson. But while His falling into the ground, with the consequent fruitfulness of His act, was unique and absolute, it provided an illustrative principle, to be realized in the lives of His faithful followers. That is His second lesson. In this respect He says **"He that loveth his life, loseth it; and he that hateth his life in this world shall keep it unto life eternal."** If the seed grain is eaten instead of being sown, it produces no fruit. If we consume our lives for our self-gratification, neither are we fruitful here, nor shall we reap the reward in the life beyond. He who sows his life for Christ on behalf of others loses much worldly advantage but keeps it in the fruit it produces unto eternal life, the effect and power of which he himself will enjoy forever.

A HIGH CALLING

Following His promise that he who hates his life shall keep it unto life eternal, a promise which He had illustrated by fruitfulness, He shows, firstly, what this means in practical experience, what kind of life we are called upon to live, and, secondly, what is the special feature of the life beyond. **"If any man serve Me, let Him follow Me."** There is emphasis on the "Me" in both clauses. It is He who is the object of the heart's true devotion and it is He who has trod the path before. His example has been set. True service means hating one's life instead of loving it. Self-love is self-destruction. He has given up His life for us; let us give up our lives to Him, cost what it may. This estimate of our life does not mean carelessness in the matter of our body and health, but it does mean absolute self-denial. It means taking up our cross and following Him, and that daily (see Luke 9:23 and 14:27). If we follow not the path He has trod we walk in darkness.

As to the future, He says, **"where I am, there shall also My servant be."** That is not merely future. It is the height of present privilege, honor and bliss. "'Tis heaven where Jesus is." That is so now. It will be so in eternity. It is Christ Himself Who will make heaven our delightful paradise.

He then says, **"If any man serve Me, Him will the Father honor."** Here the emphasis is on the verbs "serve" and "honor." It is the Father's will ever to glorify His Son; therefore service for the Son will receive honor from the Father. We should ever seek to realize what the apostle Paul calls "the prize of the high calling of God in Christ Jesus."

THE PRELUDE TO THE SACRIFICE

The Lord's mention of His approaching death leads to an utterance which has been described as the prelude of the conflict in Gethsemane. It marvelously combines the deepest trouble with the highest desire. He says **"Now is My soul troubled** [lit., has been and is troubled]; **and what shall I say? Father, save Me from this hour. But for this cause came I unto this hour. Father, glorify Thy Name"** (vv. 27, 28).

Some would put a question mark after "hour," as if the Lord meant "Shall I say, Father save Me from this hour?" While this is possible, the rendering as it stands in our versions seems right. The hour was the time of the impending sufferings of His atoning sacrifice, and of the divine judgment for sin upon His sinless soul. He knew all that was coming upon Him. That was sufficient to elicit the prayer "Father, save Me from this hour." It was an expression of the utmost stirring of His soul. It seems inappropriate to regard it as a question, as if the Lord was deliberating as to what He should say. He similarly prayed in Gethsemane, "If it be possible, let this cup pass away from Me" (Matt. 26:39). There too He said immediately "Nevertheless, not as I will, but as Thou wilt." That prayer conveyed no deviation from submission to the Father's will. So in the present instance He at once asserts the reason for His coming to that hour: "But for this cause came I unto this hour." Is not the cause the laying down of His life that the Father's Name might be glorified (combining what He had taught in v. 25 with what immediately now follows in v. 28)? Not simply in submission to the will of the Father, but in His heart's perfect devotion to Him He says, "Father, glorify Thy name."

HIS GREATEST DESIRE

That was ever His undeviating motive, and His prayer meets with an immediate double response: **"I have both glorified it, and will glorify it again."** The Father had glorified it in the past life of the obedience of His Son, reaching its climax in His death, which seems to be included in that statement as an accomplished fact. It covers both His life and His death. He would also glorify it in raising Him from the dead and seating Him at His right hand.

The crowd around imagined there had been a clap of thunder. Some thought an angel had spoken to Him. He declared that the voice had come especially for their sakes, with the object that they might believe (see v. 36). His thoughts center again in His death. **"Now is the judgment of this world."** The "now" vividly points to that which is impending. The judgment of this world means the sentence to be passed upon it, not the opinion expressed by it. While in God's love and mercy He gave His only-begotten Son to die for the world, there could be nothing else than condemnation for all rejecters, both those who actually determined upon His death, and all since who by unbelief have taken sides with them.

THE UPPER ROOM DISCOURSE

During His last meal with His disciples, Jesus prepares the eleven for what is to come. He gives them a New Commandment, urges them to love one another, tells them not to be troubled, and instructs them to believe in God. Christ warns them again of His imminent death, but reassures them that He will send a Comforter. These are His friends, and to them He says, "This is My commandment, that you love one another, even as I have loved you. Greater love hath no man than this, that a man lay down his life for his friends."

THE LORD'S SUPPER

Taking into consideration the Synoptic narratives of the institution of the Lord's Supper, and the circumstances recorded by John in chapter thirteen, it seems probable that this institution took place just after Judas had gone out, and Christ had made the immediately consequent remarks mentioned in [chapter 13] verse 32, and previously to His addressing the disciples as mentioned in verse 33. This is more probable than after what He says in verse 35, as verse 36 is linked with verse 33.

The omission is purposive. The teachings of the Lord in that room do not refer to sacrifice for sin, the body and the blood of Christ, and the new covenant. The leading subjects are our immediate relations with Him. There are manifest correspondences and connections between the institution and the Lord's discourses, as, for instance, in the instruction concerning His coming again.

A NEW COMMANDMENT

How suitably, after they had partaken from His hands the emblems of His body and His blood, the symbols of His death, and had heard His promise to return, come the words, **"Little children, yet a little while I am with you . . . A new commandment I give unto you, that ye love one another; even as I have loved you . . . I go to prepare a place for you, And . . . I come again, and will receive you unto Myself!"**

He had announced to His enemies His going, but had forewarned them of eternal separation from Him (8:21); His announcement here to His disciples of His going is accompanied by the assurance of eternal reunion. He addresses them as "little children" for the first time. John uses it seven times in his first epistle. It conveys four ideas, (1) affection, (2) parental care, (3) compassion, (4) family intimacy.

He gives a "new commandment" to love one another according to the standard of His own love (v. 34). Seven times in the whole discourse He speaks of His commandments, and in each place associates them with the subject of love (here; 14:15, 21, 23; 15:10, 12, 14 with 13). His love provides both *the motive* and *the measure* of our love. As exhibited in us it both displays *the character* of real discipleship and gives the testimony of it to the world: **"By this shall all men know that ye are My disciples, if ye have love one to another."** In this we are to be His representatives here.

The word *kainos*, "new," signifies not newness in time, recent (*neos*), but newness of nature and quality, superior to the old. The love of which the Lord speaks is therefore not obedience to the letter of the Law but the very spring and power of the new life, "the law of the Spirit of life in Christ Jesus."

Peter is occupied especially with the staggering fact that the Lord was going away. His answer elicits that disciple's impetuous but faithful assurance of the utmost loyalty. This, in turn, produces another revelation of the Lord's complete foreknowledge, and now of all that would affect the circumstances of them all.

The Lord checks mere impulse and self-confidence. His prediction of Peter's threefold denial does this. But both this prediction and other details of His disclosures produce foreboding in the hearts of all. It was all purposively preparatory on His part to the words of consolation and blessed assurance He would minister to them and to all His own ever since, and the revelation of Himself, His character, His ways and doings, which form the great essence of the following discourse.

UNITY OF THE GODHEAD

Consolation and revelation: this is His double ministry throughout. They are the features of His twofold message which opens that part of His discourse at the beginning of chapter fourteen: **"Let not your heart be troubled"**; that is the consolation; **"ye believe in God, believe also in Me"**: that is revelation. Consolation to the hearts of His followers, revelation of His own heart! Since, however, the verb rendered "Ye believe" has also the form of the imperative, and since His ministry is that of consolation to troubled hearts, it is better to regard each part as a command: **"believe in God, believe also in Me."** It is a faith that goes much further than an acceptance of a truth, it cleaves to the speaker. And what the Lord reveals is the unity between the Father and the Son. Faith in both is a necessity. Without this there is no salvation in any sense of the term.

The unity of the persons and yet their distinctive personalities are further declared: **"In My Father's House"** means that what is the Father's is likewise the Son's, and it is the prerogative of the Son both to prepare the abode and to come and convey thither those for whom it is prepared: **"I go to prepare a place for you . . . I come again** [vivid present tense in both parts, giving assurance of the future facts], **and will receive you unto Myself; that where I am, there ye may be also."** This is more than a reception to meet Him in the air (1 Thess. 4:17). That will be so, but He takes us, surely, from the place of meeting in the air, into the Father's house, to be with Him. He says, "where I am"; this is "within the veil, whither as forerunner Jesus entered for us" (Heb. 6:20). That place is "the Father's House" (see also 17:24).

HIS COMING AGAIN

The Lord is not referring to the falling asleep of the individual believer. He is speaking of the time of the Rapture of all believers at the completion of the Church. He thus, at the beginning of His discourse, carries the thoughts of the disciples right on to the time of consummation, so that this promise may cast its rays upon all that intervenes, as dealt with in the remainder of His teachings.

In His wisdom the Lord states the assumption that they know the way He is going: the R.V. is right, **"And whither I go, ye know the way."** He knew that this would cause Thomas to demur ([ch. 14] v. 5). Christ had ready His self-revelation, so personal, so comprehensive: not, "I make the way, I reveal the truth, I give the life," but **"I am the way, and the truth, and the life."** And the fact that

He is the truth and the life because He is the way, is confirmed by His additional statement, **"No one cometh unto the Father, but by Me"**; that has to do with the way alone, it is the way to the Father, and means the consequent experience of Christ as the truth and the life.

He thus goes further than the way to the Father's house. He occupies our thoughts with the Father Himself and the present experience of coming voluntarily and by faith to Him, through Christ. "By Me" conveys the twofold thought both of His immediate personal mediation and of what He has wrought so as to bring this about, that is, His incarnation, life, atoning death, resurrection and ascension (see Rom. 5:2; Eph. 2:13, 15, 18; Heb. 7:25; 10:19–21). Accordingly this statement goes far beyond what it had meant for Old Testament saints to come to God.

KNOWING THE TWO IN ONE

The Lord now presses home the profound truth He had uttered in public (8:19), but with a difference. Here He says, **"If ye had known [***ginōskō***] Me, ye would have known [***oida***] My Father also."** The first verb expresses a knowledge progressive and gained, the second a knowledge immediate and perceptive. In 8:19 the verb is *oida* in both parts. With the opposing Pharisees the very idea of getting to know Him is altogether set aside. No knowledge whatever was possible to them. To the disciples He can and does say, **"from henceforth ye know him"** (*ginōskete*, ye are getting to know); they had entered upon the process and would increase in the acquisition. Moreover they had "seen Him." Christ, as the Son, was the personal manifestation of the Father, and in reply to Philip's earnest request that Christ would show Him He says, **"he that hath seen Me hath seen the Father"** (v. 9).

Here again a different verb, *horaō*, is used from that in 12:45 (*theōreō*). *Theōreō* denotes to be a spectator of: it stresses the action of the beholder; *horaō* lays more emphasis on the object beheld, upon the direction in which the vision goes. This is especially exemplified in the Lord's word here to the disciples, that the Father manifests Himself in the Son (cp. 1:17, 18). It must be so by reason of the mutual indwelling, **"I am in the Father, and the Father in Me,"** repeated here and again in 17:23, in the prayer. The essential unity of their nature in the Godhead, involving unity of mind, will and action, is conveyed in this great foundation statement by the Lord.

OUR HIGHEST OCCUPATION

True, this unity, this mutual indwelling, exceeds the limits of natural comprehension, and for this very reason He adds **"believe Me for the very works' sake."** This He had said in public (10:37, 38), but here there is more to follow. First the person, then the works—these are the combined motives for faith. To the Jews they had been presented as alternatives; to the disciples the works provide a supplementary motive to the faith: "believe Me on account of [i.e., by reason of, not for the sake of, as in the Versions] the very works." Nicodemus draws a conclusion from the works (3:2), and that by way of observation and reasoning. The disciples acknowledge Him apart from His works (1:41–48). Our highest occupation is with Christ Himself and our personal and increasing knowledge of Him. This is strengthened by the experience of His dealings with us.

GREATER WORKS

From the mention of His works He opens their minds again to the future, but now concerning their service. He passes from Himself as the object of faith to their life of faith in dependence upon His presence with the Father. And again the greatness and newness of the theme is marked by His **"Verily, verily, I say unto you."** His self-revelation continues: **"he that believeth on Me, the works that I do shall He do also; and greater** *works* **than these shall he do; because I go unto the Father"** (v. 12). There is continuity and increase, but He is the author and means of both.

The fact that the works will be greater is due to His exaltation. They also become greater because of their extent in the world and because by them the Church, the Body of Christ, is in process of formation, the greatest of all the creative works of God.

ASKING IN HIS NAME

In this connection the Lord associates prayer with works, indicating the necessity of the former for the effectiveness of the latter. There are three factors essential in this respect: (1) requests are to be made in His name; (2) He will Himself fulfill them; (3) the Father is thus to be glorified in the Son. In this repetition of the first two He says, **"If ye shall ask Me anything in My Name"** (v. 14, R.V.), expressing in another way His unity with the Father in the Godhead.

To make a request in His Name does not mean simply appending the phrase to a petition or prayer, it involves the experience of that relationship to, and fellowship with, Him, that resemblance to His character and delight in His will which His Name implies; it means the appropriation of His merits, His rights, His claims. This imparted a new character and power and sweetness to prayer which they had not experienced hitherto.

With this His next statement is not disconnected, **"If ye love Me, ye will keep My commandments."** Asking in His Name is a mere shibboleth if we do not keep His commandments. For in departing from them we fail to represent Him and therefore fail to do anything in His Name.

THE TRINITY

But for this we cannot rely upon our own wills, however determined we may be to be obedient. Accordingly, it is just here that the Lord introduces the subject of the promised presence and power of the Holy Spirit: **"Ye will keep My**

commandments, and I will pray the Father ["make request of"—a different word from "ask" in vv. 13 and 14: *aiteō*, there, suggests the petition of an inferior to a superior, *erōtaō*, here, suggests a right to expect the fulfillment], **and He shall give you another Comforter** [not *heteros*, another of a different kind, but *allos*, another of similar nature], **that He may be with you forever, even the Spirit of truth**."

Obedience, then, is the obedience of love, love that expresses itself in an act that fulfills His will. The authority of His will and the affections of the heart are as cause and effect in those who are "in law (*ennomos*, the literal word in 1 Cor. 9:21) to Christ." For this He promises the Holy Spirit. In this matter again He reveals His oneness and equality with the Father. For in verse 26 He says, as here, "Whom the Father will send in My Name." In 15:26 and 16:7 He says, "Whom I will send." What is this but the Trinity, the three acting in one? For what He is going to reveal concerning the Holy Spirit is nothing short of a predication of His deity. The Father acts in and through the Son, the Son acts as in the Father, and the Spirit acts in perfect unison of being and action with the Father and the Son.

THE PARACLETE

The Name given to the Spirit is "the Paraclete," lit., one called to the side (of another); but the work expresses the purpose for which He comes, the kindly act He does. There are two meanings, the one signifying, as it does in the four occurrences in this part of the Gospel, one who by His presence and companionship imparts encouragement, strength and support. "Comforter" is the right rendering, only it means more than merely giving comfort. The other meaning is advocate, one who undertakes our cause and pleads for us; that is its meaning in 1 John 2:1.

When He says "another Comforter" (using the word which means another of like nature), He is recalling the fact that He has been to them all that the word signifies in the first of the two meanings just mentioned. The same ministry will be continued by the Spirit, and that "forever," both here and hereafter. He is "the Spirit of truth"; that is to say, He will be the power in their testimony to the truth, thus fulfilling both the divine counsels and human needs. For in a world of darkness, devilry and deception, man's great need is the truth. For this Christ came into the world (8:32) and He is Himself, as He has just said, "the Truth." "The Spirit beareth witness," witness to Christ and all that this means, "because the Spirit is truth" (1 John 5:7).

THE WORLD—A CONTRAST

Just here it is that the Lord contrasts them and the world. The world **"cannot receive"** the Spirit, **"for it beholdeth Him not, neither knoweth Him."** The very condition of the world rendered impossible any recognition of Him. The disciples did behold in Christ and His ways and works the manifestation of the Holy

Spirit's person and power. Instead of knowing Him, the world charged Christ with being demon-possessed (8:52). The disciples knew the Spirit, for they had already experienced His power, as well as seeing His works in their master. **"He abideth with you,"** that was already true, **"and shall be in you,"** that would be true from Pentecost onward. They would realize Him as the comforter, empowering their witness and operating in the written testimony of such as would take part in the completion of the Scriptures of truth. "With" and "in"! What a power for every experience in life!

But that did not mean that He would take the place of Christ Himself. He assures them of this immediately, and says, **"I will not leave you desolate** (lit., orphans): **I come unto you."** The Spirit Himself is the very minister of Christ. If the Spirit of Christ indwells us, Christ Himself does. This means a vision of Christ; not physical, but very real. The spiritual would replace the physical for the disciples. **"Yet a little while, and the world beholdeth Me no more; but ye behold Me."** The world had seen Him only to mistake Him, because of their sinful state. The disciples, and we like them, have a different faculty of sight, the sight of faith.

LIFE INDEED

But His presence with us and in us, according to His promise, is just the very essence and vitality of life, spiritual life: **"because I live, ye shall live also."** That means, in the later words of the apostle Paul, "To me to live is Christ." It carries with it more than mere spiritual life. It is the constant personal experience of the risen and living Christ, producing His living power within our daily life. In the present enjoyment of this it is given to us to enjoy the blessed promise, **"Ye shall know that I am in My Father, and ye in Me, and I in you"** (v. 20). For the further experience of this mutual indwelling see 15:4–7.

All this is a matter of carrying out His commandments; not mere sentiment, but the enjoyment of love as the spring of obedience, and obedience as the proof of love. So the Lord says, **"He that loveth Me shall be loved of My Father, and I will love him, and will manifest Myself unto Him"** (v. 21). This practical love on the part of a believer brings a special manifestation of the love of the Father and the Son, and not only of their love but of their very nature and character as revealed in the Son. "In the keeping of His commandments there is great reward," and there can be no greater reward than the communion enjoyed in the fulfillment of this promise. There comes a wonderful disclosure to the true heart. The verb rendered "I will manifest" is not the ordinary word *phaneroō*, it is *emphanizo*, which suggests more than an appearance, it carries the thought of a disclosure of what the person is in His own nature, character, counsel and work.

THE RELIGIOUS WORLD

This drew forth an inquiry from Judas (not Iscariot) as to what had happened to bring about this distinction between themselves and the world (v. 22). Publicity, self-advertisement to gain applause, is characteristic of mere religion; it is the negation of the character and way of Christ. Accordingly, His reply shows how utterly impossible what He had in mind for them is for the world. The world has no room for Christ all through this period, any more than it had for Him when He was on earth. It has its religious ideas of Him, but their conception of Him is radically distinct from what He is Himself. Jesus answered him, **"If a man love Me, He will keep My word** [not My words, but the whole Word as an entity]; **and My Father will love him, and We will come unto him, and make Our abode with him"** (v. 23). There is now a dwelling place on earth both for Father and Son. It is in the heart and life of anyone who carries the whole truth of the Word of God, not some particular doctrine or practice, nor a special set of doctrines, attaching importance to some while making little or nothing of others. The "Word" is the whole teaching.

This brings from the Father and the Son, not an external display of power and attractive activity, but the inward disclosure of their love, producing likeness to the character of Him who is "meek and lowly in heart," and the real power of the Spirit of God. The idea of an "abode" is not something ephemeral, but habitual and permanent. So John wrote later, "He that abideth in the teaching, the same hath both the Father and the Son" (2 John 9, r.v.). And the Lord finished His reply by combining, in a negative statement, the love and the obedience: **"He that loveth Me not keepeth not My words** [plural now, the various parts which make up the whole]: **and the word which ye hear is not Mine, but the Father's who sent Me."** It was indeed Christ's word but only as it was that of the Father, in their perfect unity.

THE HOLY SPIRIT—A PERSON

What He had told them was only a beginning. They themselves must have felt the need of more, and He assures them that the need would be met. His teaching would not end with His being here with them: **"But the Comforter, even the Holy Spirit, whom the Father will send in My Name, He shall teach you all things, and bring to your remembrance all that I have said unto you"** (vv. 25, 26). This makes clear that the Spirit is not a mere influence, He is a person, who Himself acts as the minister of comfort and instruction. The two are inseparable. Instruction imparts all that is conveyed by the comprehensive term "Comforter." He would teach all things, that is, the truth of Scripture in its entirety, and would recall all that Christ taught. This latter contains the basis of all the truth that was to follow, from the Acts to the Apocalypse (cp. Heb. 2:3). All the rest of the New Testament serves to confirm the authenticity of the Gospels.

This promise pointed to the responsibility of the disciples to recollect what Christ had taught, but this as being under the superintending control of the Holy Spirit (cp. 12:16). This places the writings of the apostles beyond the scope of mere recollection and contemplation.

THE PEACE OF CHRIST

Following this assurance the Lord ministers a word of strong comfort to them. When He says "Peace I leave with you" (v. 27), He is not giving them simply a farewell message. The word rendered "I leave" is the same in the original as when He said "I will not leave you desolate." The peace is a bequest, and that not merely of freedom from anxiety as to circumstances, but of all that makes for mental and spiritual welfare.

But there is a special character about the peace. When He further says, **"My peace I give unto you,"** He uses a phrase the force of which is not expressed in our versions. Literally it is "the peace, the Mine," a very emphatic way of speaking of His peace as that which characterizes Him in a special manner and to a special degree, an inward peace which is His own possession, a peace not to be upset by foes or by the world. More than this, it is that which He imparts as being in accordance with His own nature. It has been described as consisting of "the composure of a holy affection, the sunshine of a settled purpose, and the sunshine of unclouded communion with God." He describes His love and His joy in the same phraseology (15:10, 12).

"Not as the world giveth," He says, **"give I unto you."** There is more than one contrast. As to the mode of giving, the world gives it conventionally, and often merely superficially. As to the means, it does not possess real, lasting peace, and it cannot give what it has not got. As to the source, the peace the Lord gives has been procured for us at the cost of His atoning sacrifice; this provides the right for believers to receive it from Him. As to the nature, it is not only a peace of conscience, it is a peace of rest in the will of God, not merely resignation to it, but delight in it, rest in all His dealings.

FEARFULNESS OR LOVE

He then adds an exhortation against that which is the very negation of peace, namely, a troubled or a fearful heart. He here repeats what He said at the beginning (there in a different connection) and adds the words, **"neither let it be afraid."** The verb is *deiliaō* (here only in the N.T.), not a passing fear, but a condition of fearfulness (cp. 2 Tim. 1:7).

All fearfulness should yield place to love, for two reasons, (1) because Christ has gone to the Father, (2) because He is coming again (cp. 14:3). **"Ye heard how I said unto you, I go away, and I come unto you. If ye loved Me, ye would have rejoiced, because I go unto the Father for the Father is greater than I"** (v. 28). This last statement gives the consummating reason for love to, and joy in, Christ, as powers that banish anxiety and fear. That the Father is "greater" is not said with regard to the relations in the persons of the Trinity. The Lord has been speaking of Himself as the one sent by the Father, and who fulfills His commandments, the way that leads to the Father, and the one who reveals the Father. Of all this the Father is the authority and the object. In all these respects the Father is greater than the Son, but not greater in essence and Godhood.

That these assurances actually created the love and rejoicing to which the Lord exhorted them is told out in Luke 24:53 and in the opening chapters of the Acts. We should so live, too, that these blessings may operate in our hearts continually and give effect to our testimony.

But all is a matter of faith, faith that realizes and appropriates the unseen: **"And now I have told you before it come to pass, that when it is come to pass ye may believe"** (v. 29).

THE POWER OF DARKNESS

For the disciples the scene was about to change; this companionship and intimate converse were about to terminate for the time. The powers of darkness were mustering for the attack. **"The prince of the world"** was coming; he had come to Him with a claim to this title in the wilderness at the beginning of His public testimony. The claim was not then denied by the victorious Lord. And now with his permitted authority over rebellious man, over the world in its persistent hardness of heart against all divine revelation and command, Satan was hastening to the crucial attack, and using the leading human powers among the Jews as his instruments.

Yet if this prince of the world had claims upon men, he had none upon the Son of God: **"and he hath nothing in Me,"** He says; he could not find, as he did in the world, something that would answer morally to his own nature; the very fact that men are sinners makes them partakers with the evil one, who "sinneth from the beginning." So it was with the first human sin, and men have ever since thrown open the avenues of their being to him. But he found no means of ingress in Him in whom "is no sin." Therefore while Satan could make an attempt, subject to the permissive will of God, he had no right to do so.

THE GREAT ISSUE

That he should do so at this time was, by such permission, voluntarily granted. Therefore there must be a divine purpose in it. This is seen in the Lord's next words, **"but that the world may know that I love the Father, and as the Father gave Me commandment, so I do"** (v. 31). Therefore the doing was not merely by voluntary consent, but by loving obedience. Here was a display of grace indeed. This is something more than the fact that God so loved the world that He gave His only begotten Son for the salvation of anyone who would believe. The world was to know that, in giving up His life that men might be saved, He was giving evidence of His love to the Father. Here then was a proof of the grace of Father and Son toward a guilty world.

That the Lord now said **"Arise, let us go hence,"** does not necessitate the idea that the company immediately left the room. The greater likelihood is that they lingered there or at least in the premises while He continued His discourse and prayed His prayer. Perhaps at this point they sang the Hallel. If after they rose they stayed in the recesses of the house, there would very likely be a vine growing on the sides, and this may have led to His remarks at the beginning of chapter fifteen. What is noticeable is that immediately upon His mentioning that "the prince of the world was coming," He says, "Arise, let us go hence," suggesting His readiness to meet the attack and fulfill all that was now to be accomplished.

The purpose in the narrative, however, is clearly the continuity of the discourse; there is so much in what follows that recalls and expands what He had previously spoken of, and this He now applies by way of practical exhortation, and that not only for the Eleven but for all believers. The subject of the next two chapters is the relation of believers to the Lord Himself as the one by whose power their lives are to be lived. The relationship is fivefold; they are sharers in His life and fruitfulness as His members (vv. 1–8), in His love and joy as His friends (vv. 9, 19), in His work and ways as His associates (15:20–16:3), in His ministry and spirit as His disciples (16:4–15), in His conflict and victory as His adherents (16:16–33).

LIFE AND FRUITFULNESS

In speaking of Himself as **"the true vine"** (lit., the vine, the true one) He signifies that He is the one who is the very essence of spiritual life and fruitfulness, and from whom alone these can be possessed and produced. The nation had become barren and dead. He was the twig out of the stump (Isa. 11:1, 2). But He changes the metaphors, because now He includes all those who, as His members, partake of His life and its products, showing that there is a vital union between Himself and them.

But this union and fruitfulness must be maintained in practical apprehension by their abiding in Him. Yet fruitfulness does not lie merely within their own power. They are entirely dependent on the vine. Hence, He says, **"My Father is the Husbandman."** There are two sorts of branches, the non-fruitbearing and the fruitbearing. The former He takes away, the latter He cleanses. There is no thought here of the loss of eternal life. The Lord is picturing the use of the pruning-knife, in the one case, and the removal of such things as parasites and mildew, in the case of the other.

"He shows the disciples that, walking on earth, they should be pruned by the Father, and be cut off if they bore no fruit; for the subject here is not that relationship with Christ in Heaven by the Holy Ghost, which cannot be broken, but of that link which even then was formed here below, which might be vital and eternal, or which might not. Fruit should be the proof" (J.N.D.).

ABIDING IN HIM

The eleven disciples were already clean; their faith in Christ had made them branches in the vine. They had become clean because of the word He had spoken to them. They would yet need cleansing to bear **"more fruit."** The secret of all this lay in His command **"Abide in Me."** This implies the exercise of the will, a voluntary and conscious perseverance, and makes clear the possibility of spiritual dangers, lest anything should be allowed to interrupt or hinder the continual experience of this union. Moreover the relation is mutual. There is a promise conditional upon fulfillment of the command. He says, **"Abide in Me, and I in you."** This is a condition, not of sentiment but of activity. In 14:20, "ye in Me, and I in you" signified a state. Here the relation is that which expresses itself in practical result, the activity being the outcome of the realization of the state.

Thus soul-energy finds its effect in loving obedience to all His commands, and this is the life of Christ bearing fruit: **"As the branch cannot bear fruit of itself, except it abide in the vine; so neither can ye, except ye abide in Me. I am the vine, ye are the branches: he that abideth in Me, and I in him, the same beareth much fruit: for apart from** [i.e., severed from] **Me ye can do nothing"** (vv. 4, 5).

OUR INSUFFICIENCY

A distinction is necessary between the subject of the life of the believer as being inseparable from Christ from the day on which he receives Him by faith, and the relation of the believer to Him in the matter of spiritual fruit-bearing. As to the former the Lord made the imperishable life of the believer clear in chapter ten, in declaring that His sheep could never perish. What He is now showing is that no believer can bring forth fruit from his own resources or by his own initiative. As the apostle Paul says, "I labored . . . yet not I, but the grace of God which was with me." "We are not sufficient of ourselves to think anything as of ourselves." "I live, yet not I, but Christ liveth in me."

The Lord compares one who abides not in Him to a withered branch. That kind of branch men gather and burn. The aorist tenses of the verbs rendered **"he is cast forth"** and **"is withered,"** suggest a twofold significance, (1) the decisive character of the acts (no other course being practicable), (2) the all-knowing mind of the speaker (as one who knew what must take place before it became a fact).

The fruitlessness may be caused by lethargy of soul, or by unbelief, or by willful apostasy. The latter had been the case with the betrayer; avarice, then discontent, then definite antagonism!

CONDITIONS FOR POWER IN PRAYER

Now the Lord deals with the fruitfulness of enjoyed union and communion, and shows that the indwelling of His words means power in prayer, and that the truly prayerful life is the fruitful life: **"If ye abide in Me, and My words abide in you, ask**[1] **whatsoever ye will, and it shall be done unto you"** (v. 7). His words are vital principles; they are designed to inspire our motives and to direct our thoughts and prompt our acts. To have His words abiding in us gives us such communion with God that we can count upon His answers to our prayers. And this inevitably means productiveness. It is the very opposite to fruitlessness.

---

1 The better reading in the original is *aitesasthe*, the aorist imperative, "ask ye."

This asking and obtaining never affords self-gratulation. What it does effect is true discipleship of Christ, whose one and only motive was the glory of the Father. "Herein is My Father glorified, that ye bear much fruit; and so shall ye be My disciples" (v. 8). Their discipleship had begun, but there was to be development and progress.

THE KEY TO LOVE, JOY AND FRIENDSHIP

Passing for the moment from His subject of the vine and the branches, with its significance of vital and constant union of His members with Himself for fruitfulness, He now speaks of His love for them as His friends, and its practical effect in them. "Abiding" is the continued keynote. As they must abide in Him as their life, so they must abide in His love.

Firstly, as to the source, **"Even as the Father hath loved Me"**; secondly, as to the mediating bestowment, **"I also have loved you"**; thirdly, as to the enjoyed element, **"Abide ye in My love,"** fourthly, as to the means, **"If ye keep My commandments ye shall abide in My love:"** fifthly, as to the example, **"even as I have kept My Father's commandments, and abide in His love"** (vv. 9, 10).

All this makes clear that our obedience does not create the Lord's love, any more than walking in sunshine creates the sun's light. The light is there, His love is there all the time. Obedience gives the realization of it. Disobedience, turning from the path of His commandments, hinders our enjoyment of His love. It rests upon him who walks as He walked.

HIS JOY

It is just this which leads on to the subject of His joy, for it was His joy to do the Father's will, and in our case a life of obedience is a life of joy: **"These things have I spoken unto you, that My joy may be in you, and that your joy may be fulfilled"** (v. 11). That the former purpose means that the joy which is His own may be imparted to them (rather than that His joy in them may continue) is confirmed in two respects: firstly, by the striking character of the full phrase in the original, which describes the uniqueness of His joy, lit., "the joy, the Mine"; secondly, by His prayer in 17:13, "that they may have My joy fulfilled in themselves." It is not "that your joy may be full"; that rendering misses the important point. That His followers would live and work in full fellowship with Him in seeing the extension of His kingdom, would mean that His joy, in the outworking of the will of the Father, would be fulfilled in each of their lives.

This is abundantly illustrated in the Epistles. To take one example, when Paul says of the Thessalonian believers "Ye are our glory and joy" (1 Thess. 2:20), this is but the Lord's own joy being fulfilled in the hearts of the apostle and his fellow laborers.

HIS FRIENDS

But it is to be fulfilled by the mutual love of fellow believers, and this it is which leads to His reminder that those who act like this are His friends: **"This is My commandment, that ye love one another, even as I have loved you. Greater love hath no man than this, that a man lay down his life for his friends"** (vv. 12, 13). He uses again the same kind of striking phrase concerning His commandment as He has done of love, joy and peace: "This is the commandment, the Mine" ("that which is especially Mine").

The question has been raised as to whether, in this thirteenth verse, the Lord was actually making reference to His own atoning sacrifice, or whether, in enjoining upon the disciples the exercise of mutual love, He was simply giving the highest example of merely human self-sacrifice. This calls for careful consideration. True it is that there is no other direct reference, in this discourse in the Upper Room, to His death. It has been asked, too, whether, since Christ died for all men, "died for the ungodly," died for the whole world, He would have spoken of His death as a giving up of His life for His "friends."

THE REFERENCE TO HIS OWN DEATH

It is necessary first to consider the main purpose of the Lord's message to His disciples. One cannot read through this discourse without noticing that His great object was to comfort, strengthen and instruct them in view of their coming experiences, trials, and vicissitudes, after He had gone to the Father, and so to prepare them for their service and testimony. This would not mean the entire withholding of an intimation of His death (that would be improbable), but it would mean keeping the subject in a certain amount of reserve. The circumstances and meaning of His death they had already known to some extent ("the way ye know"), but the facts and their implications would be clear in a few hours, and in due time their full explanation would be made known to them. For that immediate occasion there was manifested therefore in His messages a divinely wise economy of treatment. To have handled the subject of His death as an offering for the world, a giving up of His life "for the ungodly," would have been to exceed the scope and method of His immediate teachings.

Consistently with this, and so far from keeping secret the subject of His death, He addresses His disciples as His "friends" in this connection. He had used that term for them long before (Luke 12:4). While therefore He is instructing them as to how they should manifest their love one to another, it is in keeping with the nature of His instructions that He should include a reference to His own death as the giving up of His life for His "friends." Such indeed it was with regard to the Eleven who were listening to Him, and there is nothing theologically erroneous, or doctrinally inconsistent with the subject of His expiatory sacrifice as set forth elsewhere in Scripture, in regarding His general statement, "Greater love hath no man than this, that a man lay down his life for his friends," as including a reference to His own act with its special significance. The fact that its general character, as bearing upon their love one to another, involved the mention of the giving up of life as the act of "a man," in no way detracts from the expiatory efficacy of His death, as if suggesting that His act was that of a mere man. On the contrary the natural illustration involved the use of such phraseology. As a matter of fact the word "man" is not in the Greek in any part of the verse. The words are "no one" and "anyone."

The crowning exemplification made the inclusion of His own deed, with its special instruction, most appropriate. And how wisely and suitably He intimated it! That His statement did not preclude an intimation of His own act, with its expiatory uniqueness, is confirmed by what His "beloved disciple" says in his first Epistle, in words which surely contain an echo of the very words of Him on whose breast he leaned, "Hereby know we love, because He laid down His life for us: and we ought to lay down our lives for the brethren" (1 John 3:16). We may observe that the apostle narrows the subject to believers, instead of referring to the world as that for which the Lord died, just as Christ Himself did on the evening when He spoke to His disciples.

THE INTIMACY OF FRIENDSHIP

In the deeper intimacy established by the Lord in this discourse He now unfolded more fully to His disciples what their being His "friends" involved. He had already made clear that it meant their doing all that pleased Him. But there was to be more than this. Accordingly He says, **"No longer do I call you servants; for the servant knoweth not what his lord doeth: but I have called you friends."**

This did not mean that they were no longer His servants. Such they continued to be, and they ever delighted so to describe themselves (*douloi*, bondservants; see 1 Pet. 1:1; Jude 5:1; Rom. 1:1). With the believer the capacity of being a servant carries with it the intimacy and communion of friendship. The servant (*doulos*) as such does not know what his master is doing; his knowledge is limited to his duty. If, however, his master takes him into his confidence, the scene is changed. There is cooperation and sympathy and fellowship. A friendship is established. And this is just what the Lord now says: **"I have called you friends for all things that I heard from My Father I have made known unto you"** (v. 15).

By this communication of the Father's counsels and ways, a communication constantly being made to us by the Spirit through the Word, Christ brings us into partnership with Himself, in His purposes, interests and operations, we are His friends. This is more than the friendship produced by loving obedience. To be partners is a greater privilege than to be servants.

His next word provides a beautiful connection. In making them His friends to share in His thoughts and purpose He it was who took the initiative: "Ye did not choose Me, but I chose you, and appointed you, that ye should go and bear fruit, and that your fruit should abide: that whatsoever ye shall ask of the Father in My Name He may give it you" (v. 16). This is not election to eternal life, it is choice for service and fruitfulness. The statement looks back to two facts, one to the immediately preceding subject of the combined service and friendship, consequent upon the communication of the Father's counsels and operations made to the disciples through the Son, the other to the first part of the chapter, where the Lord was speaking of the union with Himself as the requisite for fruitbearing.

PRIVATE COMMUNION AND VISIBLE POWER

This metaphor is resumed. The word rendered "appointed" is, literally, "set in" (*i.e.*, "I set you in Me"). But now there is more than the union of branches with the stem. There is all the consequent activity of the mission which lay before them.

With all true believers there is the double condition necessary, first the privacy of vital and intimate communion, with the realization of partnership with Him, and then, and then only, the spiritual and visible activity of producing results for His glory; not for spectacular display, but by the quiet yet earnest response to the guidance and power of the Holy Spirit. Such fruitfulness goes on from time into eternity. And the secret of it all is the power of prayer, prevailing prayer.

THE WORLD'S ENMITY

The renewal of the command in verse 17 to love one another is a connecting link between what has preceded and what now follows (cp. 14:25; 15:11; 16:1, 25, 33). As to the preceding, the one thing compatible with those who know what union and friendship with the Lord are, is that they should love one another. But this the more so owing to the antagonism of the world (cp. 1 John 3:11–14). Outer hatred! Inner love! In all this their identification with Christ is exemplified. **"If the world hateth you, ye know that it hath hated Me before it hated you"** (v. 18). This introduces certain principles, spiritual truths governing the condition; these principles are the subject of 15:18–27. In 16:1–15 the Lord gives details of actions.

We have seen how He speaks to His own, first as His *members* participating in His *life*, then as His *friends* participating in His *love*. Now He shows that they are to be His *followers*, participating in His *work*. But this last means opposition and hatred from the world and consequent experiences of suffering and trial. But that means triumph and glory through the ministry of the Comforter.

"If the world hateth you"; the "if" expresses, not a possibility, but a fact. And the explanation is clear: **"If ye were of the world, the world would love its own but because ye are not of the world, but I chose you out of the world, therefore the world hateth you"** (v. 19). There is in the world a pervading characteristic, a sort of affection for those who naturally belong to it, and this is indicated by the phrase "its own." The verb *phileō*, here used of its love, indicates what is merely natural, in contrast to *agapaō*, to love by way of moral choice. The fellowship created by Christ in choosing His disciples out of the world and uniting them to Himself, conforming them to His own likeness, is radically and essentially contrary to the spirit of the world. Therefore it hates both Him and them. The fivefold mention of the "world" emphasizes what He says of it. Similarly five times John speaks of it in his first Epistle.

The Lord now reminds them of what He had already said, **"A servant is not greater than his lord."** Before, this statement inculcated likeness to His in lowliness of service; now it speaks of identification with Him in treatment by the world: **"If they persecuted Me, they will also persecute you; if they kept My word** (which they had certainly not done), **they will keep yours."** The change to "they" is noticeable; the term "the world" suggested its oneness in nature and attitude, the plural suggests its varied antagonistic efforts: **"But all these things will they do unto you for My Name's sake** (because of My Name)." His Name is expressive of His character and ways, all being contrary to those of the world.

HIS WITNESS AGAINST THE WORLD

In both respects He revealed the Father who sent Him. In both respects His followers represent Him. Having no real knowledge of the sender, the world failed to recognize the sent. The sent one came in person and spoke to them; hence the extreme degree of their sin. **"If I had not come and spoken unto them, they had not had sin: but now they have no excuse for their sin."** The Lord thus showed that He was ready to make allowance were it possible. Their sin was unbelief. They could not plead ignorance. Their unbelief developed into hatred.

The evidence He had given was twofold and overwhelming. He had Himself borne witness that He and the Father were one. In hating Him they hated His Father also (v. 23). Then there was the witness of His works: **"If I had not done among them the works which none other had done, they had not had sin: but now they have both seen and hated both Me and My Father."** Their unbelieving malice had therefore a double condemnation.

Behind all this witness was that of the Scripture, which He speaks of as **"their law."** They boasted in it, blind to the fact that it testified against themselves: **"They hated Me without a cause."**

ADDITIONAL WITNESS

This instruction concerning the world and its treatment of them had been imparted with regard to the witness that was yet to be given in it by them. For this object adequate provision would be made. The contrasting "But" connects the past with the future: **"But when the Comforter is come, whom I will send unto you from the Father, even the Spirit of truth, which proceedeth from the Father, He shall bear witness of Me, and ye also bear witness, because ye have been with Me from the beginning"** (vv. 26, 27).

There is strong emphasis on the pronouns "I" and "He," the first stressing the Lord's own action, the second the importance of the Holy Spirit's action. The Lord speaks of Him now as "The Spirit of truth"; this is additional to what He mentioned in 14:16 and 26, and is appropriate to the subject of the witness to be given, for the truth describes the matter of the witness. Also He "proceedeth from the Father," this describes a going forth that is constant, but of which His coming at the promised time was to be a special act. The witness of the apostles would be by reason of their having been with Christ from the beginning, that is, from the beginning of His public manifestation and ministry (Acts 1:2, 21, 22; 5:32; 1 John 1:1–3).

THE ESTABLISHING WORD

The very fact that they would be witnessing to Him amidst fierce hostility produces the reminder that He was about to leave them, and that this was necessary if they were to experience the provision He was about to make for them, so that they might be both delivered and empowered. If they were to have the help they must be alive to the danger.

"**These things have I spoken unto you** [i.e., especially vv. 18–27 of chap. 15] **that ye should not be made to stumble**" (16:1); the word here is a warning, not against being tripped up in the path, but against a sorrowful reaction of thought in being disappointed at not seeing the kingdom set up in the world through the conversion of Israel. Let not their faith be staggered by the hostile fanaticism of Jewish leaders in excommunicating them, and even killing them as an act of service to God (vv. 1, 2). Let them bear in mind the reason for it all, namely, ignorance of the Father and Himself. Let them remember, when the antagonism burst upon them, that it was but fulfilling what He had foretold, and thus let the very adversities be but reminders of His ministry of love that very evening (vv. 3, 4).

"**These things**," He says, "**I said not unto you from the beginning, because I was with you.**" The phrase "from the beginning" is to be noted; it is not "at the beginning" (as in the A.V.). He *had* told them "at the beginning" (see Matt. 10:16–25), but He had not continued all along to do so and thus disconcert their minds. For He was with them, and what they needed was His person and His teachings concerning Himself. One forewarning was enough.

A WARNING

This has its lesson for us. We must never allow difficulties and distresses in the future so to preoccupy our minds that we shall lose our enjoyment of His own person and love and power. Let not dark circumstances obscure the light of His countenance and glory.

Now He was going to Him who sent Him, and, instead of faith and hope, nothing but sorrow filled their hearts. True, they had asked whither He was going (13:36 and 14:5), but the inquiries were by way of despair and perplexity, not of hope. "**Nevertheless,**" He says, "**I tell you the truth; it is expedient for you that I go away** [the pronouns "I" are emphatic]: **for if I go not away, the Comforter will not come unto you; but if I go, I will send Him unto you.**" It was expedient in more ways than one. The very loss would be gain. Sight would give place to faith, the all-important factor in present service. They would pass from a stage of training to qualified activity. Their earthly companying with the Lord would be exchanged for the power of the indwelling Spirit of God, ministering Christ to and through them.

Two different words are rendered "go" in verse 7; twice the verb *apeltho* indicates departure from the place left, i.e., from the world; the last verb *poreutho* indicates the journey to the place and the object in view, heaven and God. The former suggests the inevitable, the latter the purposive.

A THREEFOLD CONVICTION

Verses 8–15 present two contrasting operations of the Holy Spirit after His coming. The former has to do with the world, the latter with the disciples. As to the world He would convict it **"in respect of sin, and of righteousness and of judgment: of sin, because they believe not on Me; of righteousness, because I go to the Father, and ye behold Me no more; of judgment, because the prince of this world hath been judged."** The significance of the word rendered "convict," is to bring home the evils of false notions and gross errors.

The three subjects pertain to the realm of conscience. They have to do with the state and attitude of man in regard to God and His claims. They are factors in the ancient and continued controversy between God and man from the beginning of human sin onward. But the Lord shows that, since His own coming into the scene, a new and special test is applied. The test relates to, and centers in, Himself: It is applied by the Holy Spirit. As to the first, conviction in respect of sin is not of a transgression of God's law; it goes deeper, it goes to the root of sin, namely, unbelief. For all sin is essentially unbelief. That was so with Adam and Eve and had been so all along. But now, with the new test, the evil consists in refusal to believe on Christ: "because they believe not on Me."

As to the second, conviction in respect of righteousness is not because man has departed from the right ways of God. That is so. But now in Christ righteousness had been realized in man for the first time and was duly to be vindicated by His enthronement at the right hand of God: "of righteousness, because I go to the Father" (a different word again for "go": *hupagō*, which might fully be rendered "I go My way"; cp. John 8:21; 16:5). The world had refused to recognize His righteousness; they counted Him a demon-possessed blasphemer and numbered Him among the transgressors. As to His right to be raised from the tomb, with the issues at the right hand of the Father, they concocted a lying fable about that. The Lord adds very significantly "and ye behold Me no longer" ("behold," *theōreō*, is the word). That meant faith; and the life of faith is a life of practical righteousness; it is a witness to the world of what true righteousness is. Therefore, it is a veritable part of the convicting work of the Spirit in regard to the world. Appropriately therefore, the Lord associates the life of believers here with His presence with the Father, as an essential factor in this second process of conviction.

As to the third, conviction in respect of judgment is the crowning operation. The world dares to pronounce its judgment on its affairs as if its directing policy would issue in the vindication of the rights of humanity. The present is "man's day," that is, the time in which man seeks to walk by the light of his own counsels. But man's estimate is marred by his alienation from God. "The whole world lieth in the evil one" (1 John 5:19, R.V.). The world will yet find that out. But the evil one, its prince, met his doom at the Cross. Then was fulfilled the word of the Lord, "the prince of this world cometh, and hath nothing in Me." The triumph of Christ at Calvary meant the casting out of Satan (cp. Col. 2:15). Since the being who is the "the deceiver of the nations" (Rev. 20:3) has been judged, the world is to be convicted by the Spirit in respect of judgment, the falseness of its own judgment and the righteous judgment of God.

As to the Spirit's work in the case of believers, the Lord had much to say, but that was not the time: **"Ye cannot bear them now"** (*arti*, just at the present time). There is a divine economy in the process of revelation. The Lord had now disclosed matters which He had hitherto withheld. Trust is tempered to suit the mind's stage of development. The fullness of truth was to be given when further experiences relative to Christ had fitted the disciples for it. **"Howbeit when He, the Spirit of truth, is come, He shall guide you into all the truth: for He shall not speak from Himself; but what things soever He shall hear, these shall He speak and He shall declare unto you the things that are to come"** (v. 13).

FINALITY OF REVELATION

The first "He" is emphatic (*ekeinos*, the person, not an influence). He is "the Spirit of truth." Truth is His nature, and that is the guarantee of the character of what He teaches. He would not only be sent, He would "come," by His own power. He would guide into the truth, leading into its facts and their meanings by divinely arranged progress. Moreover it would be completely given to them in their lifetime. Nothing would remain to be added by the Church. It would be sufficient for all generations (Jude 3, R.V.). Just as Christ spoke that which He heard from the Father (8:38; 15:15), so would the Spirit. He is not a separate deity, originating truth. The three are one. He would declare the coming things, i.e., all things relative to this period and the coming ages.

As to the world the Lord said, **"He shall bear witness of me,"** and as to the mode of His ministry, **"for He shall take of Mine** (more fully, out of that which is Mine), **and shall declare it unto you"** (v. 14). The whole of the New Testament is the great proof of the fulfillment of this, and by means of the entire Scriptures the Spirit of truth has been fulfilling it to and through believers ever since. Yet not all has been unfolded thus far. The *ek*, out of, is to be taken literally. There remains yet more in the ages to come.

He gives a reason for this promise in repeating it, and the reason is this: **"All things whatsoever the Father hath are Mine"** (v. 15). He thus shows not only the unity between the Father and Himself in Godhood, but points out the vastness of the storehouse of divine possessions from which the revelations and unfoldings are to be made. "The Spirit searches all things, yea the deep things of God."

SORROW TO BE TURNED INTO JOY

The ministry of the Spirit would be given amidst seasons of sorrow and trial for all believers. The Lord now prepares the disciples for this. He first reminds them that He is about to leave them, but there is joy to come from His own person: **"A little while, and ye behold Me no more; and again a little while, and ye shall see Me"** (v. 16). The first "little while" was a few hours, and then after some days He would cease to be seen of them (in the sense of the verb *theōreō*, a visible beholding). He would be seen by the eye of faith indeed. But there is surely more than this in the *opsesthe*, "ye shall see (Me)." The apostle John uses this very verb and the same tense in 1 John 3:2, and the Lord doubtless had in mind His future return, as He had said in 14:3. For the time being the disciples were perplexed. The Lord noted that they were inquiring among themselves, and satisfied their questionings by His further disclosures (vv. 17–22).

They would indeed weep and lament, while the world rejoiced, but Christ Himself, first by His resurrection and appearances, would turn their sorrow into joy, and since everything centered in His death and resurrection, the very cause of their sorrow would be the cause of their joy. For Him and for them the experiences found their analogy in the birth pangs of a woman in her travail with the resulting joy in the birth of her son. His own bitter hours on the cross and the triumphant joy of the vacant tomb were to have their counterpart in their experiences, for He had identified them with Himself. He "saw of the travail of His soul and was satisfied." God loosed the birth pangs of death, because it was not possible that He should be holden of it (Acts 2:24).

He did see them again, their heart did rejoice, and no one could take their joy from them (see *e.g.*, Acts 5:41). But what was experienced in that way, and has been ever since, is not the complete fulfillment of the Lord's reassuring words of promise. The best, the complete, fulfillment will be brought about when He comes to receive us to Himself and takes us into His Father's house above.

COMMUNION, SUFFERING, VICTORY

The Lord now completes His confirmatory comfort and assurance. The intercourse they had enjoyed with Him in bodily presence was about to be changed, not to end, but to continue in a different condition. There was an intercourse during the forty days after His resurrection (Acts 1:1–8), but the new experience was to be marked by a different mode of access and by a new mode of communion. **"And in that day ye shall ask Me nothing** [margin, ask Me no question]. **Verily, verily, I say unto you, if ye shall ask anything of the Father, He will give it to you in My Name. Hitherto have ye asked nothing in My Name: ask, and ye shall receive, that your joy may be fulfilled"** (vv. 23, 24). This all combines immediate access and mediation (see Eph. 2:18; 3:12).

CONCERNING PRAYER

There is a change in the verbs to ask. The first, *erōtaō*, primarily means to ask by way of inquiry, and then by request. The second, *aiteō*, means to ask by way of petition. A nearer relation is involved in *erōtaō* than in *aiteō*. *Erōtaō* had been used of the disciples with regard to Christ (v. 19) and is used in verse 26 of Christ's address to the Father; so in 17:9, 15, 20 (cp. the change in 1 John 5:16). The Lord did not mean that no prayer must be offered to Him afterwards. They did address Him in prayer (Acts 1:24; 7:59; 9:13, etc.). What He does stress particularly is His own ministry of mediation and the effect of prayer addressed to the Father. What He gives He does so in the Name of the Lord Jesus, that is, by reason of all that the Name implies in relation to the Father (see on 14:14, 26; 15:16). The conditions for prayer being thus fulfilled, the answers are designed to fill the heart with joy, a joy of which no foe, no adverse circumstance, can deprive us.

But there was to be a change in the nature of the unfoldings of truth. The Lord would not again adopt the use of "proverbs," a word including different modes of figurative language. He would speak "plainly" of the Father. The word is to be taken in its wider sense of freedom of speech. The time for fullness of utterance was coming. No longer would the mind be needing a gradual process of training. The communications would impart a full assurance of understanding. All this became characteristic of the ministry of the Spirit to and through the apostles. The subject is "the Father," and the Lord at once communicates plain and direct truth concerning Him.

He says, **"In that day ye shall ask in My Name, and I say not unto you that I will pray [make request of] the Father for you: for the Father Himself loveth you, because ye have loved Me and have believed that I came forth from the Father"** (vv. 26, 27). Firstly, He does not say He will *not* pray the Father, He actually proceeded to do so (ch. 17), and He "maketh intercession for us" (Rom. 8:34); His negative way of putting it "I say not . . ." is simply a way of preparing for the strong positive assurance which immediately follows. Secondly, the preposition *peri* here means "concerning" ("I will pray the Father concerning you"). The same preposition He has just used in regard to telling them concerning the Father. Thirdly, He gives a reason for His interest concerning them, in that the Father Himself loves them because of their love for Christ and their faith regarding Him.

UNORIGINATED SONSHIP OF CHRIST

Now follow His plain statements concerning the Father and Himself, fundamental facts of the utmost importance, a climax in His communication: **"I came out from the Father, and am come into the world: again, I leave the world, and go unto the Father"** (v. 28). These four facts summarize the history of Christ. The first takes us to His past eternity. There is a significant change of preposition. In verse 27 He said, "Ye have believed that I came forth from (*para*, from with) the Father" (so the R.V., instead of "from God"). But now He says "I came out from

261

(*ek*) the Father." This is a deeper truth, it is more than a recognition of the faith of the disciples. The *ek* indicates a complete oneness of essence, of the Father and the Son, in the past eternity. Those who deny the preeternal Sonship of Christ fail, for one thing among others, to discern the significance of this *ek*; it definitely implies the essential relationship of Christ as the Son of the Father before He became incarnate, He did not become the Son at His birth.

The second covers the facts of His birth, incarnation, death, burial and resurrection. The third marks His ascension, the fourth His return to the Father, to the One standing in the same relation to Him as in the eternal past. His coming out and His return are each inseparable from His Sonship. The coming out does not suggest that the Father ceased to be with Him. It could not be so. He said "I and the Father are One." "The Father hath not left Me alone."

The doubts were cleared away from the minds of the disciples. They use a third form of preposition in asserting their faith that He came from God, the preposition *apo*, the least definite of the three; it gives the general view, as stated by the disciples; *para* is more close in the relation; *ek*, the Lord's other word, is the most intimate.

A CLOSING MESSAGE

His answer, **"Do ye now believe?"** (not a statement, "Ye do now believe") is not a doubt or denial. It is equivalent to an exclamation, in view of what He is going to state as to the impending danger and their being scattered: **"Behold, the hour cometh, yea, is come, that ye shall be scattered, every man to his own, and shall leave Me alone; and yet,"** He says, in giving a closing message of comfort, **"I am not alone, because the Father is with Me."** This He designed to be a reassuring word for them and for all those who, like Him, pass through conditions of trial and solitude. For He says, with reference both to this word and all that He had given them, **"These things have I spoken unto you, that in Me ye may have peace. In the world ye shall have tribulation: but be of good cheer; I have overcome the world"** (v. 33).

This sums up much of what He had said. He had given them a legacy of His own peace (see 14:27). He had reminded them of world antagonism (15:18–25; 16:1–4). He had assured them of the issue in His own case (14:3, 18, 20, 21; 16:22) and of His victory over the prince of the world (14:30). His very word "Be of good cheer" suggests that naturally there would be cause for depression of heart. But against this He is Himself the antidote. He had been through it all, and had defeated the influences of the world. He had vindicated truth and righteousness in the fact of its deceit and iniquity. The morrow was to see the crowning triumph, over the devil, the world and death, and His word "I have overcome" looks to the accomplished victory.

But they were to share the victory, and we are to share it, and the means for this is to fulfill our identification with Him and thus to obey His command of promise and assurance, "Be of good cheer." We are to be "more than conquerors through Him that loved us." And our victory that overcomes is faith (1 John 5:4, 5). It is just our joy in Christ Himself, our good cheer, that gives us to be more than mere conquerors. Christ points to this very super-victory in this His closing word. Victory can bring content. Joy in Christ gives more than the satisfaction of victory (see Rev. 3:21).

THE INTERCESSORY PRAYER

Jesus ends the Upper Room Discourse with prayer, allowing the disciples to listen in as the Father and the Son discuss the culmination of their plans. What a statement John makes by closing the major discourses with prayer! This in and of itself should speak volumes as to the importance of prayer for the believer's life.

"These things spake Jesus: and lifting up His eyes to Heaven, He said, Father the hour is come." The mention of His lifting up His eyes immediately upon His closing word to the disciples, shows that there was no break in the circumstances. The prayer follows the discourse as a consummation of the teaching given, linking it all with the throne. All that has preceded receives now its interpretation and ratification. The disciples hear how the Father and the Son contemplate their condition, how their prospects are regarded by them, how their highest interests are the subjects of effective intercession, and how others with them are to be brought into the same sphere of eternal blessing and into the bliss of ineffable oneness in both Father and Son.

In this prayer there is nothing giving the slightest intimation of infirmity, demerit or defect. Even the tone of entreaty is absent. There is nothing but the consciousness of a life of the constant, uninterrupted fulfillment of the Father's will, summed up in the statement, "I have glorified Thee on the earth." This is but one of the many such statements of the perfect accomplishment of the divine will and counsel: "I have finished the work." "I have manifested Thy Name." "I have given them the words." "I have kept (them)." These are declarations and assertions of will impossible to a mere human being. When He says "Father, I will," He expresses a claim with the complete consciousness of the right of its accomplishment, as being equally the will of Him whom He is addressing.

It is the prayer of our "Apostle and High Priest," the apostle as sent from God to men, the high priest interceding for men to God.

There are three interwoven subjects, (1) concerning Himself (especially vv. 1–5): (2) concerning His followers and messengers (vv. 6–20); (3) concerning other believers (v. 20 to end). Matters concerning Himself involve those relating to the apostles and others. These three correspond to those mentioned after Judas had gone out; (1) 13:31, 32; (2) 13:33; (3) 13:34, 35. This marks the order and connection throughout.

THE GLORY OF THE PERSONS AND THE WORK

The opening words at once indicate that everything is based upon, and determined by, the eternal relation **"Father . . . Thy Son."** There is also the consummating word of time, **"The hour."** It is the predetermined hour, fulfilling the past, conditioning the future. It is the hour of the overthrow of Satan, the hour of atonement and redemption, bearing their eternal issues. **"The hour is come; glorify Thy Son, that the Son may glorify Thee."** The answer is seen in His resurrection, ascension, and mediatorial work, and in giving Him all authority in heaven and on earth. In the exercise of this authority and work, with all that it accomplishes; the Son glorified and will glorify the Father.

LIFE ETERNAL

But this receives its especial expression in what follows: **"even as Thou gavest Him authority over all flesh** [i.e., all mankind in its weak state], **that whatsoever Thou hast given Him, to them He should give eternal life"** (v. 2). The "whatsoever" is, lit., "all that which," viewing the gift in its collective aspect and not in its individual parts (cp. 6:28 and see again 17:23, 24). But in the giving of eternal life the individual recipients are in view (cp. 10:10, 28). The life is not mere existence, it is an enjoyed possession of capacities and activities, of affection and devoted energy. This is brought out in His next words (and His own words they are, despite arguments assigning them to the writer). This is His own pronouncement of what really constitutes eternal life: **"And this is life eternal, that they should know Thee the only true God, and Him whom Thou didst send,** *even* **Jesus Christ"** (v. 3). The word *ginōskō*, "know," indicates a knowledge acquired by experience. The tense of the verb here signifies a continuous course of progressive knowledge. Moreover, it is a knowledge of persons, not simply of facts, and this involves personal contact and intercourse. It is *our* mind answering to *His* mind, *our* heart to *His* heart, our appropriating to ourselves all that God makes known to us, the Father and the Son revealing themselves to us by the Holy Spirit.

NOT THE FATHER WITHOUT THE SON

The oneness of Christ with the Father in godhood is implied in what the Lord says in regard to the experience of knowing Him, and is confirmed by the apostle's testimony, "We know that the Son of God is come, and hath given us an understanding, that we know Him that is true, and we are in Him that is true, even in His Son Jesus Christ. This is the true God and eternal life" (1 John 5:20). There is no such thing as knowing the Father without knowing the Son. No one can know the true God apart from the Son whom He sent, and who is in Himself the personal embodiment and manifestation of the true God. His two Names Jesus Christ, here mentioned by the Lord concerning Himself in His prayer, contain the title of deity, the work for which He came, and the confirmation of it by God the Father. Hence the appropriateness of the Names to His immediate utterances.

It is His coming as the Son from the Father and all that His Names convey that make the knowledge of the one inseparable from the knowledge of the other.

He is "the true God." All other objects of veneration are false gods, and any conception of God which does not accept the oneness of the Son with the Father in the Godhead, and the oneness of the Spirit in the same Godhead, as taught by the Lord and in the Scriptures of truth, is a misconception. There is no eternal life possible without the knowledge of the Father and the Son in this oneness by the operation of the Spirit.

GLORIFYING AND GLORY

The statement "whom Thou didst send" leads to the mention of the fulfillment of that for which He was sent **"I glorified Thee on the earth, having accomplished the work which Thou hast given Me to do."** Up till now he had used the third person with reference to Himself, giving an introductory review of the great facts concerning His relation as the Son, and the plan of the ministry of eternal life through Him. Now He changes to the first person "I." The contrast of circumstances is striking. "I glorified Thee:"—a life of unsullied brightness of glory in fulfilling the Father's will: "on the earth,"—a scene of grossest darkness in the human rejection of Himself and His testimony.

He finished the work, not simply bringing it to an end, but perfectly fulfilling it and achieving its object. It was His meat to do the will of Him who sent Him and to accomplish His work (4:34). This is His example for every true follower who realizes that what he engages in doing is given him to be fulfilled for His glory.

THE GLORY OF PREEXISTENT SONSHIP

And now comes the sequel, expressed in a desire certain of its fulfillment, a desire that, looking to the immediate future, goes back to the eternal past: **"And now, O Father, glorify Thou Me with Thine own self with the glory which I had with Thee before the world was"** (v. 5). There are three parts of this which call for reverent attention: (1) the bestowment of honors merited by, and consequent upon, the perfected work—"glorify Thou Me"; (2) "with Thine own self" not "by," but "with" *para*, expressing presence with (the same word as in the next clause, "with Thee"); (3) "with the glory which I had with Thee," not merely before He came as the sent One, but before the world had its being from the Creator's hands. This is the glory of essential and unoriginated deity, of a being uncreated, a personal being and not an ideal existence, and an eternal relationship as the Son; for it is a glory "with Thee," the Father—a clause in itself exposing the errors of Arianism, Socinianism, present-day cults, and the denial of the eternal Sonship of Christ. It was a glory which "I had," not which "I received."

Facts Concerning the Disciples

The Lord now mentions seven facts concerning His followers: (1) He had manifested the Father's Name to them; (2) they were the Father's gifts to Him out of the world; (3) they had kept His word; (4) they had known that what belonged to the Son came from the Father; (5) the words given them by the Son were given Him by the Father; (6) they had received them; (7) they knew that He came forth from the Father as sent by Him.

It is clear that the purpose in all this was to prepare these men for their service as instruments in bearing testimony for Him, with all its consequences. In manifesting the Name he had declared all that God is, His nature, counsels, and ways and works (cp. 1:18). His disciples were given Him **"out of the world,"** humanity in its alienation from God and in its darkness. They belonged to the Father, not merely as being foreknown by Him, but by being actually and personally related to Him. They were given to Him not merely by divine purpose, but as delivered by the Father to Him for His possession, care and instruction. With joy He could say, that they had responded to it; **"they have kept Thy word."** And not merely the teaching as a whole but the very words of which it consisted.

These teachings were not simply His; He taught every detail as that which He received from the Father. In receiving His words they had accepted the truth concerning His person as the one who came forth from the Father and was sent by Him. That was the great preparation for their mission. They were raised above the perplexities, the cavils and criticisms of false teachers.

A Radical Distinction

They were to be left, but not without the divine help they would need. So the Lord begins with His own high priestly intercession: **"I pray** [erōtaō, I make request] **for them** [the "I" is especially emphatic]: **I pray not for the world, but for those whom Thou has given Me; for they are Thine."** The distinction is solemn and radical—the disciples—the world. Not that He had not the interests of the world before Him. He was about to send them into it that all men might believe and be saved. But the uppermost and immediate interests are those of His own. They are equally the Father's and His: **"and all things that are Mine are Thine, and Thine are Mine."** To say, "whatever is mine is Thine," is possible for any believer, but no one but the Son of God could ever say, "all things that are Thine are Mine."

The next words **"and I am glorified in them"** would seem to refer to the disciples; for Christ was, and continued to be, glorified in them. It is possible, however, to read thus: "All things that are Thine are Mine, and I am glorified in them," for God orders all things so that they may be for the glory of His Son.

Kept in the Name

Now comes the special point of His intercession for the disciples as those who are to be still in the world, with all that this entails: **"And I am no more in the world, and these are in the world, and I come to Thee; Holy Father, keep them** in Thy Name which Thou hast given Me, that they may be one, even as We are" (v. 11). He had Himself experienced all the hostility and adverse conditions of the world, and He feels for those who are to be in it still. It is full of everything unholy and unwholesome, baneful to the spiritual life and antagonistic to endurance and power. All the time He was with them, He kept them, "in Thy Name," He says, "which Thou hast given Me and I guarded them, and not one of them perished, but the son of perdition; that the Scripture might be fulfilled" (v. 12). How He kept them, teaching and training them amidst all the circumstances of an adverse character in the nation's condition is brought out in the narratives of the Gospels. So to the end (see 18:8, 9).

But He kept them in the Name the Father had given Him. That is the better reading. Since the Name conveys all that God is as revealed in Christ, all the truth concerning Him, in nature, character and ways, had been the very sphere and element in which the Lord had guarded, taught and trained these men. For the subject of the Name see further at verse 26 and at Exodus 33:19 and 34:5, 6. The fullness of the Name is again and again mentioned in the Epistles as "Christ Jesus (or Jesus Christ) our Lord" (see, e.g., Rom. 5:11, 21; 6:11, 23). In all that this meant He made request that they might still be kept. And on their behalf He addresses the Father as "Holy Father," for they were, and we are to be, holy, for He is holy. They were, and we are, by nature unholy and in an unholy world.

HOLINESS

Holiness is a quality which is essential to true spiritual unity; anything short of it makes for division and discord. The unity is designed for believers, and will be manifested hereafter. It is not simply likemindedness, nor mere acknowledgment of the truth; it is the very character of God manifested in all circumstances and activities.

The "son of perdition" stands out in contrast. That kind of phrase describes the character and effect of a man's moral state, as the manner of his life (e.g., 1 Sam. 25:17; Matt. 23:31; Luke 6:35; Eph. 2:2), and not a destiny. The Scripture, being God-breathed, has the character of accurate prediction; it has never been, and could not be, falsified. Christ had shown, in regard to this very person that He, the living Word, was possessed of divine powers of knowledge (13:18).

JOY

But they were not only to be kept, it was His desire that they might be filled with joy, His own joy experienced in them: "But now I come to Thee; and these things I speak in the world, that they may have My joy fulfilled in themselves" (v. 13). This plainly intimates that the Lord purposely spoke these things in their hearing. But why does He say "in the world" instead of "in their hearing"? He had expressed the same desire to them directly (15:11). The world, however, was the scene of so much that would tend to cast down and depress (and He was leaving them in it), that He repeats this great desire, addressing it to Him to whom He was coming, that the joy that characterized Him might continue and be fulfilled in them.

But not only was His own sustaining joy to be theirs, it would be maintained by the Word He had given them, the Father's Word. The Word of God, accepted and kept, ministers joy to the heart. To keep His Word is, however, contrary to the spirit of the world and produces its hatred: **"I have given them Thy Word; and the world hated them, because they are not of the world, even as I am not of the world. I pray not that Thou shouldest take them from the world, but that Thou shouldest keep them from the evil one"** (vv. 14, 15). To remove them from the world would leave the effects of their presence and of their very mission unaccomplished. But the negative way first of making the request served only to stress the urgency of the positive desire. For the being who had sought to hinder and defeat Him was still active, and would be, in spite of his initial overthrow at the Cross. There lay, and there lies, the great danger.

THE EVIL ONE

The Lord had spoken of the evil one (Matt. 13:19), not as a sinister influence, but as a person, and the Epistles bear this out in frequent passages. The apostle Paul assures the church at Thessalonica that God would guard them "from the evil one" (2 Thess. 3:3). The apostle John speaks of him five times thus and says in the closing passage of his first epistle, in words which reecho the Lord's, "We know that whosoever is begotten of God sinneth not (present continuous tense, "doth not go on doing sin"); but He that was begotten of God (i.e., the Son of God, 4:9) keepeth him (R.V.), and the evil one toucheth him not. We know that we are of God, and the whole world lieth in the evil one" (1 John 5:18, 19).

The preposition "from" in "from the evil one" is *ek*, out of, and is used of deliverance from persons, e.g., Acts 26:17.

SANCTIFICATION

In verse 16 the Lord says again, **"They are not of the world, even as I am not of the world,"** and this precedes a request for their deliverance: **"Sanctify them in the truth: Thy word is truth."** Sanctification is a state of separation to God; all believers enter into this state when they are born of God; but sanctification is also used of the practical experience of this separation to God, and is the effect of the Word of God as learned by the Holy Spirit, and is to be pursued by the believer earnestly (1 Tim. 2:15; Heb. 12:14). In this sense of the word the Lord prays here; and here it has in view the setting apart of believers for the purpose for which they are sent into the world: **"As Thou didst send Me into the world, even so send I them into the world. And for their sakes I sanctify Myself, that they themselves also may be sanctified in truth"** (v. 18, 19). That He set apart Himself for the purpose for which He was sent, is both the basis and the condition of our being set apart for that for which *we* are sent (cp. 10:36). His sanctification is the pattern of, and the power for, ours. The sending and the sanctifying are inseparable. The words "in truth" mean "in reality," i.e., in practical experience (as in Matt. 22:16; Col. 1:6; 2 John 1).

PRAYER FOR ALL BELIEVERS

"Neither for these only do I pray, but for them also that believe on Me through their word." The Lord uses the present tense "them that believe," as He views the vast company forming the Church, the outcome of their initial ministry by tongue and by pen, the latter inclusive of the Gospels as well as the Epistles. In this connection the foundations of the future city of glory have on them the names of "The Twelve Apostles of the Lamb." The purpose of the request is the same as that made for those who were listening to Him that evening, **"that they all may be one; even as Thou, Father, art in Me, and I in Thee, that they also may be in Us"** (v. 21), lit., "one thing" in us (neuter), not indicating the elimination of individual life, but the oneness as of a body in its various members, each developing its activity as part of the whole.

The great object looks on to the time when the Church will be completed and manifested with Him in glory at His Second Advent. The world will then be brought to accept all the facts involved in His being sent, and that for the very purpose He has expressed. There are three purposes, (1) oneness in themselves as with the Father and Son; (2) oneness in them ("in Us"), the essential sphere and relation of the oneness; (3) recognition by the world.

IMPARTED GLORY EXPRESSED IN UNITY

This is confirmed and expanded in His next words, **"And the glory which Thou hast given Me I have given unto them; that they may be one, even as We are one; I in them, and Thou in Me, that they may be perfected into one; that the world may know that Thou didst send Me, and lovedst them, even as Thou lovedst Me"** (vv. 22, 23). What this imparted glory is receives an explanation from 1 Peter 1:21, "God . . . raised Him from the dead and gave Him glory." It is the glory therefore of resurrection and reception into His presence. How the Lord Jesus will impart this glory to all believers is stated in 1 Thessalonians 4:16, 17. He will "fashion anew the body of our humiliation, that it may be conformed to the body of His glory" (Phil. 3:21). At that moment and from that time believers will be one, even as the Father and the Son are one. The fulfillment and completeness is to be realized in the indwelling of Christ and the Father in each and all "I in them, and Thou in Me." The perfecting into one will be accomplished by, and consist in, our being "like Him; for we shall see Him even as He is" (1 John 3:2). There will be a participation by all in this perfect likeness. Then will be fulfilled the word, "whom He justified, them He also glorified" (Rom. 8:30).

Then will the world be made to recognize not only the great truths concerning Christ as the One sent by the Father (see v. 21), but that all that is accomplished is the effect of the love of God the Father toward believers, as definite as His love for His Son (see v. 26). For the fulfillment in regard to the world see, *e.g.*, 2 Thessalonians 1:10; Revelation 1:7. For the love of Christ as that which is to be recognized by the world, see Revelation 3:9.

THE LORD'S WILL

Thus far the Lord has said three times "I pray" (I make request); now He says "I will": **"Father, that which Thou hast given Me, I will that, where I am, they also may be with Me."** This and what follows are a consummation of all that has preceded regarding those who are His. It brings everything to the complete fruition of all the divine counsels and operations on their behalf. Accordingly His desires now find their expression in a word which conveys the equality of the Son and the Father in counsel and purpose. Again He speaks of His people first as a totality, a complete entity, **"that which Thou hast given Me,"** and then as a company of individuals, **"that they may be with Me."**

His will concerning them is twofold: (1) their being with Him, (2) that they may behold His glory, each is involved in his relation to Him. Of the first He had given them a promise (14:3), and now His will completes all that He has added: **"that they may behold My glory, which Thou hast given Me: for Thou lovedst Me before the foundation of the world"** (v. 24). This is the glory already mentioned in verse 22, a glory given, and now as a proof that the Father loved Him "before [not "from," as in Matt. 25:34, as to the earthly Kingdom] the foundation of the world." To behold His glory will be to be like Him (cp. Ps. 17:15).

THE CONCLUDING FACTS AND PURPOSE

Just as the title "Holy Father" was used as appropriate to the holiness of His followers (v. 11), so now regarding the world and its unrighteous state of ignorance of God, the Lord says, **"O righteous Father."** God had endowed man with a capacity for knowing Him, with resulting fulfillment of His will and obedience to His command. He would thus have been "right with God." The world refused to have Him in knowledge (Rom. 1:28). To the Jews He said "ye have not known Him, but I know Him" (8:55). So now He says **"the world indeed** [*kai*] **knew Thee not, but I knew Thee** [looking back on the contrast experienced in the days of His flesh]; **and these knew that Thou didst send me"** (v. 25).

Then comes the close; it is retrospective, prospective and purposive. That which He had been doing for His own, He will continue to do, and that with one great object: **"and I made known unto them Thy Name** [cp. 15:15], **and will make it known** [see 14:26 and 16:13]; **that the love wherewith Thou lovedst Me may be in them, and I in them."** He continued to make the Name known during the forty days after His resurrection; He continued to do so by the Holy Spirit through the apostles after Pentecost; He has done so ever since by the ministry of the Spirit in and through the Scriptures of truth; and this will not cease in the ages to come.

Finally, as to the purpose, the love of the Father to Him is designed to dwell in us by reason of the perpetual indwelling of Christ Himself. Were our hearts in such a condition that this love might be the controlling power over our lives, we should learn to love as He loves, to love one another fervently with a pure heart, and so to manifest the very life and character of Christ. That kind of life it is which will meet with the highest reward hereafter.

9 780310 144922